Light and Air

The camera is not a free agent as brush or pencil,

but relentlessly records things as they are. So the

artist must bring to her aid strong contrasts of light

and shade, artistic grouping and rhythmic lines.

To use a camera as a means of artistic expression,

a certain quality of spirit must be brought to aid

light and air.—*Bayard Wootten, 1926*

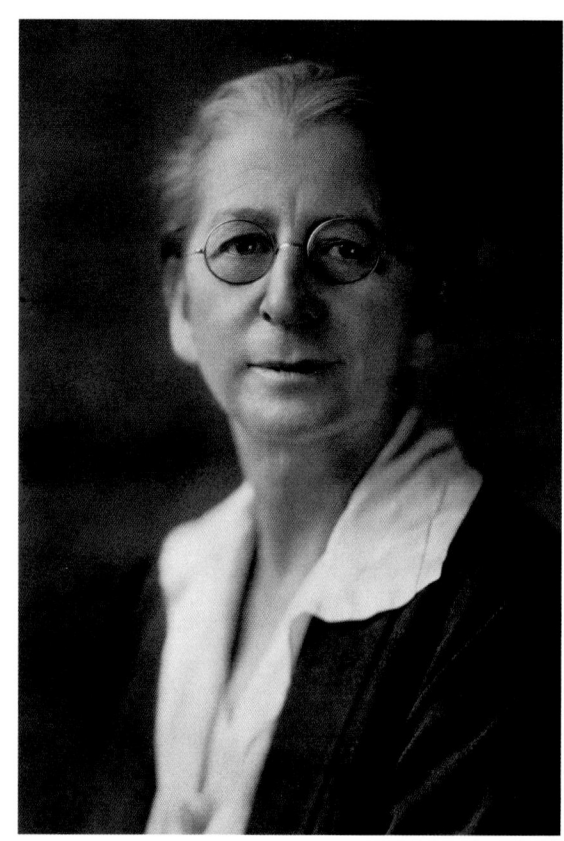

Bayard Wootten (1875–1959)

Light and Air

THE PHOTOGRAPHY OF BAYARD WOOTTEN

JERRY W. COTTEN *With a new foreword by Stephen J. Fletcher*

The University of North Carolina Press   Chapel Hill

This book was set in Monotype Garamond by Eric M. Brooks

Book design by April Leidig-Higgins

This volume was published with the assistance of the
Blythe Family Fund of the University of North Carolina
Press.

The paper in this book meets the guidelines for permanence
and durability of the Committee on Production Guidelines
for Book Longevity of the Council on Library Resources.

Library of Congress Cataloging-in-Publication Data

Cotten, Jerry W.

Light and air : the photography of Bayard Wootten /
by Jerry W. Cotten.

p.   cm.   Includes bibliographical references and index.

ISBN 978-0-8078-2445-0 (cloth : alk. paper)

ISBN 978-1-4696-3248-3 (pbk. : alk. paper)

1. Photography, Artistic.   2. Wootten, Bayard Morgan,
1875–1959.   I. Wootten, Bayard Morgan, 1875–1959.
II. Title.

TR653.C68   1998   98-3421

779'.092 — dc21   CIP

Frontispiece: Photograph courtesy of the Celia Eudy Collection.

For Bayard Wootten

and all those who went before her lens.

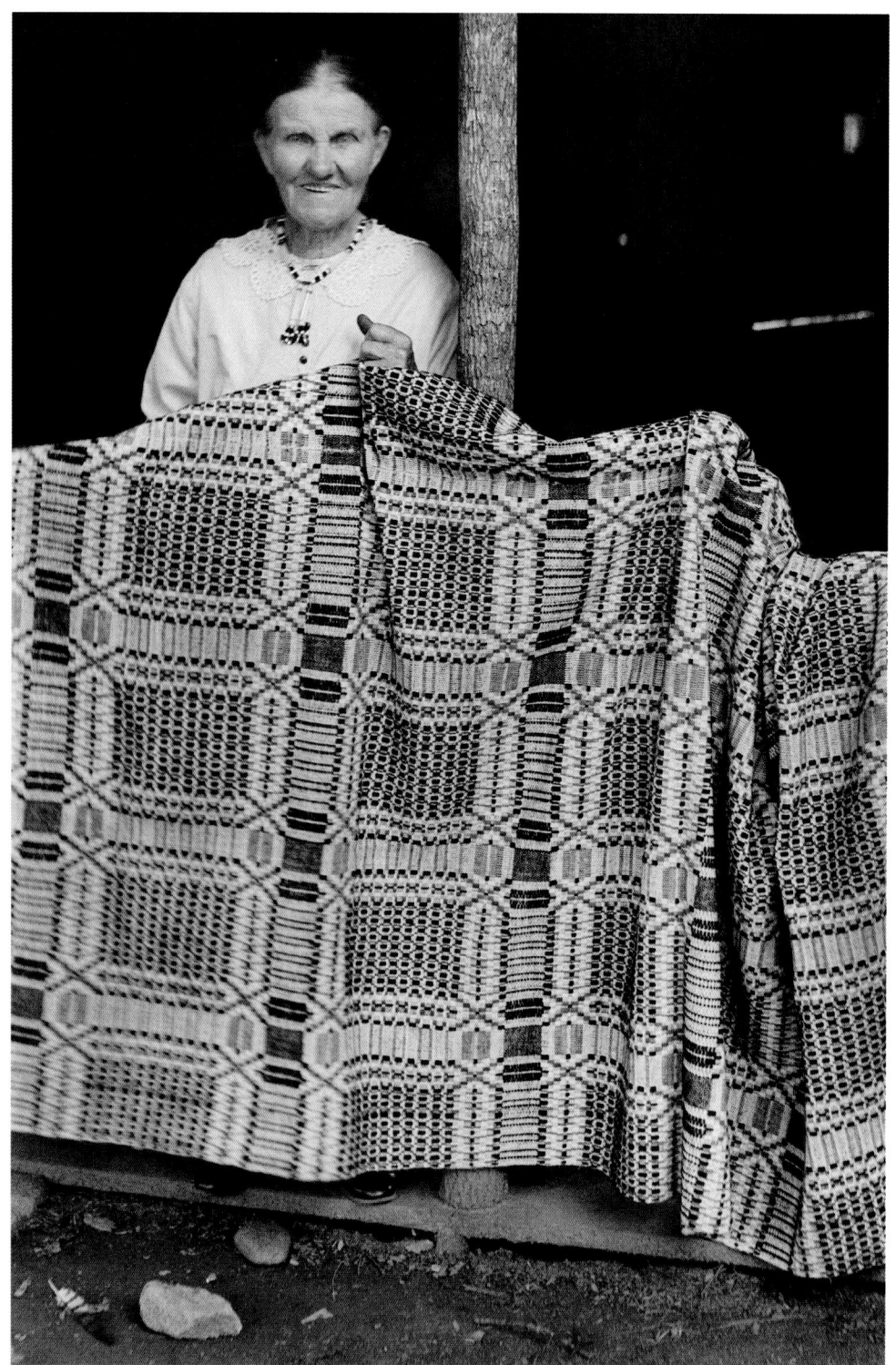

Cumi Woody

THE ANCIENT OF DAYS

Jonathan Williams

would that I
had known Aunt Cumi
Woody

C-u-m-i, pronounced
Q-my

she lived in the Deyton Bend Section of Mitchell
County, North Carolina many years ago

there is one of Bayard Wootten's photographs of her
standing there with her store-bought
teeth, holding a coverlet

she sheared her sheep, spun
and dyed her yarn in vegetable dyes,
and wove the coverlet

in indigo, the brown from walnut roots,
red from madder, green from hickory ooze, first,
then into the indigo (the blue pot)

Cumi, from the Bible
(St. Mark 5:41)

Talitha Cumi:
"Damsel, I say unto thee, arise!"

she is gone, she
enjoyed her days

Contents

Foreword

You are fortunate. Why? Because along with the good news of the second printing of *Light and Air* came the even better news that the printing plates used for the book's first printing no longer exist. You may be thinking, "So this is 'even better' news?" Yes, it is. This misfortune presented the wonderful opportunity to bring twenty-first-century digital imaging technology to the representation of Bayard Wootten's traditionally made negatives and photographs. Now we could capture even more of the richness found in her large 5 × 7- and 8 × 10-inch negatives. Today's digital cameras with high resolution image sensors, coupled with raster graphics software, have replaced the darkroom methods used nearly two decades ago. What a wonderful difference eighteen years of photographic advancements have made!

How may you enjoy these developments? Compared to traditional techniques, digital imaging technology reproduces images with improvements that are both subtle and dramatic. Spend time looking at enhanced details. Enjoy expanded tonal ranges between shadows and highlights. Appreciate skies with clouds where before they could not be reproduced. The joy is in the seeing, and all these nuances of light and air result from painstaking work by Jay Mangum, digitization support technician in the University of North Carolina Libraries' Digital Production Center. You may also explore more Wootten photographs than appear in this book. Significant portions of UNC's Bayard Morgan Wootten Photographic Collection are digitized and viewable online through UNC Libraries' collection finding aid (http://finding-aids.lib.unc.edu/P0011/), including all of her images in this book.

Stephen J. Fletcher

Preface

I saw my first Bayard Wootten photograph in 1972, not long after beginning work in the North Carolina Collection, a department of the library at the University of North Carolina at Chapel Hill. The collection is steeped in historical resources, and my explorations eventually led to an out-of-the-way cabinet of old pictures. Among the files were two large, brown envelopes labeled "Tobacco" and "Cotton." Inside were photographs of farm families, both black and white, planting and harvesting the crops. Acquired by the North Carolina Collection years earlier, the prints had attracted little notice from researchers.

These prints, however, aroused more than my passing interest. The summers I had worked on tobacco farms while growing up in nearby Chatham County were fresh in my memory. The photographs recalled a rural life that I knew, a world that had quietly slipped away with little notice.

I was not a connoisseur of fine photography, but even my layman's eye could discern a bit of artistic class in many of the compositions. An observer could absorb these photographs with little effort, the eye surveying a print and coming to rest upon subjects undisturbed by extraneous elements or stiff and awkward poses. The prints had a symmetry, a character, and a simplicity that were pleasing. They looked natural yet finely tuned, as if part of a well-crafted story. What was the origin of these photographs, and who was the photographer named Bayard Wootten who had signed each one in a distinctive block-like handwriting?

My first surprise was learning that Bayard Wootten was a woman. I never doubted that women could make great photographs, but these images dated from the Great

Depression of the 1930s, a time when most women worked at home. Wootten was also from North Carolina and largely self-taught as a photographer. One thing was certain—the more of her work I saw, the more I wanted to see.

Biographical information on Wootten in the North Carolina Collection consisted primarily of newspaper and journal articles from the 1930s through the 1950s. A small collection of prints and six books that she illustrated between 1934 and 1941 comprised the record of her camera work. Scholarly accounts of Wootten's early life did not exist, and no publication examined her contribution within the broad context of American photography in the twentieth century. In the ensuing years, however, I learned much more about Bayard Wootten and her legacy of old photographs still tucked away in closets, storerooms, and attics.

She was born in 1875 in New Bern, North Carolina. Her mother was artistically talented, and her father tried the photographic profession for several years before giving it up. He died when she was five.

Bayard's artistic skills developed under the tutelage of her mother. She attended a women's school at Greensboro in the early 1890s and then accepted a teaching position at a school for the deaf in Arkansas. Two years later she took a similar position in Georgia. She married there in 1897 and had two sons. The marriage failed, however, and in 1901 Wootten returned to North Carolina. At first she pursued drawing and painting as a cottage industry, but around 1904 the possibility of photographic orders replacing labor-intensive artwork steered her to the camera. Economic self-reliance was a necessity for Wootten, and it became a natural companion to her innate spirit of independence.

Although attracted to the medium by financial need, Wootten's passion for things artistic lingered just below the surface. The pictorial movement in photography was in its heyday during the first decade of the twentieth century, and Wootten's career timing could not have been better. She found pictorialism, with its emphasis on artistic content even at the expense of technical quality, a comfortable fit. She identified with the style throughout her half-century career, despite its steady decline in popularity after 1910.

Wootten experienced firsthand the gender discrimination within a profession overwhelmingly dominated by men. She went to a regional photographers' convention in 1907 and had attended at least one national convention by 1912. Wootten found immediate kinship with the women photographers who in 1909 formed the Women's Federation of the Photographers' Association of America. Professional meetings and publications such as the Bulletin of Photography became forums for exchanging ideas with female colleagues and learning about their work. Wootten's membership in the Federation also fortified her sense of self as a woman photographer.

Her first studio was in a small frame building beside the family home in New Bern, but over the course of her career Wootten operated branches at several other locations in North Carolina. She briefly had a studio in New York City, but the experiment proved to be a costly mistake.

Significant recognition materialized for Wootten after she moved to Chapel Hill in 1928. During this period she actively pursued subjects that complemented her pictorial style to great advantage. Her work includes beautiful gardens and spectacular landscapes, but Wootten's most notable accomplishment was the creation of a photographic record of black and white Americans in the lower reaches of society—people whom other photographers often ignored.

During the first two decades of the twentieth century the efforts of Bayard Wootten and other activist women photographers helped establish a larger foothold for women in the photographic profession. Thereafter, she settled into the niche of commercial photography, an arrangement that provided a livelihood while allowing her to pursue the medium as a form of artistic expression. She excelled at landscapes and portraits. Large billowing clouds or the gentle light of early morning and late afternoon turned her eye. On rare occasions she would backlight a subject and often used a soft focus and matte or textured photographic papers. Her longtime assistant, T. C. Moore, acknowledged Wootten's great talent at composition but also remembered that she was sometimes "at sea" in the darkroom.

Opportunities as a book illustrator unfolded for Wootten in the early 1930s and continued for a decade. She made some of her most popular photographs in the mountains of western North Carolina and the low country of South Carolina, but she also worked in other states, including Alabama and Tennessee. Wootten received frequent invitations to exhibit her work, and she assembled popular slide presentations based upon her architectural and landscape photography. Chapel Hill was the photographer's home from 1928 until her retirement in 1954. Five years later she died in New Bern at the age of eighty-four.

In 1976, on behalf of the North Carolina Collection, I made inquiries about

Wootten's negatives to T. C. Moore, her successor in the Chapel Hill studio and an employee with the firm since 1921. The studio had an estimated 94,000 negatives, but this collection included only a small portion of Wootten's best work. Moore did have over 200 11 × 14-inch exhibition prints by Wootten, many with the photographer's autograph. He was noncommittal about parting with the materials, but in 1980 the North Carolina Collection acquired all of the negatives and prints from a subsequent owner.

The library's Bayard Wootten Collection increased in size again when Mary Moulton Barden of New Bern, the daughter of George C. Moulton, Wootten's half brother and business partner, donated a collection of the photographer's glass slides. The New Bern Public Library contributed some of her glass negatives, and in 1984 the Institute of Government at the University transferred sixty-three exhibition prints by Wootten, many of which had the photographer's autograph and original titles.

Crucial additions to the collection arrived in 1986, 1995, and 1996. Wootten's niece Celia Eudy and her husband Joseph Eudy of Kinston donated prints and almost 3,000 negatives that Wootten had removed from the studio files when she retired. The negatives, made primarily between the 1920s and the 1940s, include her best work. Over the course of almost two decades the North Carolina Collection, through the generosity of Wootten's family, friends, and admirers, reassembled the bulk of her existing photographs.

A small number of Wootten's original prints and her studio camera went on exhibit at the University of North Carolina Library in the mid-1980s. The first major exhibition of her photography in forty years, however, occurred out of state. Coy Ludwig, director of the Tyler Art Gallery at the State University of New York at Oswego, bought a Wootten print of a potter from an antique shop in Syracuse. Curious to learn more about the photographer, he eventually located the Wootten Collection in Chapel Hill. From October 14 to November 13, 1988, the Tyler Gallery mounted an exhibit of more than sixty Wootten photographs reprinted from her original negatives. The exhibition attracted more than a thousand visitors.

When on the road pursuing her "camera studies," Wootten made little effort to record whom she photographed, where, or when. Identifying many of her images often involves research and guesswork. For some, identification remains elusive. The value of historical photographs, however, is not dependent on documentary facts alone. Wootten often photographed what others overlooked, and a knowledge of provenance along with the passage of time makes even the imperfect camera record significant. Wootten's best images tell a story or stand on their own as works of photographic art. Often they do both.

Wootten enjoyed success as a pictorial photographer at a time when realistic and straight photography increasingly dominated the medium. She sought out obscure people and places in North Carolina and surrounding states, creating an insightful photographic record. These images are Wootten's abiding legacy. It is my good fortune to administer this collection for the University of North Carolina Library. Even more gratifying, however, is the knowledge that these photographs have come together for preservation in one place. Wootten's artistic skills, her success as an early woman photographer, and a career spanning half a century have secured her place as a dominant figure in the photographic history of North Carolina.

Acknowledgments

I have received help from many quarters in bringing together the facts and photographs represented by this volume. The enormous holdings of the North Carolina Collection, Manuscripts Department, and University Archives at the University of North Carolina Library at Chapel Hill were invaluable. H. G. Jones and William S. Powell, former curators of the North Carolina Collection, provided editorial advice in the early stages of the project. I also gratefully acknowledge funding from the University Research Council of the University of North Carolina at Chapel Hill and from the Bayard Wootten Fund of the North Caroliniana Society Inc.

Bayard Wootten's family made available private collections and shared personal reminiscences of the photographer that filled an enormous research void. Without their help and encouragement any serious study of Wootten would have been impossible. These individuals—Mary Moulton Barden of New Bern, North Carolina; Celia and Joseph Eudy of Kinston, North Carolina; and Clare Crawford-Mason and Victor Crawford of Washington, D.C.—have studiously preserved photographs, manuscripts, and clippings. Special appreciation is also due Mary Louise Wootten Garrard of Hampstead, North Carolina, and Molli Wootten Larson of Coronado, California.

Helen Dugan Allen of Chapel Hill made her own research materials on Wootten available and shared her personal recollections of the photographer. Similarly, Samuel M. Boone, also from Chapel Hill, provided information on Wootten and her contemporary, fellow photographer Frances Benjamin Johnston, both of whom he knew personally. Useful insights were also contributed by several former employees of the Wootten-Moulton Studio, all of North Carolina: Margaret Howland Fowler of Morehead City, an employee for over two decades; Rudolph Faircloth of Wilmington, an employee in the 1930s and later a photographer for the Associated Press; and Marion Seiler of Chapel Hill, who worked at the studio during the 1940s. Ora Brock Burgin of Weaverville supplied information on her father Nace Brock, Wootten's mentor, as did Juanita Brown of Asheville, a former employee in Brock's studio.

I received research assistance from Jeannine Anderson of the Art Department of Berea College; John Hawk of the University of Oregon Library; Thomas L. Johnson of the University of South Carolina Library; Victor T. Jones Jr. of the New Bern–Craven County Public Library; Stephen E. Massengill of the North Carolina Division of Archives and History in Raleigh; Emilie Mills of the University of North Carolina at Greensboro Library; Peter Palmquist of Arcata, California; Christian A. Peterson of the Minneapolis Institute of Arts; Robin Salmon of Brookgreen Gardens in Murrells Inlet, South Carolina; and Maurice York of the East Carolina University Library at Greenville, North Carolina. David Featherstone of San Francisco and Phil Jacobs of Paris, Kentucky, provided helpful information on photographer Doris Ulmann.

I am especially indebted to Genevieve Chandler Peterkin of Murrells Inlet, South Carolina, the daughter of Federal Writers' Project field-worker Genevieve Willcox Chandler. In 1993 Peterkin identified by name many of the African Americans, including former slaves, that her mother interviewed and Bayard Wootten photographed in the rice-growing region of the lower Waccamaw River during the 1930s. She also made it possible for me to visit Sandy Island in the Waccamaw, meet some of its African American residents, and sense its remarkable history.

Others who helped in various ways include Billy Arthur, J. Todd Bailey, Lloyd Bailey, Andrew R. Cahan, Katharine W. Califf, Gladys Hall Coates, Budd Gambee, Michael Hill, William Lanier Hunt, Charles Joyner, R. Kincaid Mills, Sarah Pope, and Stephanie Slagel. I owe special thanks to Frederick N. Stipe of Chapel Hill for his skill and care in printing most of the photographs that appear in this volume. Jonathan Williams of Highlands, North Carolina—poet, writer, photographer, publisher, and founder of the Jargon Society—graciously allowed the use of his poem "The Ancient of Days." My wife Alice and son Steve always gave an extra measure of encouragement and assistance when it was needed most.

Chapel Hill, North Carolina
December 1997

Light and Air

The *Life* and Career of Bayard Wootten

S top the car, Rudolph! Stop the car!" were familiar orders to her driver and understudy, Rudy Faircloth, as they traveled together during the 1930s. A beautiful landscape, a primitive cabin, or children playing beside the road were enough to catch the eye and lens of Bayard Wootten. At the time of her death in 1959, the Associated Press described Wootten as a pioneer and one of the South's leading photographers. Her work with the camera spanned half a century and had carried her from a small town in eastern North Carolina to the streets of New York and to hollows deep in the Appalachian Mountains.

Wootten's artistic photographs in books, magazines, and exhibitions won critical acclaim. Her friends and subjects included the lowly as well as the influential and wealthy, yet in retirement she was financially dependent on others. Bayard Wootten was popular as a lecturer and famous for a dogged determination to get the photograph she wanted, and in doing so she often turned up in the most unlikely of places.

She was born Mary Bayard Morgan on December 17, 1875, in her grandparents' antebellum house, which still stands on East Front Street in New Bern, North Carolina.[1] The old home has a long porch and balcony across the front; in the distance a visitor can glimpse the Neuse River, at that point more than a mile wide. The broad expanse of water, cypress trees, and riverboats would have impressed a young girl growing up in the 1880s, especially one with an artistic eye.

New Bern already had a long history as a bustling tidewater port when Bayard Morgan was born. The town, settled in 1710, served as North Carolina's colonial and state capital from 1746 until 1792. Strategically positioned at the confluence of the Neuse and Trent Rivers, New Bern became an early objective of Union forces during the Civil War.

Bayard (pronounced "By-ard") Morgan descended from prominent Carolina families. Her maternal grandmother was the writer, poet, and editor Mary Bayard Clarke (1827–1886), often considered North Carolina's most significant female literary figure of the period. Her great-grandfather, John Devereux, was one of the state's largest slaveholders. Nonetheless, North Carolina, like much of the South, was in economic ruin following the Civil War, and her parents, Mary Devereux Clarke (1854–1931) and Rufus Morgan (1846–1880), faced financial hardship when they married in 1873.

Her father, a native of Virginia, started a photography business in New Bern four years after the war's end. He also opened galleries in Raleigh and Goldsboro. Morgan was an accomplished maker of stereographs. He often traveled around North Carolina and to nearby states in pursuit of business and was absent from New Bern when his daughter was born. A second child, Sam, arrived in 1879, also the year in which Bayard survived a bout with typhoid fever.

Rufus Morgan found that he could not support his family with the camera and gradually abandoned the profession for another of his interests, beekeeping. In 1879, he moved to San Diego County, California, to work in a large commercial apiary, planning to send for his wife and two children as soon as money became available. Many years later Wootten recalled how her mother and grandmother cried on a day in the spring of 1880 when two letters arrived from the West Coast. One letter, written by her father, discussed plans for moving his wife and children to California. It said, in part, "now that I know I am going to have you with me so soon, I feel impatient all the time to see you."[2] A second letter, from a physician, described how Rufus Morgan had suffered "untold miseries" and died after eating a meal of poisonous mushrooms.[3]

The house on Front Street was home to Bayard and her brother, mother, and grandparents. There was little in the way of income. To help support her children and parents, Mary Morgan painted decorations on small objects such as fans and invitations. Northerners who called New Bern home during the cooler months provided a convenient market. She also had a taxidermy business with a brother, and the pair

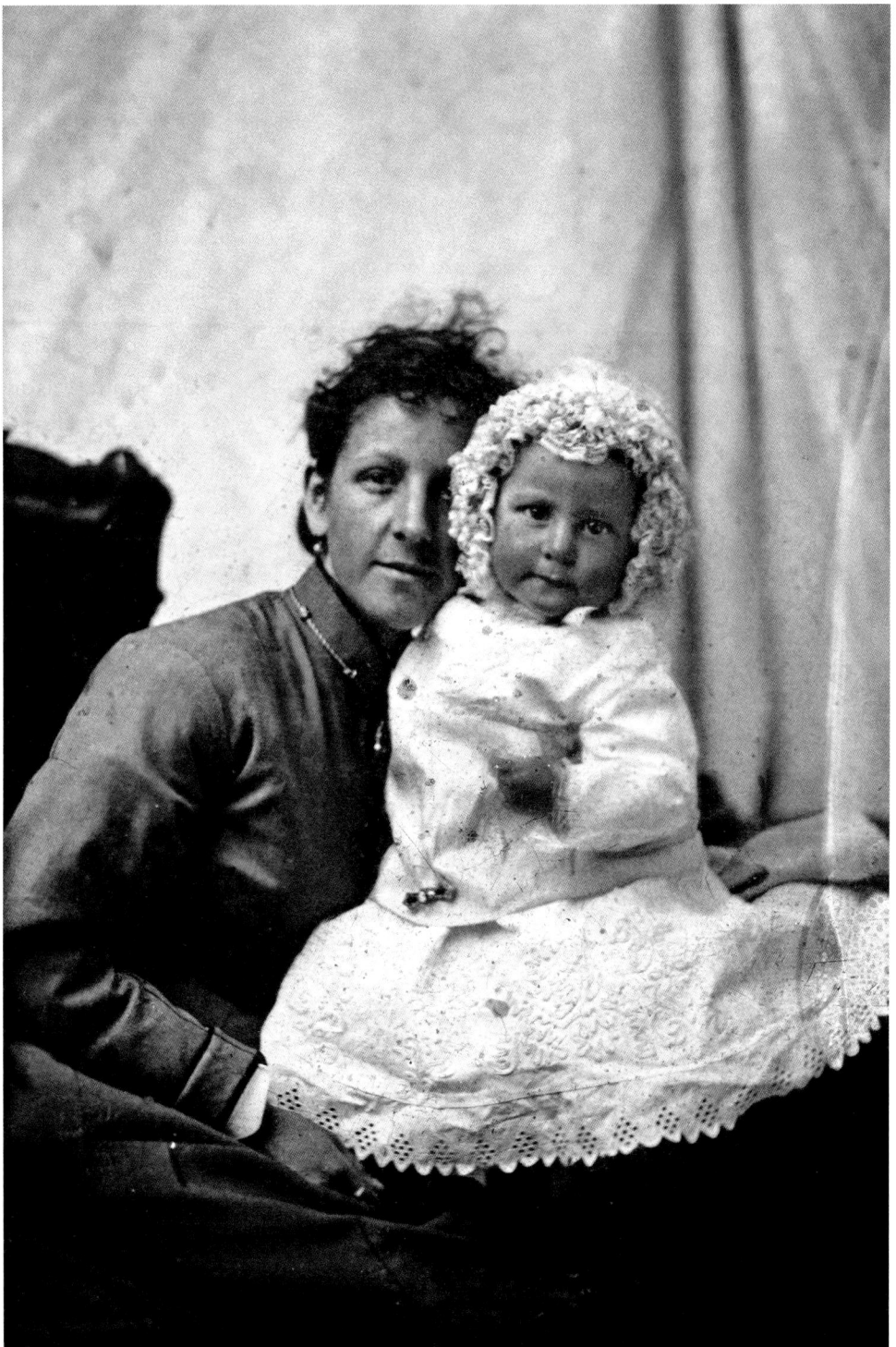

sometimes made forays to the coast to kill shore birds. They stuffed and mounted these specimens for museums and collectors or simply harvested the birds for feathers. On one occasion they mounted a twelve-foot alligator for a museum in Germany. By the end of the decade Bayard was honing her own skills with the brush, and for a time she studied photograph retouching in the studio of New Bern photographer Edward Gerock.

In 1886, Mary Morgan remarried at the bedside of her ailing mother. The groom was George Moulton, an itinerant merchant and 44-year-old bachelor from New Hampshire. Income increased, but so did the size of the family. George Clarke Moulton, who later joined his half sister Bayard in her photography business, was born to the couple before the year ended. Another son, Warren, arrived in 1894, and a daughter Celia four years later.

Bayard was the oldest of the children and the first to leave New Bern. In the summer of 1892, after attending the New Bern Collegiate Institute, she applied to the North Carolina State Normal and Industrial School at Greensboro, now the University of North Carolina at Greensboro. In a letter to Charles Duncan McIver, president of the school, she wrote that her family was "very poor" and said, "I am determined to make my own living, and if I cannot do it by teaching I shall have to do it by sewing, and therefor [*sic*] I am very anxious for an education."[4] A New Bern lawyer and former classmate of McIver as well as the town's mayor sent letters of support. The attorney noted that she was from a "naturally talented family," and the mayor stressed her "extraordinary talents for drawing and painting."[5]

In the fall of 1892 she entered the college, where much of her instruction was in art. An uncle, Francis Devereux Clarke, paid most of her expenses at the school. About a year and a half later, Clarke helped his niece secure a teaching job at the Arkansas Deaf-Mute Institute in Little Rock where he was superintendent, and she left Greensboro, apparently without a degree. The stay in Little Rock was short. By late 1894, she had moved to Georgia to teach art at a state school for the deaf in Cave Spring. Her time there was longer and had a far greater impact on her life. In 1897 she described the work at Cave Spring to a relative:

I have drawing classes from eight to ten-forty. They [my students] draw in charcoal from castes [*sic*] and objects, and eight of the most advanced ones started in water-colors a few weeks ago. From 2:30 P.M. to 3:30 I have a class in wood-

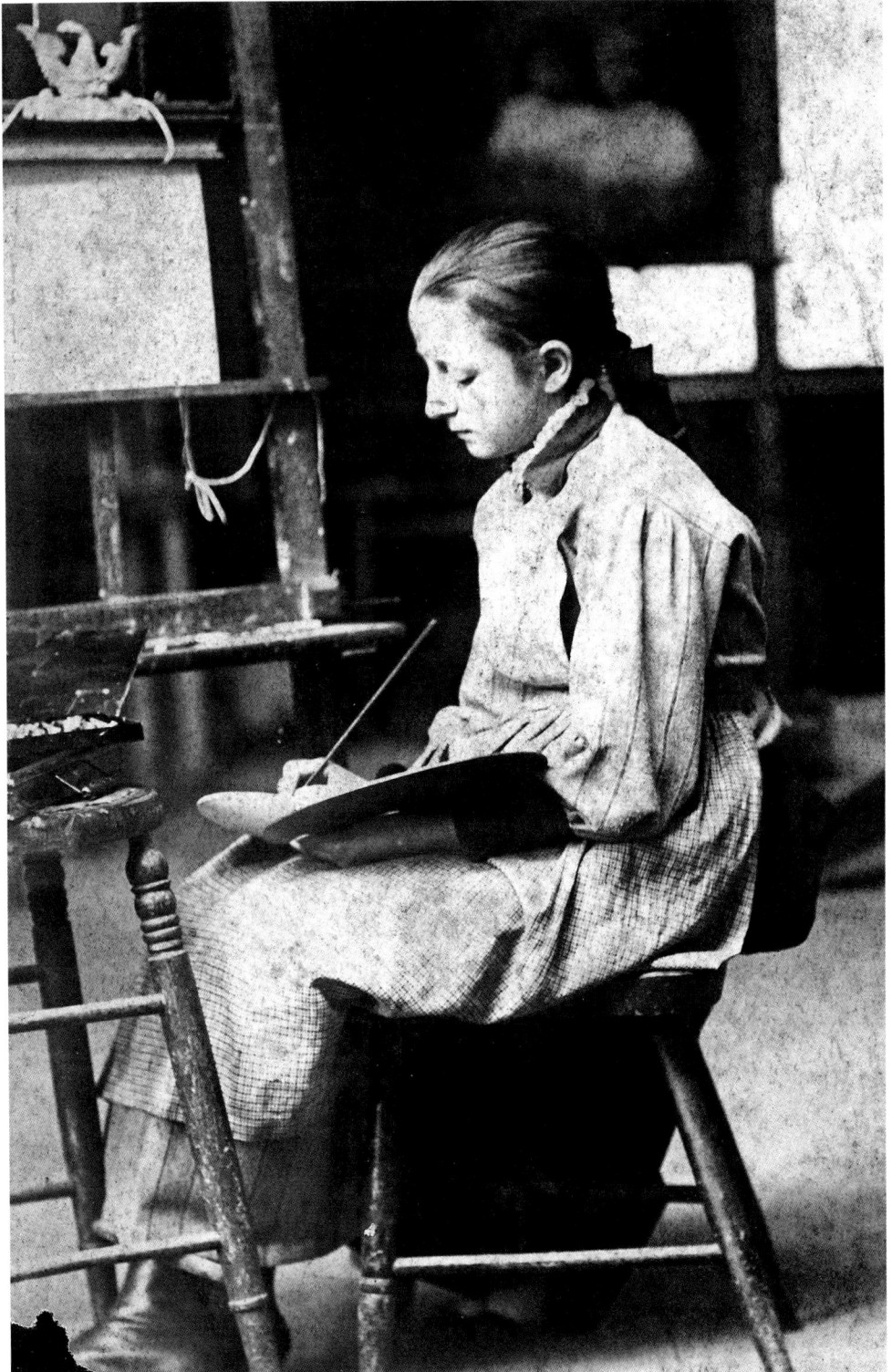

FIGURE 2
*Bayard was only
about fourteen years old
in 1890 when she was
photographed working
with paints in Edward
Gerock's New Bern stu-
dio. A decade and a half
later she had her own
photographic business
in the town. (North
Carolina Collection)*

FIGURE 3

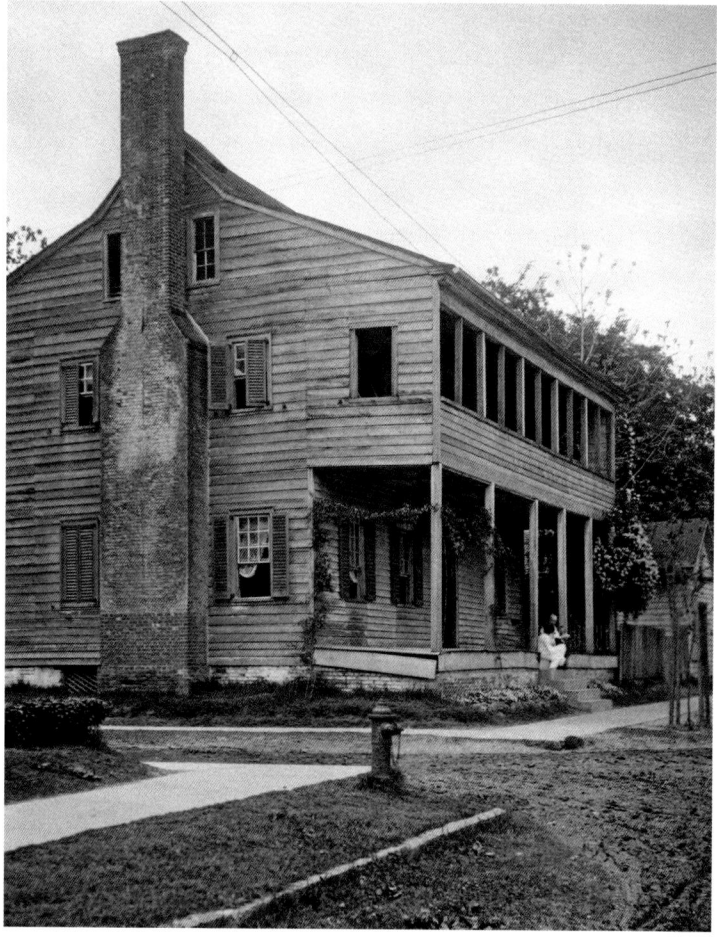

carving, and I enjoy it more than any of the others. We have just finished a handsome cabinet mantel for one of the school parlors. Then they carve screens, bread-platters, picture frames, boxes, etc. I do all the designing for them and find it very interesting.[6]

While working at Cave Spring, she met Charles Thomas Wootten, a man nine years her senior who worked at odd jobs and occasionally practiced law in the nearby towns of Wadley and Louisville. A courtship followed, and the couple visited Morgan's family in New Bern. They announced plans for a future marriage but set no date. Bayard wrote to an aunt in New Hampshire revealing her intentions and predicted, "From the present out-look everything [is] bright, and my married life will be most happy."[7]

A few months later, on November 21, 1897, the couple married in the school chapel at Cave Spring without informing relatives in North Carolina. Her family received news of the event from an account picked up by a local newspaper. The episode hurt them deeply. Within weeks of the wedding, Charles Wootten wrote a letter to his mother-in-law seeking to make amends.

> I know that I have unfortunately caused you much pain, and while that cannot be undone, yet I feel satisfied that I can convince you it was not without consideration of you, and regret that your wishes could not be followed. There is no longer a reason why you don't come down and help Bayard boss me. She will need very little assistance as she seems already an expert on that line; and I feel that I have much reason to be proud of her executive ability. I am easily the best managed man in Wadley. Like a pillar of fire by night and a pillar of cloud by day your disappointment at the circumstances surrounding our marriage has haunted her mind, casting a shadow where else all were sunshine. She knows that your love for her is the cause for your disappointment, and her love for you makes this estrangement very hard for her to bear.[8]

Charles Thomas, the first of the couple's two children, was born on October 8, 1898. Wootten gave up teaching but continued to draw and paint. She took orders for custom-made party favors, occasionally sold paintings, and colored photographs.

The couple had a difficult marriage, due in part to finances, but personal differences likely played a role as well. The relationship ended in 1901 when an unpaid landlord locked Bayard out of her home. Charles Wootten had gone out of town on business, leaving behind a check that proved to be worthless. A local minister gave Bayard money for a train ticket to North Carolina, and his wife packed food for the trip. In Sandersville, Georgia, Wootten and her toddler son were short of the needed train fare by less than a dollar. She begged the remaining money from a stranger.[9] In an interview decades later, Wootten reminisced about the failed relationship: "Before we were married Charlie visited my home at New Bern. It was a substantial old place and was filled with beautiful, expensive furniture we had inherited. My husband thought my family was wealthy and that I'd eventually come into some money. When he found out later that we had no money he left me."[10] Wootten's divorce became final in 1907, and she never again married or became seriously involved with anyone.

Bayard Wootten's return to New Bern put more people in the house on East Front Street than ever before. On New Year's Day 1902, she gave birth to a second son, Rufus. Charles, the older of the two, described their extended family: "Mama and her mother called themselves 'the Firm,' raising four children, Rufus and me and Grandma's two youngest, who were one and five years older than I. With Father Moulton and two older children of Grandma's, Sam Morgan and George Moulton, this made a family of nine!"[11]

Small children to care for made work outside the home impractical for Wootten. The brush, a previous source of income, continued to provide meager support. Both Wootten and her mother pooled their talents to paint designs on anything that would sell, including fans, dresses, calendars, parasols, cards, and invitations. Orders came from as far away as New York and Massachusetts. In 1904, a hand-painted fan sold for seventy-five cents; fifty cents bought two calendars.

According to Charles Wootten, his mother also designed the first trademark used by Pepsi-Cola. "[The drink] was the creation of C. D. Bradham, owner of two drug stores in New Bern. . . . He lived next door to us in what I'm pretty sure was the largest and handsomest [sic] residence in town. He had mama design the Pepsi-Cola labels."[12] Bradham filed an application with the U.S. Patent Office to register a Pepsi trademark in 1903 and indicated that his design had been in use since 1901, the year in which Wootten returned to New Bern.

About 1904 she began working with the camera, seeing it as a faster medium than the brush. "Mr. Garrett [Gerock], the local photographer, loaned me a little 4 × 5 camera and said I was welcome to experiment in his shop. He was always shaking his head, saying I'd never make the grade."[13] By 1905, however, Gerock viewed Wootten as a competitor, and he stopped her from using his equipment. She then bought her own camera and formed a partnership with a "Mr. Grant," possibly John Lewis Grant of New Bern. They opened a small studio beside her home, but the partnership dissolved the next year.

Drawing and painting greatly diminished in importance for Wootten. She sought photographic instruction from any available source, including Eastman Kodak salesmen and representatives of other photographic companies that passed through New Bern. In the fall of 1905, she went to Asheville to study photography under Ignatius

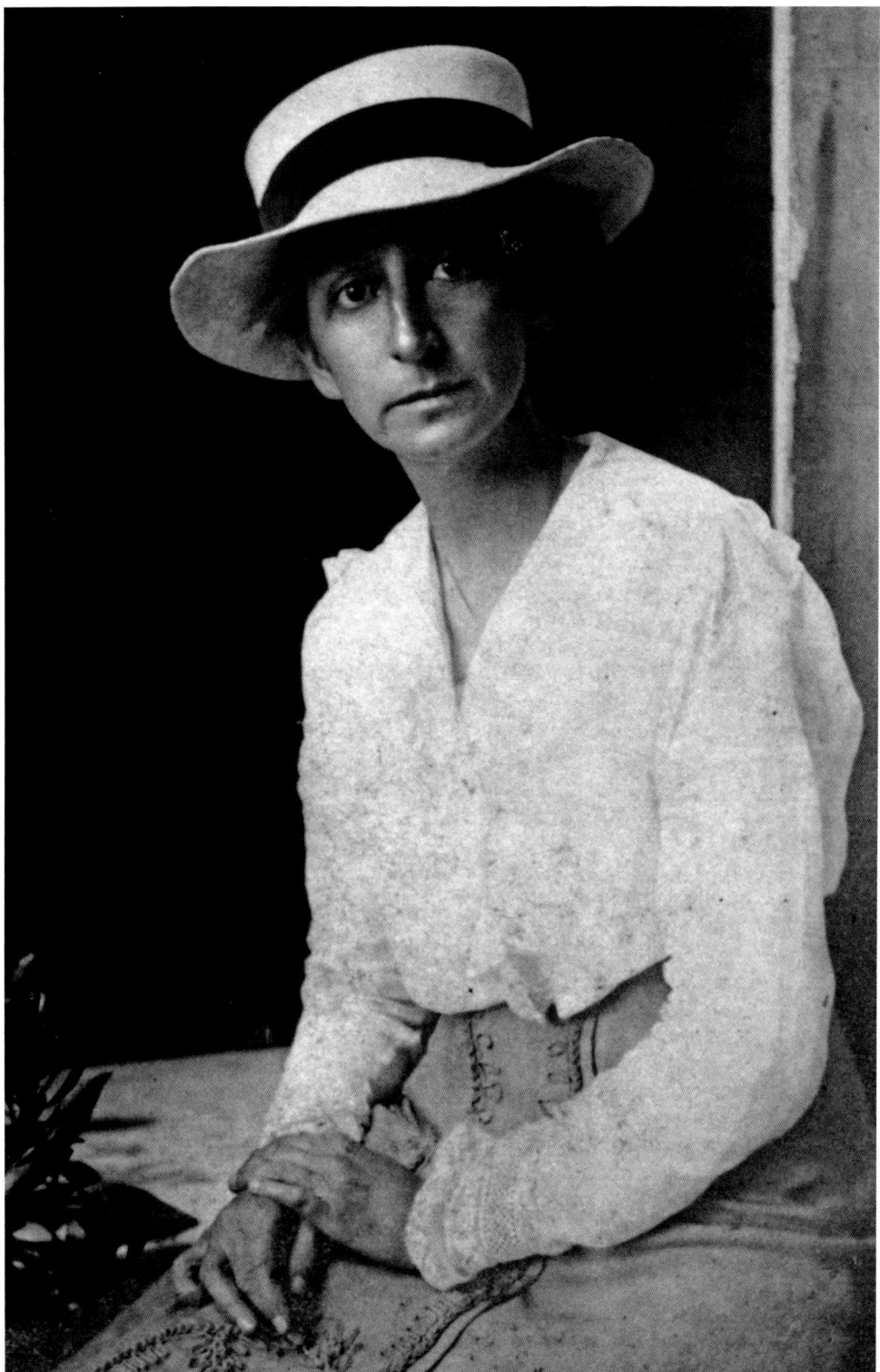

FIGURE 4
*This somber portrait
of Wootten, taken
after her 1901 return to
North Carolina, perhaps
has subtle overtones of
the personal difficulties
that she faced as a
divorced single mother.
(Clare Crawford-Mason
and Victor Crawford
Collection)*

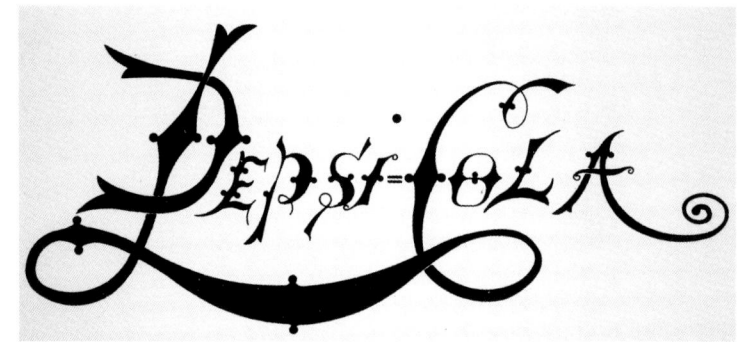

(Nace) Wadsworth Brock, who, more than any other person, served as a mentor. This talented painter, photographer, and amateur poet was born on a Jones County farm near New Bern in 1866. He studied art at Cooper Union in New York City and worked as an apprentice at Edward Gerock's studio in New Bern. Around 1897, Brock opened his own studio in Asheville after visiting the mountain town on his honeymoon. He lived there until his death in 1950.

Wootten first met Brock about 1890 or possibly earlier. An assistant in Brock's studio remembered a conversation in which Brock mentioned visiting Wootten's grandmother, Mary Bayard Clarke, to discuss poetry. Clarke died in 1886. One of Wootten's sons recalled a description of Brock as his mother's childhood "beau." The two photographers remained lifelong friends, and in her sixties Wootten signed letters to Brock with the words "affectionately, Bayard." In a 1956 interview, Wootten spoke of her friend's abilities with the camera and brush:

> I met him when I was a young girl . . . at a New Bern photographer's, Mr. Gerock, where I was studying retouching. He strolled in . . . dirty, unkempt, unshaven. His work was the only thing he was interested in. When I decided to go into photography, I went to Asheville and had a month in his studio. The artistry of his posing, his graciousness to his subjects, was entirely out of keeping with his appearance. He is the most talented artist that I have ever had the privilege of knowing,

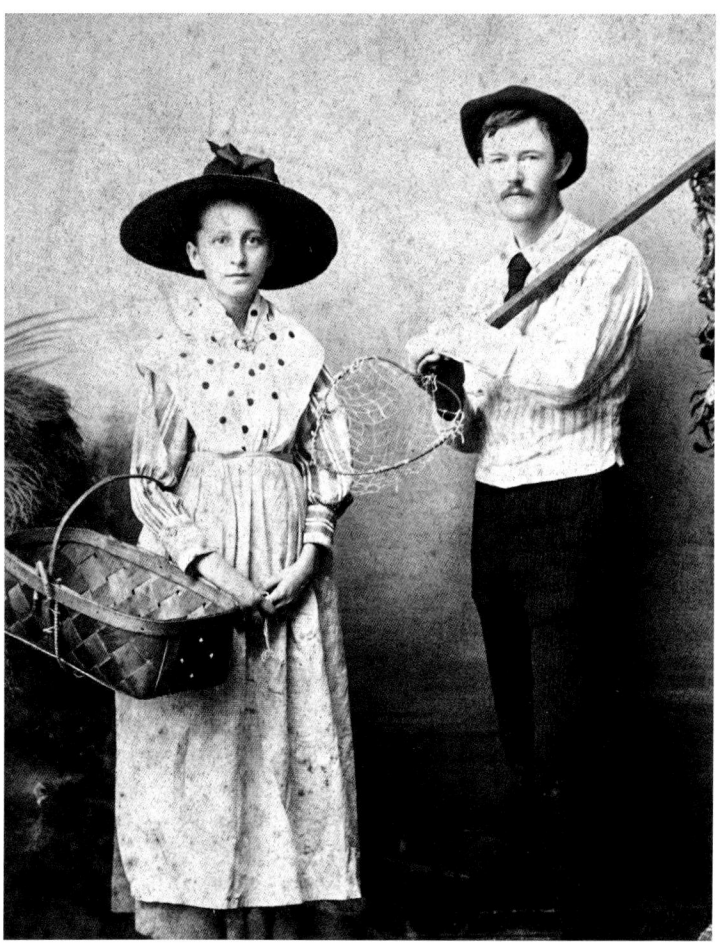

FIGURE 6

Bayard and Nace Brock posed for this photograph in New Bern around 1890, when the two were allegedly sweethearts. (Photograph by Edward Gerock, North Carolina Collection)

equally at home with paints or a camera. I consider that I personally owe him a greater debt than anyone who has influenced my life; his beautiful landscapes showed me what could be done pictorially with a camera.[14]

WOOTTEN AND THE TIDE OF PICTORIALISM

The introduction of faster film and lenses and smaller cameras toward the end of the nineteenth century had a liberating effect on photography. Picture taking became easier and the ranks of those who called themselves photographers swelled. When Wootten entered the profession in 1904, a movement was already underway to redefine the medium as well as the relationship of photographers to it.

Known as pictorialism, the movement began in the 1890s with the objective of elevating photography to a true art form rather than a simple trade. Pictorialists took inspiration from impressionist painters, and their photographs often appear heavy with artistic effects. Softness of contrast and tone, a diffused "atmospheric" look, and even dreamlike appearances were popular. Pictorial photographers preferred matte or textured print surfaces, and they experimented with a broad medley of papers and processes. Some high-art pictorialists physically altered negatives and prints for visual effect.

To give images an emotional dimension, pictorial photographers often chose quaint, picturesque, and sentimental subjects. They objected to "straight" and realistic photography. Personal expression permeated every aspect of the photographic process from subject selection to printing. The overriding objective was to create an artistically beautiful image, even if mood eclipsed reality in the process.

In the 1890s, photography clubs and exhibitions promoted the pictorial style, and the movement gained an international following. New York photographer Alfred Stieglitz was an influential leader of organized efforts on behalf of pictorialism in the United States. In 1902, he founded a group known as the Photo-Secession, which published an illustrated journal titled *Camera Work* and opened a gallery at 291 Fifth Avenue. Among the early pictorialists were many now associated with the development of twentieth-century American photography, including Edward Weston, Edward Steichen, Gertrude Käsebier, Alvin Langdon Coburn, Imogen Cunningham, and Clarence White. Bayard Wootten's friend and mentor Nace Brock, talented with both the camera and the brush, was also North Carolina's earliest pictorial photographer.

Pictorialism flourished during the first decade of the century. An exhibition held at the Albright Art Gallery in Buffalo, New York, in November 1910 came at the movement's crest. This exhibit included contemporary as well as retrospective works and was international in scope. The size of the exhibition, 606 photographs, was fully equal to its breadth.

There were no prints by Wootten in the Buffalo exhibit, and there is no indication that she had any direct connection with New York pictorialists at this time. Indeed, her artistic skills with the camera were still in their adolescence. Most pictorialists gradually abandoned the style and progressed toward a photographic approach that was more "straight" and purely photographic in the modern sense. There were exceptions, however, and one of these was Bayard Wootten.

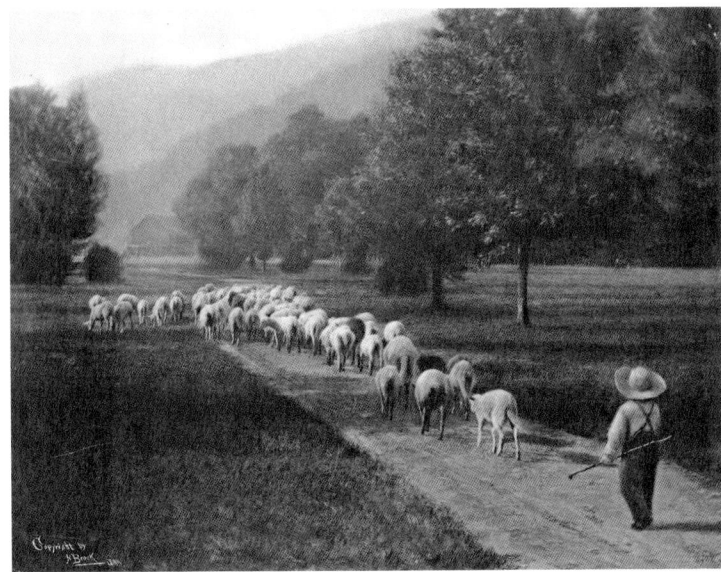

FIGURE 7

Nace Brock's pictorial photography influenced Wootten during her formative years. Typical of his artistic work is this 1899 composition, "Return of the Sheep," originally printed on platinum paper. (North Carolina Collection)

In 1916, photographers Clarence White, Gertrude Käsebier, and Alvin Langdon Coburn founded the Pictorial Photographers of America (PPA) to carry the movement onward in the face of declining popularity. White became the group's first president. The PPA mounted exhibitions and published an attractively printed annual titled *Pictorial Photography in America* containing articles and photographs. Issues appeared in 1920, 1921, 1922, 1926, and 1929.

Exactly when Bayard Wootten joined the PPA is uncertain, but her name appears on the membership roster of 1918. She made an ill-fated effort to establish a studio in New York City the previous year and may have joined the organization during her brief residency. No articles or photographs by Wootten appear in any of the five PPA annuals.

Clarence White operated a photography school and commercial studio in New York City, and he exerted a forceful influence on behalf of pictorialism. Among his students were Doris Ulmann and Dorothea Lange, photographers who later had outstanding careers that on occasion brought them to North Carolina. White, like Wootten and many other pictorialists, tried to combine artistic and commercial photography. They believed that pictorial images would gain popular acceptance and carry artistic photographers to financial success. In spite of the efforts of White and others, however, the style continued its decline. By the mid-1940s when Wootten's own career had begun a descent, due in large measure to her age, pictorialism was little more than a colorful footnote on the photographic page. Its emphasis on intense composition and depiction of a subject's character, however, had an enduring influence on portrait photography.

The importance that pictorialism placed on visual appeal complemented Wootten's artistic training. Her photographic style evolved over a period of years, but it never became the hand-manipulated and painting-like approach of some high-art pictorialists. Wootten's photography was fundamental photography. She composed scenes for aesthetic effect and used the basic ingredients of camera work—light, shadow, focus, and perspective—to carry out artistic objectives. Some pictorialists used special camera lenses to create diffused images. Wootten's negatives, however, are sharply focused. She softened images at the enlarger with matte or textured photographic paper, filtration, or slightly out-of-focus printing.

PHOTOGRAPHY AS A BUSINESS

Wootten's motives for entering the profession were economic. The idea of combining photography as a business and as an art form appeared increasingly plausible to Wootten as her skills increased and the studio prospered. Purists such as Stieglitz saw this philosophy as an aesthetic compromise. In 1907 he criticized Gertrude Käsebier, a member of the Photo-Secession and a photographer of international stature, when she joined a trade organization, the Professional Photographers' Association of New York. Like Käsebier and many other pictorialists, Wootten had no reservations about using the camera as a source of livelihood and as a medium of personal expression.

She attended a convention of the Photographers' Association of Virginia and the Carolinas in 1907. It may have been her first professional meeting. Wootten sent a glowing account to her stepfather: "Last week I went to the photographer's convention at Norfolk, and I had such a good time. And just think of it. I was elected third vice president of the association. That means I am in line for the presidency, and some day can hope to be president. This was a great compliment as I am one of the most inexperienced members. And the big men made speeches and complimented my ability and I felt very proud."[15] However, Wootten's name does not appear in a list of officeholders in a report on the group's meeting held the following year in Greensboro, North Carolina.[16] She did not become president of the organization and always believed that her sex prevented this achievement.

In the early years of her career, Wootten concentrated on routine trade photography. Beginning in 1898, the U.S. Post Office Department permitted privately made postcards to go through the mail at the one-cent rate. The medium exploded in popularity, and the years 1907 to 1914 saw more than a billion cards produced. Wootten adopted the popular format, and it helped establish her business. To a relative she wrote: "We are doing well in the studio, but not turning the earth over yet. Just now I am trying to make a run of postals of 'critters' with people's heads. I hope to make a success of it."[17] Six months later Wootten confidently predicted that, except for Nace Brock in Asheville, "I expect to have the biggest photo business in the State."[18]

Photography in New Bern was seasonal. Orders dwindled in summer months when some residents moved away to escape the heat of eastern North Carolina and farmers tightened their belts until crops of tobacco and cotton went to market. Wootten needed another outlet for photographs, one that did not wither during summer doldrums. The North Carolina General Assembly provided a solution.

In 1906 the Assembly established Camp Glenn, a National Guard summer training camp at Morehead City, only a few miles from New Bern. Wootten packed her equipment and went to the camp in search of photography business. She used the words "timid" and "forlorn" to characterize her first visit to the post.[19] She met a soldier from New Bern, and he confidently assured the photographer that taking pictures would be a good idea. The commander, General Laurence W. Young, however, branded Wootten a "camp-follower," prohibited any pictures of the officers, and provided what she later recalled as a "horrible dressing down."[20]

Wootten eventually prevailed, though, and in her first summer at the camp sold 2,300 postcards. A soldier could buy six cards of a single pose for fifty cents. Views of companies and battalions on parade or taking rifle practice were a nickel each. Her pictures appeared on walls and billboards at the camp, and soldiers mailed them home to family and friends. General Young decided that photographs were good for morale and promoted National Guard interests. Wootten later recalled that he "spent the next 15 years trying to make amends."[21]

The large volume of work prompted Wootten to ask permission to build a small photo hut at the camp, and Young consented. He sanctioned the decision by designating the photographer a member of the Guard with the title "Chief of Publicity." Thereafter she enjoyed the distinction of being known as the first woman in the North Carolina National Guard.

FIGURE 8

Wootten's first studio was in a small frame building beside her home on New Bern's East Front Street. By 1911, she had moved to these larger quarters at 96 Middle Street in the main business district. (Clare Crawford-Mason and Victor Crawford Collection)

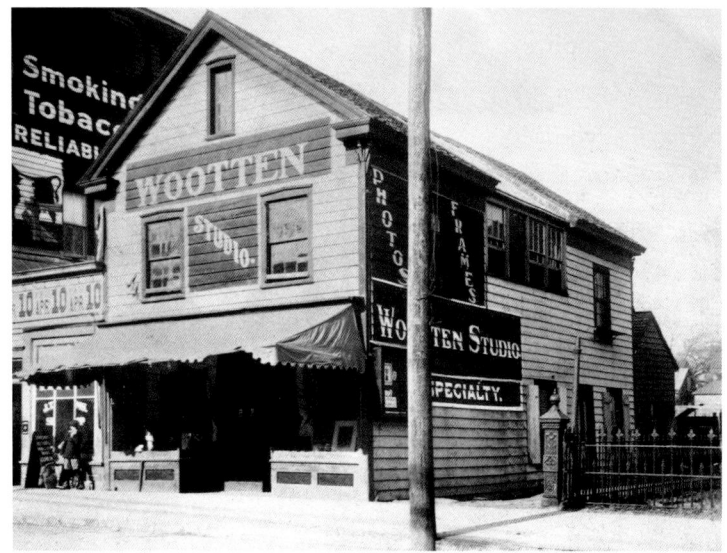

A woman in her early thirties at a military camp full of men invited problems. The Guard responded by issuing Wootten a uniform. She later recalled that it "was a great joy for me, and I think an affliction to my family. And I wore it all the time for 12 of the 16 years that I made pictures for the National Guard."[22]

The military subsequently informally named Wootten an "adjutant general," but enlisted men fondly gave her nicknames such as "Sandfiddler," "Morehead," "Aunt Ruth," and "Ole Campaigner." On one occasion she photographed a drunken recruit holding six bottles of beer when he entered the photo hut and requested a picture. A day later he returned to apologize and asked that the photographs be destroyed. Wootten consented, but "in the rush" a print ended up on the commissary wall. "I've never seen anyone so furious," she remembered. "He said to me: 'God, but I wish you were a man.' I told him I was glad for once that I wasn't."[23]

The opportunities at Camp Glenn led Wootten to expand the studio. She opened a small branch in Morehead City, and her family, including her two small sons and mother, often stayed overnight to help with the work. In a letter to her half brother, George C. Moulton, then living in New Hampshire, Wootten wrote enthusiastically of the profession. "I am certain there is a big fortune in it. We propose to get out postals for every town of any size in N.C."[24] Wootten prodded Moulton to return to North Carolina and join the venture, an offer that he subsequently accepted. "We have a deluge of orders," she wrote, "& need help badly right now. Suppose you go in with us. We will bear your expenses and by Xmas will give you $5.00 a week. Next summer at the encampment will pay $15 a week. Will teach you the whole business from A to Z. Every paper in the state has noticed our work for the last two or three weeks so we are well advertised & we are going to follow it up."[25]

Camp Glenn with its white sand and bright summer sun gave Wooten useful experience in working under primitive conditions and handling difficult lighting situations with the camera. She met soldiers from all parts of North Carolina, and her photographs received wide geographic distribution. In 1910, her studio marketed a series of special postcards to coincide with the New Bern Bicentennial and two years later offered same-day "rush" photographs during the Eastern North Carolina Fair.

In the early years of the studio, Wooten established a pattern of traveling to other cities and towns in search of business. This strategy persisted to some degree throughout her career. Going on the road became a way of life on which she thrived, both professionally and personally. Her children accepted their mother's absence as a necessary inconvenience. "Mama was frequently absent on business trips," remembered her son Charles. "Her friends used to ask me when she was away, 'Don't you miss your mother?' For some strange reason, I didn't miss her, but I was always joyous when she returned, because her first afternoon at home she took a walk across the Neuse River bridge. . . . We did this alone, and I don't think two people, especially child and adult, ever got closer together."[26]

Wooten's National Guard experience, informal personality, and hands-on approach to work influenced the way that she dressed. Although she sometimes donned elegant attire for special occasions, Wooten was out of place in fine feathers. A bandanna or visor around the head, trousers, loose print dresses, or dark skirts and heavy cotton stockings often defined her appearance. Her hair was kept short and combed straight back, perhaps to minimize the investment of time in a perfunctory chore. When she bought a new hat in 1938, the local newspaper took note of the "sensational event."[27]

Boldness with the camera took equal billing with Wooten's penchant for travel. On May 28, 1914, during New Bern's homecoming celebration, Wooten joined a visiting pilot in an open Wright Brothers Model B airplane and made aerial pictures of the fairgrounds and surrounding countryside. "I was present," recalled her son Charles, "when Mama made the first picture-taking plane flight by a woman. Mama used a Graflex camera and could point it straight down between her feet in the

FIGURE 9

Photographing National Guardsmen at Camp Glenn was so successful for Wootten that she expanded the studio and brought her half brother George Clarke Moulton into the business. In this scene at the camp she is wearing a military-type uniform provided by the Guard to help maintain proper decorum at the post. (Clare Crawford-Mason and Victor Crawford Collection)

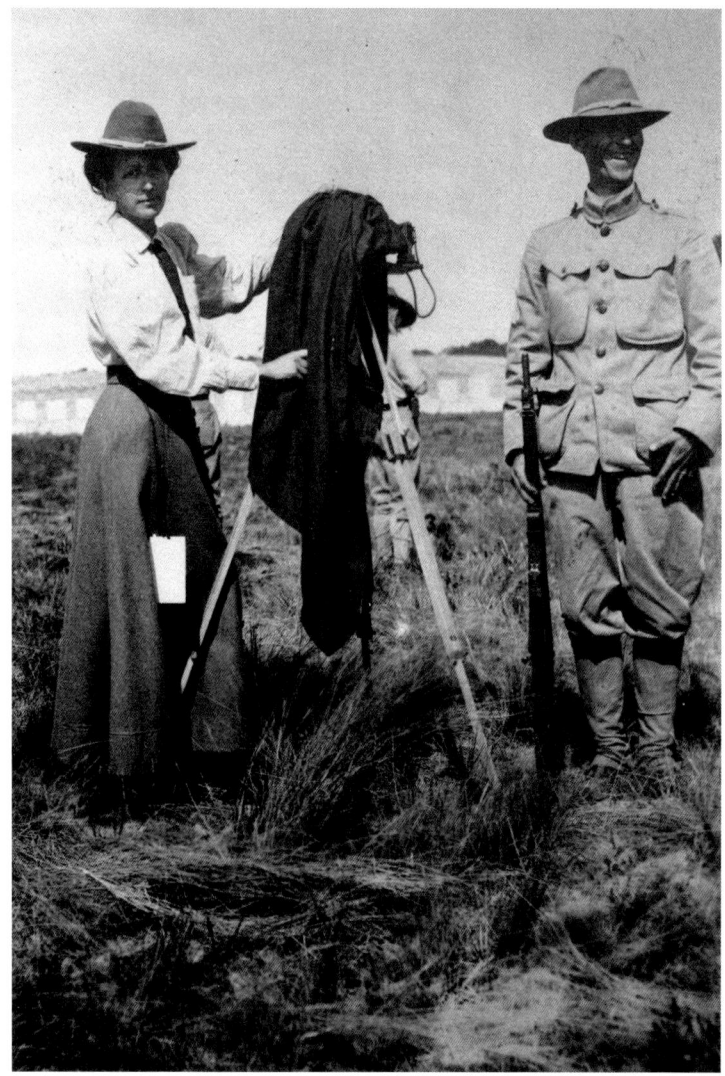

plane."[28] The New Bern *Daily Journal* gave the event front-page coverage. "Mrs. Wootten is probably the only lady in New Bern who has been up in an aeroplane," wrote the paper, "and she is very proud of this fact. As the big machine soared over the race track far into the clouds, the spectators craned their necks and followed its flight with their eyes until it had alighted and Mrs. Wootten had alighted amidst the cheers from many throats."[29]

Deliberation over whether she made the first aerial photographs by a woman perhaps obscures a more basic point. Bayard Wootten would stubbornly pursue a

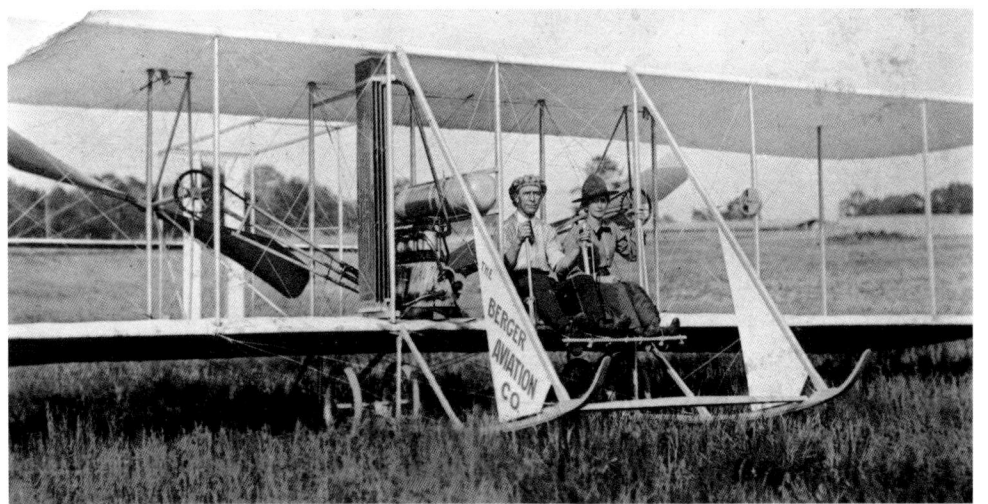

photographic opportunity that others might ignore. Her family and friends learned to tolerate the photographer's persistent quest for unusual subjects, dramatic land-scapes, and the best angle for the camera.

THE WOMEN'S FEDERATION

Women entered the American labor force in increasing numbers toward the end of the nineteenth century. About 2.6 million were present in 1880. By 1900 the number of female workers had climbed to 5.1 million, and a decade later the total stood at 7.8 million. Women photographers attended meetings of the Photographers' Association of America (PAA) in the 1890s, but their numbers were small compared to the men, and their presence produced little in the way of personal or professional recognition. The influence of women grew, however, in response to an increasing number of female photographers who saw the profession as a viable career.

At the Detroit meeting of the PAA in 1908 about twenty women came together in an informal group known as "the Circle." The following year when the convention met in Rochester, New York, the Women's Federation of the Photographers' Association of America was established under the leadership of Philadelphia photographer Mary Carnell. Membership in the Federation was open to "white women who are engaged in the practice of photography in any of its branches."[30] Dues were one dollar a year.

FIGURE 11

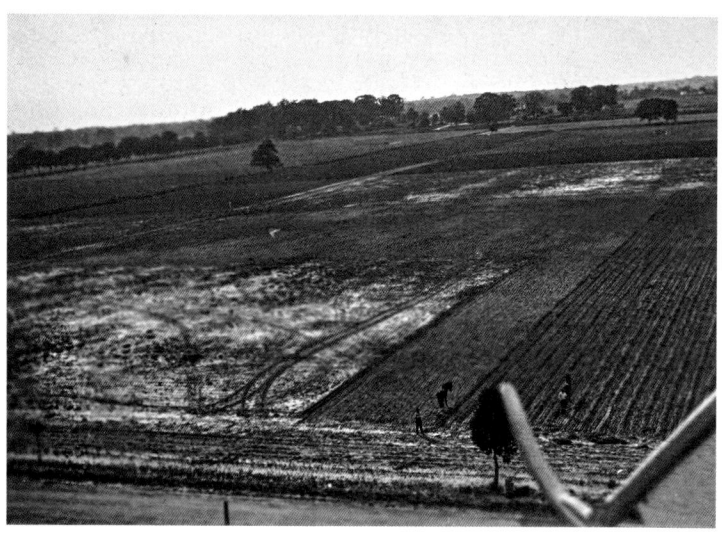

Farmers plowing in a field paused as Wootten photographed them from the air. Part of the plane's ski-type landing gear is visible on the lower right. (North Carolina Collection)

The male leadership of the Association supported the Federation and incorporated the women's group into the program for the 1910 meeting in Milwaukee. At this gathering the first collective exhibition of photographs by the Association's professional women photographers took place. Wootten was an exhibitor, but it seems unlikely that she was present because of the distance from New Bern and the travel and lodging costs the struggling photographer would have had to bear.[31]

Wootten wrote the following short piece for the *Bulletin of Photography* endorsing the Federation. Titled "The Outlook for Women," it expressed her vision of the role women should play in the profession and protested the widespread gender discrimination in the workplace and among photographic professionals. Several years after her death in 1959, Wootten's son Charles commented that "mama was a woman's liberation movement all by herself."[32]

> Most cheerfully do I welcome the coming of the Women's Federation, for I think it means more for the uplifting of the individual woman photographer than we realize. It is a step toward placing us on a secure footing and where we belong, and where we will rise to the merit of our work and capacity for business. I truly believe, if we grasp this opportunity, and each woman will give her heartiest support to these women who have so generously given their thought and time for this movement, we will accomplish more than our most enthusiastic friends anticipate. Now to be a woman and a photographer means to be a photographer

handicapped, but this is but transition. A few years ago, at a State convention, I was nominated as Third Vice-President of the association. Immediately a man was on his feet. "We do not wish Mrs. Wootten because she is a woman." If he had said, "We do not wish her because she is not fit" he would have voiced the truth, and I would have congratulated him on his clear judgment, but to try to throw me out on account of sex was both unjust and a rank of injustice. This illustrates how the profession-at-large feels towards the woman worker. Her sex scores a point against her when she enters the professional field. The Women's Federation will do much to overcome this prejudice, and I hope the men will be wise enough to appreciate our efforts. Will they? It means an impartial showing and gives us an opportunity of gaining the recognition we deserve. We are in the dawn of a new régime and the fit will survive, regardless of sex. This is our opportunity. If we grasp it and if every woman supports this Federation to the best of her ability there will be many and more women to be with the fit when the time of reckoning comes, and I am going to fight.[33]

The Federation existed solely for the benefit of women photographers. They exchanged information, studied one another's photographs by formally circulating portfolios, and cultivated social and professional bonds. Following the Federation's establishment, the number of women attending PAA meetings increased markedly. Naomi Rosenblum's *A History of Women Photographers* indicates that thousands of women belonged to the Federation by 1913. New York photographer Pearl Grace Loehr wrote that "the Federation was the answer to a silent heart cry for professional recognition, which every progressive woman worker knew she must have before she could be a real power in her profession."[34] Another member put it even more succinctly: "Before we came—now we belong."[35]

There seems to be no record of Wootten's association with the Women's Federation until her name appeared as a print exhibitor at the PAA meeting in 1910. When the group met at St. Paul, Minnesota, in 1911, they appointed Wootten chair of a Federation section. As was the case a year earlier, however, she may not have been present.

Wootten did attend the Philadelphia convention in July 1912. She gave a brief report and exhibited two prints. One of these, a photograph of a boy reading a book, appeared in the September 18, 1912, issue of the *Bulletin of Photography*, and it may have been her first published photograph of professional merit. John Bartlett, editor of the *Bulletin*, critiqued the work, noting that "the subject is well posed, but the disposition of the curtain is unfortunate. The dimensions of the mount give an impression to the spectator of restraint."[36] A partially opened curtain in the background cut a diagonal line across the print that may have appeared distracting, but the use of diagonal elements in photographs became a common trait in Wootten's work.

More than sixty women photographers, representing a broad cross section of the profession, exhibited their work in the Philadelphia exhibition, a reflection, no doubt, of the growing appeal of photography as a career for women and the increasing popularity of the Women's Federation. The exhibitors ranged from prominent and established photographers such as Frances Benjamin Johnston and Gertrude Käsebier to relative newcomers like Wootten and Seattle photographer Imogen Cunningham.

Wootten began serious camera work three years after Cunningham made her first photograph in 1901. Both women opened studios during the first decade of the century and were part of a tide of women photographers entering the profession. Cunningham and Wootten, like many other women, came under the influence of pictorialism, but Cunningham later embraced straight photography while Wootten continued marching to the pictorial drummer.

The September 18, 1912, issue of the *Bulletin* contains a short article by Wootten titled "As Seen by One of the Throng," in which she discusses the contribution of women to the Federation and profession. Wootten is also the likely author of an unsigned article titled, "A Woman by a Woman." This piece describes the plight of a struggling woman photographer "in a little Southern town" and the importance of membership in the Federation.

Wootten remained active in the group, and Federation members elected her secretary-treasurer in 1914 and reelected her to a second term the following year. The 1916 *Bulletin* did not list Federation officers, and World War I led to the cancellation of national conventions in 1917 and 1918.

The level of Wootten's activity in the organization appears to have subsided after her service as a Federation officer. There is no indication that Wootten held other offices, and her photographs are absent from the *Bulletin of Photography* until 1920. This lull may have resulted in part from the professional setback she suffered in 1917 when her New York City studio failed. Nonetheless, the late 1910s were a period of

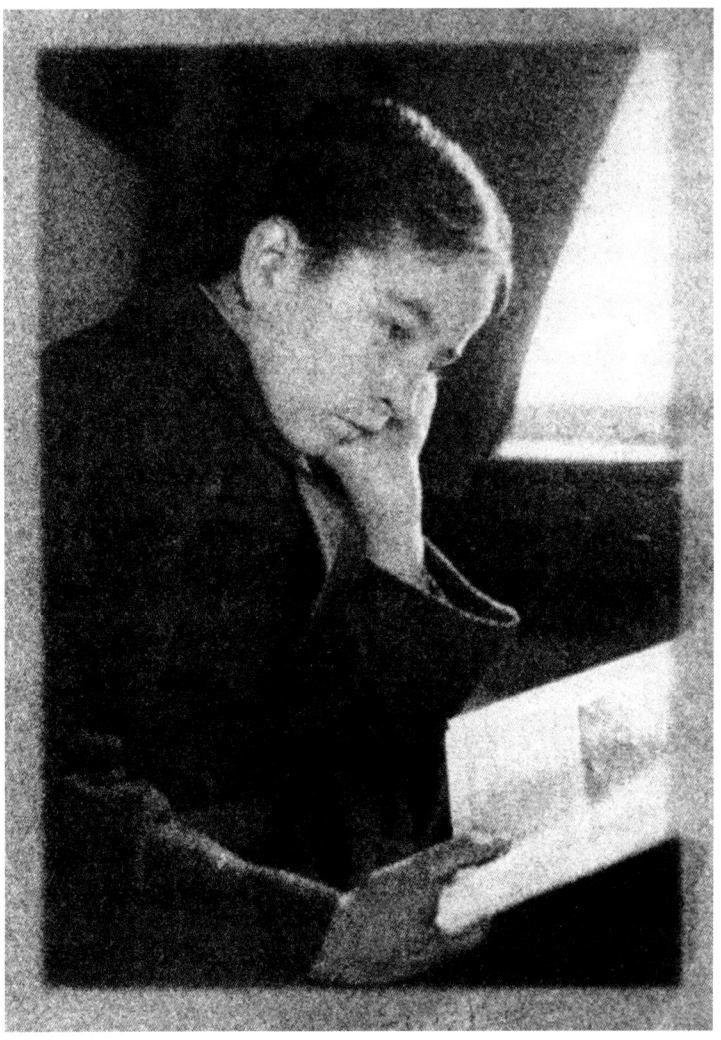

FIGURE 12

One of Wootten's earliest published portraits was this view of a young boy reading a book, which appeared in the September 18, 1912, issue of the Bulletin of Photography.

general improvement in the status of women both in and out of the photographic profession.

In 1919, both houses of the U.S. Congress passed a constitutional amendment granting women the right to vote, and the requisite number of states approved the measure the following year. Wootten had long been a supporter of women's suffrage. As early as 1913 she had a reputation in New Bern for "asserting her rights and doing as she sees fit."[37] Her scrapbook also contains photographs made in that year during a tumultuous suffragette demonstration in Washington, D.C., that coincided with Woodrow Wilson's inauguration as president. These photographs suggest that she attended.

FIGURE 13

Wootten (far left) and other members of the Women's Federation posed for a group photograph in Atlanta during the 1914 convention of the Photographers' Association of America. At the meeting, Federation members elected Wootten secretary-treasurer. This print is from Abel's Photographic Weekly, *July 18, 1914. (North Carolina Collection)*

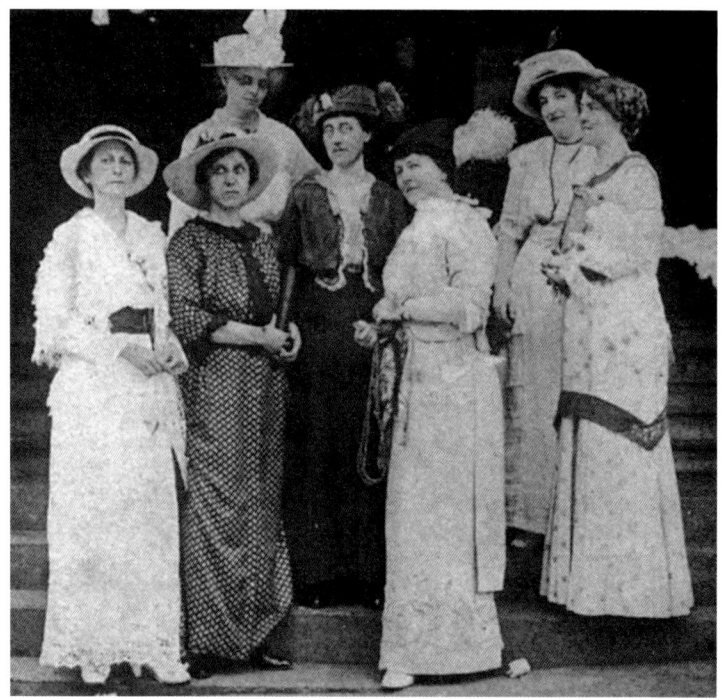

Also in 1919 a proposal went forward to change the constitution of the Photographers' Association of America. Article III listed the governing offices of the organization—president, first vice-president, second vice-president, and treasurer. The suggested changes included a statement that "one of these officers shall be a woman photographer."[38] At the 1919 convention, Mamie Gerhard of St. Louis became the first woman elected to the board of the PAA.[39]

The formal disbanding of the Women's Federation at the 1919 convention was an even clearer indication that women photographers had won much of the professional acceptance they had sought by establishing the organization a decade earlier. Bayard Wootten supported the Federation for most of its life. Professional involvement at the national level helped Wootten define her role as a photographer and helped mold her vision of what a good photograph should be.

Wootten endured the slow professional climb of women photographers, and by the 1920s her photographic business was stable, if not prosperous. Discrimination did not cease, however, with the professional gains that culminated as the second decade of the century drew to a close. The public could still ignore meritorious photographs, dismiss proven abilities, and silently channel work to male competitors.

For example, in 1923 Wootten suggested to University of North Carolina officials that the campus be photographed from the air to show its "bigness." In reporting the story, the newspaper in Chapel Hill noted that the school was "looking around for a man who will do the work well."[40] Wootten's activist years in support of women photographers gave way to a period of normalcy in which she concentrated on the growth of her studio. Its financial soundness in the 1920s enabled the photographer to pursue an artistic stirring from within. North Carolina was the source of her economic well-being; it also became the primary focus of Wootten's creative photography.

MAKING NORTH CAROLINA HER FIELD OF WORK

Bayard Wootten's photographic ambitions eventually encompassed an entire state and beyond. Her pursuit began at New Bern and Camp Glenn and spread outward, creating a checkerboard of career successes and failures. Among these was a futile effort to compete in the New York City market.

Around 1912, James A. Bryan, a New Bern banker and one of North Carolina's wealthiest men, hired Wootten to make promotional photographs for a mammoth sale of lake and forest property near New Bern. She made hundreds of pictures, and Bryan employed an agent from Boston, Albert R. Rogers, to manage the sale. Rogers came to New Bern to see the property and compile Wootten's photographs. He liked her work and assembled thirteen volumes, each containing about 200 prints.

This assignment provided Wootten with an opening that she could not have anticipated. During a 1917 visit to New York she got in touch with Rogers, who was then general manager for the Grand Central Palace, one of the city's major exhibition halls. He promised her "a lot of work" if she was good at photographing interiors. Wootten offered to make pictures of the New York Flower Show then booked at the Palace, but another photographer already had the job. Rogers agreed to let Wootten take photographs, however, if a newspaper or magazine asked her to do so.

Wootten persuaded the editor of a photographic publication to which she had previously submitted work to request pictures of the show. She rented camera equipment from Allison and Hadaway, a Fifth Avenue firm that also allowed her the use of a darkroom. Working one night at the Palace until 3:30 A.M., Wootten made negatives on 8 × 10-inch glass plates. "I shall never forget the thrill of it all," she wrote, "working in those vast halls alone, except for the occasional passing of a watchman as he made his rounds."[41]

The quality of Wootten's prints convinced Rogers that he needed a new photographer, and she received the contract. He later wrote, "the work that you did at the Flower Show is without question the best photography work that has ever been done in this building. I hope it will be possible for you to take photographs at other exhibitions here, for you certainly have the artistic eye for grouping and you thoroughly understand the art of photography."[42]

Two sons to educate, the challenge of something new, and simple excitement convinced Wootten to give New York a try. She obtained a five-year lease on space in the Printing Crafts Building at Eighth Avenue and Thirty-fourth Street across from Pennsylvania Station. To fund the effort Wootten spent part of a $1,000 inheritance. The studio lasted only a few months. Of the New York experience she reminisced:

> "I learned that I could not live in a city and be happy; that if I worked in New York, all my creative something would be crushed, and I would find myself doing one small specialty, photographing hats, or pictures, or statues, or maybe just babies. Best of all, it showed me what I had in my Old North State, the acre of diamonds that lay at my door. I had a vision of making all North Carolina my field of work, as it was no greater effort for me to go from Asheville to New Bern than from Harlem to the Bowery."[43]

The New York failure was undoubtedly a personal and professional setback for Wootten, but it redirected her attention to North Carolina and the South. She returned to New Bern intent on renewing old business contacts and making new ones. Wootten again went on the road and advertised portraits made "in the homes."

The strategy of taking photographs in a subject's home rather than in a studio was not uncommon among women photographers, but Wootten may have been the first person to practice it extensively in North Carolina. Articles on "home photography" appeared in literature to which Wootten had access. She was also in the audience when New York photographer Pearl Grace Loehr gave a talk on the subject at the PAA meeting in 1912. Home photography enabled Wootten to cover a large geographic area and compete with established photographers on their home turf. She set up a chain of local agents, such as drugstore clerks, in towns across the state and paid a commission for portrait appointments they arranged.

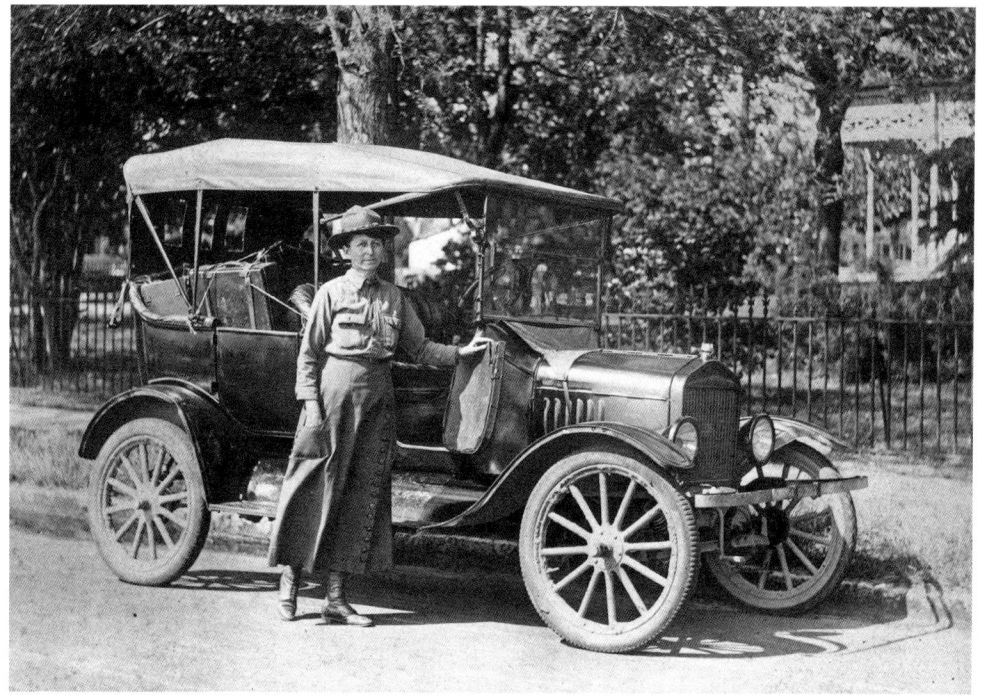

FIGURE 14

Wearing her National Guard uniform, Wootten posed beside the Ford that she drove on photographic assignments. Boxes tied down on the car's back seat likely contain her photographic gear. (Clare Crawford-Mason and Victor Crawford Collection)

In the fall of 1918, while working in Chapel Hill, Wootten met Frederick Henry Koch, a young and enthusiastic drama professor in his first year of teaching at the University of North Carolina. Koch had founded a new theatrical group that he called the Carolina Playmakers. He wanted their performances documented and approached Wootten about doing photography. The pair negotiated an arrangement under which the Wootten-Moulton Studio would charge only for photographs that turned out well. When her half brother and business partner heard about the agreement, he was certain they would lose money, but Wootten believed it could open a lucrative market at the university. Her hunch was correct.

Early in 1919, one of the photographer's first assignments for the Playmakers was to make pictures of a young student from Asheville acting in a play he had written about the North Carolina mountains. The play was *The Return of Buck Gavin*, and the student was future novelist Thomas Wolfe. Eight years later, Wolfe would be among the parade of notables who posed in the New York studio of another woman photographer and pictorialist, Doris Ulmann.

The Carolina Playmakers used Wootten's pictures in promotional publications and compiled scrapbooks of newspaper clippings, playbills, and photographs. By

FIGURE 15

After Wootten's New York studio failed, she came home to North Carolina and resumed traveling by automobile in search of photographic work. This advertisement appeared in the Elizabeth City Independent *on October 31, 1919. (North Carolina Collection)*

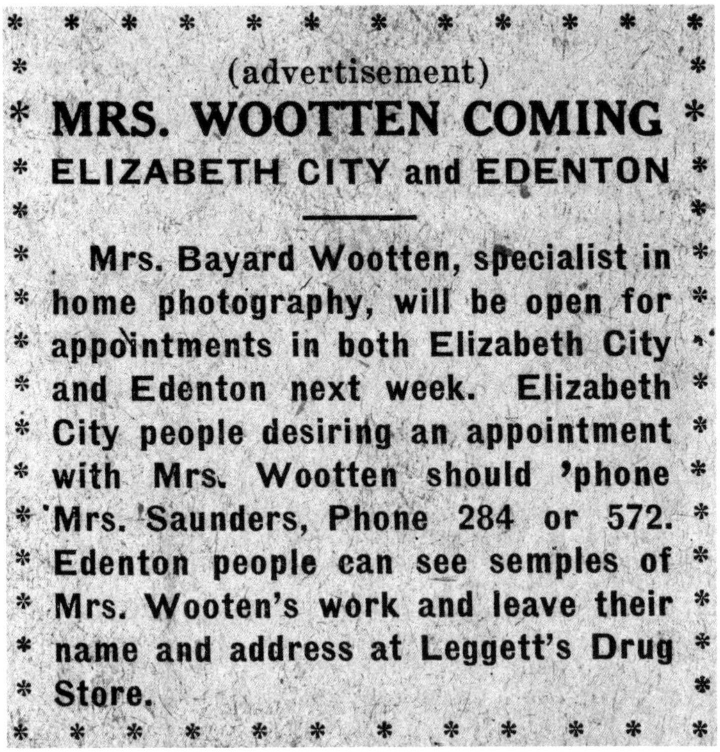

(advertisement)

MRS. WOOTTEN COMING
ELIZABETH CITY and EDENTON

——————

Mrs. Bayard Wootten, specialist in home photography, will be open for appointments in both Elizabeth City and Edenton next week. Elizabeth City people desiring an appointment with Mrs. Wootten should 'phone Mrs. Saunders, Phone 284 or 572. Edenton people can see semples of Mrs. Wooten's work and leave their name and address at Leggett's Drug Store.

1922, she had won the contract for the university's yearbook, *The Yackety Yack*, and except for one year her studio kept it until after World War II. The year in which she lost the contract, 1923, it went to the studio of New York pictorialist Clarence White.

Wootten's pursuit of photography business at military posts in North Carolina also continued periodically until after World War II. The 1918 opening of Camp Bragg (Fort Bragg after 1922), a hurriedly built U.S. Army facility near Fayetteville, provided such an opportunity. The commander, General Albert J. Bowley, saw examples of Wootten's photography during a tour of Camp Glenn and in 1921 invited her to come to Bragg.

Wootten's move to Camp Bragg came none too soon for Bowley. The government considered closing the post, and he used her photographs of military activity in a successful lobbying effort to keep it open. Bowley gave the photographer wide latitude to travel around the camp and take pictures, and on one occasion she wandered onto an artillery range by mistake. Years later she recalled the incident vividly:

I asked one of the officers if I could go over to where Battery F was firing to get some shots. He told me to go ahead. I followed the directions and went a half-mile to a lone pine, then headed to the right for the battery, which was supposed to be another half-mile away. That was the dangerous part of the trip and when they started firing over my head I lost my nerve and became hysterical. They were using real shells that day. I must have been out there for 30 or 40 minutes.[44]

When a new commander arrived at the post in 1928, he objected to the security risks of having a civilian photographer on the base, and Wootten had to leave.

During the years at Fort Bragg, Wootten became interested in theosophy, a system of religious and philosophical thought whose tenets included a belief in reincarnation. She had grown up in the Episcopal Church and maintained nominal ties to the denomination throughout her life, but Wootten liked other religions, including Christian Science. By the 1920s, "occultation and theosophy" had her interest. She joined the Theosophical Society, and weekly meetings were held in her studio at Fort Bragg. Colonel T. E. Merrill, stationed at the post, shared Wootten's interest and presented the photographer with his collection of books on the subject when he moved away. Her fascination with theosophy did not wane, and in the years that followed she continued to enlarge this personal library.

It may also have been in the 1920s that Wootten first became interested in the potters living around Jugtown in North Carolina's central piedmont northwest of Fort Bragg. She developed a warm friendship with two of the potters in the area, Jacques and Juliana Busbee. The Busbees were not descendants of the native potters that had lived in the region for generations; they were outsiders from Raleigh who moved to the area in 1917. Like Wootten, the Busbees had studied art, and their travels often carried them outside the state. Although their professions differed, they had much in common with the photographer. In her visits to the Jugtown region, Wootten recorded on film potters who are now legendary in the state, including Ben Owen, Jacon B. Cole, Nell Cole Graves, Waymon Cole, and Charlie Teague. Their colorful ware also greeted visitors to Wootten's home.

The Wootten-Moulton staff traveled over much of North Carolina to supply the studios in New Bern and Fort Bragg with work. In 1923 Wootten wrote her step-father from Winston-Salem in the western part of the state, describing her daily routine: "I am making pictures for the annual of Salem College. I make three pictures

In the aftermath of success at Camp Glenn, the Wootten-Moulton Studio built a "Photo Hut" at Camp Bragg (later Fort Bragg), an army post near Fayetteville. Wootten and her half brother George Moulton, fourth and fifth from the left in this 1924 photograph, worked together for almost half a century. (North Carolina Collection)

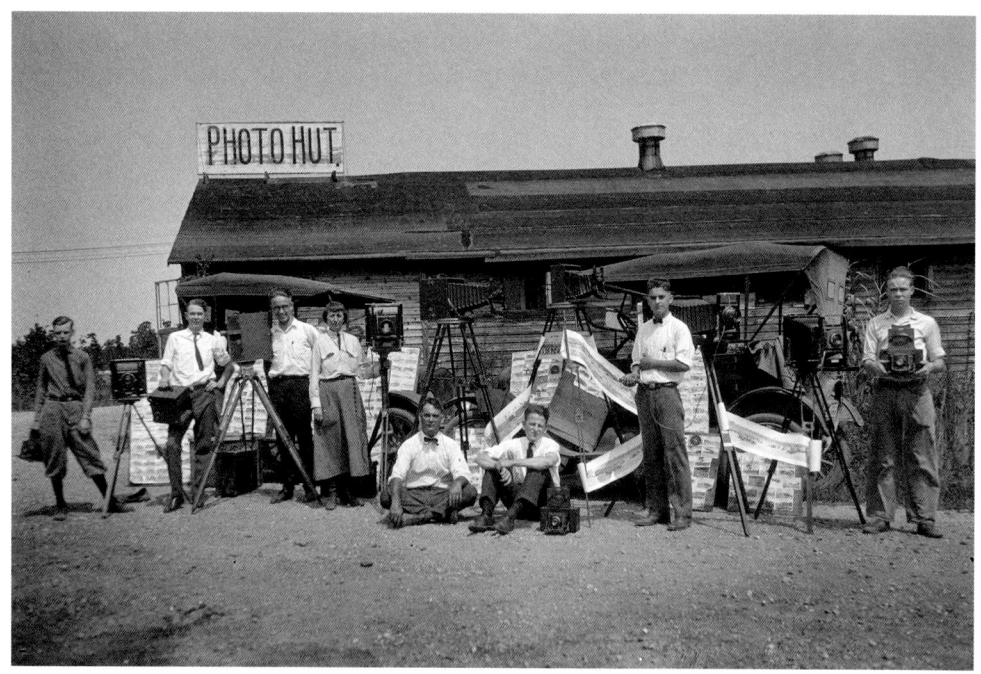

of one girl every ten minutes. It gets to be monotonous, but I am very glad to have the job."[45]

The studio prospered, and both of Wootten's sons received a good education. Charles, the older, gained admission to the U.S. Naval Academy and son Rufus attended Harvard. In the 1920s she opened two more branches of the studio in addition to those at New Bern and Fort Bragg. Friends of Wootten living in Greensboro, insurance executive Julian S. Price and New Bern native Maude Latham, encouraged Wootten to open a studio there. She did so in 1925, but within two years the Greensboro operation closed. Latham, who later became chief benefactor for the restoration of Tryon Palace in New Bern, the stately home of two of North Carolina's royal governors, remained a close friend. Following Latham's death in 1951, the photographer received a $1,000 bequest from her estate.

Wootten and her half brother George Moulton opened a studio in Chapel Hill in 1928 to accommodate the growing photography business in the university town. They rented space on the second floor of a building located in the main business district and shared a house a few blocks away. Initially the studio sent negatives to New Bern for processing and printing, but by the early 1930s the Chapel Hill branch had its own darkroom.

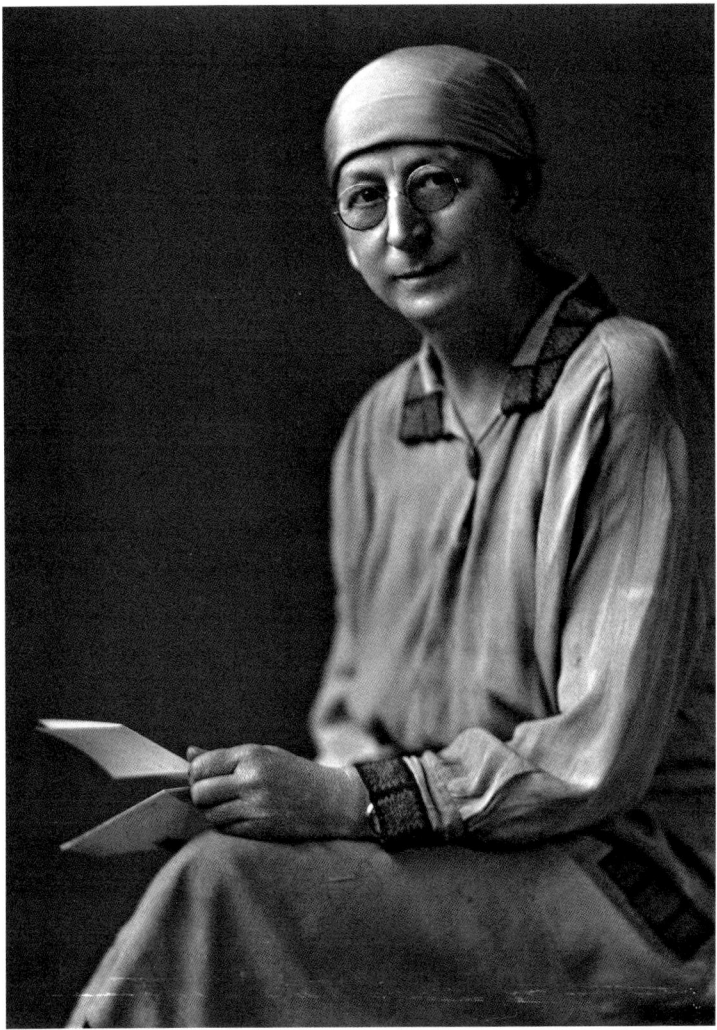

FIGURE 17

The Wootten-Moulton Studio shared in the general prosperity of the 1920s. Wootten, shown here during that period, increasingly found the time and resources to pursue an interest in artistic photography. (Celia Eudy Collection)

A fire that struck the New Bern studio on the morning of January 2, 1932, may have prompted the change. The blaze started in an adjoining business, and much of the damage to the studio was from water. Losses totaled $10,000, of which insurance covered only $1,250. Among the casualties were negatives recently made for the yearbooks of Davidson College and the University of North Carolina. Perhaps the greatest loss, however, was among the older negatives, which spanned the entire quarter century of the New Bern studio's existence and documented Wootten's early career.

The partnership between Moulton and Wootten sometimes brought the pair into sharp conflict over management issues, for their operating styles differed markedly.

Wootten was a visionary and a dreamer. Moulton was a conservative businessman whose skill often kept the studio in the black. At times they had heated disagreements. Wootten discussed one of these in a letter to their sister Celia:

> Sometimes I want to say a word to you that I do not care for George to read. . . .
>
> I enclose a letter from Sussman that completely relieves George of any responsibility for the purchase or payment of the Lares Printer. I am sorry that George is making himself unhappy about the purchase of this printer, but I cannot help it. I will never buy a piece of equipment for the business that I do not stand ready to pay for personally if he objects to it, but I shall make such purchases whenever I consider the business needs equipment for its development. As for his not liking my way, that is nothing new. He never has. It is about time he was getting used to it. It is also about time that he is realizing that my way has often brought the business success. This business probably means more to me than any of you realize. It is not only my means of livelihood, but it is my source of entertainment and amusement. For many years I have been so strapped, and felt the responsibility of the family so keenly that I could not do many of the things I wanted to. This is changed now. We are making money enough for me to reach out for larger opportunities, and I do not feel the weight of responsibility. Everybody can make a living for themselves now, and I can take changes [chances] with my own future that I would not have when there were people dependent on me. I shall go after the opportunities that call me, but I shall be careful not to drag George into anything that he does not wish to go into. . . . I am hoping to make money. I shall count it a success, however, if I have happiness and entertainment, even if the money does not materialize.[46]

Not long after the Chapel Hill studio opened, a young man named William A. Lively started working for the company. His father, Joseph, had opened a studio in Asheville in 1928; his grandfather, William S. "Daddy" Lively, was at the time something of a dean of southern photographers. Daddy Lively was already working as a traveling photographer when Bayard Wootten was born in 1875. She likely met him early in the century at one of the regional or national photographic conventions, where he was often a fixture.

In 1904, Daddy Lively and Kentucky photographer W. G. McFadden opened the Southern School of Photography in a vacant academy building in McMinnville, Tennessee. The school was only modestly successful in attracting students, although some came from as far away as California and Canada. The institution lasted until 1928, when the old academy burned down.

Young William A. Lively learned photography at his grandfather's school. After starting work at the Wootten-Moulton Studio, he began courting Wootten's half sister Celia, who worked at the branch in New Bern. The couple eventually wed and had a child, but in 1931 they separated and put an end to the storybook union that briefly joined two of the South's leading photographic families.

By the time Wootten opened the Chapel Hill studio, her pictorial style had fully matured, but significant recognition of her talent remained elusive. The roots of her photography were in drawing and painting, and she knew the works of the old masters. Symmetry, form, and balance were meaningful ingredients in her application of artistic principles to photographic composition. Wootten was particularly fond of diagonal arrangements. These led the viewer's eye to a main subject or simply countered the vertical and horizontal motif of the rectangular photograph. The placement of a fence or even a trail of footprints in the sand served her purpose. Wootten's highly controlled camera technique was time-consuming, but it worked effectively in landscape and architectural photography where time limits on camera work often are not critical. Wootten's books—*Charleston: Azaleas and Old Bricks*, *Old Homes and Gardens of North Carolina*, and *New Castle, Delaware, 1651–1939*—are replete with examples of this well-crafted style of photography.

In portraiture Wootten tried to discern the essential traits that defined subjects and to pose individuals in a way that revealed what she visualized. Here too, she was at her best in static settings, creating insightful portraits with a moody tone. Her unhurried approach was a distinct liability, however, in recording human activity or almost any subject that required a prompt response by the photographer. Awkwardness and stiffness easily crept into these images.

REACHING A WIDER AUDIENCE

Two events in the 1920s paved the way for the most successful period of Wootten's career, the 1930s. One of these was her move to Chapel Hill in 1928. While she lived in the university town, exhibitions of her most creative photography cast Wootten into the public eye, and publishers became interested in her images for their illustra-

FIGURE 18

Diagonal elements frequently appear in Wootten compositions. In this example, footprints in the sand lead a viewer's eye to the main subject. Wootten made the photograph about 1921 as her half sister Celia Moulton stood on a sand dune near Beaufort, North Carolina. (North Carolina Collection)

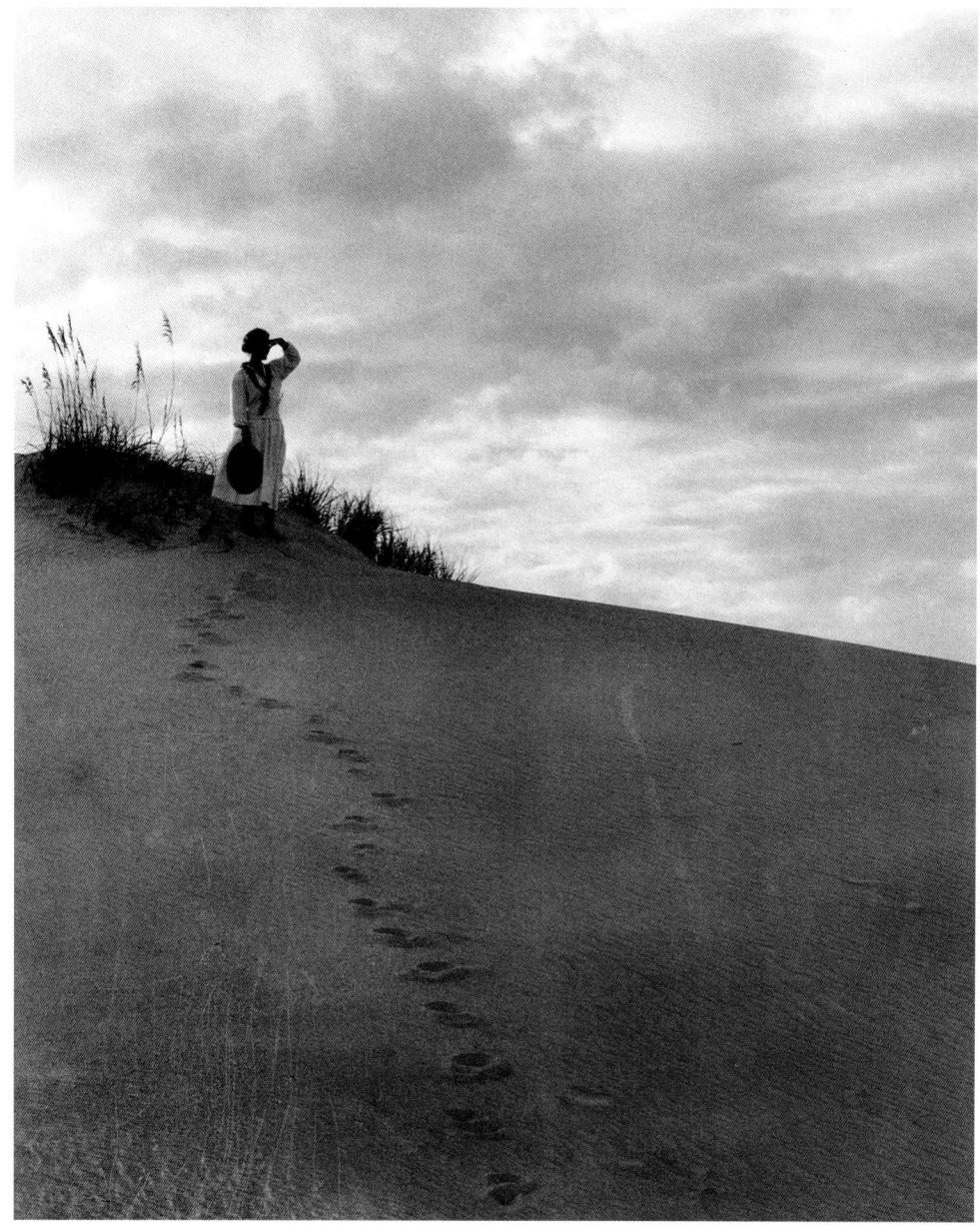

tive value. These developments provided Wootten with outlets for her best work. A second event, and one of equal consequence, was a visit Wootten had with her cousin, Lucy Morgan, at the Appalachian School (later Penland School) in the mountains of western North Carolina. This region possessed an abundance of fresh and novel subject matter that sparked Wootten's creative spirit.

The *Life* and Career of Bayard Wootten

The Episcopal Church had founded the school in 1914 in the rural Mitchell County community of Penland, and it initially provided instruction only for children. In 1920 Lucy Morgan moved to Penland as a primary teacher. Two years later she took a course in weaving at Berea College in Kentucky and returned to Penland to teach the craft to children at the school. Morgan soon became interested in reviving weaving among women in the community, and the school added adult instruction to its curriculum. The weavers marketed their products in nearby towns, and in 1924 Morgan carried an exhibit to the North Carolina State Fair in Raleigh. At this fair or one soon thereafter, she encountered her cousin Bayard Wootten.

With her father Rufus Morgan having died almost half a century before, Wootten had not stayed in close touch with Morgan relatives living in western North Carolina. Sometime after meeting Lucy Morgan at the state fair, however, Wootten received an invitation to visit Penland and take pictures for the school's catalog. This was probably around 1927. Wootten accepted the offer and many years later provided a colorful account of her introduction to a region that was pivotal in elevating her career.

She made the cross-state drive from New Bern to the mountains accompanied by her mother and half sister. They arrived in the foothills by late afternoon and made a stop in the town of Marion to ask for directions to Penland. Continuing, Wootten recalled, "we ascended a marvelous gorge, the road seeming to hang on the side of the mountain. Never shall I forget the thrills of that drive! It was my first experience on a mountain road."[47]

After dark and still with no Penland in sight, they reached the village of Linville Falls. Stopping again to ask the way, the party learned that the directions they had received in Marion were for Penland Hotel, some thirty miles from their real destination. There was little choice but to spend the night. The next morning they walked to the ninety-foot waterfall that cascades into rugged Linville Gorge. Wootten described the falls as "marvelous," and visited the spot again on subsequent trips. On one of these she was lowered by rope over a cliff to make pictures of the view from what appeared to be the best angle.

Resuming the search for Penland, Wootten and her companions eventually came to a fork in the road and a faded sign that read "Appalachian School." She described the final trek:

The road started bravely, but after the first turn around the mountain it was so narrow it could not by any chance accommodate another car. I did not think about it at first, but as I pushed on, ever ascending, the mountain on one side and the valley on the other, I began to get very nervous. Suppose we should meet a car. . . . as I pushed on, going higher, the road bending and coming back above itself as it toiled up the mountain, the valley below fading in the distance, my nervousness almost amounted to terror. As my car clung to that thread of road, hugged the mountain, I glanced down in the valley hundreds of feet below us and realized that if I lost control of my car and it left the road it meant death for all of us—and the loss of a perfectly good Ford.[48]

Wootten found her cousin Lucy Morgan and returned to the magical Penland many times. The school was a hub for mountain crafts and a focal point of surrounding communities. Many of those who worked and studied at Penland sat for a Wootten portrait. They also introduced the photographer to family, friends, and acquaintances willing to do the same. Penland served as a window that provided Wootten an intimate look at the region. It was also a catalyst that freed her from artistic obscurity.

SUCCESS AS A CAMERA ARTIST

Early in her career Bayard Wootten exhibited photographs at fairs in North Carolina and at regional and national photographic conventions. Her name appears in an undated catalog describing an exhibit of women's photography at the studio of E. Blanche Reineke in Kansas City, Missouri. The titles of her two prints were "Our Future Statesmen" and "Playmates."[49] These may have been part of a traveling exhibit sponsored by the Women's Federation, for it also included works by other members, including Mary Carnell, Katherine Jamieson, Belle Johnson, Maybelle Goodlander, and Pearl Grace Loehr.

A Wootten photograph titled "The Elements" appeared in the tenth annual Pittsburgh Salon of Photography exhibition at the Carnegie Institute in 1923.[50] The first major solo exhibition of her work to attract widespread attention, however, did not occur until nine years later, in June 1932. The site was the Fine Arts Theatre in Boston.

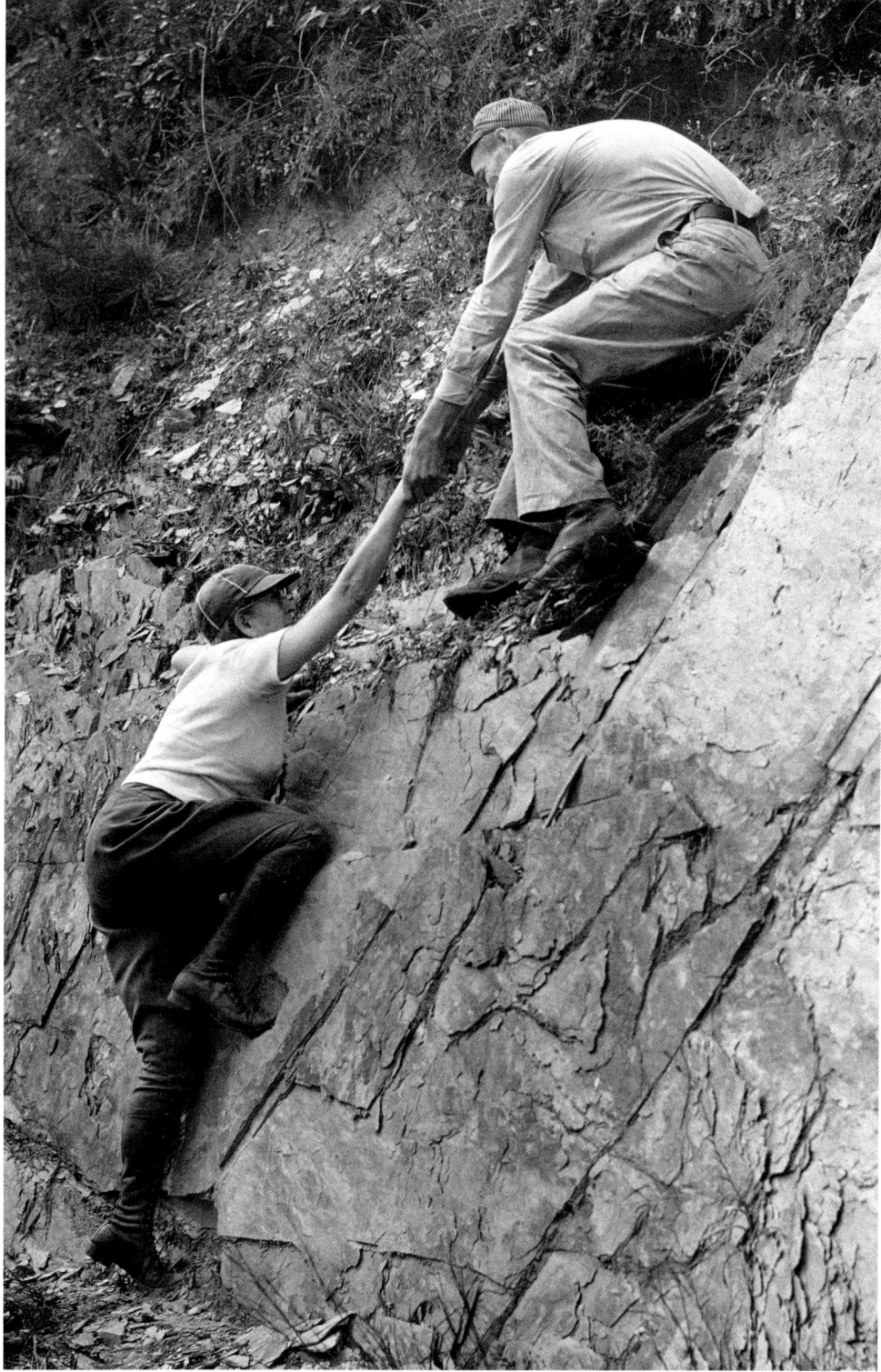

FIGURE 19
A companion hoists Wootten up a rocky slope in the southern Appalachians in the 1930s during one of her numerous missions of discovery to the area. (North Carolina Collection)

Elmer Hall, an assistant director of the Carolina Playmakers who had Massachusetts connections, helped arrange the exhibit. Wootten sent a collection of forty prints that included both landscapes and portraits, but it was the latter, particularly her views of mountain people, that attracted the most interest. Complimentary articles on the exhibit appeared in Boston newspapers. One of the reviews picked up by the *Charlotte Observer* described Wootten's photography as "natural" and "picturesque." Another characterized the show as "an unusually fine exhibition of photography."[51]

This public recognition was a springboard for Wootten's career. A collection of images made around Charleston, South Carolina, went to the Fine Arts Theatre in the summer of 1933. Always the businesswoman, she advertised the photographs in her exhibit catalog as "moderately priced." Other invitations to exhibit her work came from throughout the East.

Wootten exhibited prints at the Chicago World's Fair on September 7, 1933, North Carolina Day, and by year's end there were also venues in Richmond, Virginia; Charleston, South Carolina; and Washington, D.C. Over the remainder of the decade, exhibitions took place in Tennessee, Alabama, Arkansas, Georgia, New York, Ohio, California, and in many parts of North Carolina. Wootten's print "Live Oaks" won the American Forestry Association's 1933 North Carolina Award for the "most beautiful photographs of trees in America."

By 1935 she was experimenting with color slides. Landscapes and flowers were a common theme in watercolors that Wootten painted at the turn of the century, and she pursued similar subjects in slide photography. She toured the southeast coast photographing grand homes and formal gardens, sometimes processing black-and-white film in hotel bathrooms as she traveled. Her itinerary included Orton Plantation near Wilmington, North Carolina; Wormsloe Plantation near Savannah, Georgia; and Bellingrath Gardens in Mobile, Alabama. The historic city of Charleston, South Carolina, however, was a favorite, as well as the low-country gardens of Magnolia, Belle Isle, Middleton, and Cypress.

Wootten visited Charleston in 1932 and possibly earlier, sometimes traveling in the company of Maude Waddell, a poet and feature writer for the *Charlotte Observer*. Waddell, although born and reared in North Carolina, kept a home in Charleston for three decades. Wootten, perhaps benefiting from Waddell's social connections in the city, often partook of its cultural life.

She established a reputation as a photographer of the South Carolina low country well before the 1937 publication of her book, *Charleston: Azaleas and Old Bricks*. The guest list for a Charleston party held in Wootten's honor a year before the volume appeared included New York industrialist and art collector Solomon R. Guggenheim. Wootten also knew sculptress Anna Hyatt Huntington and her husband, Archer, a respected Hispanic scholar and adopted son of nineteenth-century railroad builder Collis P. Huntington. At Brookgreen Gardens, the couple's 9,000-acre preserve near Murrells Inlet, Wootten photographed their renowned collection of outdoor sculpture.

The studio funded her travel and photography, but often to the chagrin of her partner George Moulton. Wootten received frequent speaking invitations, especially from garden clubs and women's groups in North Carolina and South Carolina. For these occasions, she bought a slide projector and put together programs on the historic homes of North Carolina and "Gardens of the Low Country." Her slide-and-lecture combination was informative, entertaining, and popular. These programs undoubtedly provided some viewers with their first look at color photography. During 1934, Wootten pasted in her scrapbook almost two dozen newspaper clippings describing lectures and exhibits for the year. On one occasion she even went to New York City to address the Women's National Republican Club on the gardens of Charleston.

Wootten herself was not a gardener. Her modest frame home in Chapel Hill had just a smattering of cultivated flowers, but a profusion of naturally occurring dogwoods made a springtime walk by the place an appealing pastime. Wootten's circle of friends, however, included well-known Chapel Hill horticulturist William Lanier Hunt. It was Hunt who knew the important gardens of the South and many of their owners as well. He provided a valuable link to the gardens and to the garden clubs that often served as forums for Wootten's lectures and slides. Many of Hunt's own botanical insights undoubtedly enlivened her presentations.

These lectures produced little in the way of income for Wootten, and her studio's financial condition was tenuous during the depression years. Employees sometimes received scant wages, occasionally none at all. Two of the staff lived in the Chapel Hill studio for a time because they could not afford other housing. At one point the business lost credit with Eastman Kodak and had to buy supplies through Foister's Camera Store, a business located down the street. At the beginning of each fall season, the studio sometimes borrowed cash from George Moulton's wife Myrtle in New Bern to restock with film, paper, and chemicals. Both Moulton and his wife were adept in business matters, and she owned considerable rental property in New Bern.

In the late 1920s, Moulton and Wootten moved to Chapel Hill to operate the new branch. Myrtle Moulton, whose numerous close ties to New Bern included an aged father, stayed behind. Wootten and Moulton initially shared a small house on Pittsboro Road in Chapel Hill, but in 1930 they moved into a larger home at the northeast corner of Cameron Avenue and Mallette Street, purchased by Mrs. Moulton. Wootten paid no rent, and a former employee of the studio believed that the Moultons were the financial backbone of the business.

The Moultons undoubtedly had little enthusiasm for a disrupted family life, but with studios in New Bern, Chapel Hill, and Fort Bragg, travel and frequent separation were an accepted part of the enterprise. Except for summers, weekends, and holidays, or when business in Chapel Hill was slow, George Moulton did not live at his home in New Bern year-round until the early 1940s.

Moulton appreciated his half sister's skill with the camera, but he had little of the passion for artistic photography that drove Wootten. For Moulton, the glue of financial livelihood, family loyalty, and endless patience held the sometimes difficult partnership together. Myrtle had less enthusiasm for the arrangement and a smaller degree of tolerance for Wootten in general. Wootten's regard for her sister-in-law was equally measured.

Wootten was not the conservative photographer exemplified by her half brother. She typically followed her own photographic agenda, little deterred by financial considerations or other obstacles. She was sometimes absent from the studio on "another expedition" for days or even weeks at a time. On these photographic outings Wootten preferred using a large-format camera that required necessarily expensive film. "I work with an 8 × 10 camera with a 5 × 7 back as well as the 8 × 10. I use a Wollensak f/4.5 lens with a 12 inch focus whenever possible. When this will not cover, I have two other lenses, one a medium wide-angle Goerz and the other an extreme wide-angle Wollensak. I lug this heavy equipment around with me wherever I go. I do not do much trimming—except on the ground glass. In no instance is the print taken from a part of the negative."[52]

Friends or relatives usually traveled with Wootten to drive the car and help with equipment. Often her companions were young men from the Chapel Hill studio, particularly Rudy Faircloth, Sherman B. Smithey Jr., and Arline Carawan. On the road

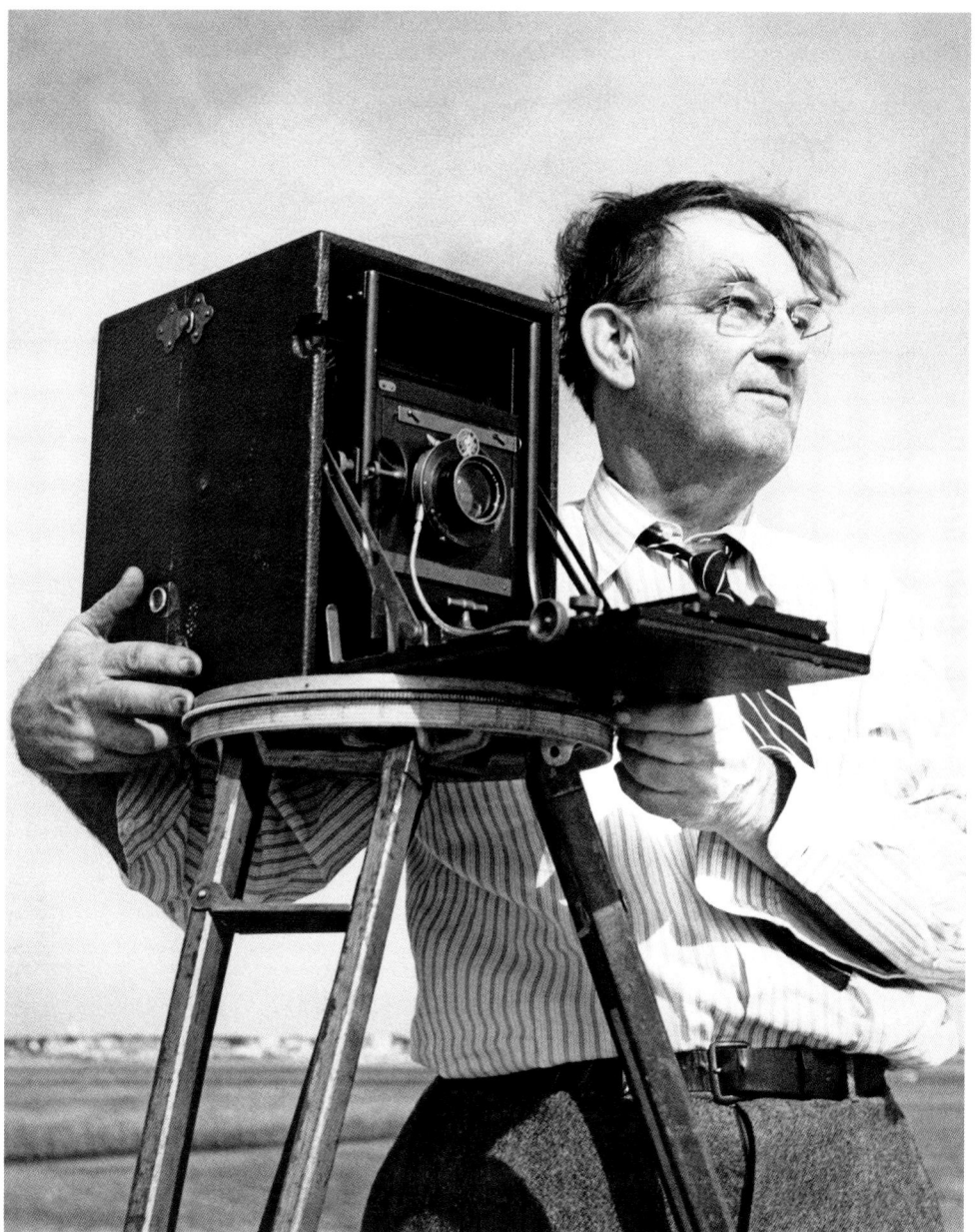

she loaded film holders in dark closets and bathrooms or used a changing bag in the backseat of the car. Even an experienced photographer occasionally produced poor negatives, and Wootten was no exception. In the darkroom she sometimes increased the density of underexposed negatives by arranging ground coffee on them at the time of printing.

The University of North Carolina Press took advantage of Wootten's photographic skill soon after she moved to Chapel Hill. Several of her pictures appeared in the Press's 1933 book, *The Story of North Carolina* by Alex Mathews Arnett and Walter Clinton Jackson. Charles Morrow Wilson's *Backwoods America* (1934) contained over thirty photographs by Wootten, and she contributed more than a hundred images to Muriel Earley Sheppard's *Cabins in the Laurel* (1935).

The University of North Carolina Press arranged with Wootten to illustrate *Cabins* months before turning to her for help with *Backwoods America*, the volume that appeared first. Wilson had supplied photographs for his book, but the Press director, William Terry Couch, found them unacceptable and enlisted Wootten's help. The first printing of *Backwoods America* arrived just before Christmas 1934. Couch mailed out review copies after the holidays and released the volume to the public in February, only a month before the release of *Cabins in the Laurel*.

Cabins, with 128 photographs, eclipsed the earlier volume in popularity and became the work most often associated with Wootten. The photographs included portraits and landscapes made primarily in the largely rural North Carolina mountain counties of Mitchell and Yancey. The images represent some of the best of Wootten's pictorial photography. A host of favorable reviews followed the book's appearance. A writer for the *New York Herald Tribune* called Wootten's photographs "truly magnificent."[53] The *Baltimore Evening Sun* described the images as "astonishing" and suggested that Wootten be counted among "the country's gifted photographers."[54] Later in the year the *Detroit News* featured several of the photographs in a special rotogravure section of the paper.[55]

Newspapers in the photographer's home state were even more lavish in their praise. Walter Spearman reviewed *Cabins in the Laurel* for the *Charlotte News* and wrote that "it is Mrs. Wootten with her splendid series of 128 photographs who injects the real life blood into the volume."[56] Maude Minish Sutton, a reviewer for the *Raleigh News and Observer*, compared the book's photograph of Arthur Woody to the work of Rembrandt. "It is impossible to exaggerate the beauty of the illustrations," she said, "and they add immeasurably to the value of the book."[57]

A copy of *Cabins in the Laurel* reached the desk of Allen H. Eaton with the Russell Sage Foundation in New York. Sage, a wealthy railroad and stock investor, died in 1906, and a year later his wife had established the foundation to work for the improvement of "social and living conditions in the United States." The book interested

Eaton for its documentary value, and in a letter to Wootten he declared *Cabins in the Laurel* a "fine event" in which author and illustrator had achieved a perfect fit.[58] Two years later in 1937, the Foundation published Eaton's own book on the Appalachians, *Handicrafts of the Southern Highlands*.

Some of the people living in the North Carolina mountain counties depicted in *Cabins in the Laurel* reportedly felt used. Many persons undoubtedly opened themselves to Wootten, a relative of Mitchell County's Lucy Morgan and a well-known North Carolina photographer, when they might not have done so for someone else. Critics also draw attention to a stereotypically backward and primitive view of mountain life presented by the volume.[59] Like a historical novel penned from both fact and fantasy, Wootten's photographs in their own small way nurtured myths about the South.

Much of the unhappiness with *Cabins in the Laurel* derived from the author's text, but Wootten was an accomplice who faced a dilemma indigenous to photographers. Private persons often feel invaded, exposed, and manipulated when their likenesses reach the public media. Nonetheless, *Cabins in the Laurel* has been through several printings, and a large-format edition released in 1991 places greater emphasis on the photographs.[60]

Wootten and UNC Press director Couch enjoyed a working relationship that was mutually beneficial. Under the New Deal's Works Progress Administration, Couch became assistant state director for the Federal Writers' Project in North Carolina. Wootten was one of several photographers chosen to illustrate the agency's 1939 book, *North Carolina: A Guide to the Old North State*, and Couch provided guidance in the selection of subjects to photograph.[61]

In 1937, Wootten and George Moulton went to Roanoke Island on the North Carolina coast to make publicity photographs during the first season of Paul Green's pioneering outdoor drama *The Lost Colony*. Wootten also worked for the Tennessee Valley Authority to carry out photographic surveys in Shelby County, Alabama, and at Norris Dam in Tennessee.

Wootten attempted to penetrate the publishing business further by placing photographs with the New York agency of R. I. Nesmith and Associates, but her reputation and personal contacts were more effective. Wootten's photographs of Charleston, South Carolina, for instance, came to the attention of the Houghton Mifflin Company after Leroy Barker, an employee, admired several prints in the home of Fant Thornley in Columbia, South Carolina. Thornley probably met Wootten when he was a library science student at the University of North Carolina. Houghton Mifflin published *Charleston: Azaleas and Old Bricks* in 1937, and the volume highlighted, through photographs and text, the grandeur and quaintness of the historic port city. Wootten's name appeared prominently on the book's spine and title page along with that of Samuel G. Stoney, author of the text. She dedicated the volume to Thornley.

Reproductions in the Charleston book were by photogravure, and the volume was much larger in format than any previous one to which Wootten had contributed photographs.[62] She considered it her crowning achievement. "This is my great adventure," she declared. "In a way it is for me the fruition of my long career as a photographer. But I'm still a young woman you know."[63] Wootten was sixty-two at the time.

One volume led to another. In 1939, Houghton Mifflin published *New Castle, Delaware, 1651–1939*, with photographs by Wootten and text by Anthony Higgins. For both the Charleston and New Castle books, Wootten received a 10 percent royalty from Houghton Mifflin for each copy sold. This was only half what she received for *Backwoods America*, published three years earlier by the University of North Carolina Press, an indication, perhaps, of how favorable her relationship with the local publisher became. In addition, Wootten had to pay $500 to Samuel Stoney for the text that he wrote on Charleston, and Anthony Higgins received a third of her royalty for his composition on New Castle, Delaware.[64]

In 1939, Wootten provided landscape and architectural photographs for *Old Homes and Gardens of North Carolina*, published by the University of North Carolina Press and the Garden Club of North Carolina. The last book that she illustrated was Olive Tilford Dargan's *From My Highest Hill: Carolina Mountain Folks*. Published by J. B. Lippincott Company, it appeared in 1941 and, like *Cabins in the Laurel*, was set in the mountains of western North Carolina.

Old Homes and Gardens of North Carolina is notable as the first volume to attempt a systematic photographic documentation of many of the historic homes in the state. University of North Carolina mathematics professor and historian Archibald Henderson wrote the text, and Wootten took over 500 photographs, of which 100 made the final cut. The book had a limited-edition printing of only 1,000 copies, and North Carolina governor Clyde R. Hoey autographed each one. A reviewer in the *New York*

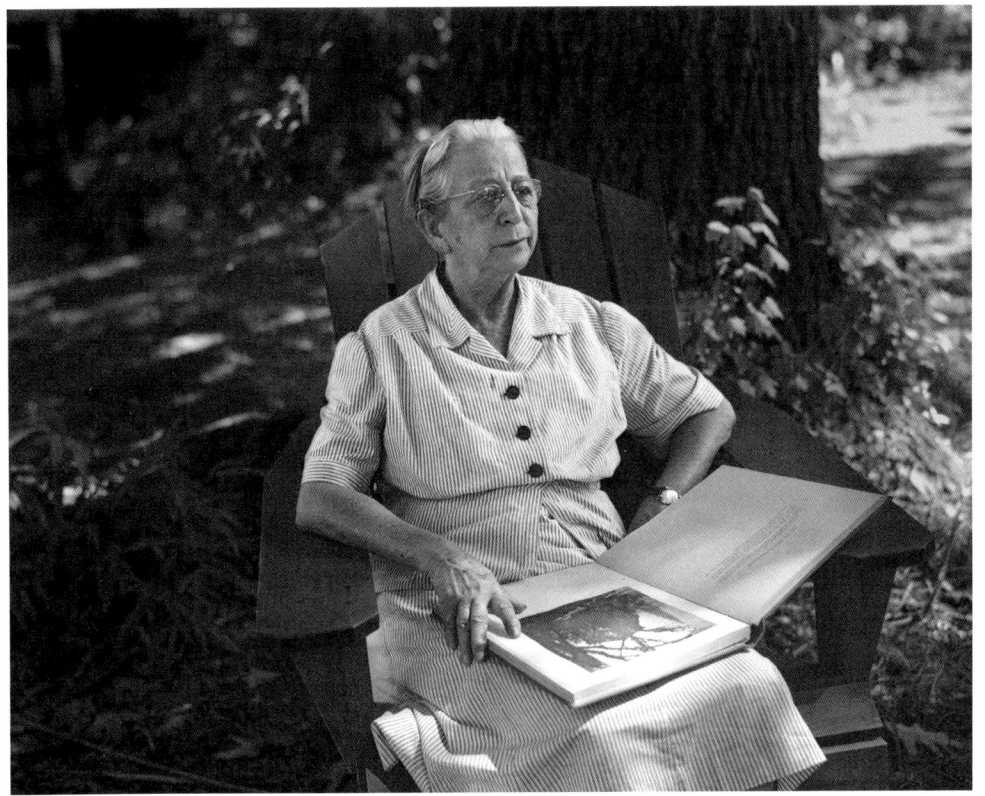

FIGURE 21

Wootten holds a copy of
Charleston: Azaleas
and Old Bricks. *Of*
the six major books that
she illustrated, this was
reportedly her favorite.
Wootten sat for this
photograph not long after
the volume appeared in
1937. (North Carolina
Collection)

Times Book Review characterized it as "beautiful and evocative," and it enjoyed widespread approval across North Carolina.[65]

The UNC Press never reprinted *Old Homes and Gardens*, but only two years later it published a second book on the state's historic buildings, *The Early Architecture of North Carolina*, with text by Thomas T. Waterman and photographs by Frances Benjamin Johnston, one of the most eminent of women photographers. Johnston and Wootten knew one another, but their friendship was only casual. The two women had little in common but the camera, and even here their styles diverged.

Johnston was born in 1864 in West Virginia. Her family moved to Washington, D.C., when she was still a child, and she grew up in an atmosphere of economic well-being and high social standing. She studied art in Paris and Washington and in 1890 opened a photographic studio at her family's home in the nation's capital. She later had a studio in New York City. Johnston worked as an apprentice in the photographic section of the Smithsonian and documented five presidential administrations, from Cleveland's to Taft's. She made the last photograph of President William McKinley before his assassination and recorded many other notables on film, including Admiral George Dewey, Booker T. Washington, George Washington Carver, Susan B. Anthony, Alexander Graham Bell, and Mark Twain.

Johnston's early work established her reputation as a photographer and photojournalist. Subsequent photographic projects, including a study of Pennsylvania coal miners, women factory workers in Massachusetts, and much admired images of the schools of Washington, D.C., reinforced her already lofty stature. Commissions took Johnston to Europe to carry out architectural photography, and in 1927 she documented the architecture of Fredericksburg, Virginia.

A 1929 Library of Congress exhibit of Johnston's Fredericksburg assignment led to a series of Carnegie Corporation grants in the 1930s to photograph early architecture in nine southern states. *The Early Architecture of North Carolina* was one culmination of this effort. Johnston passed through Chapel Hill in 1938 and photographed several buildings in the area. Whether she visited Wootten at the time is unknown.

Wootten's *Old Homes and Gardens of North Carolina* and Johnston's *The Early Architecture of North Carolina* look very different. The two women photographed the exteriors and interiors of many of the same structures, but the Johnston book contains almost 300 photographs, compared to just 100 in *Old Homes and Gardens*. This numerical advantage enabled Johnston to cover a larger number of structures and include more photographs of each.

Wootten set out to document the old homes and to do so artistically. Johnston simply tried to document. Johnston's photographic perspective was straightforward and direct, and her work is often superior in rendering fine detail. The Wootten photographs are generally more appealing visually. Wootten did not crop images as tightly as Johnston did, and she often included enough of a home's surroundings to define the environment in which it existed. Moving the camera farther away from a subject also clarified its architectural scale.

Photographs made from a direct and one-dimensional perspective clashed with Wootten's desire for artistic composition. Her views of homes, therefore, often include trees, walkways, and hedgerows—elements that give the photographs depth and perspective. The differences in the two women's photographic styles are also apparent in their photographs of interiors. Johnston's views of such features as staircases, mantels, and walls are typically frontal and direct. Wootten often photographed these from an angle, sometimes including an adjoining wall or placing the main subject off-center in the image.

The Early Architecture of North Carolina is printed on coated paper, and its glossiness enhances the perception of high photographic detail. Photographs in *Old Homes and Gardens of North Carolina*, like the Wootten books on Charleston and New Castle, are photogravures. These also show excellent detail but possess a grain pattern and matte surface that is visually soft, an effect that pictorial photographers like Wootten found appealing. Wootten was at her height as a photographer by the end of the 1930s when *Old Homes and Gardens* appeared. The National Arts Club in New York elected her a member early in 1939, and in the fall she served as a judge in a print competition for the Atlanta Camera Club.

During the summer of 1939 Wootten visited the New York World's Fair, where North Carolina, like many other states, had an exhibit. A "Court of Tourism" section in the state's 3,000-square-foot exhibition hall included several large, three-sided, rotating panels outfitted with photographic murals that formed a continuous panorama when the panels moved into proper alignment. Smaller photographs were superimposed on the three large panoramas to illustrate geographic features or activities. The North Carolina exhibit received numerous complimentary reviews, but after Wootten saw the murals she issued a criticism that was uncharacteristically harsh.

The trouble with the exhibit . . . is that it was put on by a bunch of amateurs, and poor ones at that. The theme is twelve large prints, approximately eight feet by four, which revolve on three shafts. The idea is good, but making prints of this size is a highly technical job. Not a professional photographer in the state was consulted, and these prints are the worst that I have ever seen anywhere at any time. If these enormous prints had been of outstanding beauty spots, or if they had depicted our mammoth industries, the effect would have been dramatic. As it is, they tell nothing of the beauty of our marvelous State. . . . Besides the large prints that fill the center of the space, there are many 8 × 10 prints tacked up at random, not one of which was made by a professional photographer for this exhibit. They look very much as if the Carolina Motor Club had gathered up all the prints they have accumulated in their many years in business, and shipped them up to fill in. Many of them are printed too dark, others too light, some are turning yellow.[66]

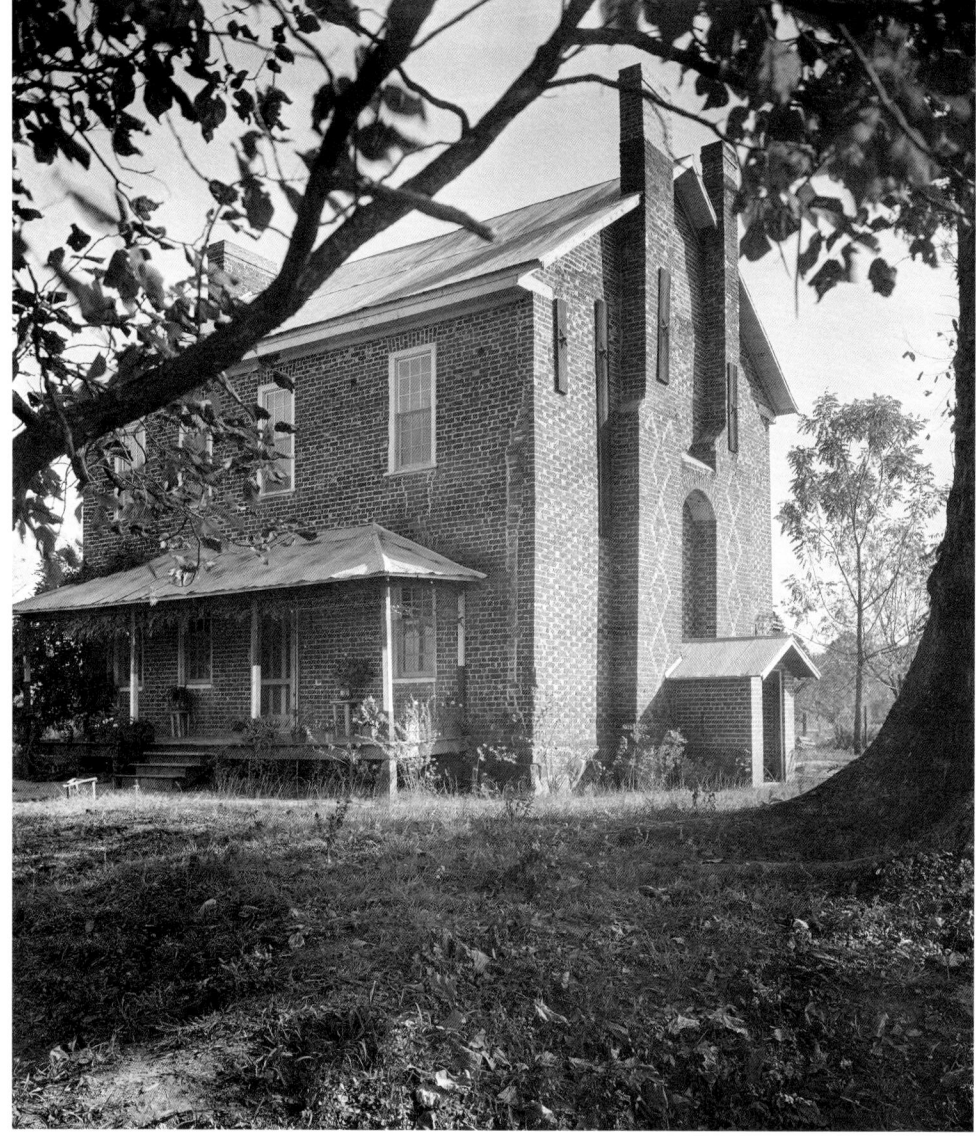

The major shortcoming of the designers may simply have been funding, for the North Carolina General Assembly of 1937 provided no financial support. The state's exhibit depended largely on corporate donations and work contributed by the North Carolina Department of Conservation and Development. Wootten undoubtedly scrutinized the World's Fair exhibit far more critically than typical fairgoers—photographic murals later became one of the services offered by her own studio. In December 1939 she supervised the installation of a major collection of these in the new

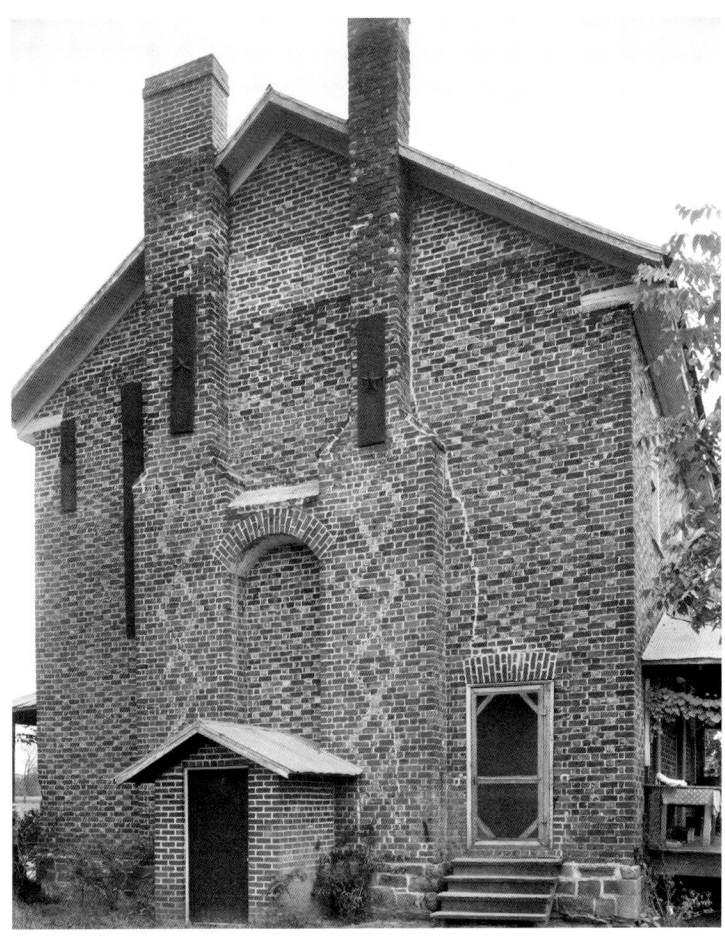

Institute of Government building at the University of North Carolina. Wootten and
Gladys Hall Coates, the wife of the Institute's founder, selected scenic images made
by the photographer from the North Carolina mountains to the coast. Some of the
murals were seven feet in height and as long as nine feet.

Over the next several years, murals made from Wootten's photographs appeared
in private homes and even courthouses. In 1946, in the twilight of her career, she
mounted several murals at the governor's office in the state capitol. According to a
secretary who worked in the studio, a commercial photographic company actually
printed the largest of the murals from negatives that Wootten supplied. Today, a few
of the murals remain in private hands; all but one of those in public buildings, however, are thought to be gone. Wootten mounted one of her largest murals, a view of
an apple tree at Little Switzerland, North Carolina, in the Craft House at Penland

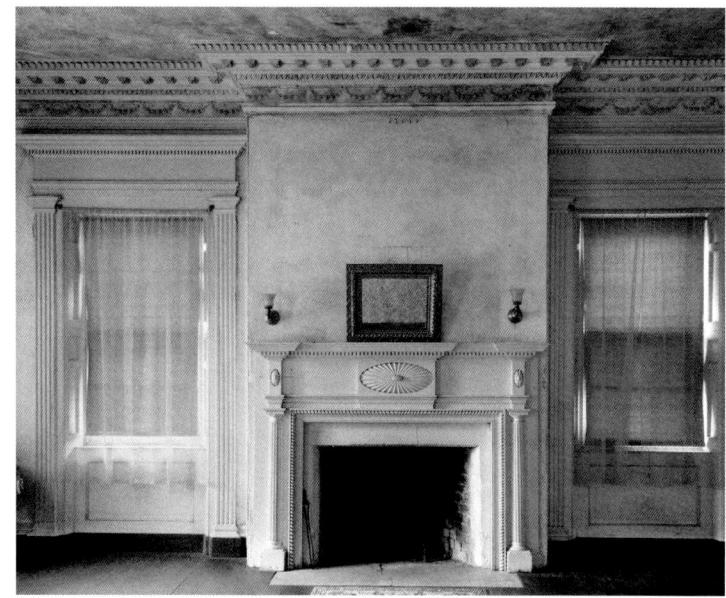

FIGURE 24

A comparison of interiors photographed by Johnston and Wooten reveals the same dichotomy between artistic and straight perspective as in their exterior views. Johnston's picture of this drawing room at Ingleside in Lincoln County is a direct view of a wall with fireplace and mantel, windows, and decorative molding. (North Carolina Collection)

School. This mural survived until about 1990 when it fell victim to a renovation of the building, a loss indicative of the decline in Wootten's once imposing reputation in North Carolina.

A PICTORIALIST AT HEART

Her small white business card read "Bayard Wootten, Pictorial Photographer." In the late 1930s when Wootten's career peaked, pictorialism was becoming a photographic anomaly. The final yearbook of the Pictorial Photographers of America had appeared a full decade earlier, and two leading advocates, Clarence White and Gertrude Käsebier, had died in 1925 and 1934, respectively. Nonetheless, pictorialism remained at the core of Wootten's love affair with the camera. It was a lofty vision, a path on which to travel, and the catalyst of her creative energy. Her pursuit of artistic photography was the common thread in a lengthy career, one that endured even as popular styles changed and horizons for the medium expanded.

Seeds for the decline of pictorialism were in place even before the movement peaked in 1910. It never lacked for critics, especially of the heavy image manipulation often practiced by high-art pictorialists. Many of the movement's early supporters

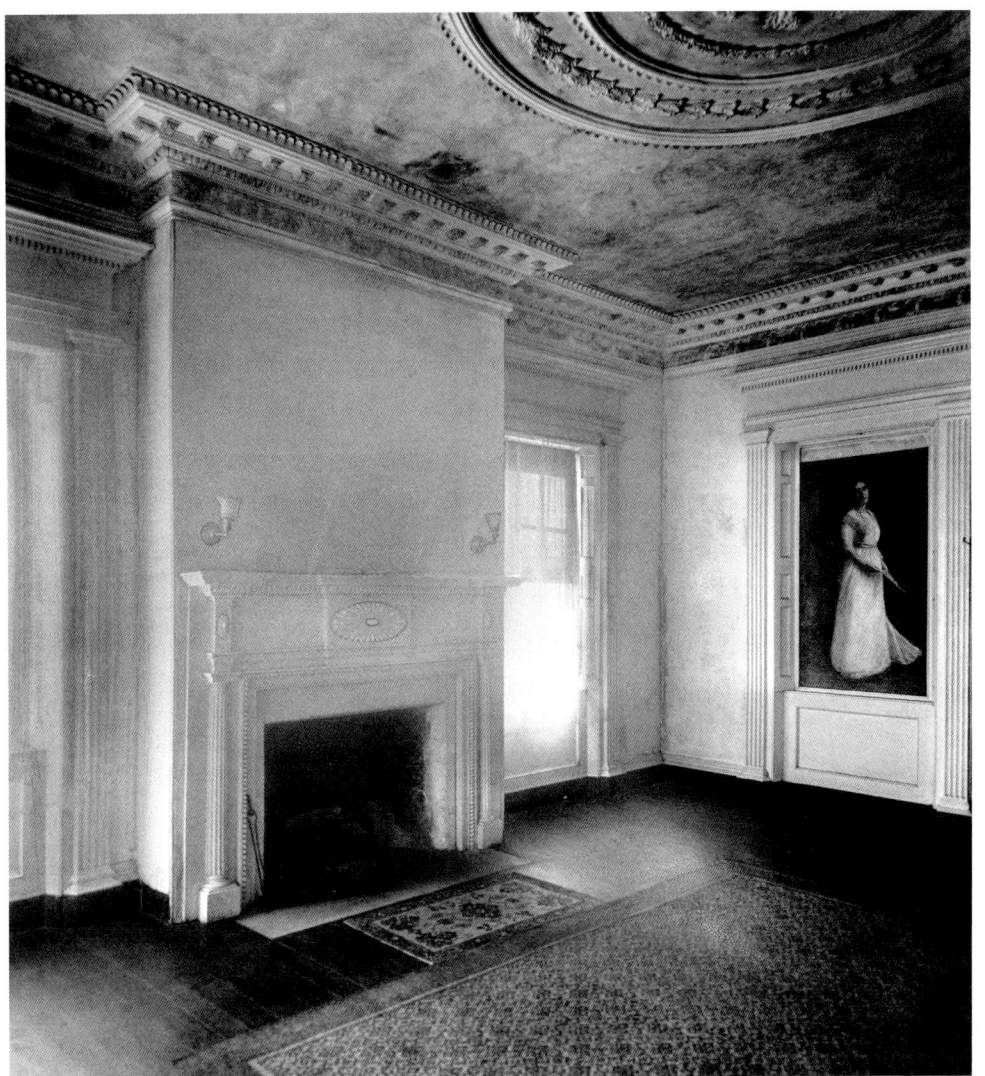

FIGURE 25

Wootten's photograph of the drawing room at Ingleside shows parts of two walls, giving the view a sense of depth. A carpet is visible on the floor, the curved lines of an elaborate ceiling ornament are prominent, and a painting of a woman in evening dress hangs on the far wall. The Early Architecture of North Carolina includes Johnston's photograph shown in Figure 24 and a separate photograph of the ceiling ornament. Wootten, however, skillfully combined the major components of the room into one photograph, suggesting to the viewer a grander place than is evident in the two individual views by Johnston. (North Carolina Collection)

eventually questioned basic assumptions about the influence of the traditional arts in photography. This was true even of Alfred Stieglitz, the founder of the Photo-Secession and pictorialism's most effective advocate in the early years.

The photographic technique of many pictorialists evolved toward an approach that was more allied with the nature of photography itself. This decline in the influence of other forms of art on the medium was gradual, and holdouts like Bayard Wootten were not uncommon. The images of celebrated American photographers

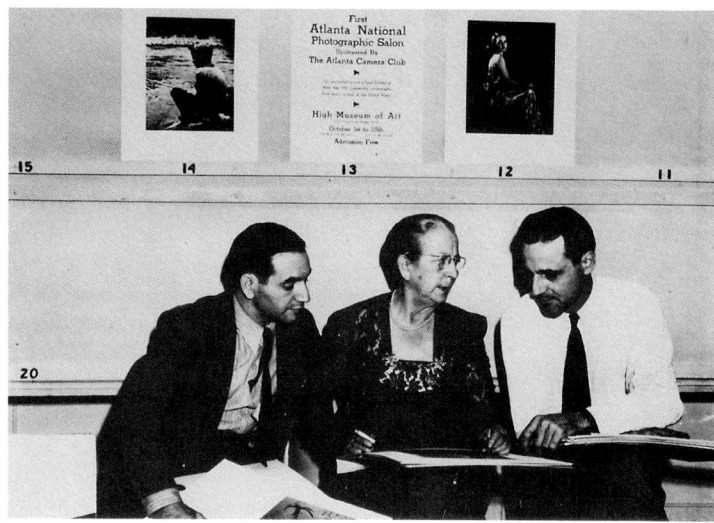

such as Stieglitz, Paul Strand, Edward Weston, Imogen Cunningham, and others document the transition.

Imogen Cunningham, a West Coast photographer who entered the profession at
about the same time as Wootten, joined the Pictorial Photographers of America in
1923. In less than a decade, however, she teamed with Californian Ansel Adams and
five other photographers including Edward Weston to form Group f/64, an organization dedicated to the complete antithesis of pictorial photography.

Adams did not settle on photography as a profession until 1930, but in time he
became perhaps the best known of all American photographers. His technique was
unabashedly straight and pure photography. Adams objected to photographs with a
stylistic link to other forms of art, and he saw pictorialism as something artificial and
burdensome.

Group f/64 advocated creative photography based exclusively on the medium
itself. They promoted sharp images and glossy photographic papers instead of the
soft look and matte or textured paper dear to the pictorialists. The group's manifesto
stated in part that "pure photography is defined as possessing no qualities of technique, composition or idea, derivative of any other art form. The production of the
'Pictorialist,' on the other hand, indicates a devotion to principles of art which are

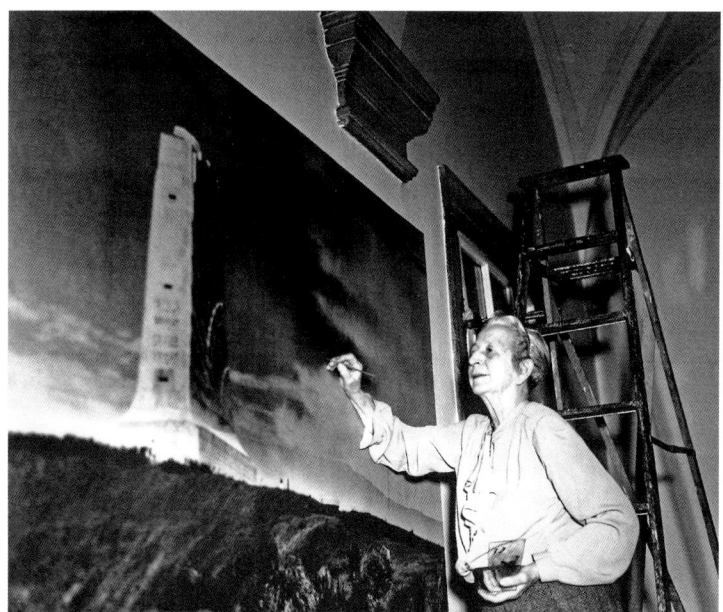

directly related to painting and the graphic arts."[67] Wootten, by contrast, in a news-paper article pasted in her scrapbook and dated August 11, 1939, paid homage to her artistic roots. Photography, she asserted, is an "interpretive art" and "the study of art plays a tremendous part in composition and composition in turn in interpretation."

In late 1932, Group f/64 mounted its first exhibit in San Francisco. As an organi-zation, however, it soon declined, even though straight photography and the careers of straight photographers continued to ascend. Adams proselytized the straight phi-losophy in articles for *Camera Craft* and *Modern Photography*, and his 1935 book *Making a Photograph* found a welcome audience. Over the next five decades, other books and articles by Adams, as well as workshops, lectures, and exhibitions of his superlative landscape photographs, helped to shape the modern conception of photography as a fine art in its own right.

Improvements in technology also aided the realistic photographers and contrib-uted to pictorialism's decline. Film speed and resolution steadily increased, and in the 1920s the appearance of small cameras such as the Leica opened the door to photog-raphy that was more spontaneous, candid, and oriented to action. This development nourished the increasingly modern idea of journalism wedded to photography. Newspaper and magazine readers responded favorably to photographs with a story and a message.

Photograph-dependent magazines such as *Look* and *Life* began in the 1930s, and new career openings for photographers blossomed in the worlds of fashion and advertising. Realistic and straight photography fueled the expansion. Ironically, it was also in this decade that Wootten achieved her greatest success as a pictorial photographer, an indication of the opposing currents and dynamic changes swirling within the medium. Bayard Wootten had little reason to seriously deviate from her course.

The photographs of the New Deal's Farm Security Administration exemplified the movement of straight photography to center stage. The subject matter chosen by FSA photographers was often identical to that pursued by Wootten. The techniques and philosophy that lay behind the images, however, were different, and so were the uses for the photographs.

In 1935, the Resettlement Administration (the name changed to Farm Security Administration in 1937) established its Historical Unit to create a photographic record of the agency's work and to document a nation struggling with the Great Depression. The Unit's director, Roy Stryker, possessed a genuine social consciousness, which influenced the group of about a dozen young, talented photographers that staffed the unit over its seven-year life. It was particularly the photographs made by Arthur Rothstein, Walker Evans, Dorothea Lange, Russell Lee, Marion Post Wolcott, Jack Delano, Ben Shahn, and Carl Mydans that established the unit's lasting recognition.

The work of the FSA photographers revealed innocent people caught in a desperate plight. Their images were alive with human endeavor, credible to the viewer, and often stark in their reality. They were photographs with a perspective that documented problems and stirred viewers to respond. The FSA prepared exhibits and distributed copies of the photographs for publication. Their massive archive numbered a quarter of a million pictures when the project ended in 1942.

Images made by the FSA photographers struck a responsive chord with the public and contributed to a rising appreciation for the power of straight, realistic photography to communicate facts and, in turn, influence events. This was not an overriding objective of Bayard Wootten's photographs. She wanted to make an artistic statement, not a social or political one. Her images are nonjudgmental and for the most

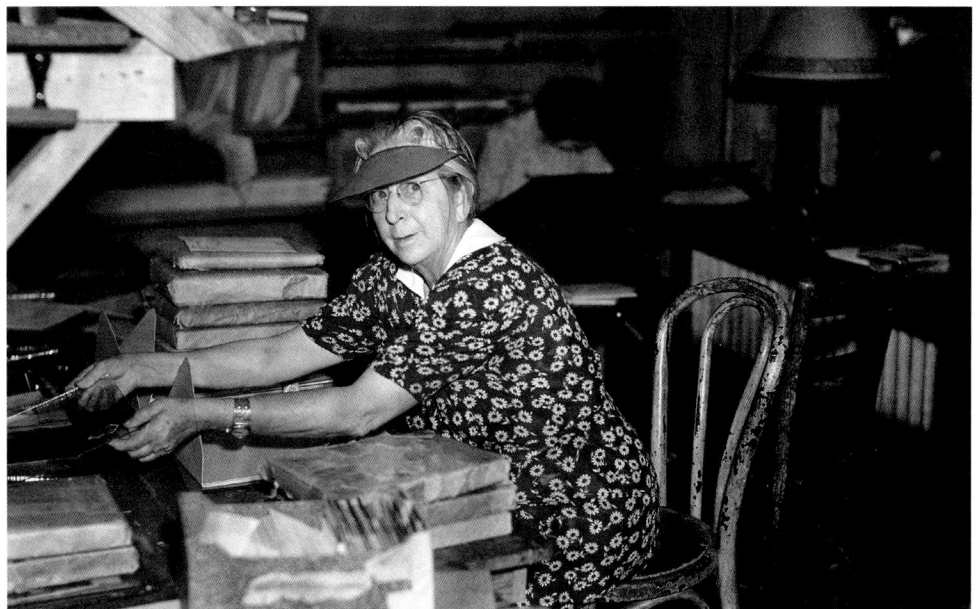

FIGURE 28
At work in the studio during the 1930s, Wootten gingerly reaches for a piece of glass for use in framing a photograph. (North Carolina Collection)

part have a tone of optimism or social neutrality. Exposing economic and social ills that she had frequent occasion to observe was never part of Wootten's plan. She did not simply photograph the South the way it was but the way she wanted it to be. Even a Wootten photograph of convict laborers in Alabama possesses a touch of artistic verve.

The FSA photographers who worked in North Carolina included Marion Post Wolcott, Jack Delano, Dorothea Lange, and Arthur Rothstein. Wolcott, Delano, and Lange came to the state under the auspices of the FSA and the Institute for Research in Social Science at the University of North Carolina. The Institute's director was Howard W. Odum, a respected sociologist and prolific writer. Odum sat for portraits at Wootten's studio, but it seems unlikely that she shared his progressive ideas on social planning and race relations.

Wootten's racial attitudes were typical of those prevalent among many whites of her generation. Born in 1875, she reached maturity at a time when Jim Crow laws were being passed across the South. In 1900, when Wootten was twenty-five, North Carolina voters approved a constitutional amendment that disfranchised African Americans. Some of her photographs reflect the racial stereotypes of the period, and as late as the 1930s she gave the title "Pickaninnies" to an exhibition photograph of black children. Wootten's images, however, probe the character of those she photographed whether they were black or white. With few exceptions, she depicted subjects with dignity and charm even when bare feet and tattered clothes spoke of unseen hardships.

Howard Odum and FSA Historical Unit chief Roy Stryker had deep roots in academia and shared a social perspective to which Wootten did not subscribe. Stryker had taught economics at Columbia University before joining the FSA, and Odum earned his doctoral degree in sociology at Columbia. In the 1930s much of Odum's work at the University of North Carolina focused on the study of regionalism. He identified a thirteen-county area in north central North Carolina and south central Virginia as a "subregional laboratory for social research and planning." Odum and his colleagues at North Carolina identified places and subjects for a photographic study of the subregion, and in 1939–40 Stryker's photographers came to the area.

They photographed some of Wootten's traditional subjects—rural life, farm and domestic scenes, and people at the bottom of the economic ladder. Tobacco farming, a major source of livelihood in the area and a defining element in the region's culture, received heavy emphasis. The FSA photographs appear unrehearsed and provide an honest representation of rural and small town life. There is no pretense of artistry. In contrast to Wootten, who kept only sparse records, the FSA photographers usually noted who and what they photographed, along with dates and locations. This information significantly enhances the documentary value of their images.

In the spring of 1940 the Institute for Research in Social Science hosted a conference in Chapel Hill on "population research, regional research, and the measurement of regional development." Roy Stryker attended the meeting, and the FSA prepared an exhibit from the work carried out by Wolcott, Delano, and Lange.

The exhibition may not have been open to the general public, for it received no local publicity. Even if Wootten did not see the FSA photographs in Chapel Hill, however, she knew of the work FSA photographers had done in North Carolina and elsewhere. Her own photographs, along with those of the FSA, appeared in the Works Progress Administration's *North Carolina: A Guide to the Old North State* (1939). Two Wootten photographs and one by Carl Mydans appeared two years earlier in *An Exhibition of the Rural Arts*, a book commemorating the seventy-fifth anniversary of the U.S. Department of Agriculture.

Pictorial photographers exercised a freedom in subject manipulation that was less accessible to strict documentary photographers, and Wootten took advantage of these liberties. At Penland School, for instance, on property owned by the Episcopal Church, she had a fake moonshine still constructed for use in a photograph and then posed herself in the picture as a moonshiner. Wearing a man's work clothes, including a hat that partially obscured her face, Wootten sat guard-like, holding a rifle. The image appears in *Cabins in the Laurel*.

The staging of photographs is a practice dating from the dawn of photography. Mathew Brady's photographers, for example, reportedly moved bodies around on Civil War battlefields for visual effect, and manipulating a scene for the camera was not an uncommon procedure for Wootten and many of her contemporaries. The ethics of this custom came into question in the 1930s, however, in a controversy involving the FSA.

While FSA photographer Arthur Rothstein was in the Dakotas in the spring of 1936 to document the region's drought, he happened upon the skull of a steer lying on dry and cracked earth. The skull likely predated the drought, but Rothstein photographed it and then moved the skull a few feet away and took more pictures. The FSA released both versions to the public.

In August, as the presidential election neared, the Roosevelt administration sent a delegation to visit states stricken by the drought. The day they reached North Dakota, a Republican newspaper in Fargo printed a front-page story that characterized the Rothstein photographs as inaccurate fakes. It portrayed the skull as a prop that the photographer simply moved about. Wire services carried the story, and it appeared in newspapers around the country. The truthfulness of the Unit's photographers and, indeed, that of the agency itself, came into question. Although politically inspired, the skirmish over photographic accuracy was slow to subside, and it tarnished the reputation of the Unit. The incident undoubtedly tightened the unwritten standards of documentary photography as well.

Less than two years before the Rothstein episode, Wootten had participated in a photographic hoax that passed without question. In 1934 she supplied thirty-two prints to the University of North Carolina Press for Charles Morrow Wilson's volume, *Backwoods America*. The book's setting was the Ozark mountains of Arkansas and Missouri, but none of the photographs were from either of the two states. Instead, they came from the Appalachian mountains of western North Carolina and eastern Tennessee. Wootten even made one of the photographs, a couple making

FIGURE 29

*One of the most repro-
duced photographs by a
Farm Security Adminis-
tration photographer is
this image by Dorothea
Lange of a migrant
mother with her children
at Nipomo, California.
The image conveys the
desperateness of the
Great Depression, deliv-
ering in resounding tones
a message of personal
hardship, uncertainty,
and fear. Although pov-
erty is evident in many of
Bayard Wootten's photo-
graphs, her images do not
make a biting social com-
mentary. (Library of
Congress)*

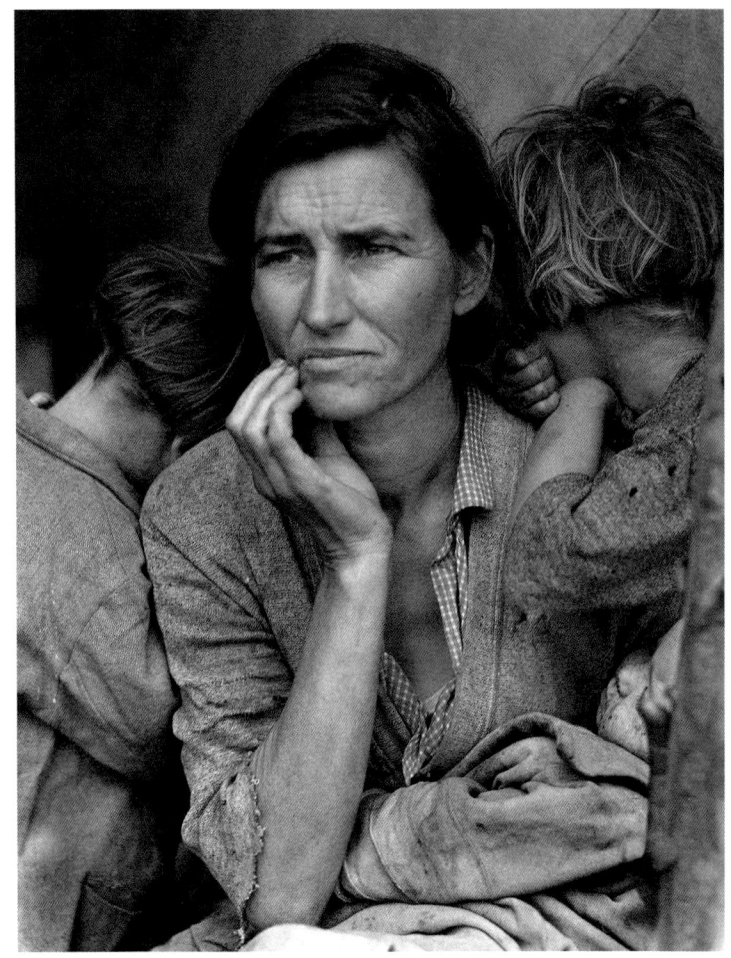

soap in a large pot, on the outskirts of Raleigh, far from the Appalachians and farther
still from the Ozarks. The University of North Carolina Press, the author, and the
photographer approved the use of photographs in a context that a later generation
would question.

William T. Couch, the Press's director, felt that illustrations were essential for
Wilson's book and wrote the author in July 1934 that the Press's willingness to publish
his work might rest on "the attractiveness of the photographs you can secure."[68] Wilson had thirty-eight prints by Arkansas photographer J. H. Field sent to the Press.
Couch turned them down, supposedly because they did not closely illustrate themes
discussed in the manuscript.

In September, the Press mailed Wilson forty-three prints by Wootten along with

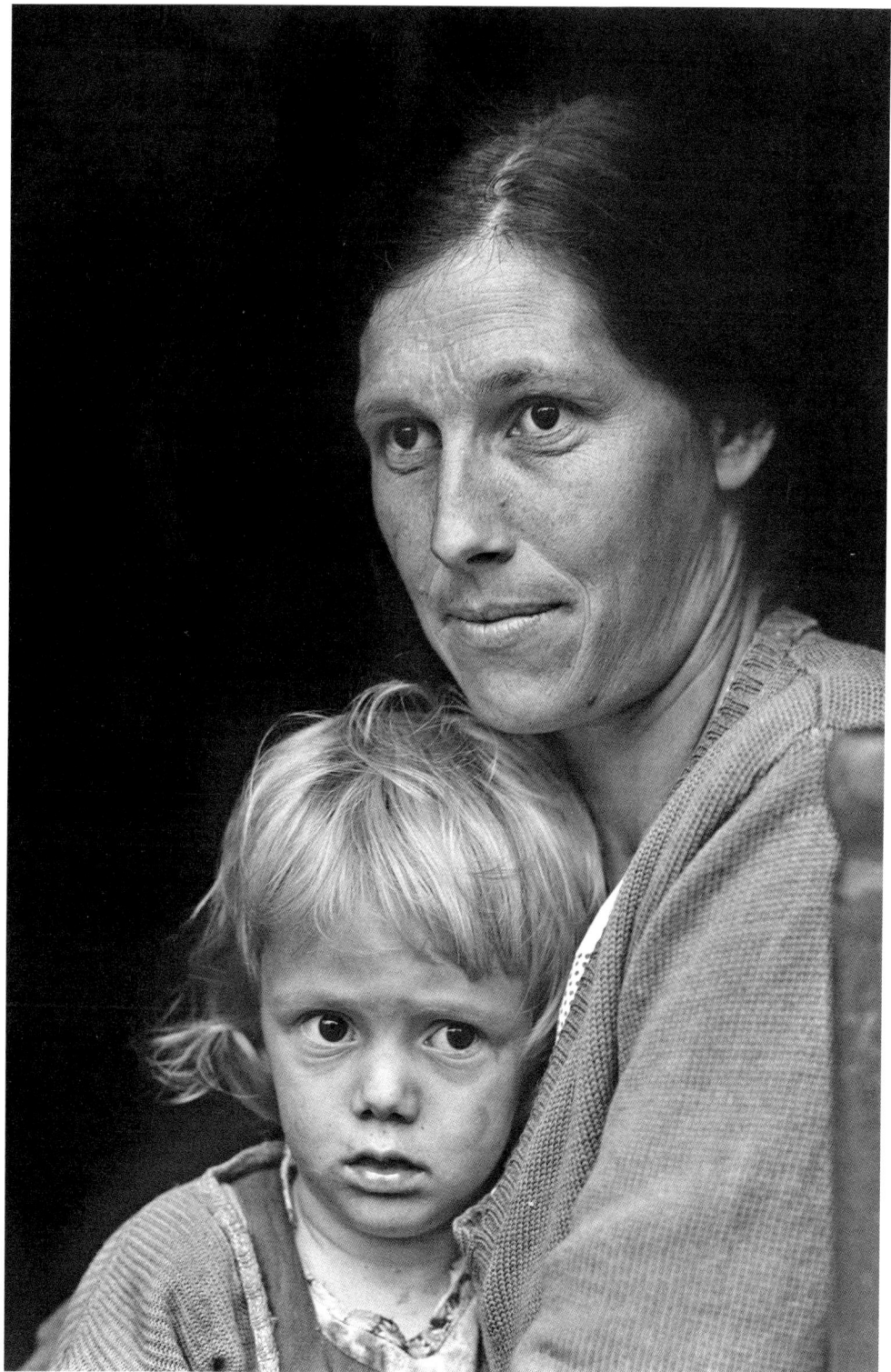

FIGURE 30

Wootten, like Lange, carried out some of her best photography during the 1930s. Wootten's photographs, however, often skirt the trauma of the time. Her view of a mother and child at Penland, North Carolina, contrasts markedly with the hopelessness portrayed in Lange's photograph of the California migrants. Although the child in Wootten's photograph looks apprehensive, the mother projects an aura of self-assurance and serenity. (North Carolina Collection)

Bain's Store in Person County, North Carolina, was the subject of a Lange photograph on a Sunday afternoon in July 1939. She stood directly in front of the building as a white man and several blacks chatted informally on the porch. The scene recorded by Lange appears spontaneous, animated, and realistic. (Manuscripts Department, University of North Carolina Library at Chapel Hill)

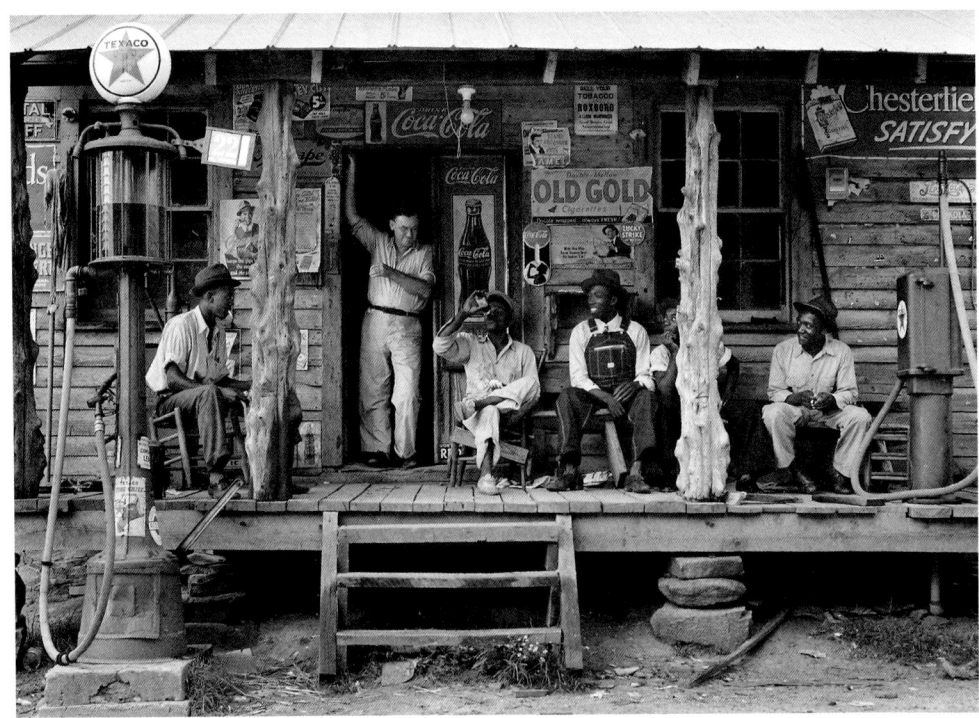

a list of where she made each one. "I believe that practically all of them are suitable for illustrating a book entitled *Backwoods America*," wrote Couch. "Her work is widely known and we cannot use it without paying her a portion of the royalty and giving her recognition as illustrator on the title page."[69]

Wilson agreed, and he replied to Couch, "they will fill the purpose very well indeed."[70] There is no indication that Wootten had any misgivings about using her photographs to depict a region they did not represent with complete accuracy. She was, after all, trying to sell photographs in the Great Depression. Her name appeared on the title page of *Backwoods America*, and she received 20 percent of the royalties.

Following the book's publication, the public library in Little Rock, Arkansas, unaware or unconcerned with geographic inaccuracy, asked the Press to send copies of Wootten's photographs for an exhibition. It is not difficult to surmise that perhaps Couch and Wootten glanced over their shoulders a few months later as the uproar over Arthur Rothstein's use of a skull unfolded in the media.

There is no indication that the growing popular taste for straight photography influenced Wootten significantly, and she undoubtedly found FSA-like camera work to be awkward. Her preference for large-view cameras with 5 × 7-inch or 8 × 10-inch

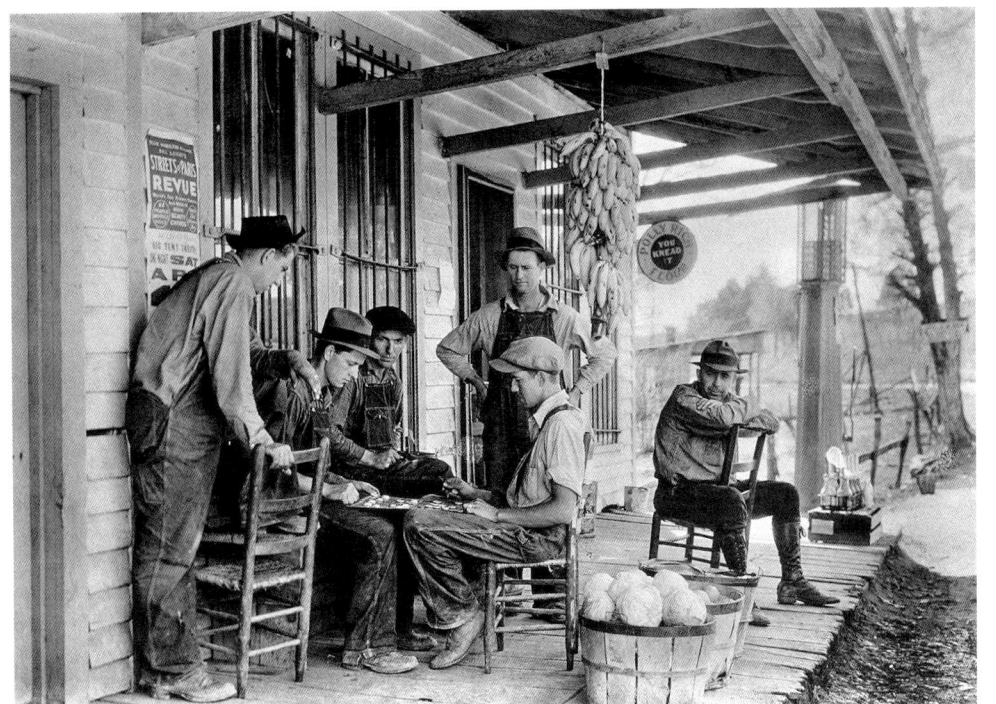

FIGURE 32

In contrast to Lange's photograph at Bain's Store, Wootten's photograph of checker players on the porch of a store near Sevierville, Tennessee, is a study in stationary composition. She arranged the men in a way that focuses attention on the checkerboard and photographed the scene at an angle, providing the image with depth. (North Carolina Collection)

sheet film restricted mobility and hampered the impromptu camera work often required for documentary photography. Subjects had ample time to respond to Wootten's presence, and her deliberate, planned, and slow approach to composition helped to define what she could photograph. For Wootten, the line between photographs as creative interpretations and as documentary records was indistinct. When printed in sharp focus on glossy paper, however, many of her images look strikingly like those of FSA photographers and other 1930s contemporaries such as Margaret Bourke-White. Although this signals a stylistic overlap and also demonstrates Wootten's versatility, her published photographs do not frequently appear within the same documentary context as those of the FSA. The Farm Security Administration images are often critical social documents. Wootten's folk portraiture is documentary in human terms that are more broad and nebulous.

The final volume illustrated by Wootten, Olive Tilford Dargan's *From My Highest Hill: Carolina Mountain Folks* (1941), hints at a degree of transition for the photographer. In making photographs for this book, Wootten experimented with a smaller and lighter camera. The book's photographs supposedly date from about 1940, but the images are on a mixture of film formats. Negative sizes include those used by

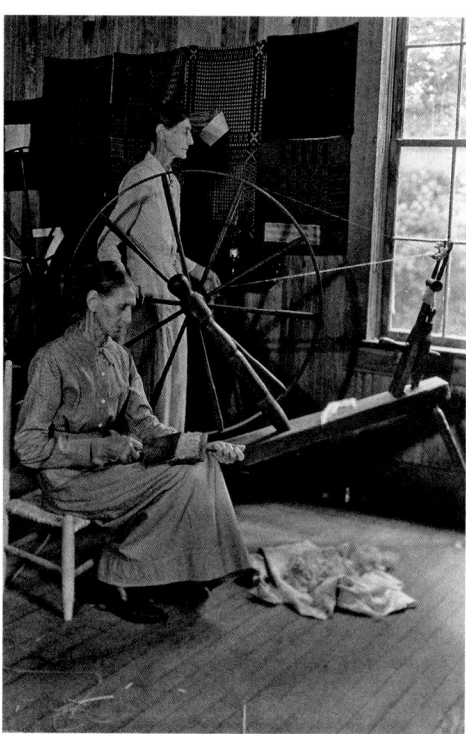
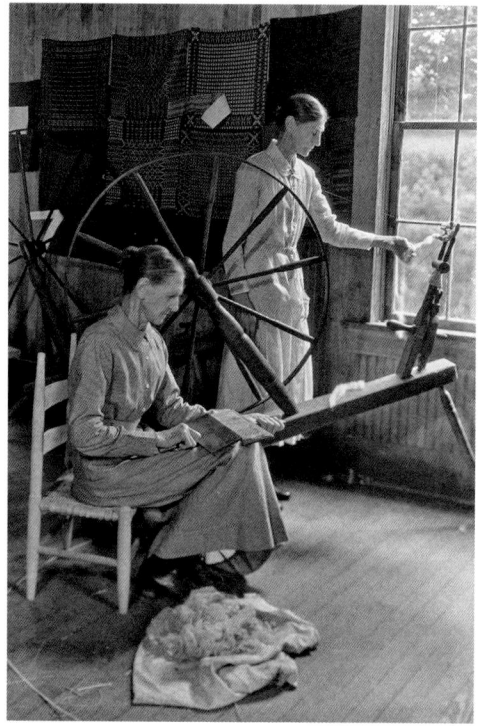

Wootten since the 1920s, the 5 × 7-inch and the 8 × 10-inch. Other negatives, however, are 4 × 5-inch and are on a thin film base. The use of a smaller and lighter 4 × 5 camera suggests a willingness on Wootten's part to experiment with something new, but strong ties to her traditional camera equipment remained. The mixture of film sizes also raises the possibility that a few of the book's photographs were made several years earlier than 1940.

Some of Wootten's photographs in *From My Highest Hill* reflect the freedom made possible by a less demanding camera. Though subtle, differences in the book's images are apparent when compared to those in *Cabins in the Laurel* and *Backwoods America*. Although a few of the people in Dargan's book have the same stoic appearance as in earlier volumes illustrated by Wootten, smiling faces are more prevalent in *From My Highest Hill*, and several scenes involve action. Wootten took many of these photographs using the 4 × 5 camera. The result is a mild collision of photographic styles within the book. What is not present in the volume, however, is a departure from the backward-looking nature of Wootten's photography. As in her earlier works, the photographs are nostalgic and skirt themes of modernism. Nonetheless, the im-

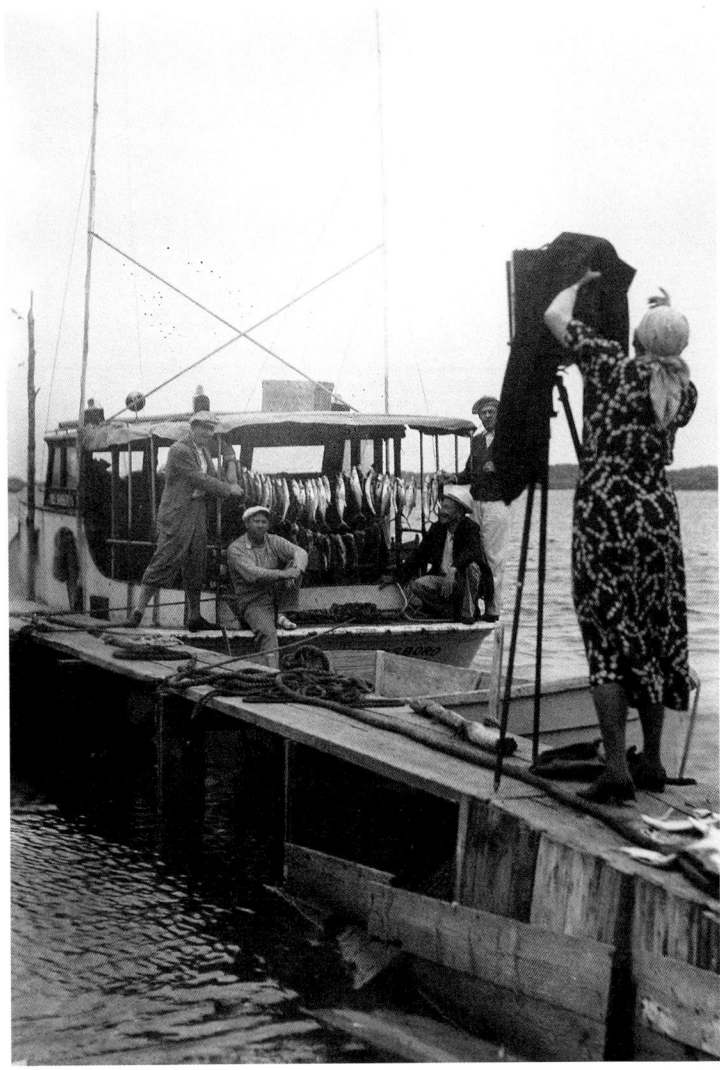

FIGURE 34

*An assistant photo-
graphed Wootten as she
prepared to make her
own picture of a fishing
party with their catch at
Swansboro, North Caro-
lina. Wootten's bulky
camera and the time
required to operate it
restricted her capacity as
a documentary photogra-
pher. (North Carolina
Collection)*

ages in *From My Highest Hill* have more of a genuine documentary quality than those in either *Backwoods America* or *Cabins in the Laurel.*

Wootten's creative photography rested heavily upon a shrinking pictorial niche, and her photographic vision—the romanticism, the quaintness, the optimism, and the endless quest for artistry—defined Wootten's relationship with subject, camera, and print. When the FSA photographers started their documentary work in 1935, Wootten was already sixty years old—perhaps too old to seriously pursue new frontiers with the camera.

The photographic opportunities of the 1930s provided Wootten with a creative spark and lifted her career above the commercial doldrums of a small-town southern photographer. The decade also saw the maturation of forces that helped to modernize photography and move it well beyond the confines of pictorialism. As Bayard Wootten's career peaked on a blend of art and realism, the photographic world was brimming with new life. There were more ways to use photographs, and a greater need for action and literalism emerged. In turn, the value of pictorial interpretation slowly ebbed.

THE PHOTOGRAPHY OF WOOTTEN AND DORIS ULMANN

The mountains of western North Carolina have provided photographers with a wealth of photographic opportunities since the nineteenth century. This picturesque region with lofty peaks and a cool summer climate became a popular tourist mecca that supported a thriving photographic trade. Wootten's father, Rufus Morgan, marketed stereographs of the mountain area in the 1870s. Beginning in the 1880s several Asheville-based photographers—including Thomas H. Lindsey, Nat. W. Taylor, and W. T. Robertson—mass-produced scenic landscapes and quaint views of mountain people.

Nace Brock, Wootten's mentor, opened his Asheville studio in the late 1890s. Another, the Baker-Barber Studio, operated for several generations at nearby Hendersonville, and the region also supported many small-scale photographers. Notable among these was Paul Buchanan. Between the 1920s and 1950s, he worked in the counties of Avery, McDowell, Mitchell, and Yancey, an area crisscrossed by Wootten beginning in the late 1920s.

Except for a link with the pictorial photography of Nace Brock, Wootten was not cut from the same mold as the local photographers who pursued mountain subjects. These were men for whom the profession was essentially a trade. Wootten appreciated photography as an expressive medium and incorporated genuine artistic skills in her work. This was also true of two other women with photographic ties to the region.

New England photographer Chansonetta Stanley Emmons (1858–1937) visited North Carolina and South Carolina in 1897 and again in 1926. On both occasions she documented her travels with photographs. Her inventive brothers owned the Stanley Dry Plate Company, a manufacturer of glass photographic plates. They also made the Stanley Steamer automobile, and most of Emmons's income derived from the family enterprises. Like Wootten, Emmons received training as an artist, and domestic life, particularly in rural areas, attracted her as a photographer. Children, African Americans, and elderly men and women were favored subjects. A viewer is struck by the sensitive posing and idyllic settings of Emmons's work. She often made photographs within the homes and workplaces of her subjects using only natural illumination, a technique that sets Emmons's work somewhat apart from much of Wootten's photography.

Another talented woman photographer, active in the southern Appalachians after Chansonetta Emmons and more a contemporary of Wootten, was Doris Ulmann of New York City. Ulmann was largely unknown in North Carolina, but leading pictorialists held her work in high regard.

It is uncertain whether Wootten and Ulmann ever met, but they undoubtedly knew of one another's work. They may even have crossed paths more than a decade before working in the southern Appalachians. Wootten lived in New York City briefly in 1917, and both women were members of the Pictorial Photographers of America. Both also had prints in the 1923 Pittsburgh Salon of Photography exhibition at the Carnegie Institute.

In April 1936, less than two years after Ulmann's death, Berea College, now home to the Doris Ulmann Foundation, held a joint exhibition of southern Appalachian photographs by the two women. Wootten supplied prints from her personal collection. Ulmann's photographs came from the Russell Sage Foundation in New York.

Many of the photographs by Ulmann and Wootten are strikingly similar in both style and content. In personal respects, however, the women were worlds apart. Ulmann, born in New York in 1882, was several years younger than Wootten. She attended the public schools and made childhood visits to Europe with her father, a German immigrant and the founder of a textile company. She entered Columbia University Teachers College and in the course of her studies enrolled in a photography class led by prominent pictorialist Clarence White. Ulmann later attended the New York photography school that White established in 1914, and his influence was significant in her embrace of the pictorial style.

Ulmann's interest in the medium was reinforced by her marriage to another photographer, Charles Jaeger, also reportedly White's personal physician. Jaeger, like

FIGURE 35

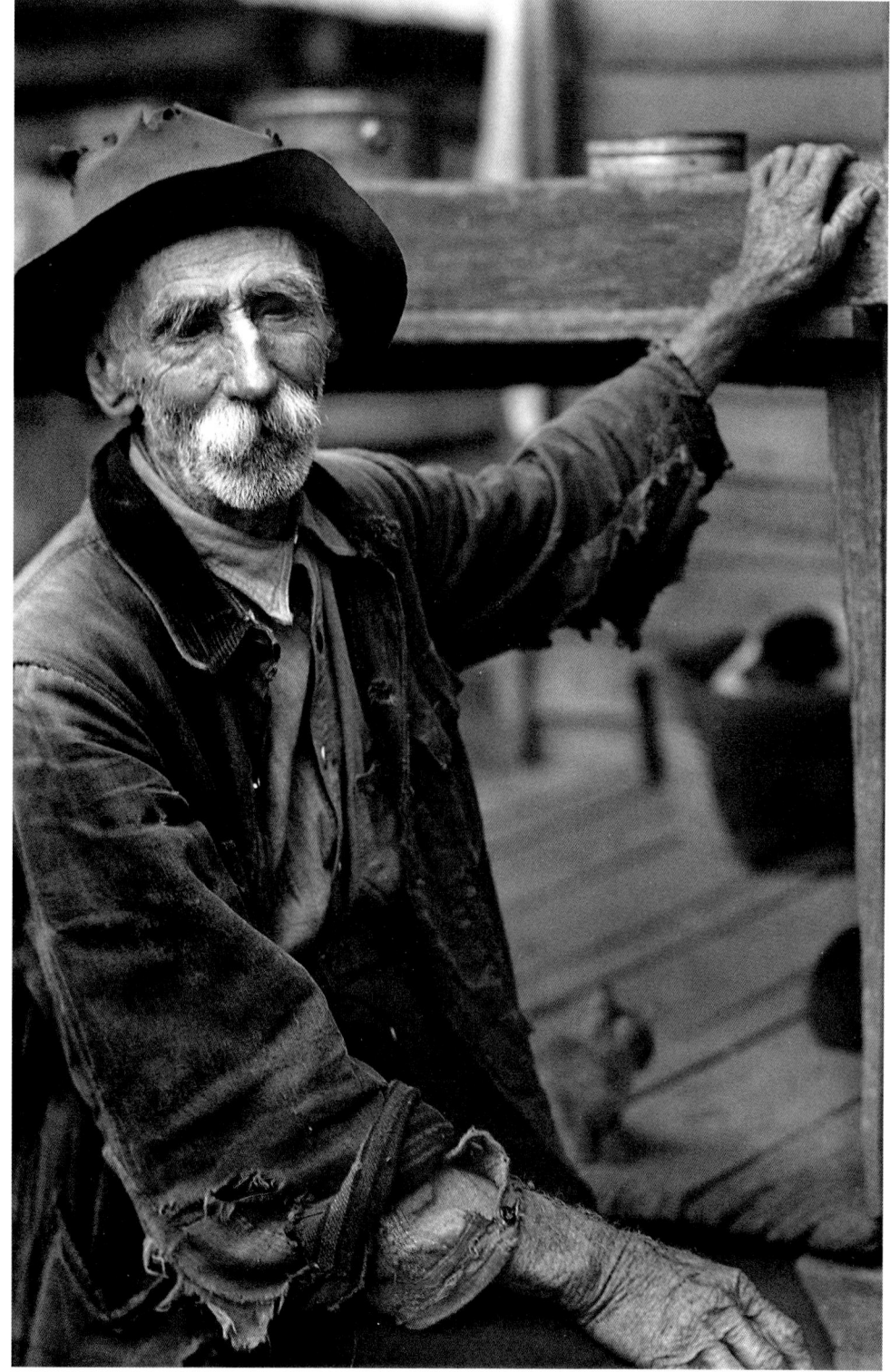

The *Life* and Career of Bayard Wootten

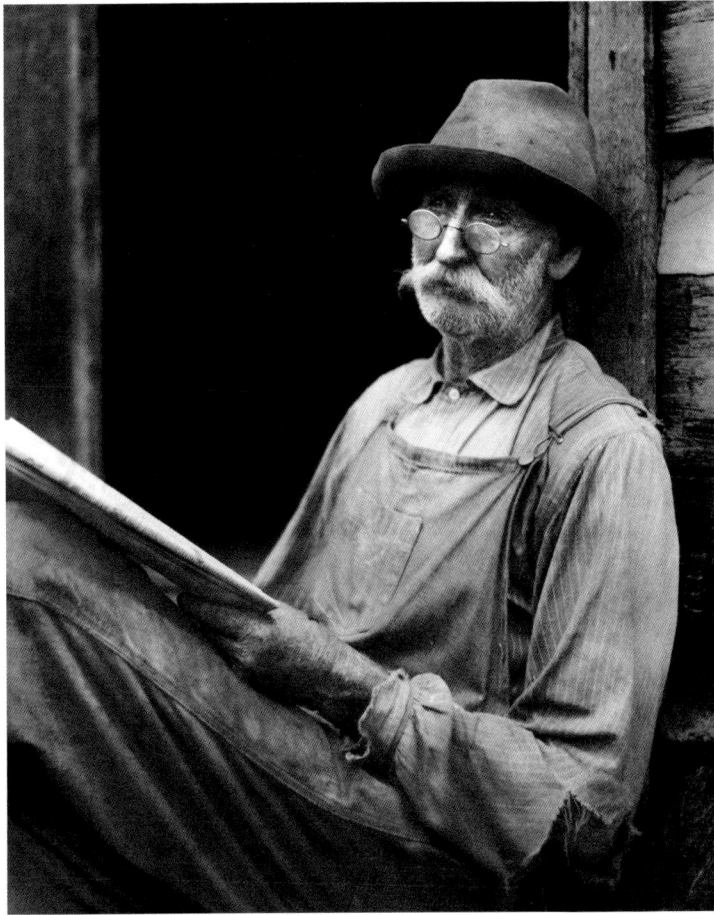

FIGURE 36

A portrait by Ulmann, remarkable in its similarity to the Wootten image in Figure 35, illustrates the close thematic bond shared by the two photographers. (Used with the special permission of Berea College and the Doris Ulmann Foundation)

Ulmann, belonged to the Pictorial Photographers of America. From their base in New York City, the couple often explored small towns and rural areas within a convenient driving distance in search of pictorial subjects. They experimented with a variety of printing media, but platinum photographic paper with its characteristic matte surface and delicate tones was a predominant choice. Although preferred by many art photographers, the increasingly high cost of platinum restricted the paper's use. There is no clear evidence that Wootten ever worked with platinum.

For Ulmann, the camera was a recreational pursuit, and one that was unfettered by the financial considerations affecting Wootten. Ulmann received a large inheritance from her father's estate in 1917, and her life in New York was one of comfort and ease. Her economic and social standing as well as a genuine appreciation for literature and the arts often provided access to celebrities who came to the city. Many of them accepted Ulmann's invitation to sit for a portrait at her Park Avenue studio, among them Anna Pavlova, Max Weber, Paul Robeson, Lillian Gish, William Butler Yeats, Sinclair Lewis, Robert Frost, Thomas Wolfe, Helen Keller, and Albert Einstein, to name but a few. Wolfe, photographed by Wootten in 1919 while attending the University of North Carolina, used his 1927 Ulmann portrait on the dust jacket of his first novel, *Look Homeward, Angel*.

Ulmann and Jaeger separated in the early 1920s and later divorced. By the time of the 1923 Carnegie Institute exhibit in which she and Wootten had prints, Ulmann was again using her maiden name. The 1920s was a decade in which folk portraiture became a major thrust in the photography of both women. Ulmann's interest in portraiture, also like that of Wootten, transcended the studio. They pursued subjects of a similar type, particularly elderly men and women living in rural, agrarian settings. Ulmann's photographic excursions of the mid-1920s went as far south as the Shenandoah Valley of northern Virginia. She had visited western North Carolina by 1929.

The 1926 issue of *Pictorial Photography in America* included Ulmann's print titled "Old Virginia Type," which showed a man seated on a bench and holding his pipe. The book's commentary drew attention to Ulmann's portrayal of his "character," a word that appears frequently in later descriptions of Wootten's photography. The novelist and poet Hamlin Garland used the phrase "character portraits" in a July 1927 article about Ulmann that appeared in *The Mentor*. He noted her "special interest in the patient wives of farmers, in the ruminative old tinkers, philosophical blacksmiths and other sturdy primitive types."[71]

Wootten's portraiture elicited similar comments. Her 1932 exhibition at the Fine Arts Theatre in Boston included prints with titles such as "Mountaineer," "The Reaper," and "Mr. Woody, Chairmaker." Walter Spearman, book review editor of the *Charlotte News*, in his critique of *Cabins in the Laurel*, described the book's photographs as "either a character portrait of a rugged and interesting individual or a landscape of incomparable beauty."[72] "Character studies" and "character sketches" are other phrases commonly applied to the images that Wootten made. One newspaper even referred to her Chapel Hill business as a "folk studio."[73] Wootten sometimes labeled negative envelopes with terms such as "mountain people," "darkey women," and "darkey men." She grouped the negatives accordingly, suggesting an overriding interest in the types of people whom she photographed rather than in their individual identities.

The accomplishments of both Ulmann and Wootten rested in part upon strategic friendships that provided each photographer with a stream of good subject matter. Lucy Morgan of Penland School linked Wootten with rural communities in the mountains of western North Carolina. Similar connections were crucial for Ulmann.

Wootten had made the transition from glass negatives to the far lighter cellulose nitrate film by 1921. Ulmann, however, continued to use the heavy glass plates. In 1925 she met John Jacob Niles, an actor and singer born in Kentucky who agreed, two years later, to help her with camera work. Niles provided much-needed assistance with the bulky camera gear and film, but his ties to Kentucky were equally significant in steering Ulmann to the "primitive types" that she sought.

Ulmann's success in locating subjects to photograph in the North Carolina mountains stemmed in large measure from her work with the Russell Sage Foundation based in New York. The Foundation's concern with economic and social life in the Appalachians led to an interest in the native crafts of the region. Doris Ulmann's photography received close scrutiny after Allen Eaton, an employee in the Foundation's Survey Department, saw her prints on exhibit at the Mountain Workers Conference in Knoxville, Tennessee, in 1930. Two years later, while working on a book on native crafts, Eaton approached Ulmann about providing illustrations. Viewing the project as a way of getting further access to people in the Appalachians, she readily consented. Eaton's work culminated in 1937 with the publication of *Handicrafts of the Southern Highlands*. Fifty-eight of the book's photographs are by Ulmann. The remaining ninety-two are from other sources, including one by Wootten.

Eaton directed Ulmann in her photographic agenda in much the same way that William T. Couch of the University of North Carolina Press guided Wootten. Eaton wanted certain craft activities documented, and he provided an itinerary of places to go and people to see. In the summer of 1933, Ulmann and Niles visited the John C. Campbell Folk School at Brasstown, North Carolina, for the first time. The school was founded in the mid-1920s by Olive Dame Campbell, who named the institution for her husband, the secretary of the Southern Highland Division of the Sage Foundation until his death in 1919. At Brasstown, Ulmann found a crafts community similar to the one encountered by Wootten at Penland and responded in much the same way. Ulmann photographed the students and then sought out their families and friends in nearby communities in a search for individuals whom she considered interesting.

FIGURE 37

Historical interest in the work of Ulmann and Wootten derives in part from the photographic record they made of handicrafts practiced in the southern Appalachians during the late 1920s and early 1930s. Wootten photographed this basket maker at Penland, North Carolina, and the image has a quality that is more documentary than pictorial. The woman appears actively at work, her partially completed basket prominently displayed against a dark background. (North Carolina Collection)

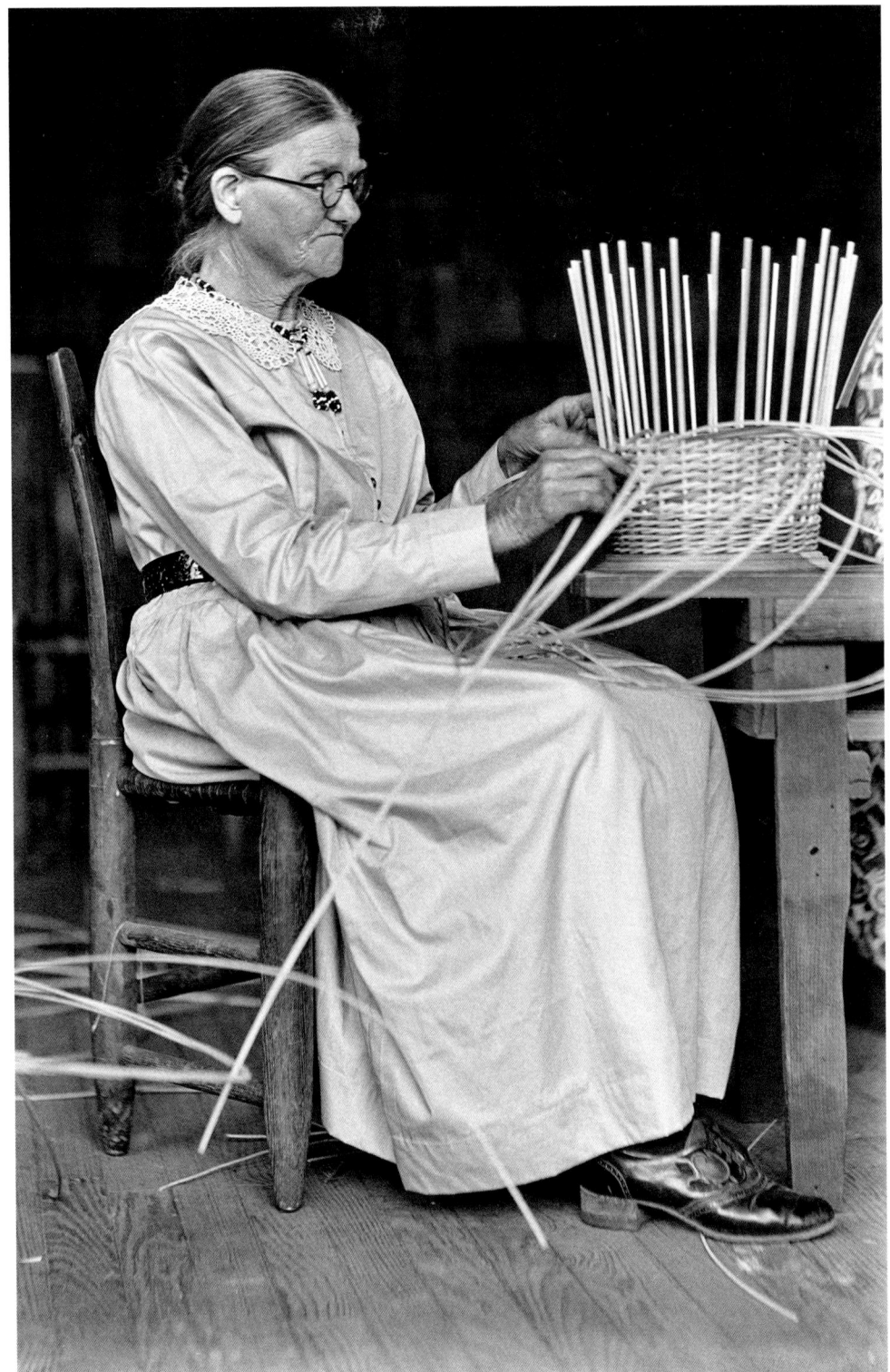

The *Life* and Career of Bayard Wootten

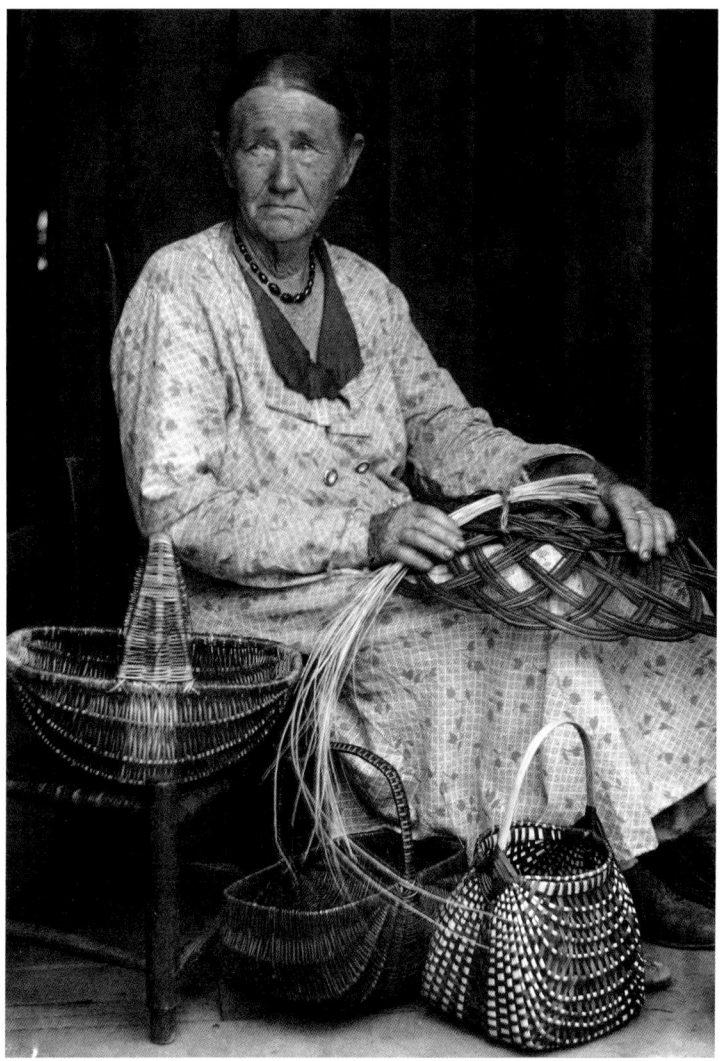

FIGURE 38

This Ulmann photograph of a basket maker at Hindman, Kentucky, appears staged. Three baskets, placed in the foreground in a curved arrangement, are presumably her work. The woman holds a sheaf of what might be weaving material, even though the basket on her lap appears finished. (Used with the special permission of Berea College and the Doris Ulmann Foundation)

The compensation provided by Wootten and Ulmann to most of the persons they photographed in these settings likely consisted of no more than complimentary prints, if that. Wootten told an interviewer that she gave sitters a photograph of the "conventional posed type" in exchange for permission to make other photographs "as she wished."[74] Ulmann reportedly adhered to this commitment faithfully, but for both women long periods may have elapsed between the making of negatives and the actual delivery of prints to sitters.

On photographic outings, Ulmann preferred staying in towns with comfortable hotels. She typically traveled in a chauffeur-driven Lincoln loaded with camera equip-

FIGURE 39

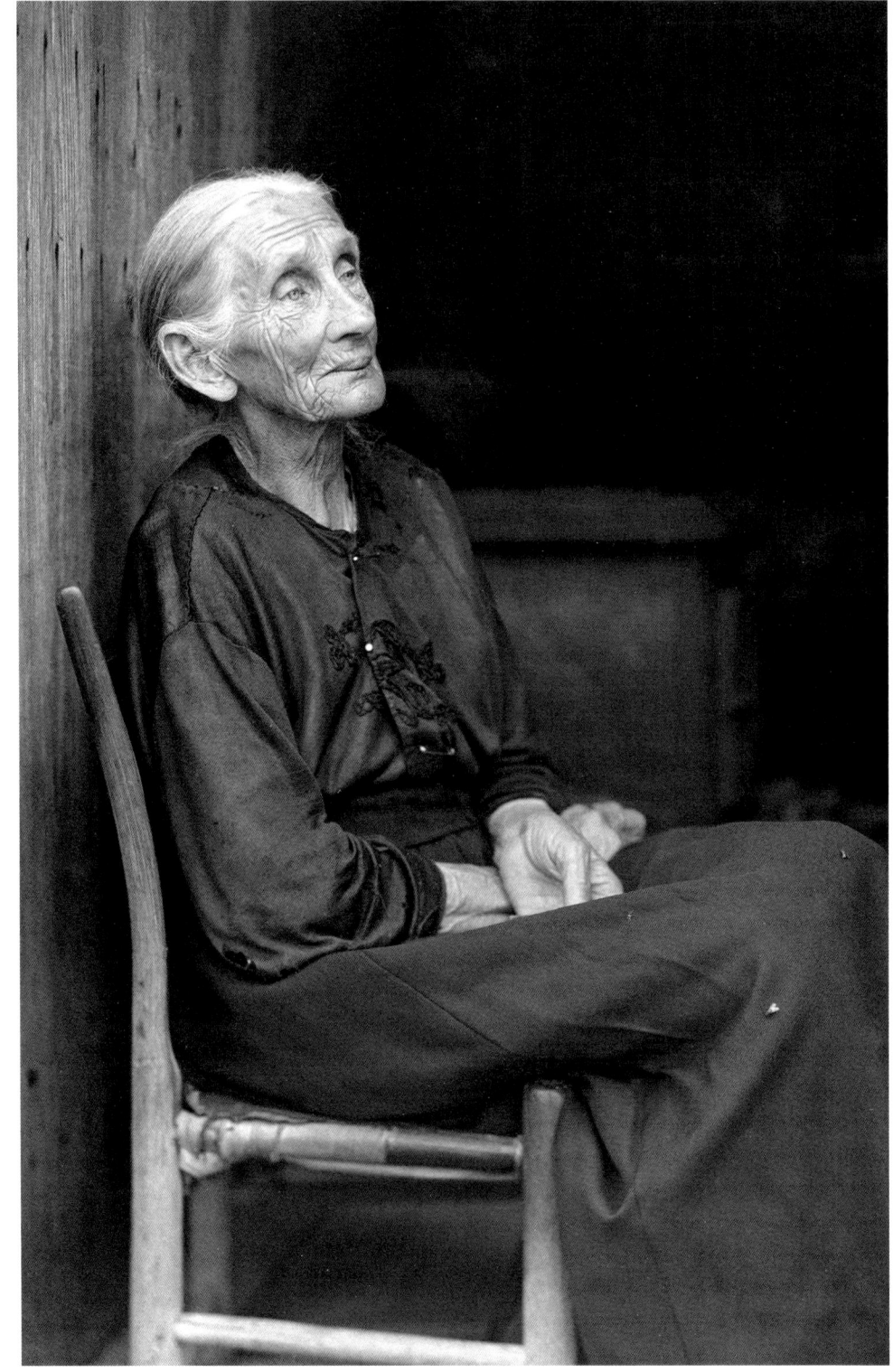

The *Life* and Career of Bayard Wootten

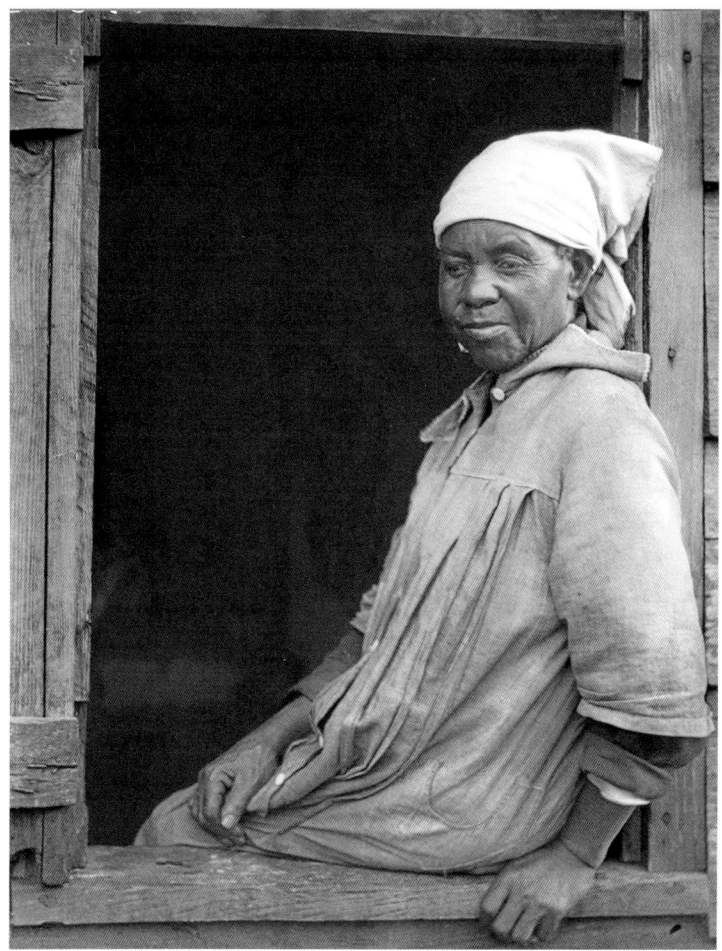

FIGURE 40

Ulmann also relied on dark interiors to emphasize many of her subjects. Details in the face of this African American woman contrast markedly with the smooth, rich blackness of the background. Without this backdrop, the photograph's dramatic presentation would be lost. (Ulmann Collection, University of Oregon Library)

ment and a courtly wardrobe sufficient to permit a clean outfit each day. Niles drove his Chevrolet for the pair to use on roads that were too rough for the Lincoln.

To what extent camera subjects respond to a photographer's appearance and demeanor is a matter of conjecture. By all accounts both Ulmann and Wootten could engage in the small talk that often put strangers at ease. Ulmann's image of wealth and elegance, however, differed sharply from Wootten's informal, unpretentious, and at times untidy appearance. Hamlin Garland's article in *The Mentor* mentions Ulmann's difficulties in trying to prevent rural subjects from dressing up for a photograph. She wanted them to wear clothes that were ordinary or old, a reality that for many persons must have struck a sharp contrast with Ulmann's own appearance.

The experiences of Wootten and Ulmann in photographing African Americans arose from different origins. Ulmann had spent a lifetime in the ethnically diverse and relatively open culture of New York, where blacks were not uncommon subjects for photographers. The culture of the South was more closed, and suspicion of outsiders, especially in rural areas, was widespread. Interacting with African Americans in the South in a way that might easily produce the same sensitive and artistic photographs that characterized Ulmann's work elsewhere initially proved to be challenging.

The chance to pursue African American portraiture in the South materialized for Ulmann after she met South Carolina novelist Julia Peterkin in 1929. Peterkin won the Pulitzer Prize in that year for her novel, *Scarlet Sister Mary*. A close friendship between Ulmann and Peterkin developed quickly, eventually resulting in a collaboration between the two on *Roll, Jordan, Roll*, a book Peterkin authored on "Negro life in the South."

Ulmann made at least three trips to South Carolina in 1929–30, visiting Peterkin at Lang Syne, the author's plantation near Columbia. Ulmann's photographic itinerary included African American subjects at Lang Syne and the coastal region around Charleston. Ulmann also visited Louisiana and Alabama, and photographs from those states appear in *Roll, Jordan, Roll* in addition to the South Carolina images.

Ulmann encountered unfamiliar customs in South Carolina and a black culture less than open to strangers with a camera. David Featherstone, in *Doris Ulmann: American Portraits*, quotes a letter the photographer wrote from Charleston in the fall of 1929 that recounted the problems: "It seems to be exceedingly difficult to get the studies in which I am interested here," Ulmann said. "The place is rich in material, but these negroes are so strange that it is almost impossible to photograph them. So this is rather a strenuous affair and then I do not feel satisfied! . . . I think the people of Charleston are rather difficult because they are so very self-conscious."[75]

For the most part Ulmann adapted to the difficulties that frustrated her early efforts in South Carolina. *Roll, Jordan, Roll* appeared in late 1933, and the trade edition included seventy-two of her photographs. Ulmann posed subjects artistically, and the photographs are reminiscent of her earlier pictorial work.

A few of the photographs, including one of blacks walking into a church, appear decidedly rigid and unnatural. The limitations of controlled composition to depict themes normally characterized by movement are evident in the photography of both Ulmann and Wootten. A preference for heavy, large-format cameras and meticulous posing limited the range of their photographic repertoire. Ulmann's use of glass plates and a primitive, shutterless camera made the task even more daunting.

The reproduction quality of images in the trade edition of *Roll, Jordan, Roll*, printed by offset, is poor. Photographs are often so dark that faces are indistinguishable. Even though Ulmann's sensitive and artistic style is apparent in the photographs, the published result surely disappointed the photographer. Although a higher quality gravure edition containing ninety photographs appeared later, its publication run was less than 400 copies.

Bayard Wootten's experience with African Americans was both lengthy and frequent. Wootten lived in a state that was roughly one-fourth black. In eastern North Carolina, the location of her hometown, the black population exceeded 50 percent in some counties. Although racial inequality was the norm, black and white populations in the small towns and rural areas of the East were always near to one another.

The photographic record of Wootten's early work with African Americans is thin, due to the 1932 fire that destroyed negatives in her New Bern studio. Some newspaper accounts of the photographer's entry into the profession mention that she borrowed a camera to photograph blacks working in a cotton field for use on calendars. In 1907, Wootten marketed a series of postcards showing African Americans. Giving them titles such as "From de white folks kitchen" and "One of the Boys," she undoubtedly intended these racially tinged cards for a white audience.

Throughout the 1930s, Wootten photographed black agricultural laborers involved in the production of tobacco, cotton, and other crops in many parts of North Carolina and the South. She was only a step behind Doris Ulmann in pursuing African American subjects in South Carolina. Wootten was in Charleston in 1932 and possibly earlier, and she spent a month in the area in the spring of 1933 making photographs for her second exhibition at Boston's Fine Arts Theatre. Other visits to the Charleston area took place over the next four years as Wootten enlarged a portfolio that culminated in 1937 with the publication of *Charleston: Azaleas and Old Bricks*. The volume was principally of architectural interest, but eight of its sixty-one photographs included blacks.

Many of Wootten's most intriguing images of African Americans did not originate in Charleston, however, but along the lower Waccamaw River in Georgetown County to the north of Charleston. This part of South Carolina was economically and ethnically unique. Many of the great antebellum rice plantations had been in

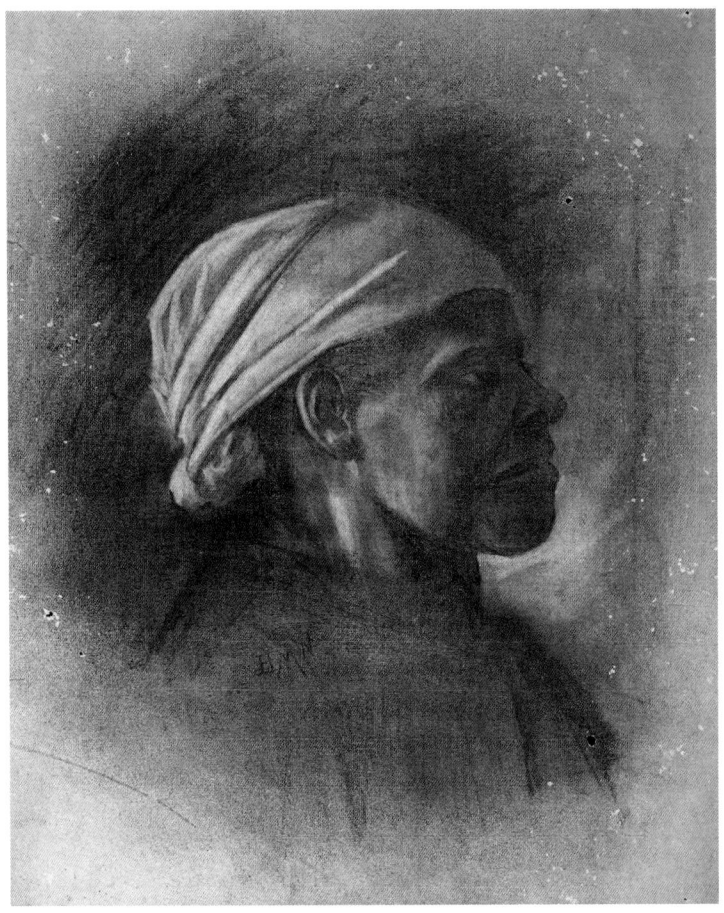

Lower All Saints Parish, a neck of land between the Waccamaw River and the Atlantic Ocean.

The Waccamaw rises in North Carolina and flows drowsily across the state line into the counties of Horry and then Georgetown before reaching the ocean at Winyah Bay. The land is flat, low, and in places swampy. The river is the color of weak tea and along its shores are forests of cypress, pine, oak, sweet gum, and wax myrtle that have reclaimed ancient rice fields once cultivated by generations of African Americans. On the eve of the Civil War the Georgetown district produced a third of all rice grown in the United States. Charles Joyner, in *Down by the Riverside*, identifies more than thirty plantations located on the lower Waccamaw before the war. Joshua Ward, the owner of seven of these, had more than 1,000 slaves.

In the mid-nineteenth century, the population of Lower All Saints Parish was 89 percent black and included many slaves who were African-born or had come by way of the Caribbean islands. After the war, the relative isolation of the lower Waccamaw contributed to the persistence of a black culture that was strong with African and Caribbean influences. When Wootten went to the area in 1937–38, her itinerary included Sandy Island, an isolated outpost in the Waccamaw River that even today is accessible only by boat. Its permanent population is all black, and the state of South Carolina has taken steps to protect the island from development.

Wootten came to the lower Waccamaw with decades of experience interacting with blacks as neighbors, friends, and camera subjects. The challenge of carrying out a successful photographic mission in the region, however, depended upon having a local contact who knew the area and its people. Genevieve Willcox Chandler of Murrells Inlet served as Wootten's companion and guide.

Chandler was a field-worker for the Works Progress Administration's Federal Writers' Project, a government-sponsored effort to provide work for unemployed writers. It was Chandler's assignment to compile oral history and folklore from the lower Waccamaw, and she conducted interviews with former slaves who had lived on the rice plantations that once clustered along the river. Chandler likely knew most of the people whom Wootten photographed in the area.

How Wootten learned about these African American communities and met Genevieve Chandler is a matter of speculation. What is certain is that the two women knew one another by January 1937 when Wootten visited Murrells Inlet to photograph Brookgreen Gardens. The following year the Washington office of the Federal Writers' Project encouraged its South Carolina bureau to produce a book based upon Chandler's work. Both Wootten and Chandler believed that a publication would emerge from their combined efforts. Some of Wootten's surviving photographs from the area even have the inscription "for Chandler book."

Regrettably, no volume resulted from this collaboration. In the fall of 1938 the Works Progress Administration directed that WPA workers who qualified for Social Security be released from the agency. Chandler, although only in her forties, qualified as a widow with dependent children. With her continued employment in doubt, Chandler secured work in the private sector, and in January 1939 her work with the Federal Writers' Project ended.

If a publication had emerged, it might well have been of genuine historical interest. Among the people photographed by Wootten and interviewed by Chandler were

FIGURE 42

Wooten, on the right, stands beside Federal Writers' Project employee Genevieve Willcox Chandler of Murrells Inlet, South Carolina. Chandler served as Wooten's guide in the late 1930s when she photographed African Americans living along the lower Wacca-maw River. A book anticipated by the two women never material-ized. (North Carolina Collection)

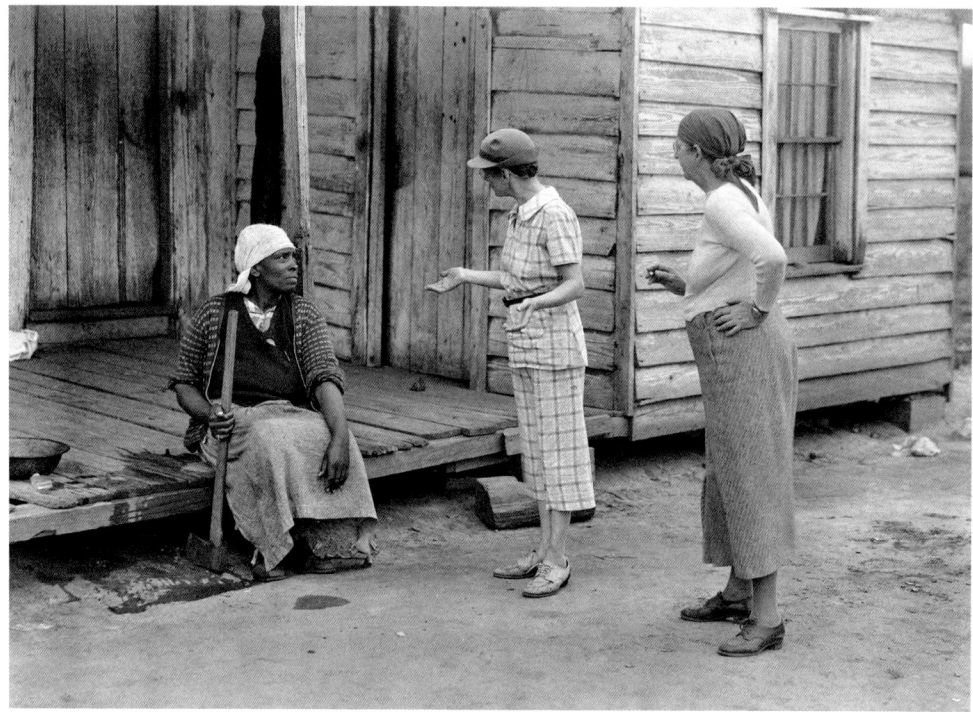

Welcome Beese, a former slave born on the Oatland Plantation about 1833; Mariah Heywood from the Midway Plantation, who as a child was a wedding gift from her owner to his daughter; and Hagar Brown from The Oaks, who described to Chandler the beatings and other punishments inflicted upon the slaves.

Doris Ulmann's friend, South Carolina writer Julia Peterkin, also knew about the black communities of the lower Waccamaw. In 1909 Peterkin and her husband bought a cottage at Murrells Inlet, and it became a favorite summer retreat for the couple. The author's collection of short stories, published in 1924 under the title *Green Thursday*, drew upon her experiences with African Americans, and the setting of Peterkin's next work, *Black April*, was on Sandy Island and adjacent Brookgreen Plantation. Her Pulitzer Prize–winning novel *Scarlet Sister Mary* was based upon events at Brookgreen, Sandy Island, and Lang Syne Plantation. Ulmann and Peterkin visited Murrells Inlet on at least one occasion between 1929 and 1931. Ulmann photographed African Americans living in the area but apparently did not tap the region's photographic richness to the extent that Wooten did. The joint effort of Julia Peterkin and Doris Ulmann in *Roll, Jordan, Roll* (1933) set the stage for later collaborations between writers and photographers working in the American South.

Pictorial imagery was paramount in Ulmann's work, and Wootten's photography for *Backwoods America* (1934) and *Cabins in the Laurel* (1935) followed in much the same vein. The southern Appalachian and African American photographs of Ulmann and Wootten blend documentary features with pictorial tradition. Ulmann's camera equipment was rudimentary by almost any standard. Wootten's was less so, and she pursued a more challenging photographic agenda. Photographs by the two women vary in historical accuracy, for both took artistic liberties with subject content as well as with composition. Ulmann reportedly posed women beside spinning wheels they had rarely used, if ever. She also dressed subjects in old clothes that were not their own. Wootten is said to have engaged in similar orchestration in her photography for *Cabins in the Laurel*. For both Wootten and Ulmann, subjects were like actors on a stage responding to a director's commands.

The best of their photographs represent a coherent union between subject matter and pictorial effect. Their purpose with the camera was to create pictorial documents, not to advance a social agenda or to necessarily be objective as photographers. The careers of Ulmann and Wootten coincide with the Great Depression, but little about their images suggests the scale and human despair of the national experience. Instead, their photography celebrates human character and is optimistic in the face of an immense economic crisis. Within a pictorial framework they photographed people of a certain type. Their subject selection was deliberate and concentrated. It implied a recognition that something meaningful about American life survived in quiet places where people had a simple existence close to the earth and to each another.

Differences in many of their photographs are minor. Ulmann often gave prominence to a subject's hands, and Wootten's fondness for visual diagonals is well documented. Wootten also seems to have photographed children more often than Ulmann and chose on occasion to make extreme close-ups of a subject's face. The two women typically avoided themes of industry and technology, preferring to emphasize manual labor in settings that were often rural and agrarian. Their Appalachian and African American photographs are frequently backward-looking, sometimes resurrecting themes from times past. When viewed against the backdrop of the highly realistic photography of the 1930s and later, the work of Wootten and Ulmann appears to flow outside the mainstream of photographic development. In essence, however, they sat astride a transitional era in photographic evolution, an intersection between pictorial photography and modernism.

FIGURE 43

Although not documented, it is possible that Wootten and Ulmann had met. In 1936, two years after Ulmann's death, Berea College mounted an exhibition of Appalachian photographs taken by the two women. Wootten pasted this newspaper clipping from the April 23, 1936 issue of the Berea Citizen *into her scrapbook. (Clare Crawford-Mason and Victor Crawford Collection)*

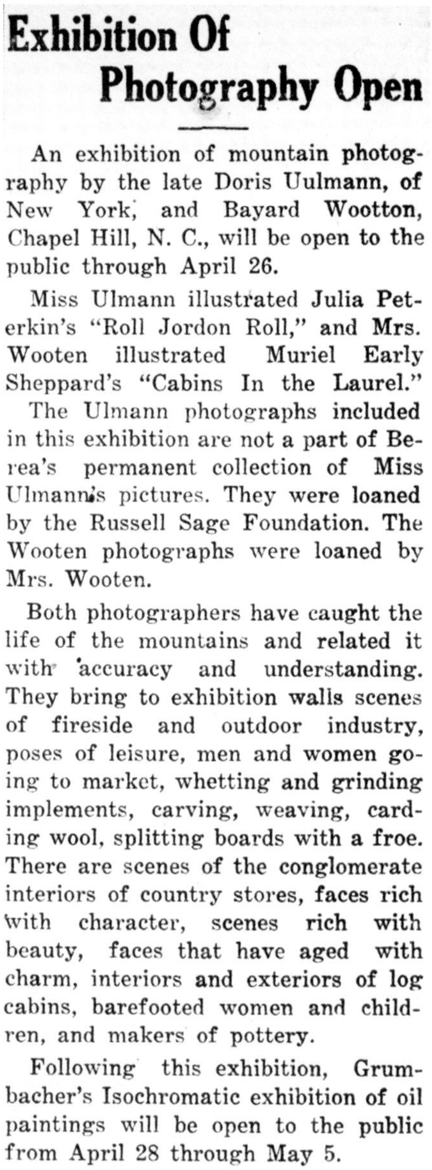

Exhibition Of Photography Open

An exhibition of mountain photography by the late Doris Uulmann, of New York, and Bayard Wootton, Chapel Hill, N. C., will be open to the public through April 26.

Miss Ulmann illustrated Julia Peterkin's "Roll Jordon Roll," and Mrs. Wooten illustrated Muriel Early Sheppard's "Cabins In the Laurel."

The Ulmann photographs included in this exhibition are not a part of Berea's permanent collection of Miss Ulmann's pictures. They were loaned by the Russell Sage Foundation. The Wooten photographs were loaned by Mrs. Wooten.

Both photographers have caught the life of the mountains and related it with accuracy and understanding. They bring to exhibition walls scenes of fireside and outdoor industry, poses of leisure, men and women going to market, whetting and grinding implements, carving, weaving, carding wool, splitting boards with a froe. There are scenes of the conglomerate interiors of country stores, faces rich with character, scenes rich with beauty, faces that have aged with charm, interiors and exteriors of log cabins, barefooted women and children, and makers of pottery.

Following this exhibition, Grumbacher's Isochromatic exhibition of oil paintings will be open to the public from April 28 through May 5.

Photographic history might have taken more note of latter-day pictorialists had death not claimed the talented and influential Ulmann in 1934 when she was still relatively young. Often in frail health, Ulmann spent much of that summer working in the southern Appalachians assisted by a nurse. Her condition deteriorated as the weeks wore on, and Ulmann made her last photographs on August 4 at the home of a rural family near Asheville, North Carolina. She returned to New York and died within the month.

Books that appeared later in the decade tapped the wealth of social documentary photography that was largely outside the Ulmann and Wootten realm. These publications forcefully combined thoroughly realistic images with authoritative reporting. *You Have Seen Their Faces* by Erskine Caldwell and Margaret Bourke-White appeared in 1937, followed by Archibald MacLeish's *Land of the Free* a year later. Dorothea Lange collaborated with Paul Taylor on *An American Exodus* (1939), and Walker Evans and James Agee produced *Let Us Now Praise Famous Men* in 1941.

Viewer empathy for a pictorial vision of reality, however, inspires a degree of timeless appreciation for photographs like those by Wootten and Ulmann. Their character studies give expression to admirable human qualities with which an observer can identify. They found enchantment and beauty in people and localities that by any measure were ordinary, commonplace, and overlooked. Their photography is a reminder of simple living, innocence, the dignity of work, and the eternal beauty of human endurance recorded in weathered faces and wrinkled hands.

THE JOY IS IN THE GOING

Stories of Bayard Wootten's camera adventures became almost as much a part of her photographic legacy as the images themselves. "I am amused how really childish I am underneath," she once said. "It gives me a greater thrill to put myself across to these two grown sons, who have known me all their lives than it does to impress the public. It's fun to send them clippings and roto pages that prove: 'See what mother has done now.'"[76]

Wootten's independence and picture-taking excursions sometimes took her to places that were unusual for a woman. On an outing in the North Carolina mountains she spent several days with lumbermen at a logging camp near Shining Rock seeking photo opportunities that would "tell the story of N.C. industries."[77] The camp could be reached only by means of a hand car traveling on a narrow-gauge railroad. Lumbermen riding with Wootten described the car's previous mishaps, adding to her apprehension. She reached the camp without incident and described as "thrilling" the 3,000-foot climb that took her across a bridge that "swayed under our weight."[78]

Some eighty lumbermen lived in the camp. Wootten received lodging in the railroad car of an absent superintendent and joined the men for meals in the diner. The

FIGURE 44

Obstacles that might sidetrack other photographers were a challenge that Wootten appeared to enjoy. In this scene dating from about 1940, farmers used oxen to pull her car along a primitive mountain road. (North Carolina Collection)

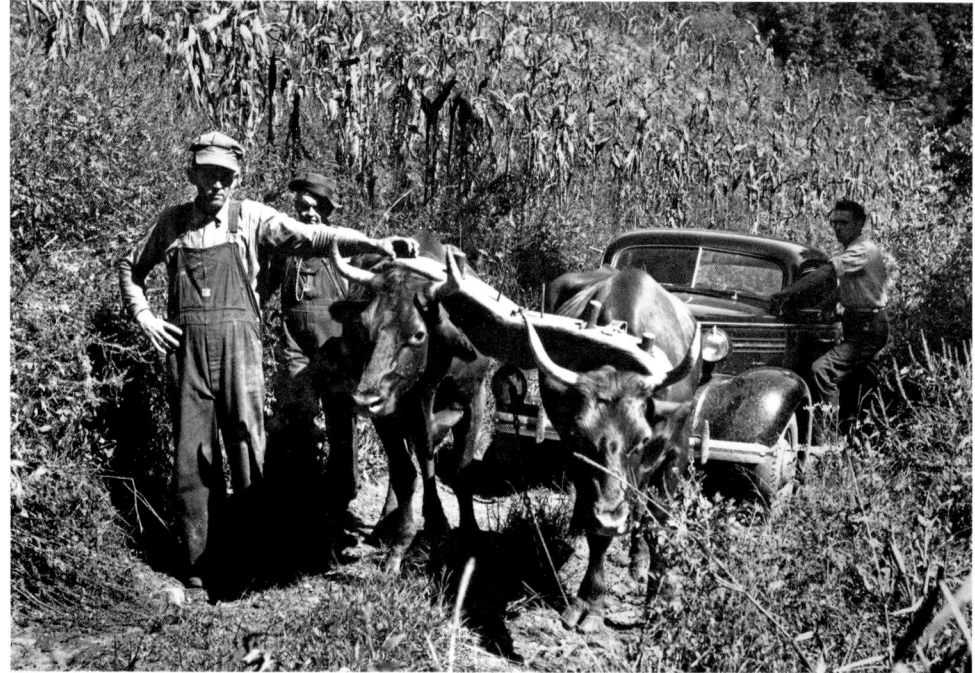

fare she judged as "right royal." After taking pictures for several days, Wootten learned that the superintendent was returning and that she had to vacate his quarters. The photographer then moved into one end of a car occupied by the two camp cooks, who were male. With their quarters separated only by a hanging quilt, Wootten spent just one night "bunking with the crew." The following day she headed for home.

The sixteen-mile return trip was more precarious than the ascent several days before. Though traveling slowly, the hand car jumped the tracks, and Wootten landed on the ground. "I felt a jerk, a jar, things went black, and I did not know what else happened until light came back, and I found myself on all fours on the ground looking over a precipice. I felt faint and blood was trickling in my eye. My hand was wet, a red splotch on the ground."[79] The injuries were minor, and Wootten completed her trek without further mishap.

In her sixties, she went to the Smoky Mountains to shoot pictures for *From My Highest Hill*, her final job as a book illustrator. A team of oxen pulled her car out of mud on four occasions as she made her way up one of the peaks. Once at her destination, Wootten braved a swarm of angry honey bees to photograph men raiding a bee tree.

In 1940 she positioned a view camera on the banks of the Yadkin River to photograph a new bridge that spanned the stream. Her activity aroused security guards at a nearby factory, and they briefly detained Wootten on suspicion of being a spy. Her occasional misadventures also occurred in the darkroom. The Chapel Hill studio was above a clothing store on the town's main street. A former employee recalled the day an incorrect mixture of chemicals foamed over a sink and seeped through the floor to apparel hanging in the shop below. Wootten paid for the damages.

Traveling along North Carolina's picturesque coastline was a favored pastime for Wootten, and she often had her drivers go near the shore, even on the narrow barrier islands fronting the Atlantic. On one excursion her car became mired in sand just beyond the breakers. The tide was rising, and Wootten frantically sought the aid of nearby fishermen. They came to her rescue and saved the automobile. In 1937 she boasted to an interviewer, "I will climb a mountain, row a boat, ride a horse, hike cross-country, wade in mud and water, or do anything necessary to get a picture and get it from the angle that I want."[80]

Wootten produced an impressive body of photographs, but her investment in time, effort, and material was substantial. Failure inevitably punctuated the successes. Even these episodes, however, she recalled with the flair of an adventurer. An expedition to take pictures from the summit of North Carolina's Mount Mitchell, the highest peak in the eastern United States, was the fodder for one of her tales.

With her aunt and a cousin as traveling companions, Wootten drove her automobile to a camp a mile below the 6,000-foot summit. They hand-carried the large, heavy camera equipment the remaining distance, only to find the peak engulfed by clouds. Wootten wanted late afternoon or early morning light for a proper landscape photograph. If they returned to the car with all the equipment, there would not be sufficient time in the morning to again reach the summit. The trio decided to sleep on top of the mountain and share a crude cabin with a ranger and two Boy Scouts.

Wootten, hoping the afternoon sky would clear, lingered in the observation tower until dark. Exhausted after the long day, she finally made her way down a path to the cabin, where her aunt and cousin, the ranger, and the two scouts were preparing for an evening meal. Wootten described the scene:

> The cabin was the type that had two rooms made of logs connected by a covered
> way between. When I stepped up in that covered way, my heart sank. A cheery

FIGURE 45

*True to her words,
"anything necessary to
get a picture," Wootten
stands in water beside the
large view camera used
for most of her photogra-
phy. It held 5 × 7-inch
or 8 × 10-inch sheet film.
(North Carolina
Collection)*

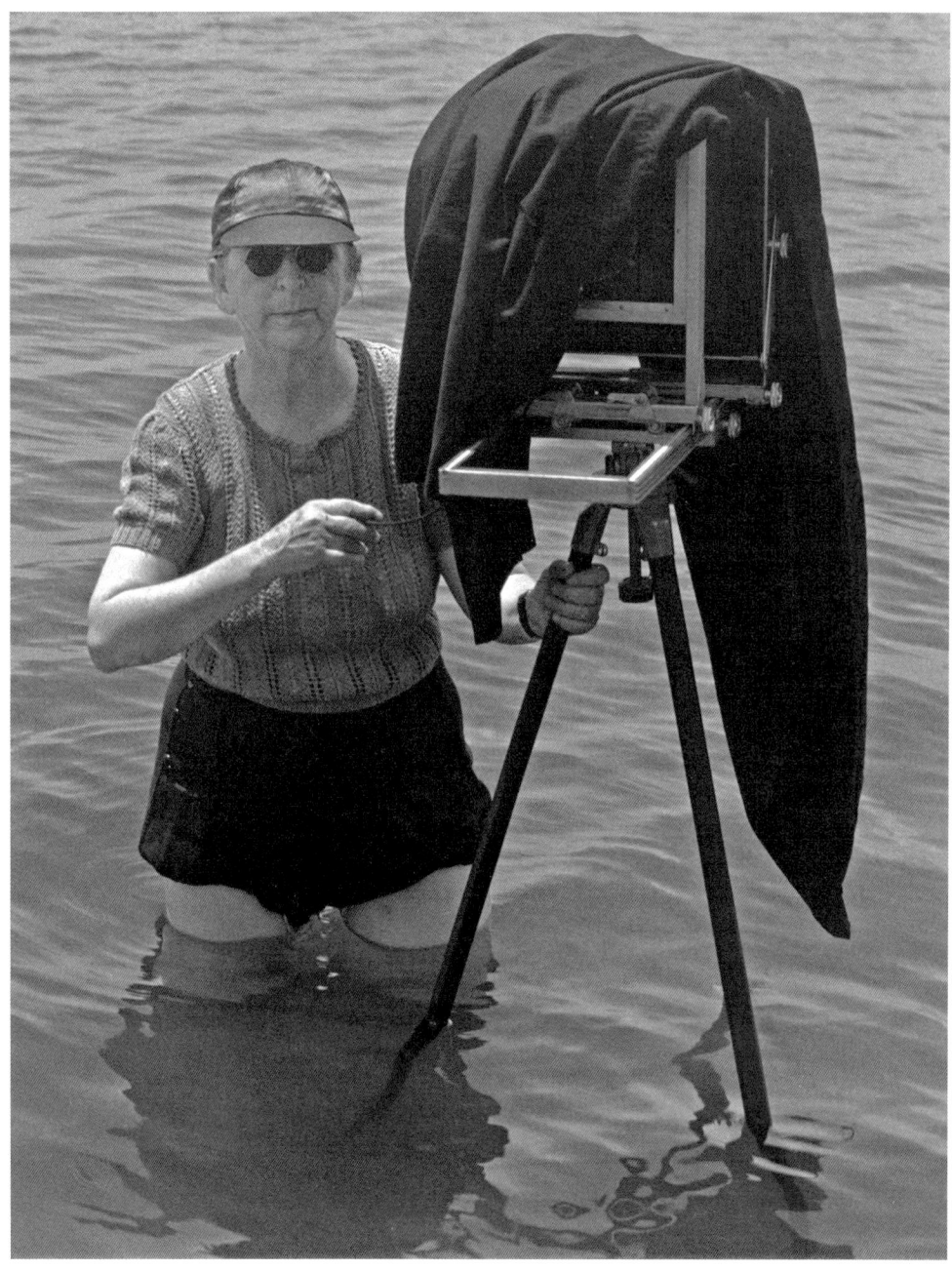

stream of light poured from the room . . . and fell in several holes in the floor of the covered way, and on a pile of old empty tin cans. An uninviting entrance to say the least. I peeped in the dark room wishing to see inviting beds. What I saw was the stars shining down through holes in the roof, a pile of straw on the floor and a pile of dilapidated old mattresses thrown in a corner. Forlorn and weary, I sought the other room to find several of the dirtiest, most repulsive beds that it has ever been my lot to come upon.[81]

The scouts cooked dinner and she pronounced the result "good." At bedtime the two boys offered Wootten's party the straw to sleep on, but they graciously declined. Instead they chose the old mattresses, rented blankets from the ranger, and then went to bed. "The weather turned cold as the night wore on," she reminisced, "and I awoke with an uncomfortable sensation of being mashed nearly as thin as a wafer. The row of campers with whom I had gone to sleep, which had reached all but across the room, had contracted to a very compact mass of human beings. I never was so cold in my life, and never more uncomfortable. The morning revealed clouds and rain, and we journeyed down about as depressed and unhappy a group as I have ever seen."[82]

Wootten readily approached strangers about taking photographs, and her presence invited more than casual notice. When she went by foot to photograph a man living in an isolated mountain home, he did not at first realize that she was a woman because of her short hair and masculine dress. Traveling with Wootten revealed to companions the intimacies of a personality that was dynamic, spontaneous, and philosophical. Her car would be laden with camera gear and luggage, and occasionally Wootten carried along a typewriter, even though she could type with only two fingers.

Burn holes sometimes accented her clothing because she smoked cigarettes and often ignored the accumulation of hot ashes until they fell. A colleague remembered a drive to South Carolina in which Wootten lit a cigarette with the car's new electric lighter and then tossed it out the window as she always did with matches. Friends and relatives along the way often gave Wootten free lodging. If none was available, hotels, at times cheap ones, sufficed. Frequent stops were in order if photographic opportunities presented themselves, but Wootten typically proceeded with a sense of anxiety and urgency—until she reached a destination. Once there, she went about her camera work with infinite patience and deliberation.

FIGURE 46

*Her warm personality
often enabled Wootten to
get an intimate view of
how people lived. At this
home in the mountains
of western North Caro-
lina, she (far left) sits
with a family at a dinner
table illuminated by a
kerosene lamp in a room
wallpapered with news-
print. (North Carolina
Collection)*

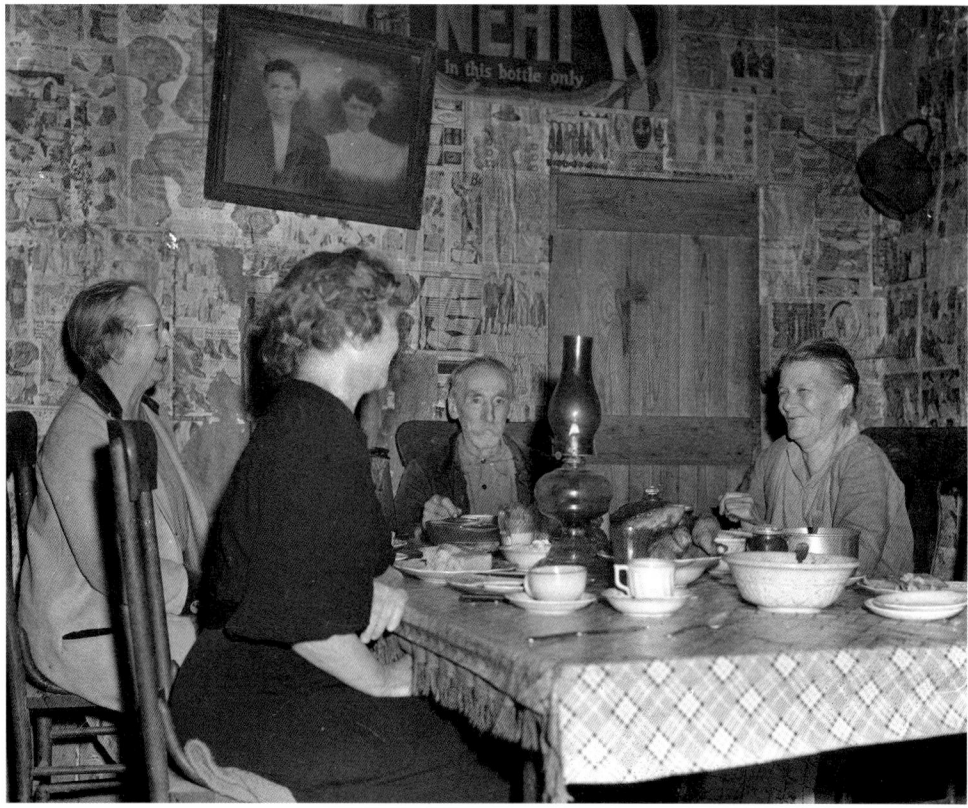

Wootten had little time or inclination for household chores and paid a black maid or handyman to clean and cook. Her culinary ability was elementary at best, being limited to such basic fare as Spanish omelets and coffee. The latter she often saved for reheating the next day. A drink or two was the preferred ending of a typical day, and Wootten sometimes joined in the revelry of University of North Carolina students who rented rooms in her home. A former neighbor remembered seeing a student passed out in Bayard's yard on a football Saturday. Although it may never have been spoken in her presence, a member of the studio staff gave the high-spirited photographer the nickname "Wootten Tootin'."

In the early 1940s the North Carolina Photographers Association honored Wootten with an award for her many years of distinguished work, and *Who's Who* included her biography in its September 1944 supplement. By that time the camera artist was almost seventy, smoked heavily, and suffered from a partial loss of hearing. There would be no other exhibitions to mount and no other books to illustrate.

During World War II, the Wootten-Moulton Studio reopened a branch at Fort

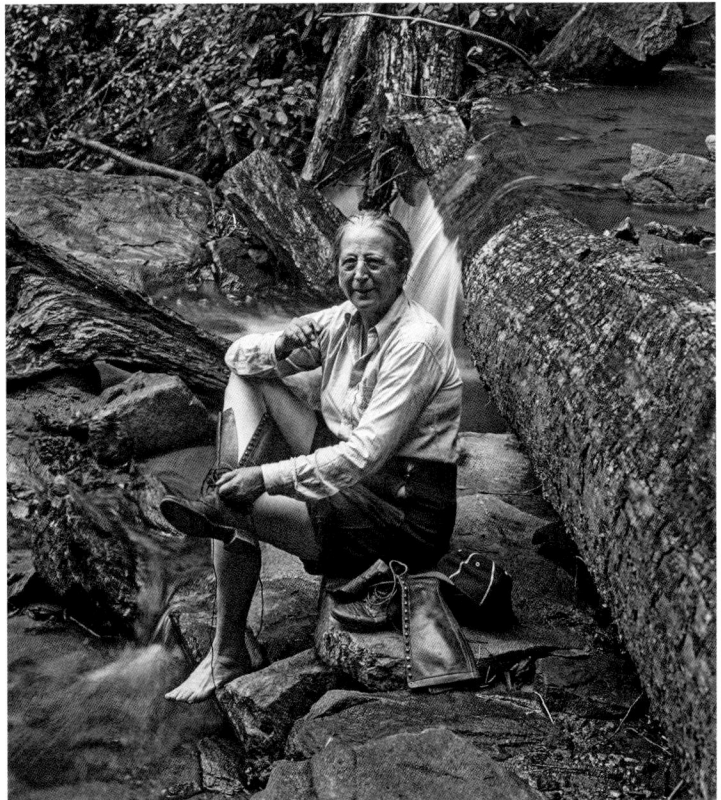

FIGURE 47

In 1938 at the age of 63, the indomitable Wootten, with a cigarette in hand, prepares to soak her feet in a mountain stream. (North Carolina Collection)

Bragg and established another at Camp Butner north of Chapel Hill to tap the influx of soldiers. Management of the business was largely out of Wootten's hands; her son Rufus moved to Chapel Hill in 1945 and directed the studio for the next four years.

In 1947, Wootten wrote to her old friend Nace Brock in Asheville, confiding, "I guess I'm getting old. I do not have the pep and energy I used to."[83] Less than a year later Wootten suffered an eye hemorrhage, which ended serious work with the camera. She continued to be a fixture at the Chapel Hill studio, greeting the public, typing, making proofs, or washing and drying prints. The days of adventure with the camera, however, were over.

Wootten belonged to the Business and Professional Women's Club and also the Altrusa Club, a local and international service organization. In 1949, the Altrusans held a reception in Chapel Hill to honor the veteran photographer, and 400 people attended. In 1954, Wootten sold the Chapel Hill studio to longtime associate T. C. Moore, formally closing a half-century career in photography. Before turning over the business, she sorted through the studio's vast collection of negatives and identi-

FIGURE 48

The staff of the Wootten-Moulton Chapel Hill studio joined Wootten in a birthday celebration about 1940. George C. Moulton, her half brother, stands on the far left. In front of him and leaning over the table is T. C. Moore, Wootten's successor in the business. Margaret Howland Fowler, a secretary in the studio for two decades, is to Wootten's right. (Mary Moulton Barden Collection)

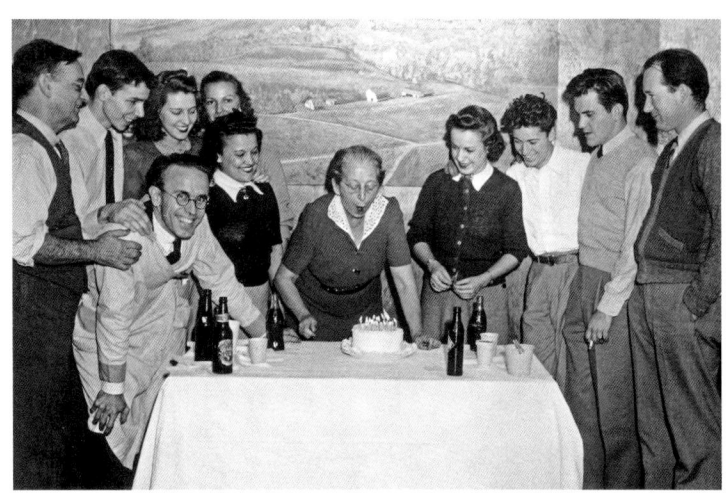

fied some 2,000 of her favorite images. She moved these negatives along with her other belongings to the family home on East Front Street in New Bern, and there, in the house in which she was born, Wootten spent the remaining years of her life. She died on April 6, 1959. The funeral, two days later, coincided with the long-awaited opening of the restored Tryon Palace in New Bern. It was a restoration project she encouraged and then followed with great anticipation. Its opening was an event Bayard Wootten would surely have captured on film in an earlier day.

Over the decades the Wootten-Moulton Studio had remained financially viable but often precariously so. Wootten made her mark in photography with less of the education, cultural advantages, and monetary resources enjoyed by some of her better known contemporaries. At best the camera provided only a modest income for Wootten, and in retirement she depended on relatives for support. Photography was sufficient, however, to help Wootten emerge from a divorce and support a family. It immersed her in the campaign by women to achieve parity with men as professional photographers and ultimately became the expression of Bayard Wootten as an artist. She was perhaps the most widely known North Carolina photographer in the first half of the twentieth century, and photographs are her enduring legacy. They survive

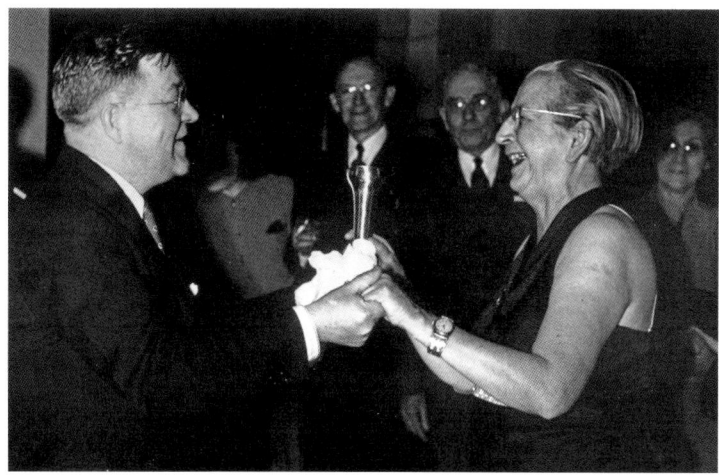

in the six major books she illustrated and in thousands of individual prints and negatives.

Many persons learned photography under Wootten's tutelage, but none possessed her artistic skill and stubborn determination to use it. When she put aside the camera, the Wootten banner of pictorial photography also came to rest. Wootten set a high standard of aesthetic quality in the medium. Her ability to embrace a subject and compose it artistically was sensitive and strong. "The camera is not a free agent as brush or pencil," she said, "but relentlessly records things as they are. So the artist must bring to her aid strong contrasts of light and shade, artistic grouping and rhythmic lines. To use a camera as a means of artistic expression, a certain quality of spirit must be brought to aid light and air."[84]

Simply working in a studio never quenched Bayard Wootten's thirst for the medium of photography. She was a free spirit, and the camera became an avenue to a world of art and exploration that stretched far beyond the darkroom. Photography was a way to meet new people, it was the means to tell a story, and most of all it was the practice of a fine art. "There is nothing in the world quite as satisfying as this business of photography," she said. "Far outweighing the financial return to me is the happiness I've found as a by-product of my interest in photography. The people I've met, the places I've been, and my adventures on the road all mean more to me than any dollars I have made."[85]

Wootten's reputation as a photographer extended across North Carolina and beyond. If some doors closed because she was a woman, others surely opened for the

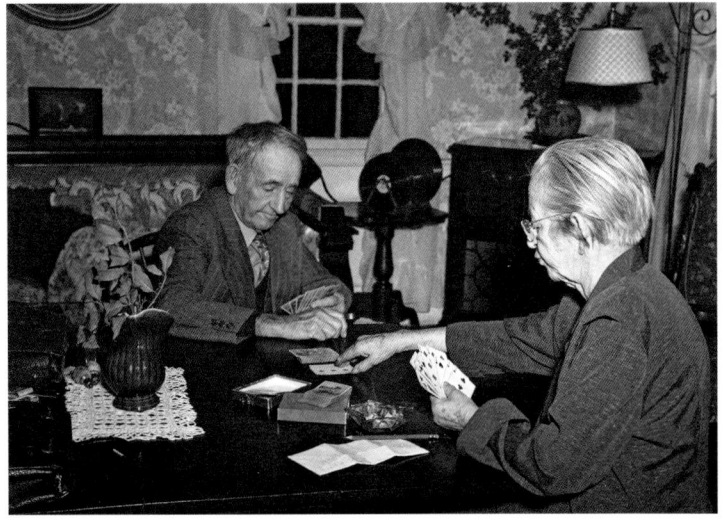

Gin rummy was a favorite game for Wootten when she had a partner, but when alone she also enjoyed solitaire. In this photograph, identified as Christmas 1950, her brother Sam Morgan joined her for cards at the family home in New Bern. (North Carolina Collection)

same reason. She made the large and intimidating camera less so, and strangers often revealed a personal side for Wootten that male photographers may never have seen. She could elevate the simple, reveal the familiar, and capture the elusive. "I have found excitement in the most commonplace people and localities," she declared. "True, they have been the same kinds of people and places you see about you every day. We all see them, but we do not think about the beauty of a timeworn face, a workworn hand, or a God-driven wind. I love people and places and they have told me a lot about living."[86]

Photography and art thrived in the Wootten studio more so than any other in North Carolina. She was a standard-bearer of pictorial photography in the state for decades and the first North Carolina woman photographer to achieve genuine recognition. Newspapers characterized Wootten as a "distinguished artist" and an "eminent American photographer." Beyond the Southeast, however, she remained little known or appreciated, and her contribution to photographic history even in North Carolina became a dusty memory after the 1950s. For Bayard Wootten, photography was the zest of life. Without her passion for the camera, some secluded corners of the South now alive in old photographs would forever be lost and forgotten. "I have always been chasing something," she wrote, "but one of the surprises that life has held for me is that I am happier as an old woman than I ever was as a young one. Perhaps the reason for this is that I realize now it does not matter whether we arrive. The joy is in the going."[87]

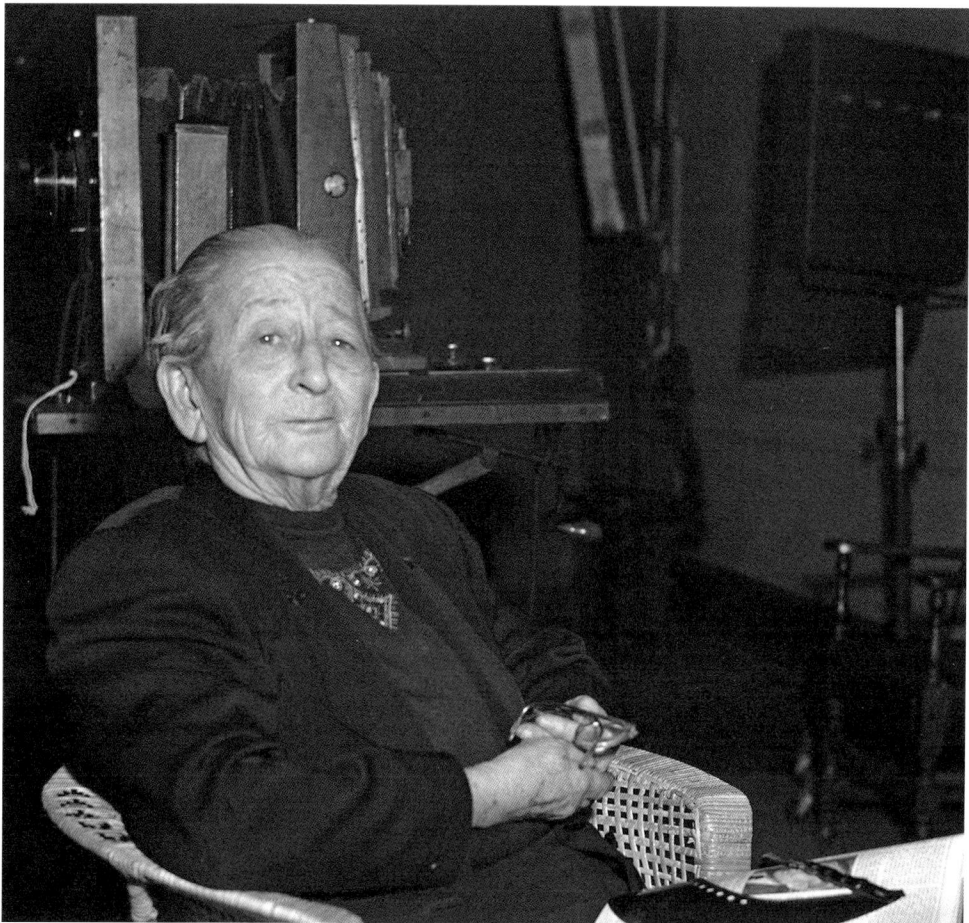

FIGURE 51

As in so many of the photographs that she made of others, age along with contentment and satisfaction seem present in one of the last photographs of Wootten. This image was taken in 1955 as she sat in the New Bern branch of the Wootten-Moulton Studio. (North Carolina Collection)

NOTES

1. Many sources, including the tombstone on her grave in New Bern's Cedar Grove Cemetery, list the year of Bayard Wootten's birth as 1876. However, a telegram sent to her father announcing the event is clearly dated 1875. William J. Clarke to Rufus Morgan, Dec. 17, 1875, Mary Moulton Barden Collection.
2. Rufus Morgan to Mary Morgan, Apr. 4, 1880, Mary Moulton Barden Collection.
3. M. C. Woodson to Mary Morgan, Apr. 5, 1880, Mary Moulton Barden Collection.
4. Bayard Morgan to Charles Duncan McIver, July 13, 1892, Charles Duncan McIver Papers.
5. Charles R. Thomas to Charles Duncan McIver, July 9, 1892; M. Manly to Charles Duncan McIver, undated letter; Charles Duncan McIver Papers.
6. Bayard Morgan to Josephine Graves, Apr. 3, 1897, Mary Moulton Barden Collection.
7. Ibid.
8. Charles Wootten to Mary Moulton, January 27, 1898, Mary Moulton Barden Collection.

9. Allen interview.

10. *Durham Morning Herald*, July 27, 1952.

11. Charles Thomas Wootten to Helen Dugan Allen, May 9, 1974, Helen Dugan Allen Collection.

12. Ibid.

13. *Raleigh News and Observer*, Dec. 5, 1937.

14. *Asheville Citizen-Times*, Jan. 22, 1956.

15. Bayard Wootten to George Moulton, Oct. 10, 1907, Mary Moulton Barden Collection.

16. "Photographers' Association of Virginia and the Carolinas," 190.

17. Bayard Wootten to George C. Moulton, Feb. 11, 1906, Mary Moulton Barden Collection.

18. Bayard Wootten to George C. Moulton, Aug. 22, 1906, Mary Moulton Barden Collection.

19. *Charlotte Observer*, Oct. 22, 1933.

20. *Raleigh News and Observer*, Dec. 5, 1937.

21. Ibid.

22. *Charlotte Observer*, Oct. 22, 1933.

23. *Raleigh News and Observer*, Dec. 5, 1937.

24. Bayard Wootten to George C. Moulton, Aug. 22, 1906, Mary Moulton Barden Collection.

25. Ibid.

26. Charles Thomas Wootten to Helen Dugan Allen, May 9, 1974, Helen Dugan Allen Collection.

27. *Chapel Hill Weekly*, Dec. 2, 1938.

28. Charles Thomas Wootten to Helen Dugan Allen, May 9, 1974, Helen Dugan Allen Collection.

29. *New Bern Daily Journal*, May 29, 1914.

30. "Woman's Federation of the P. A. of A.," 432.

31. Wootten wrote New Bern banker James A. Bryan to ask for a twenty-five dollar credit, saying "I have not any money." Bayard Wootten to James A. Bryan, Mar. 12, 1909, Bryan Family Papers.

32. Charles Thomas Wootten to Helen Dugan Allen, May 9, 1974, Helen Dugan Allen Collection.

33. Wootten, "Outlook for Women," 360–361.

34. Loehr, "Benefits of the Woman's Federation," 425.

35. Van Fleet, "Now We Belong," 429.

36. Bartlett, "Exhibit of Woman's Federation."

37. *New Bern Daily Journal*, July 8, 1913.

38. "Important to Every Member of the P. A. of A.," b.

39. Chambers, "Woman's Auxiliary at the National," 253.

40. *Chapel Hill Weekly*, Oct. 23, 1923.

41. *Charlotte Observer*, Oct. 22, 1933.

42. Albert R. Rogers to Bayard Wootten, Apr. 12, 1917, Wootten-Moulton Collection.

43. *Charlotte Observer*, Oct. 22, 1933.

44. *Raleigh News and Observer*, Dec. 5, 1937.

45. Bayard Wootten to George Moulton, Oct. 9, 1923, Mary Moulton Barden Collection.

46. Bayard Wootten to Celia Moulton, Jan. 3, 1924, Mary Moulton Barden Collection.

47. *Charlotte Observer*, Dec. 31, 1933.

48. Ibid.

49. *Showing of Work by Women Photographers* (Reineke studio show catalog), n.d., Clare Crawford-Mason and Victor Crawford Collection.

50. *Catalogue of the Tenth Annual Pittsburgh Salon of Photography* (1923), Clare Crawford-Mason and Victor Crawford Collection.

51. *Charlotte Observer*, July 1, 1932.

52. *Detroit News*, Nov. 24, 1935.

53. *New York Herald Tribune*, May 5, 1935.

54. *Baltimore Evening Sun*, June 1, 1935.

55. *Detroit News*, Dec. 8, 1935.

56. Spearman, "Backwoods America Comes to Life."

57. Sutton, "A Mountain World Sits for Its Picture."

58. Allen H. Eaton to Bayard Wootten, Mar. 27, 1935, Clare Crawford-Mason and Victor Crawford Collection.

59. Watkins, "Merchandising the Mountaineer."

60. In preparing the 1991 edition of *Cabins in the Laurel*, the UNC Press borrowed the original files relating to the book's production from the University of North Carolina Library at Chapel Hill. A fire at the UNC Press in 1990 destroyed these documents.

61. William Terry Couch to Bayard Wootten, Apr. 28, 1937, Federal Writers' Project Papers.

62. Photogravures are created from a metal plate etched with a photographic image. They have a matte surface and a fine, irregular grain pattern that produces excellent image detail.

63. *Raleigh News and Observer*, Dec. 12, 1937.

64. Houghton Mifflin Papers.

65. "Some Old Homes of North Carolina."

66. *Raleigh News and Observer*, Aug. 6, 1939.

67. Adams and Alinder, *Ansel Adams*, 112.

68. William Terry Couch to Charles Morrow Wilson, July 24, 1934, UNC Press Records.

69. William Terry Couch to Charles Morrow Wilson, Sept. 22, 1934, UNC Press Records.

70. Charles Morrow Wilson to William Terry Couch, Sept. 26, 1934, UNC Press Records.

71. Garland, "Doris Ulmann's Photographs," 44.

72. Spearman, "Backwoods America Comes to Life."

73. *Winston-Salem Twin City Sentinel*, Dec. 30, 1932.

74. *Knoxville News-Sentinel*, July 29, 1934.

75. Featherstone, *Doris Ulmann*, 43.

76. *Detroit News*, Nov. 24, 1935.

77. *Charlotte Observer*, Dec. 31, 1933.

78. Ibid.

79. Ibid.

80. "Introducing Bayard Wootten."

81. *Charlotte Observer*, Dec. 31, 1933.

82. Ibid.

83. Bayard Wootten to Nace Brock, Dec. 1, 1947, Ignatius Wadsworth Brock Collection.

84. *Greensboro Daily News*, Aug. 1, 1926.

85. *Raleigh News and Observer*, Oct. 9, 1949.

86. *Greensboro Daily News*, Apr. 25, 1948.

87. Bayard Wootten to Nace Brock, Sept. 12, 1941, Ignatius Wadsworth Brock Collection.

Plates

B ayard Wootten appreciated the American South as a photographic study. The region is geographically, racially, and culturally diverse, yet its people are connected and intertwined by common elements of a shared past. Wootten knew the South and she knew southerners. Her photographs reflect the breadth of this knowledge, and they tap the South's rich visual landscape at numerous points.

A 1932 studio fire destroyed much of Wootten's early photography. Fortunately, her period of greatest recognition occurred afterward, and the bulk of these later photographs survive. *Charleston: Azaleas and Old Bricks* (1937), *New Castle, Delaware, 1651–1939* (1939), and *Old Homes and Gardens of North Carolina* (1939) document Wootten's abilities as an architectural photographer. These volumes, as well as *Backwoods America* (1934), *Cabins in the Laurel* (1935, 1991), and *From My Highest Hill* (1941), also include landscapes.

It is not architectural and landscape photography, however, that continues to arouse most of the interest in Bayard Wootten. At the core of her appeal today are the photographs that provide insight into the lives of ordinary men, women, and children of a bygone era. These personal images first popularized Wootten as a photographer in the early 1930s, and they still beckon viewers from across the years. Consequently, such photographs compose the main body of images selected for this volume. A few of the photographs have appeared in earlier publications, but many others are presented for the first time here.

Wootten's surviving exhibition prints are on matte-surface, silver-gelatin photographic papers, some with a grid-like texture, which helps give the photographs a soft and moody appearance. Most of the plates in this volume are from modern prints made using Wootten's original negatives and do not have the same appearance as her exhibition photographs. The use of reprinted photographs is a presentation compromise made in order to escape the effects of deterioration in the original exhibition prints, to show previously unknown images, to include images for which Wootten studio prints do not exist, and to provide a degree of consistency in the appearance of the plates. Frederick N. Stipe of the Photographic Services Section of the University of North Carolina Library at Chapel Hill carried out most of this photographic work. The late L. C. Scarborough, also of the Section, made a few of the prints in 1988.

The arrangement of the photographs is topical and broadly chronological. Titles or captions found on Wootten's prints or negative jackets appear in italics. Also included are the names of individuals and geographic locations, if known. Information thought to be in doubt is bracketed. Wootten occasionally used more than one title for the same photograph and at other times applied the same title to different photographs. When appropriate titles from negatives or original prints did not exist, captions previously published with some of the photographs have been used. Such captions appear inside quotation marks, and the list of credits includes their respective sources. All other captions have been provided by the author.

Plates

I know a land of Elizabethan ways, an America of

cavaliers and curtsies, a land of mystic allegiances and

enduring frontiers, where moods of yesterday touch

hands with the probable ways of tomorrow. Smooth,

timbered hills painted green-golden by the magic of

sunlight. Hillsides and green valleys, lost ravines and

forest lands. Clear rivers, fast running and gay. Farm

roads that smile in good fellowship. Fence-rows, open

fields, and a comforting, life-giving earth.

—Charles Morrow Wilson (*Backwoods America*, 1934)

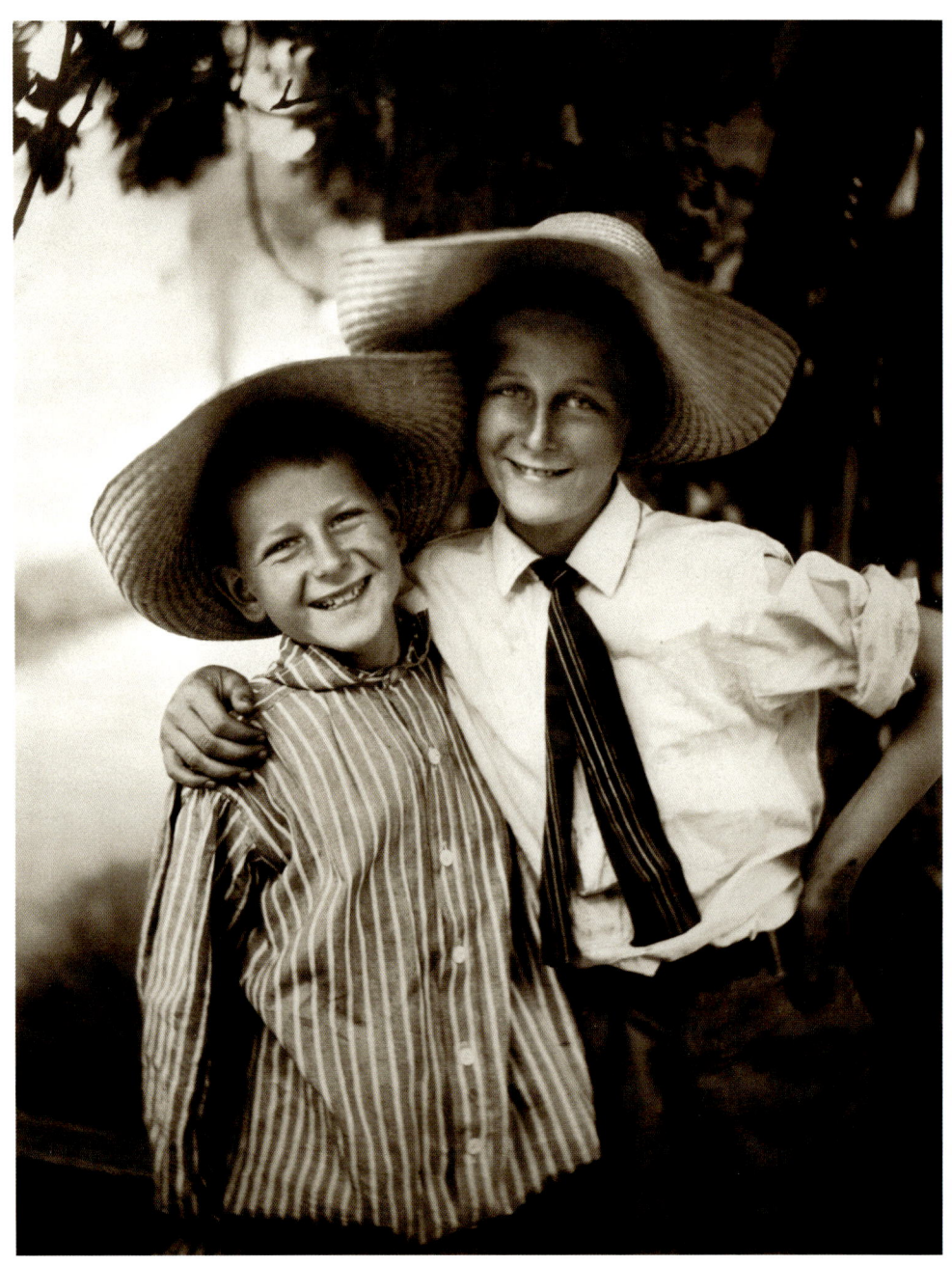

PLATE 1   Rufus and Charles Wootten. New Bern, North Carolina, ca. 1914.

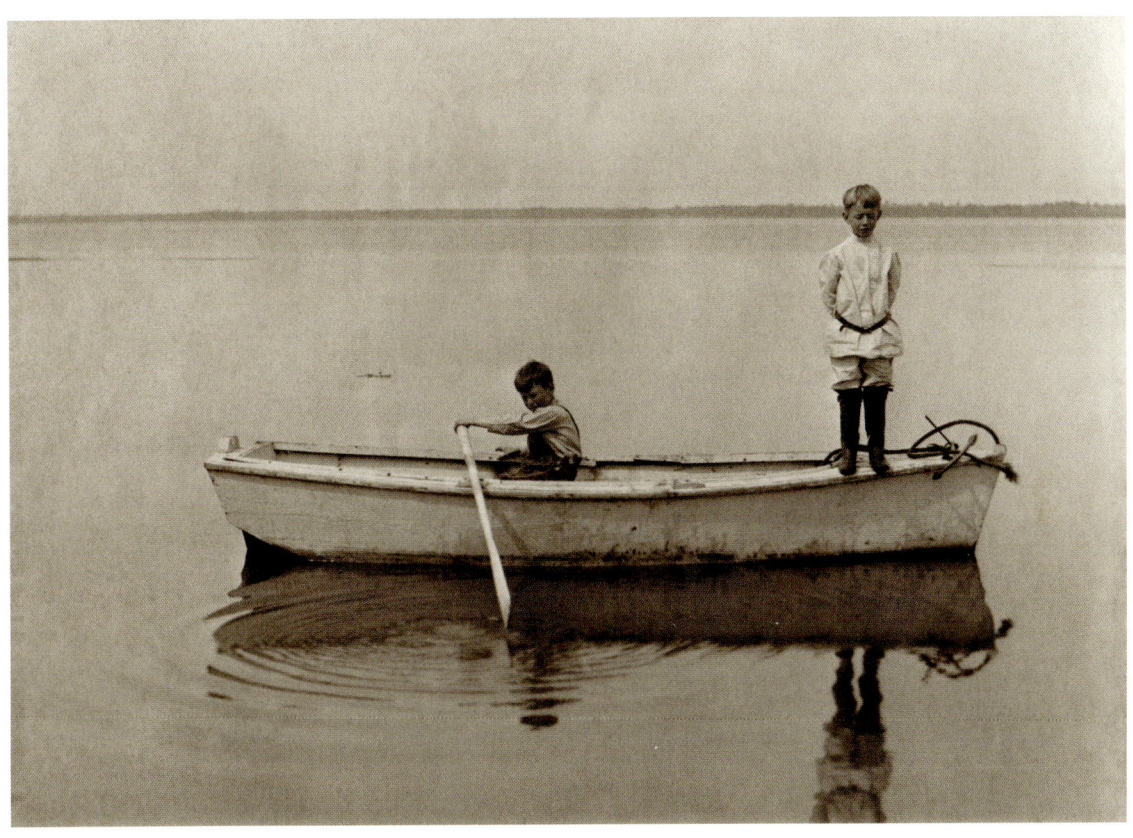

PLATE 2   Boys in a rowboat. New Bern, North Carolina, ca. 1915.

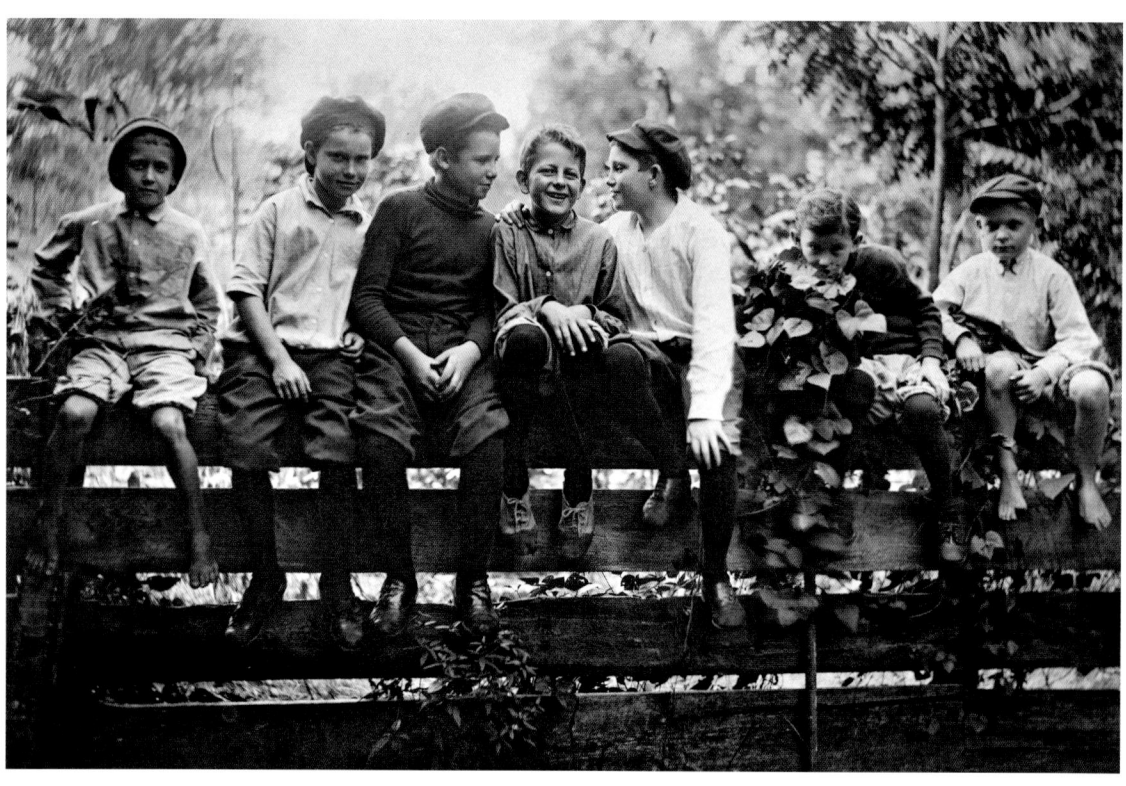

PLATE 3   [*Playmates*]. New Bern, North Carolina, ca. 1914.

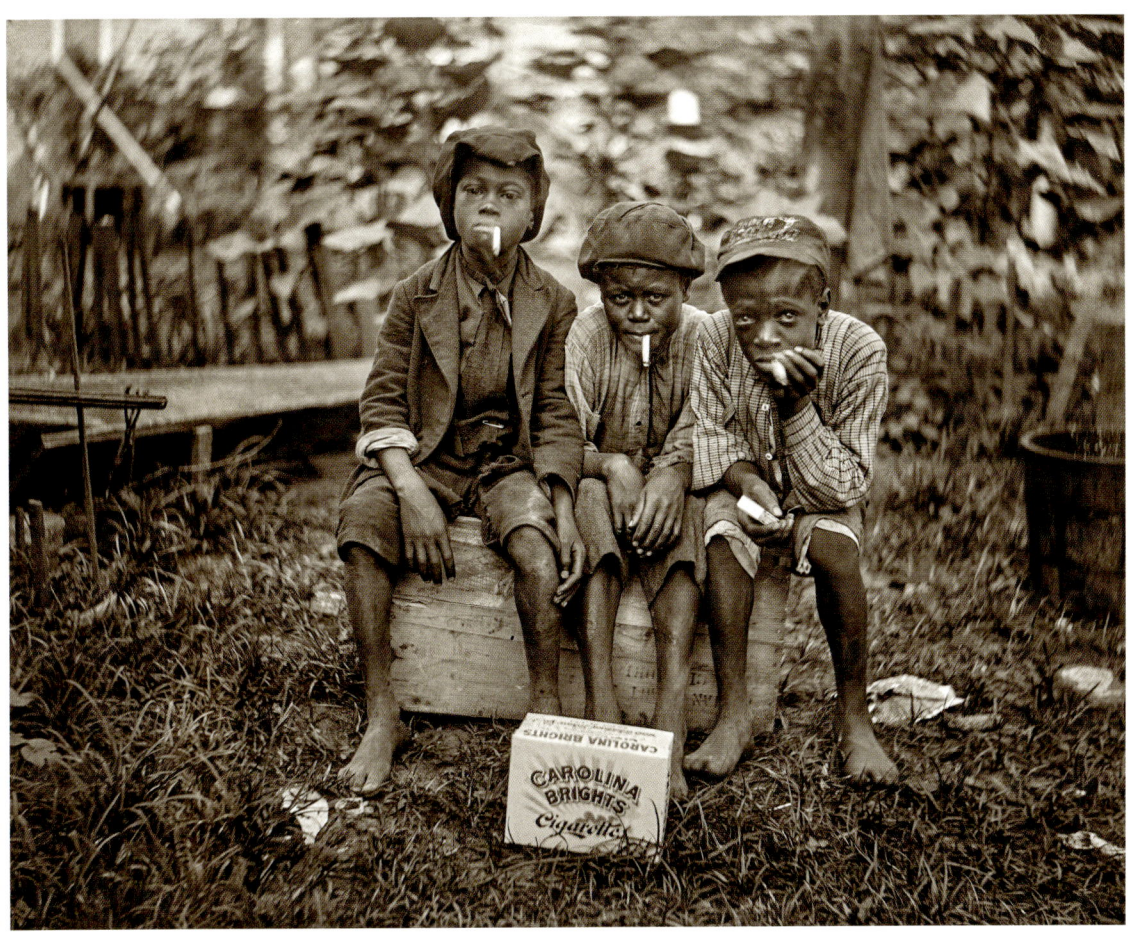

PLATE 4   Children smoking Carolina Brights. New Bern, North Carolina, ca. 1912.

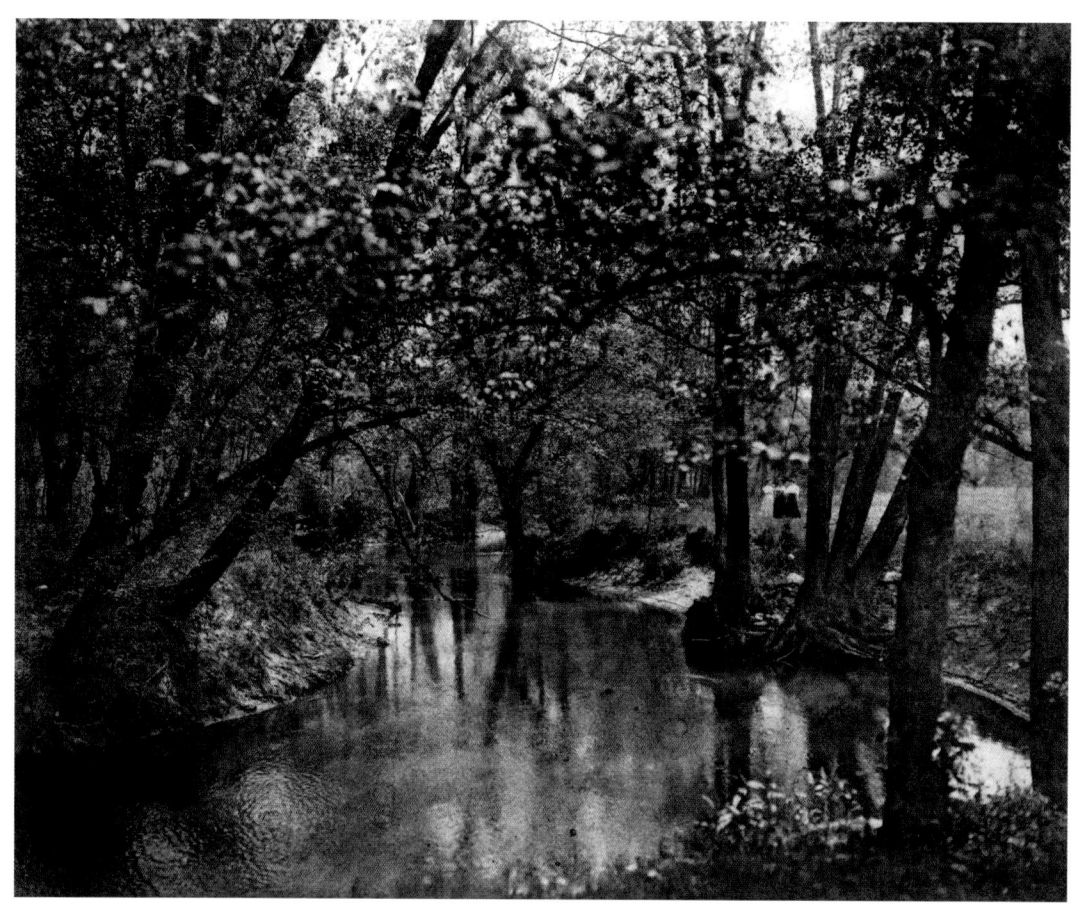

PLATE 5   Woodland stream. [New Bern, North Carolina], ca. 1915.

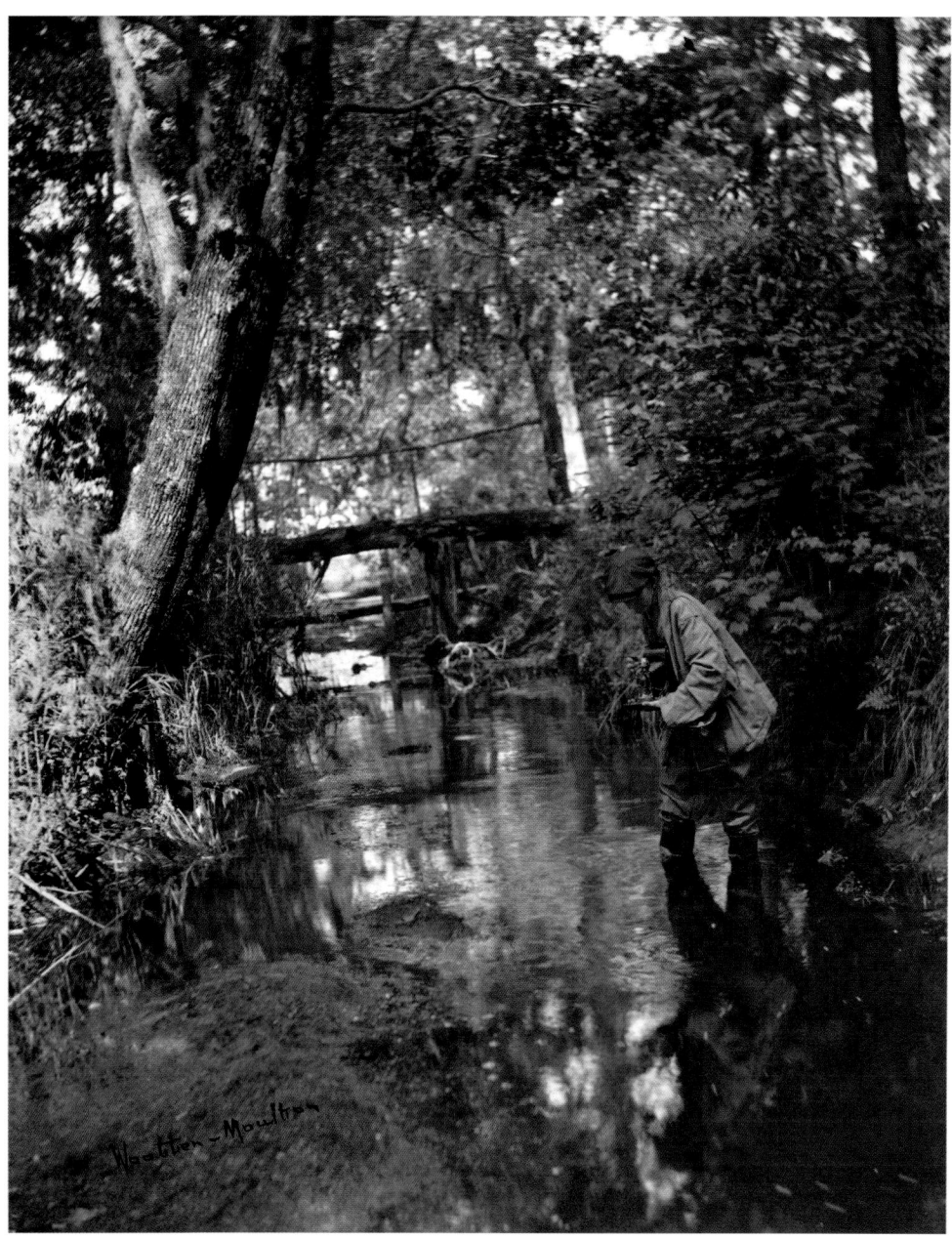

PLATE 6   An amateur photographer. New Bern, North Carolina, ca. 1915.

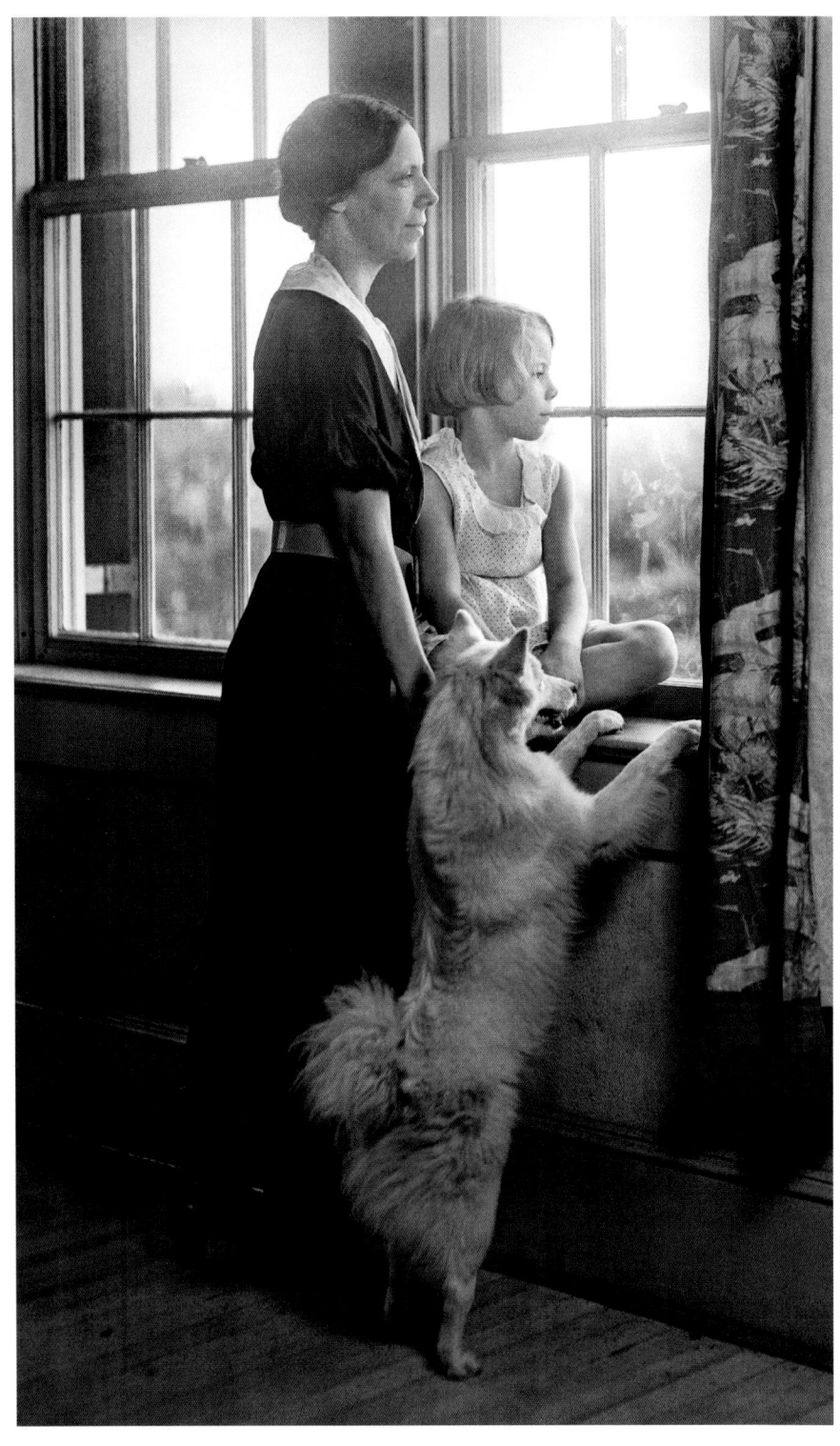

PLATE 7 *Mother Nature's Storm*. Celia M. Lively and Celia W. Lively. New Bern, North Carolina, ca. 1937.

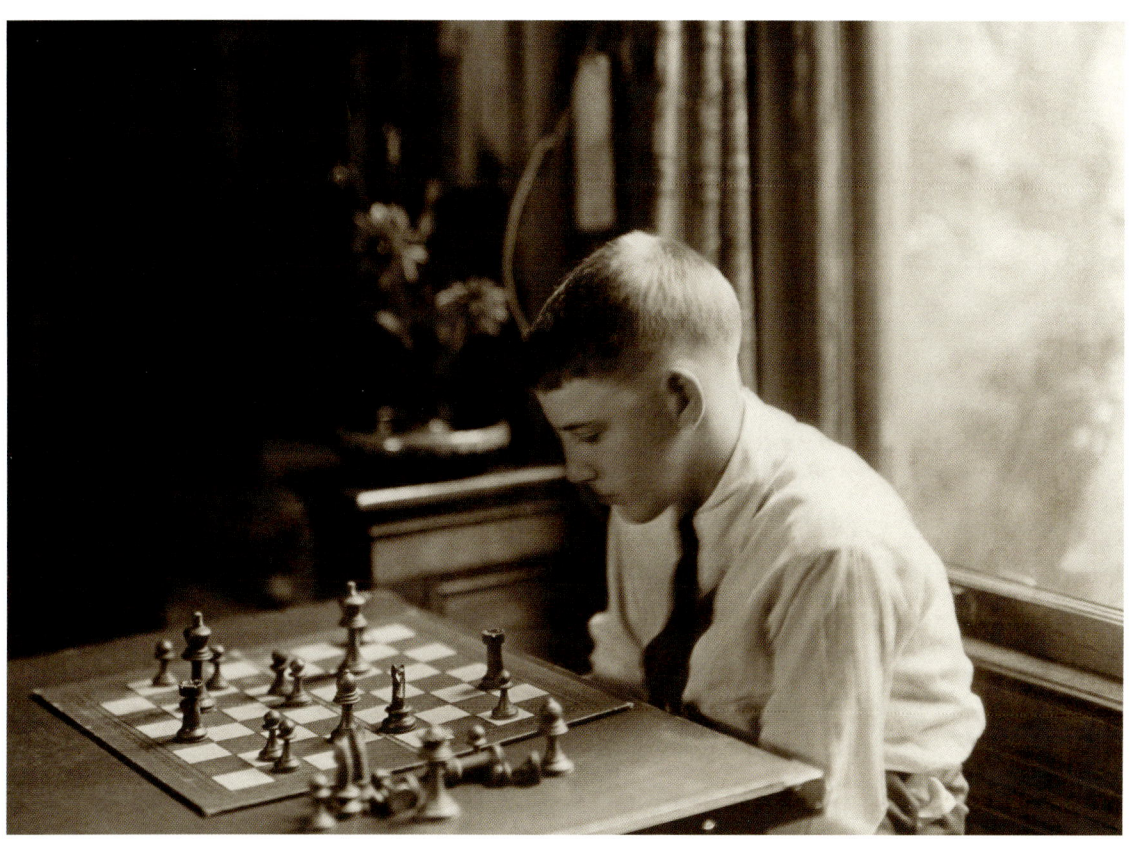

PLATE 8   Charles S. Mangum Jr. Chapel Hill, North Carolina, ca. 1918.

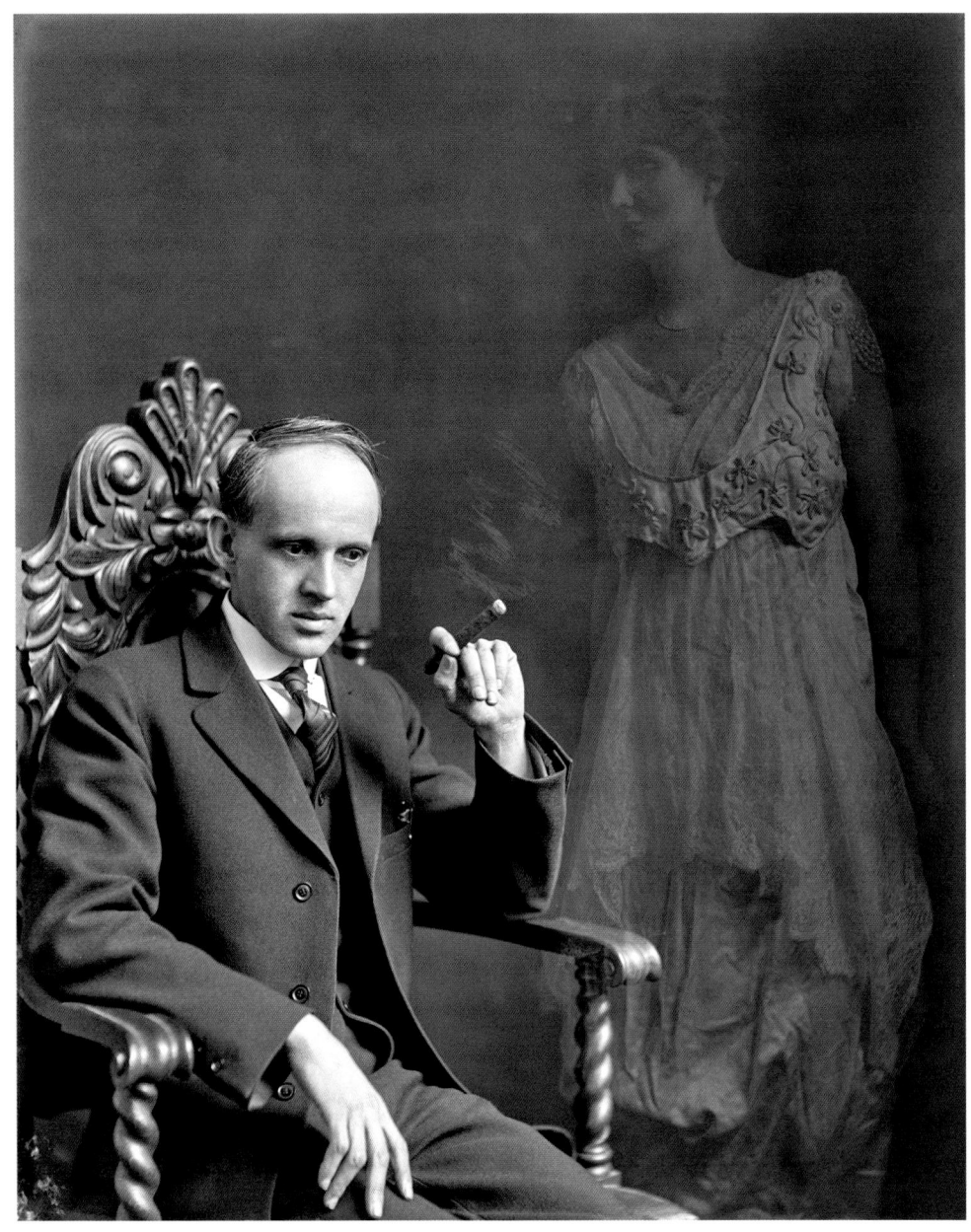

PLATE 9   *Dream*. Douglas and Amanda Creech. New Bern, North Carolina, 1916.

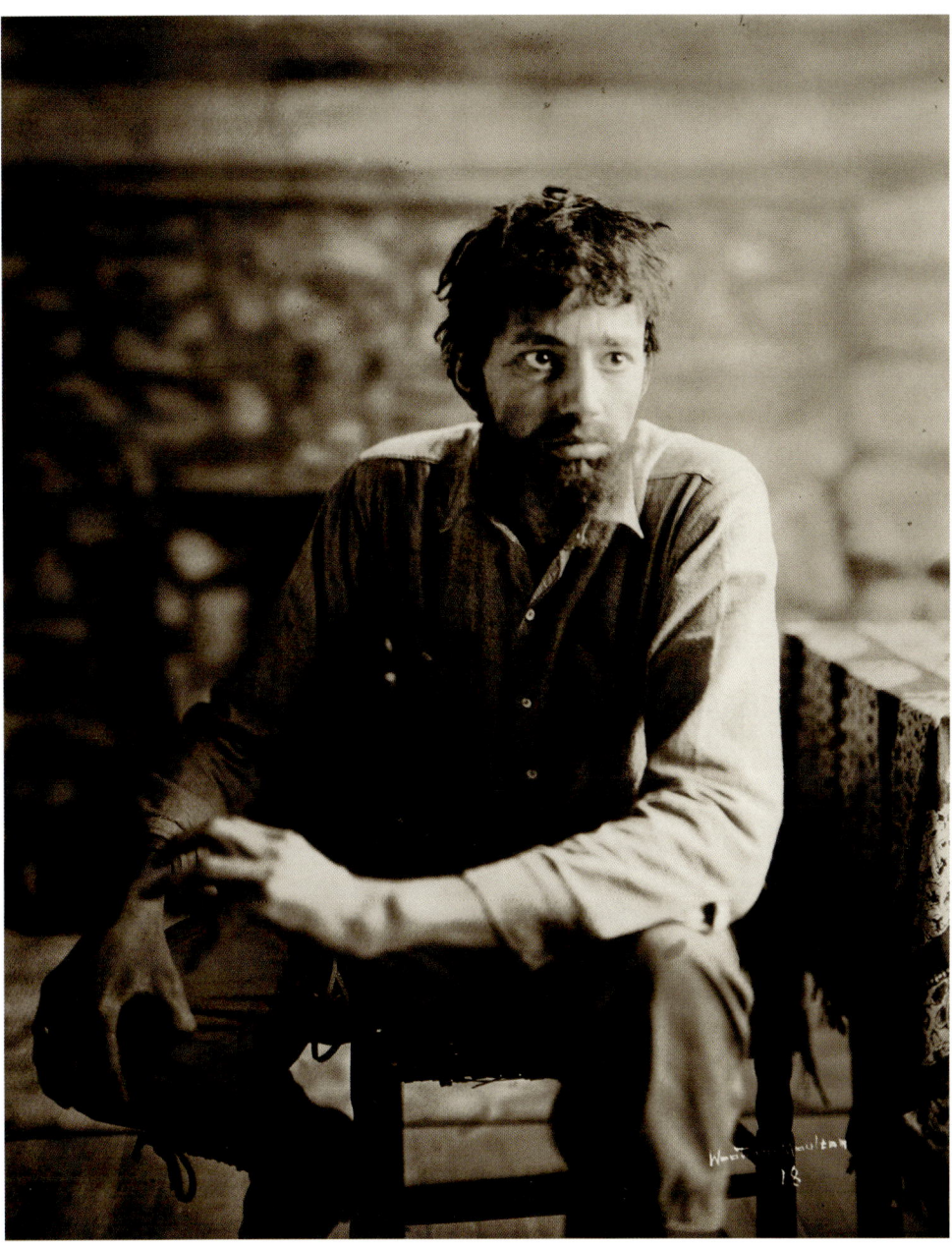

PLATE 10   Thomas Wolfe in *The Return of Buck Gavin*. Chapel Hill, North Carolina, 1919.

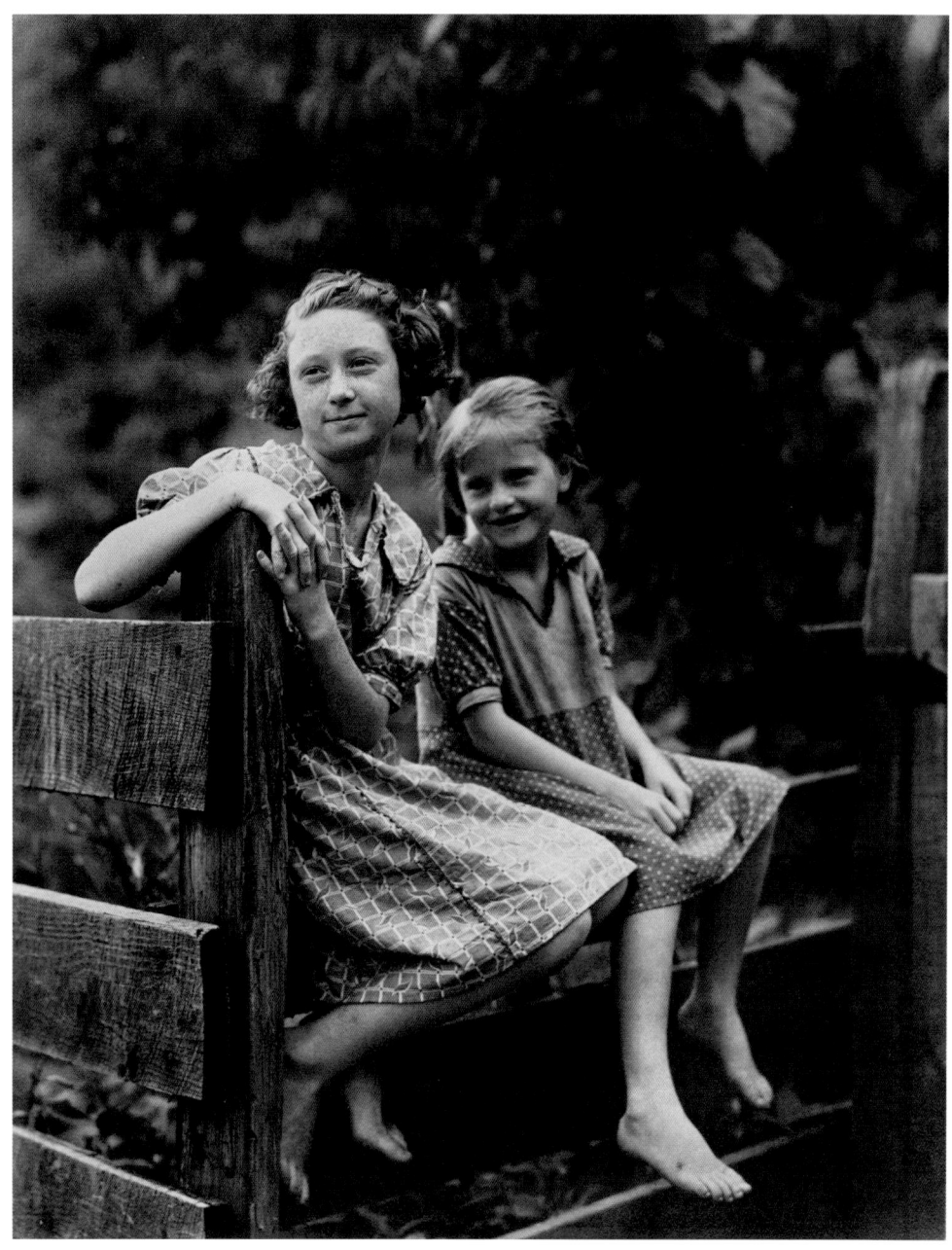

PLATE 11   *Watching the Passing World Go By.* [North Carolina], 1930s.

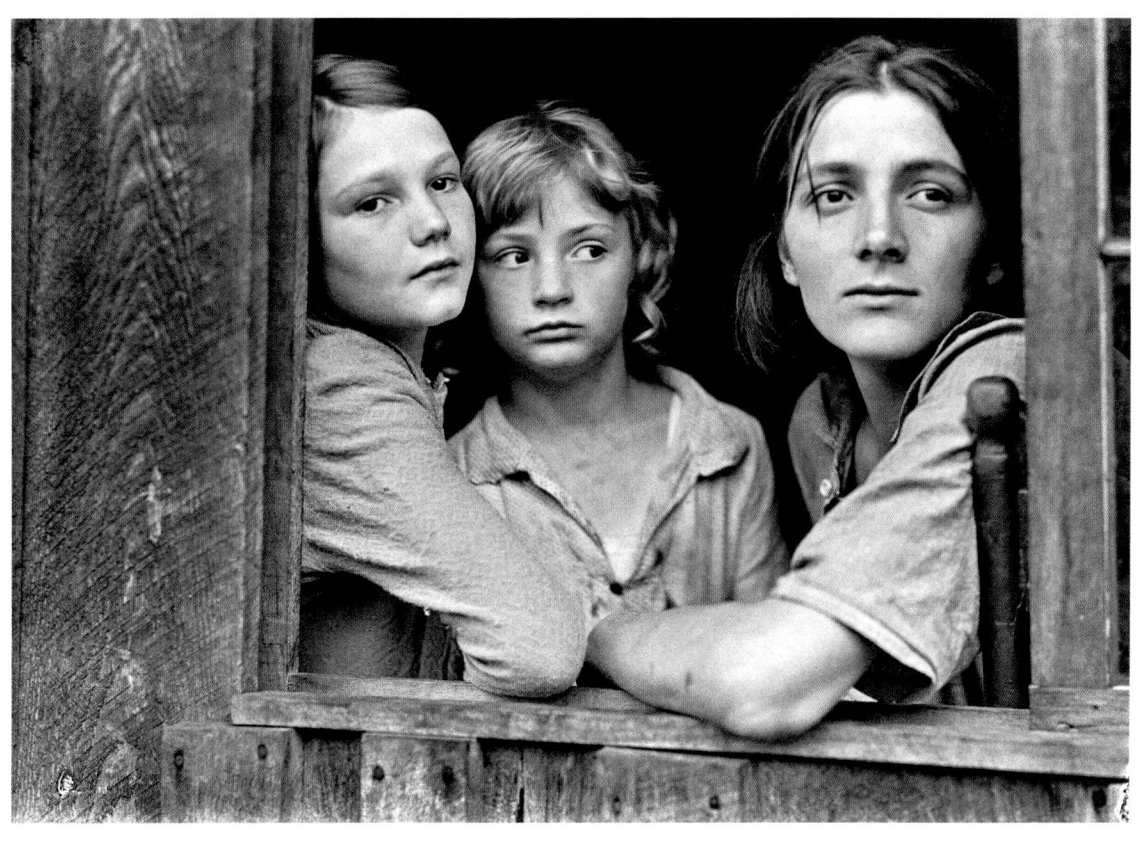

PLATE 12   Group in a window. Western North Carolina, 1930s.

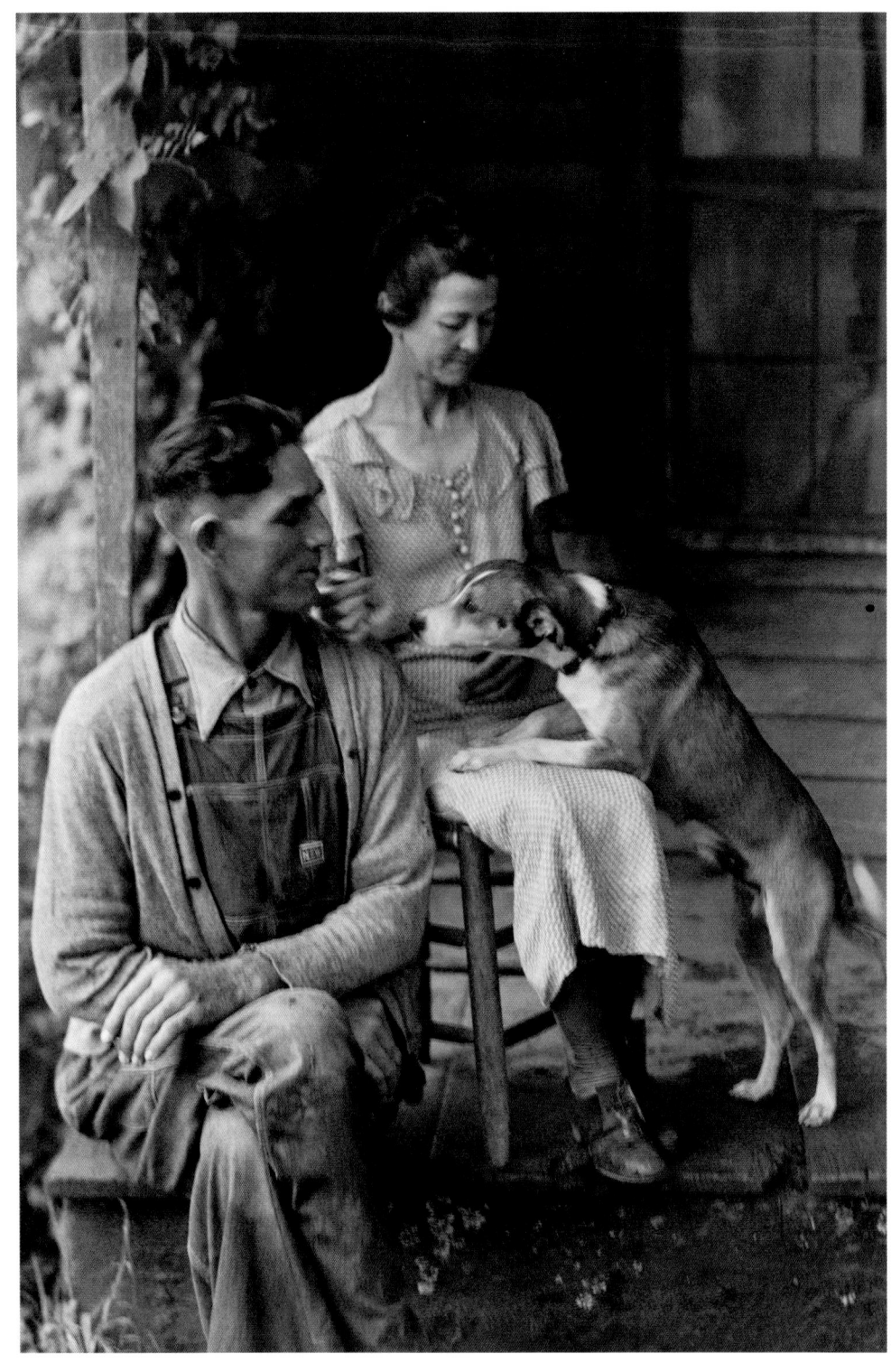

PLATE 13 Wilma McNabb's porch. [Western North Carolina], 1930s.

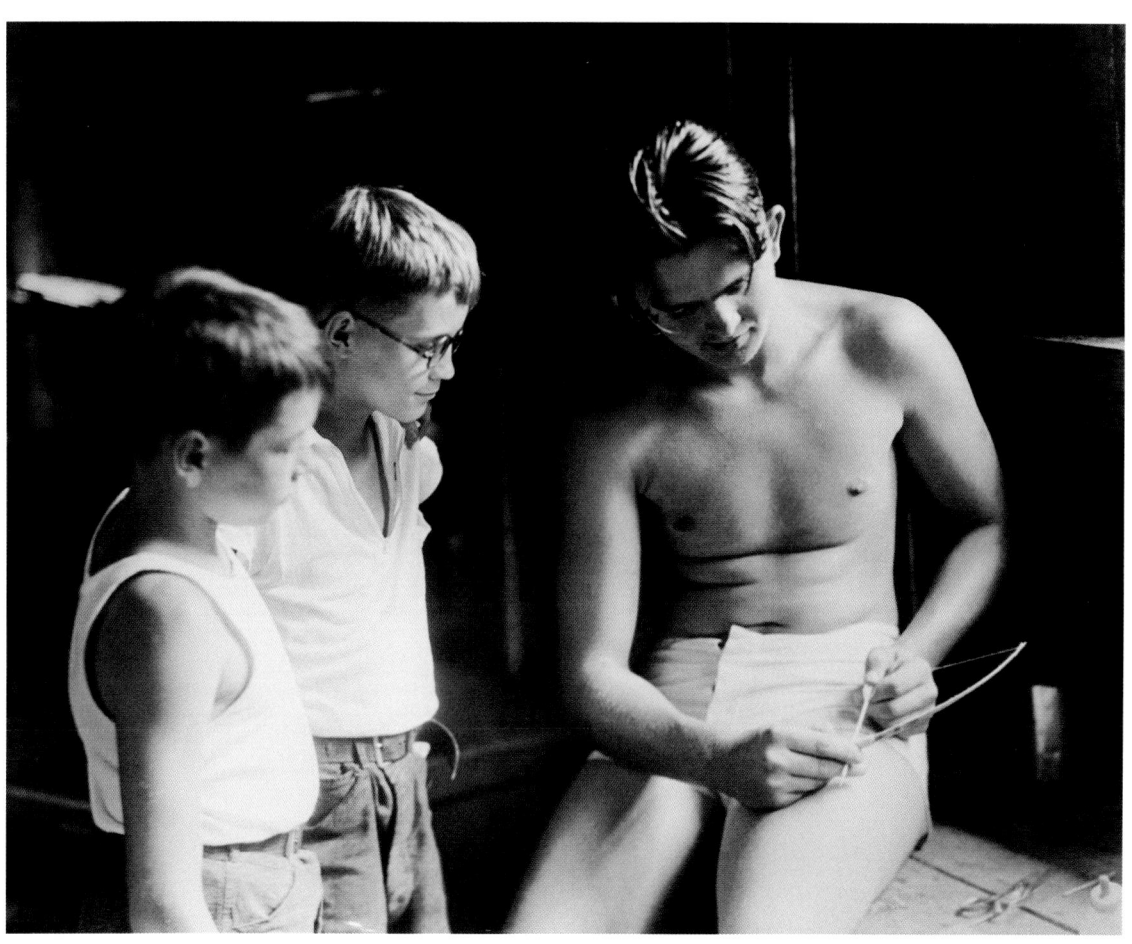

PLATE 14   *At a Boys' Camp.* [North Carolina], 1930s.

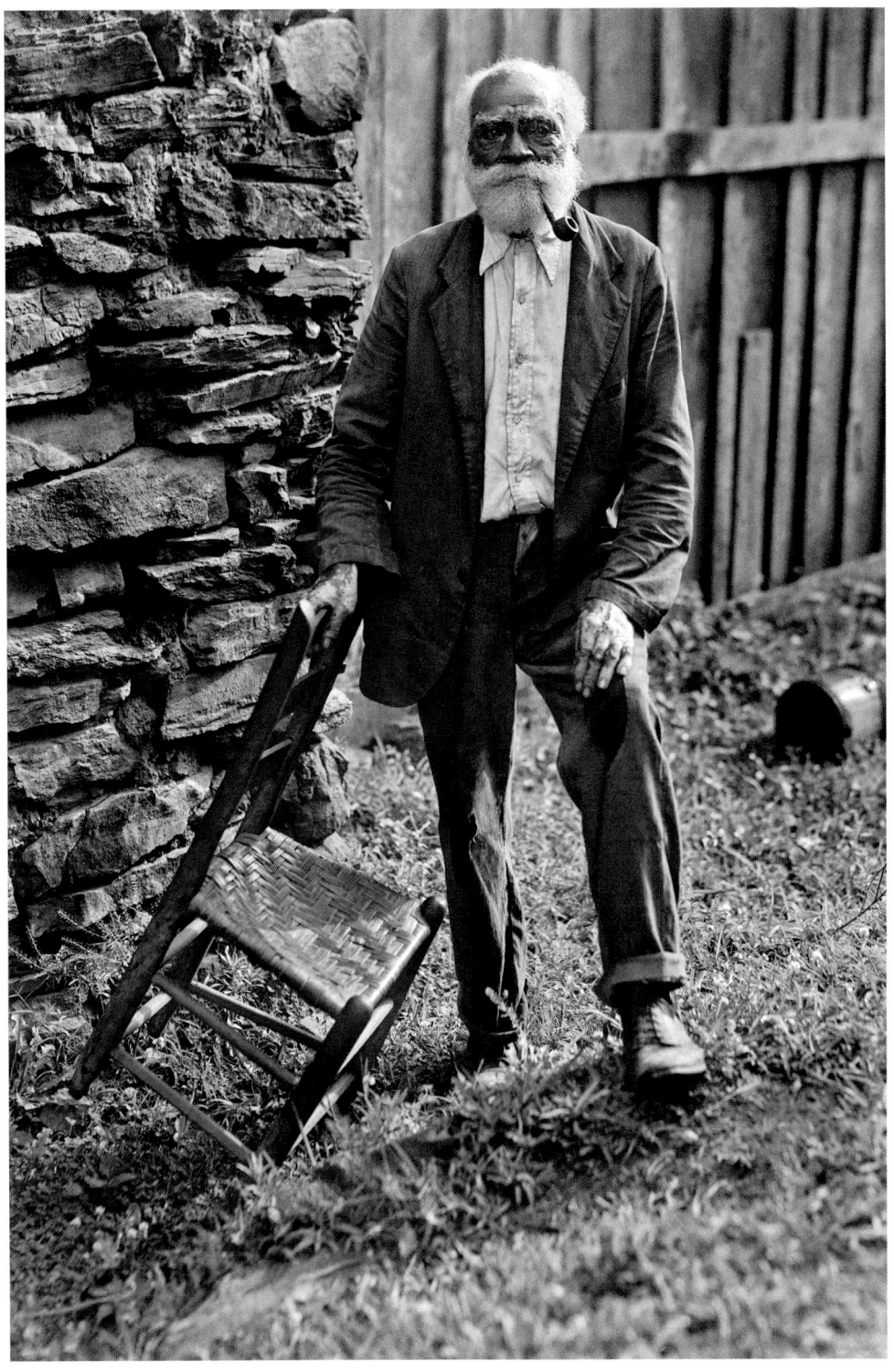

PLATE 15   Man with pipe and chair. Murphy, North Carolina, 1930s.

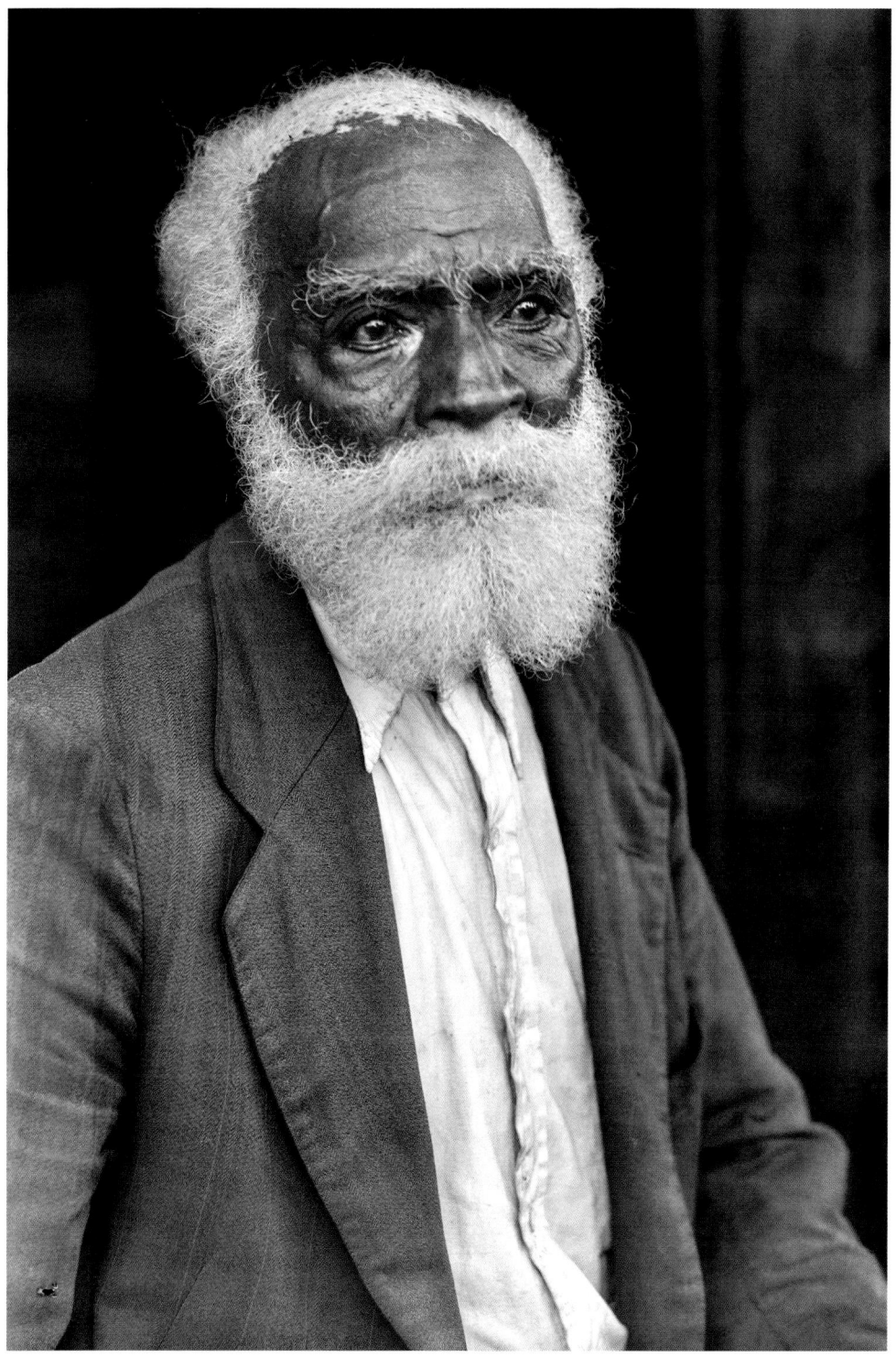

PLATE 16   Portrait of an African American man. Murphy, North Carolina, 1930s.

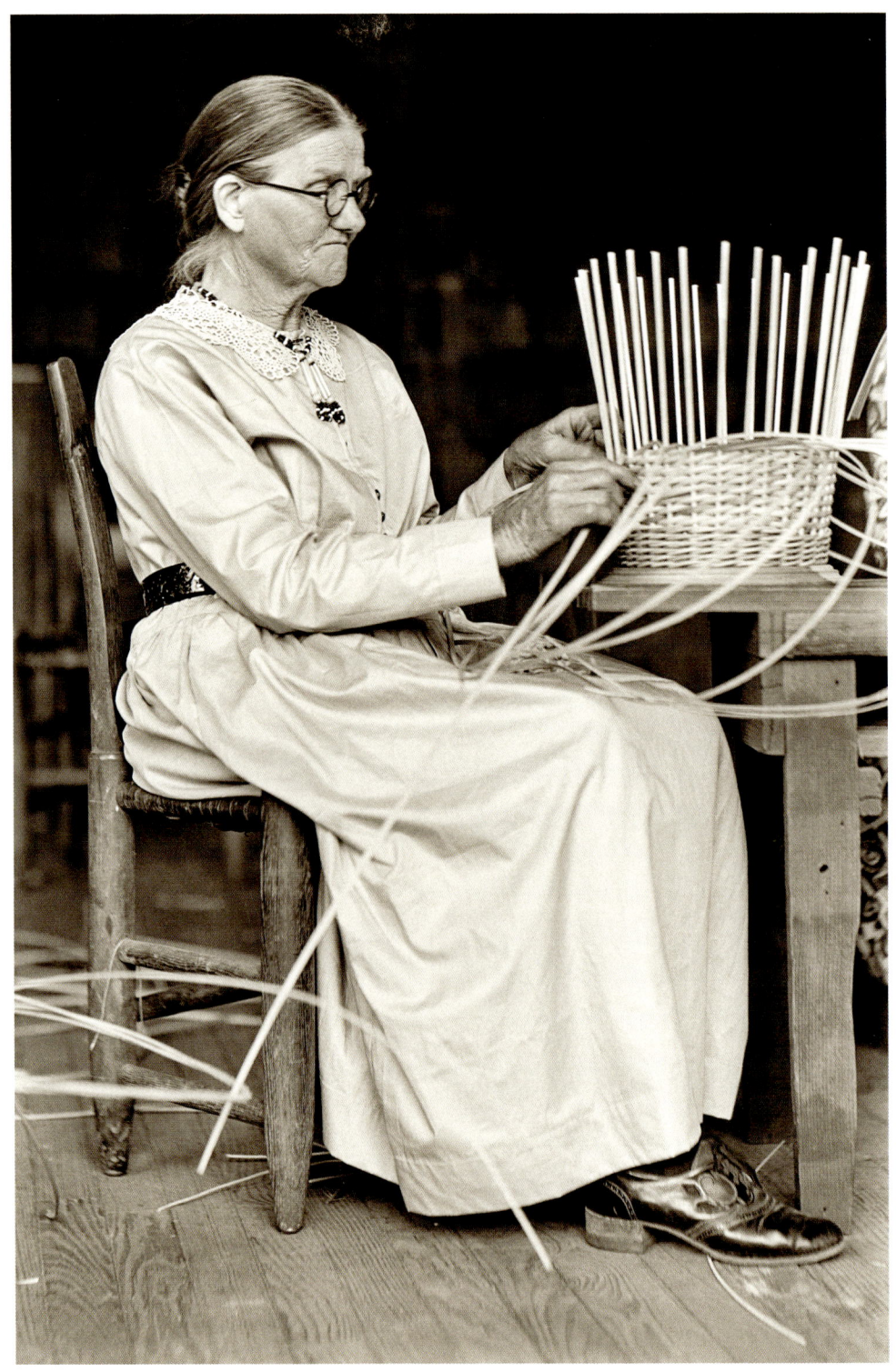

PLATE 17   A weaver of baskets. Penland, North Carolina, 1930s.

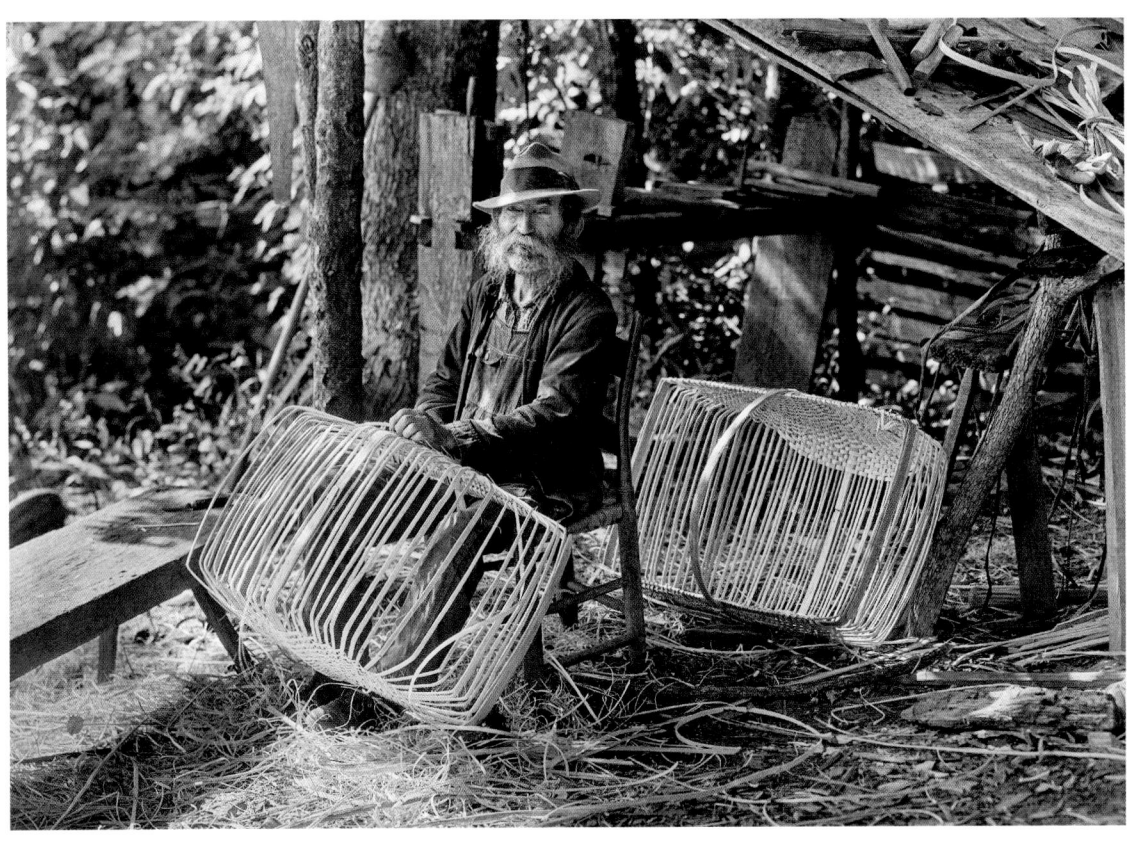

PLATE 18   George Queen making baskets. Mitchell County, North Carolina, 1930s.

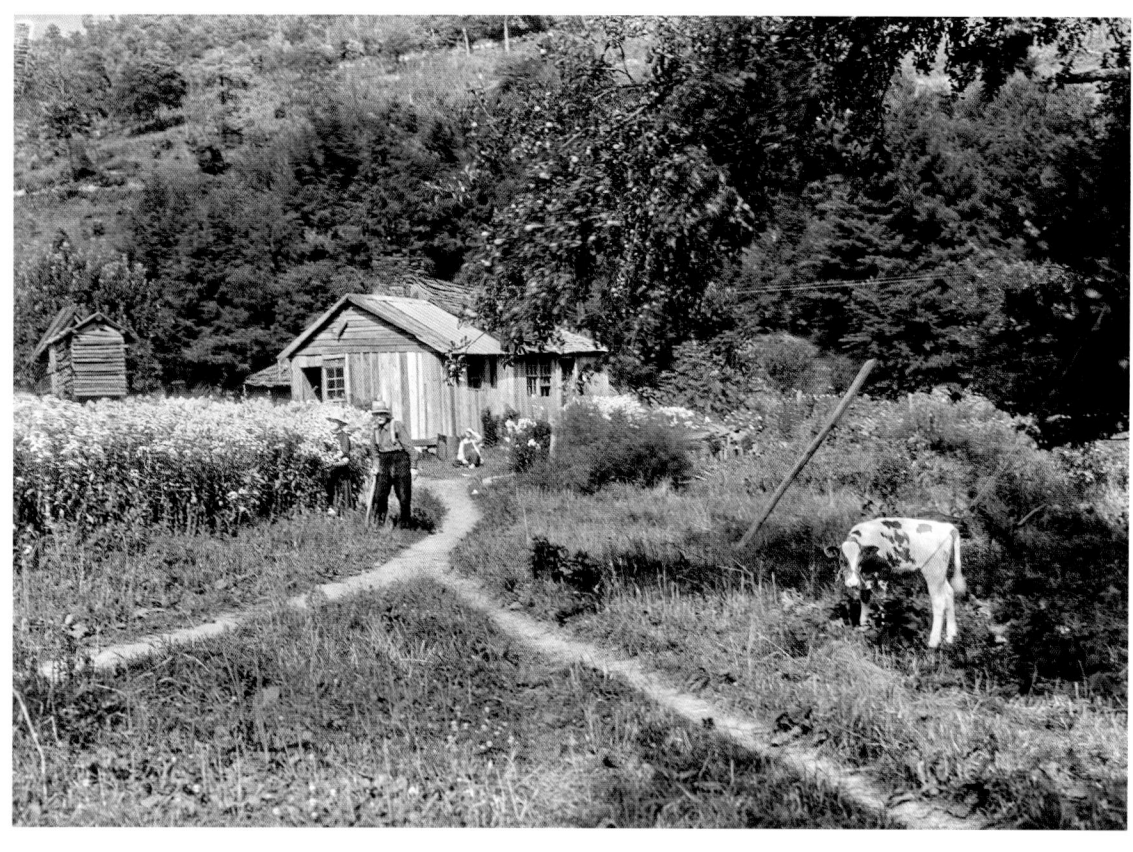

PLATE 19   A rural home. Mitchell or Yancey County, North Carolina, ca. 1934.

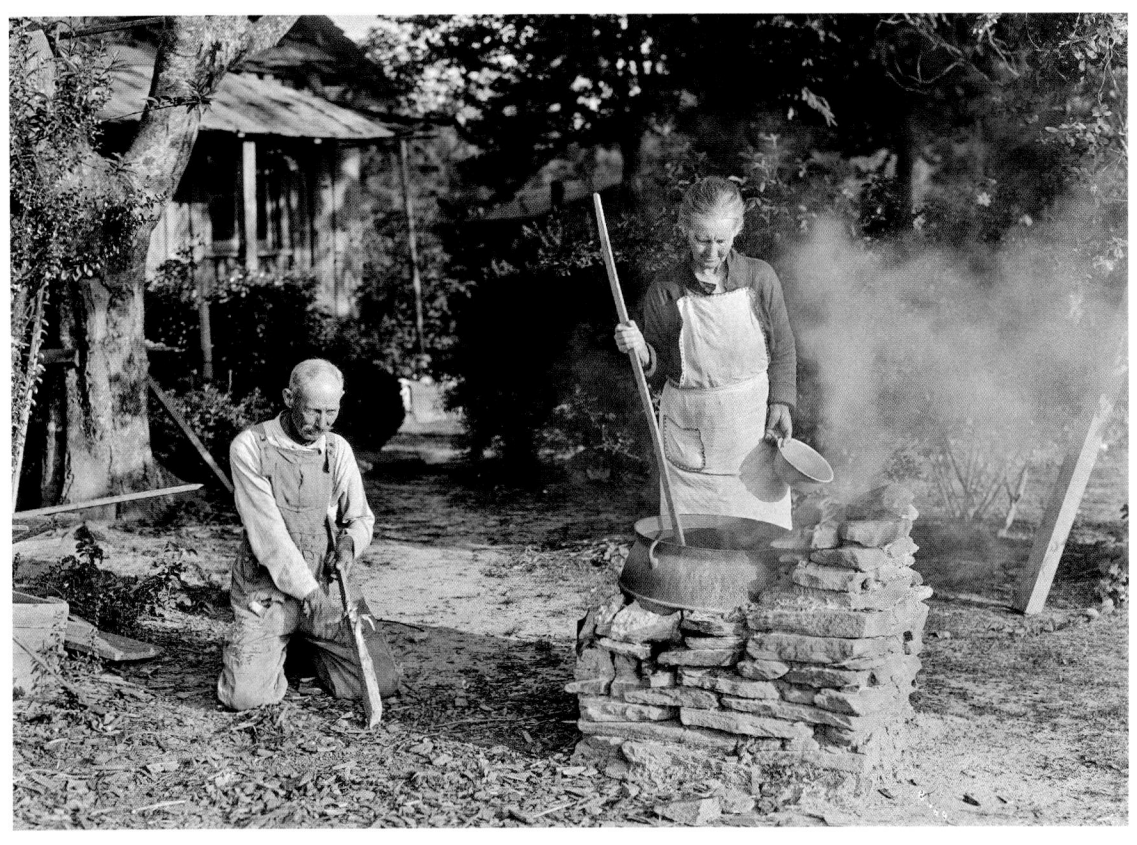

PLATE 20   Eugene and Rebecca Jones making soap. Wake County, North Carolina, 1930s.

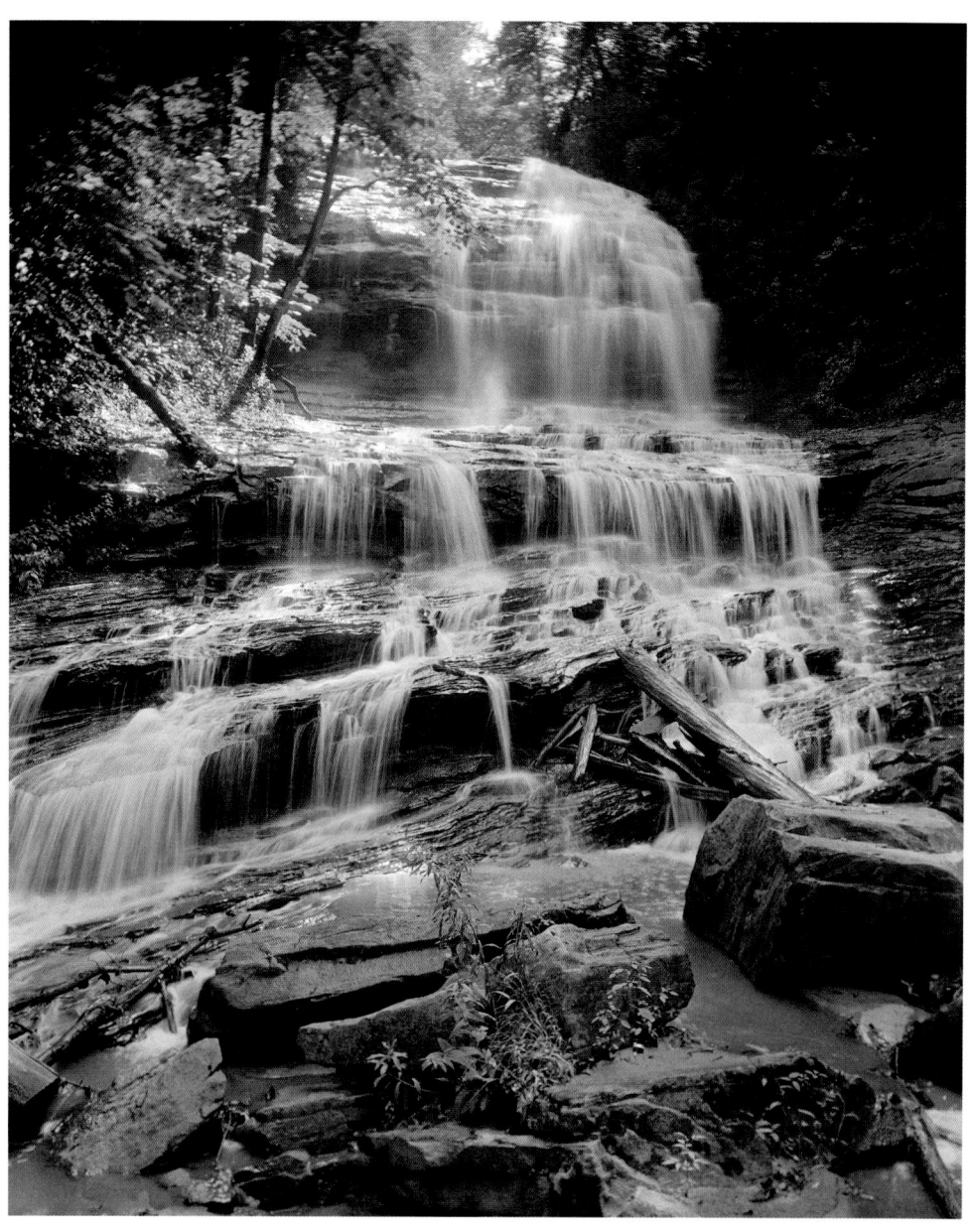

PLATE 21   Pearson's Falls on Colt Creek. Polk County, North Carolina, 1930s.

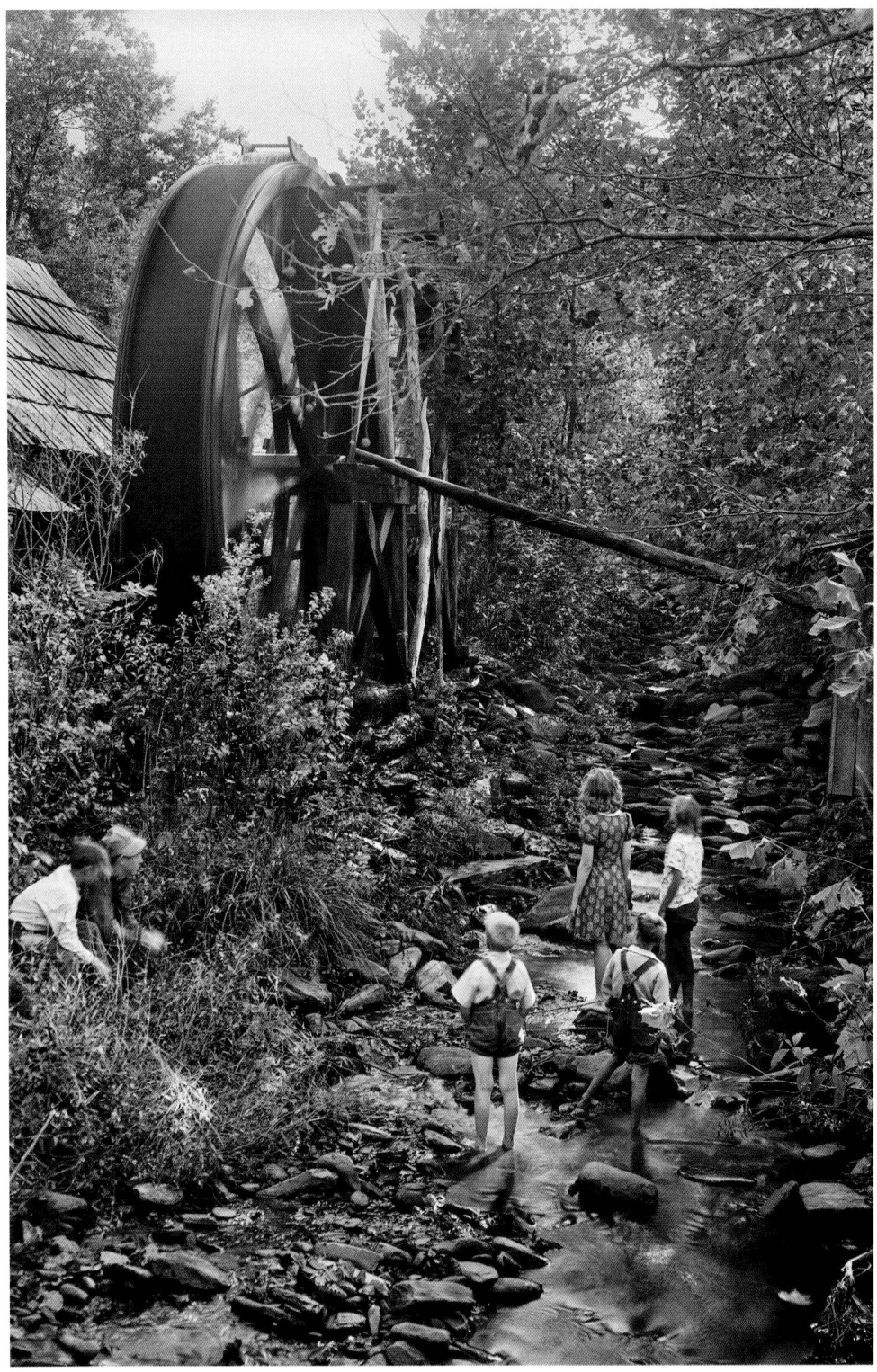

PLATE 22   Children at a gristmill. Eastern Tennessee, 1930s.

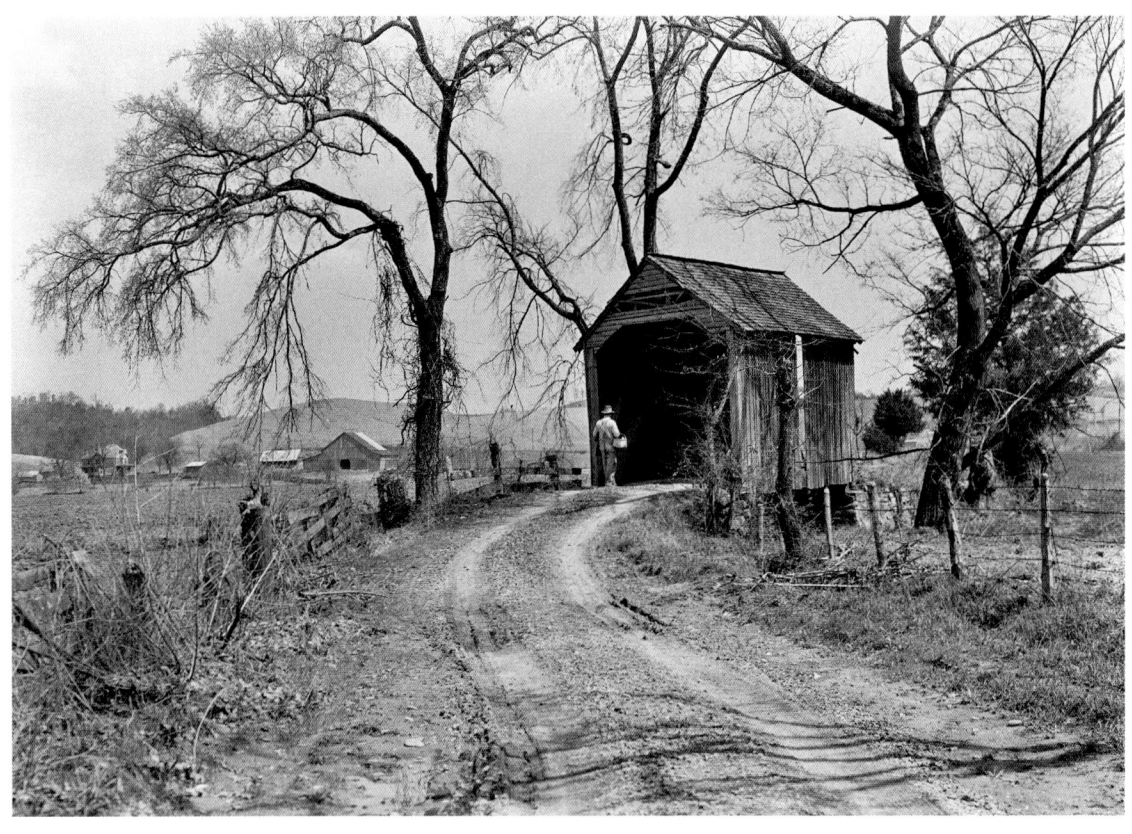

PLATE 23   Covered bridge in the Smoky Mountains. North Carolina or Tennessee, 1930s.

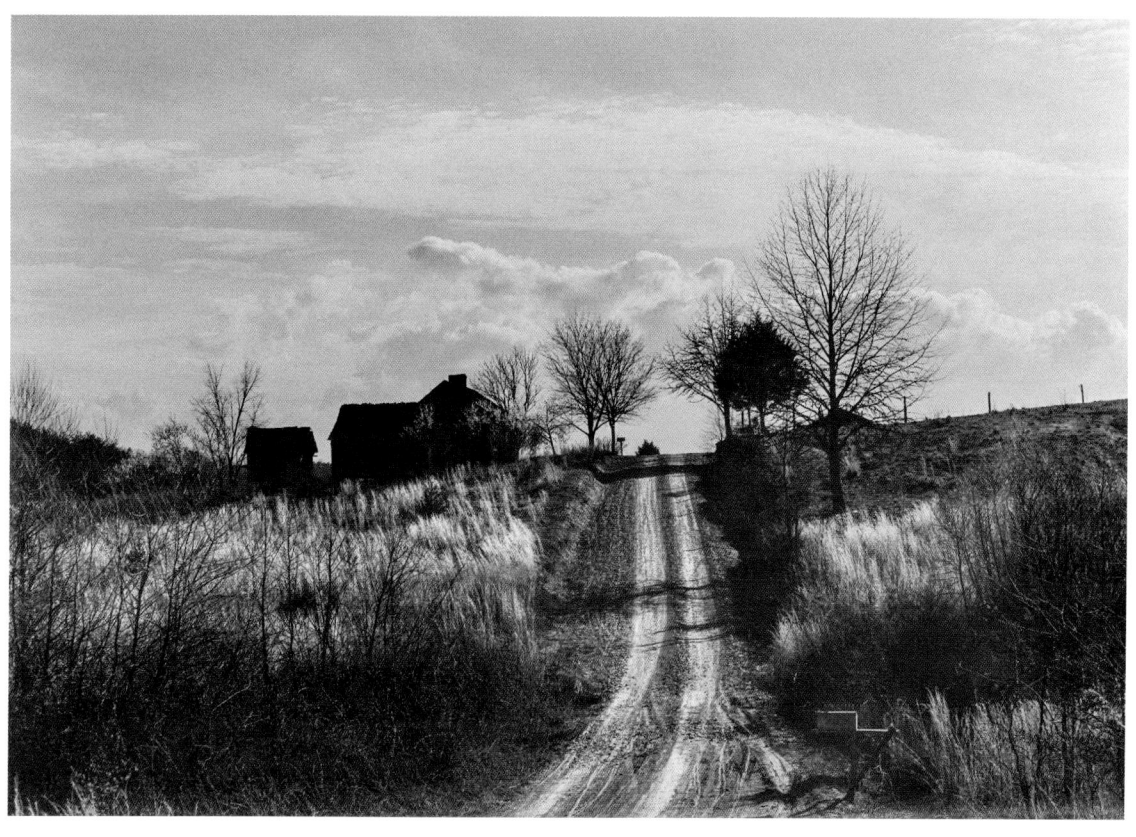

PLATE 24   Evening landscape. Vicinity of Norris, Tennessee, 1930s.

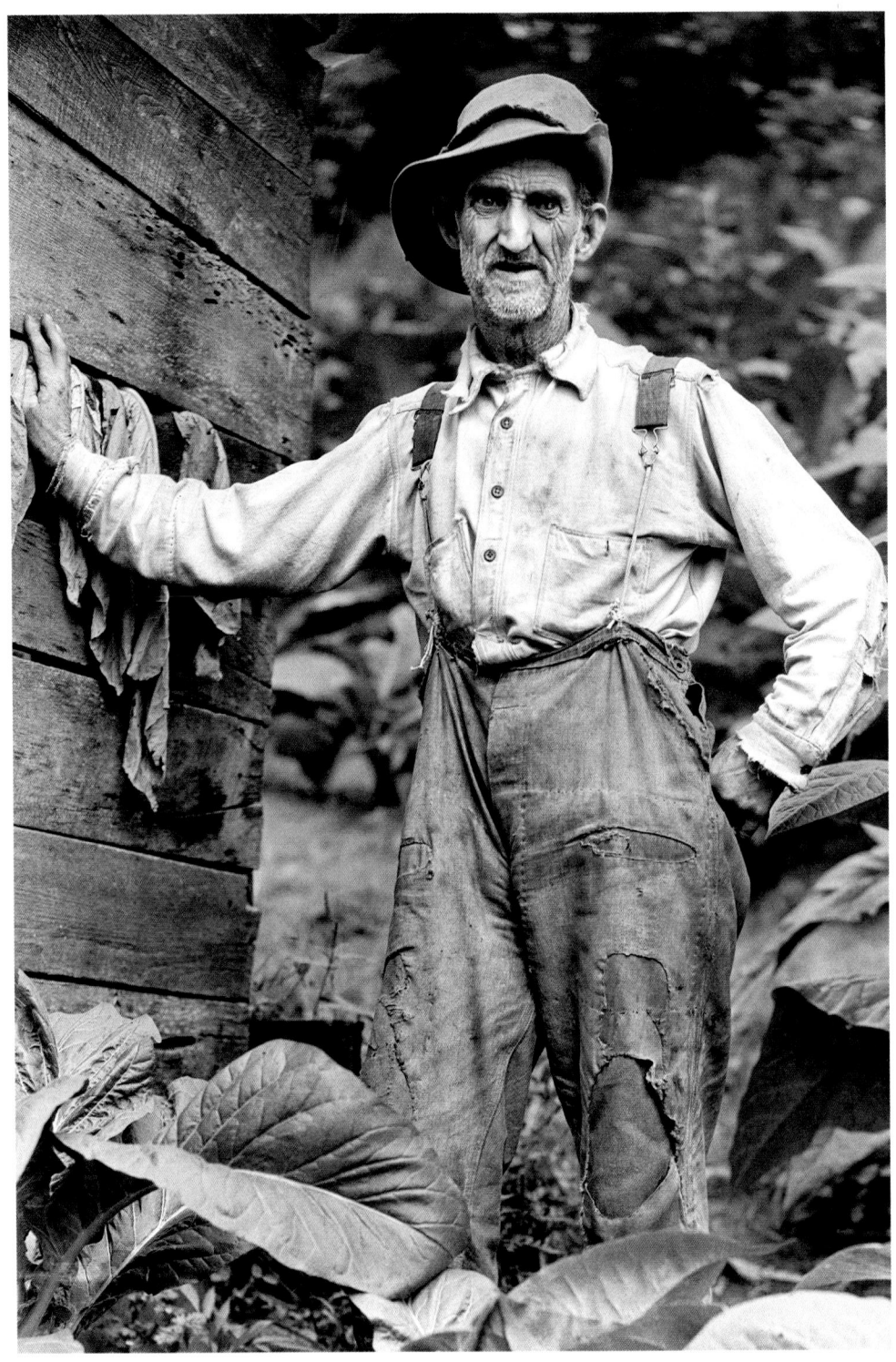

PLATE 25   *Governor Hensley*. [Yancey County, North Carolina], 1930s.

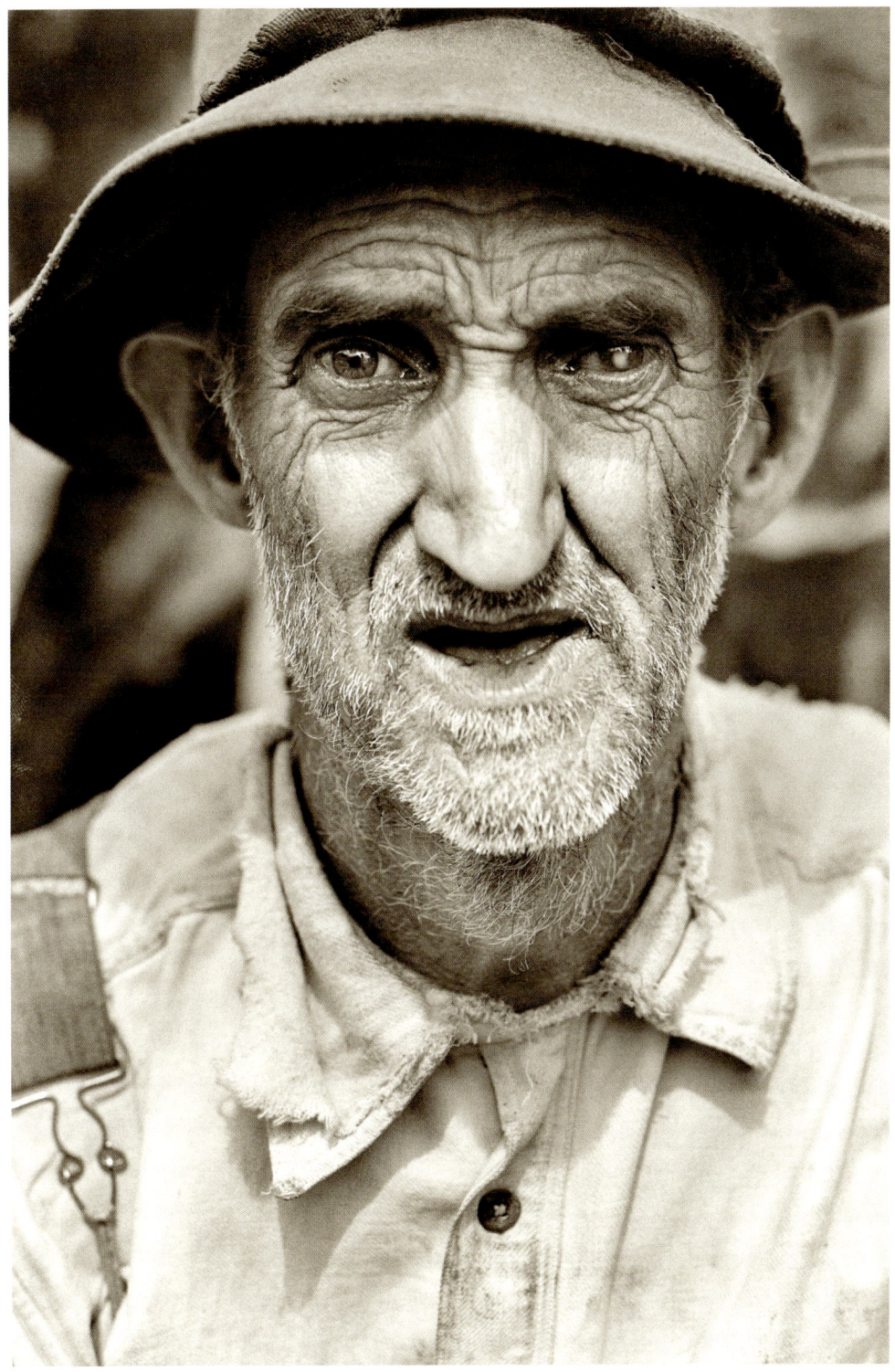

PLATE 26 *Governor Hensley*. [Yancey County, North Carolina], 1930s.

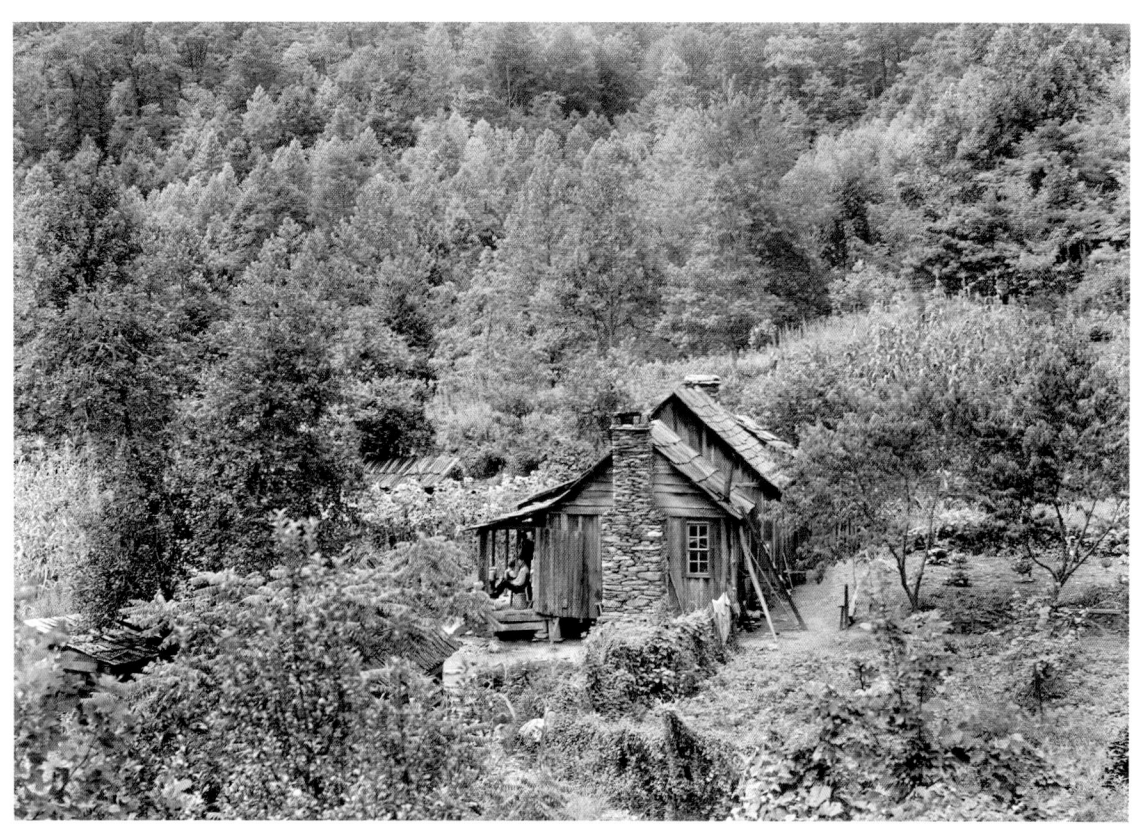

PLATE 27   West Johnson cabin on Buck Creek Road. Mitchell County,
North Carolina, 1930s.

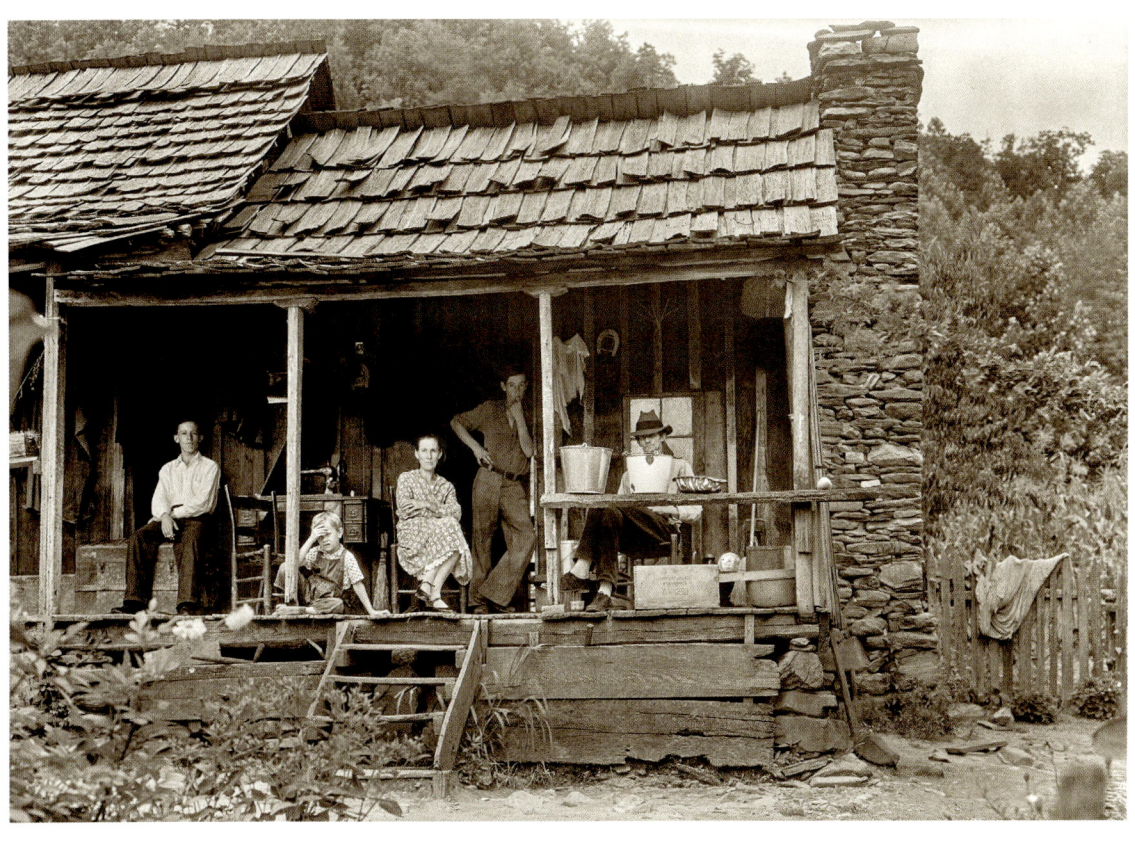

PLATE 28   Porch of the West Johnson cabin. Mitchell County, North Carolina, 1930s.

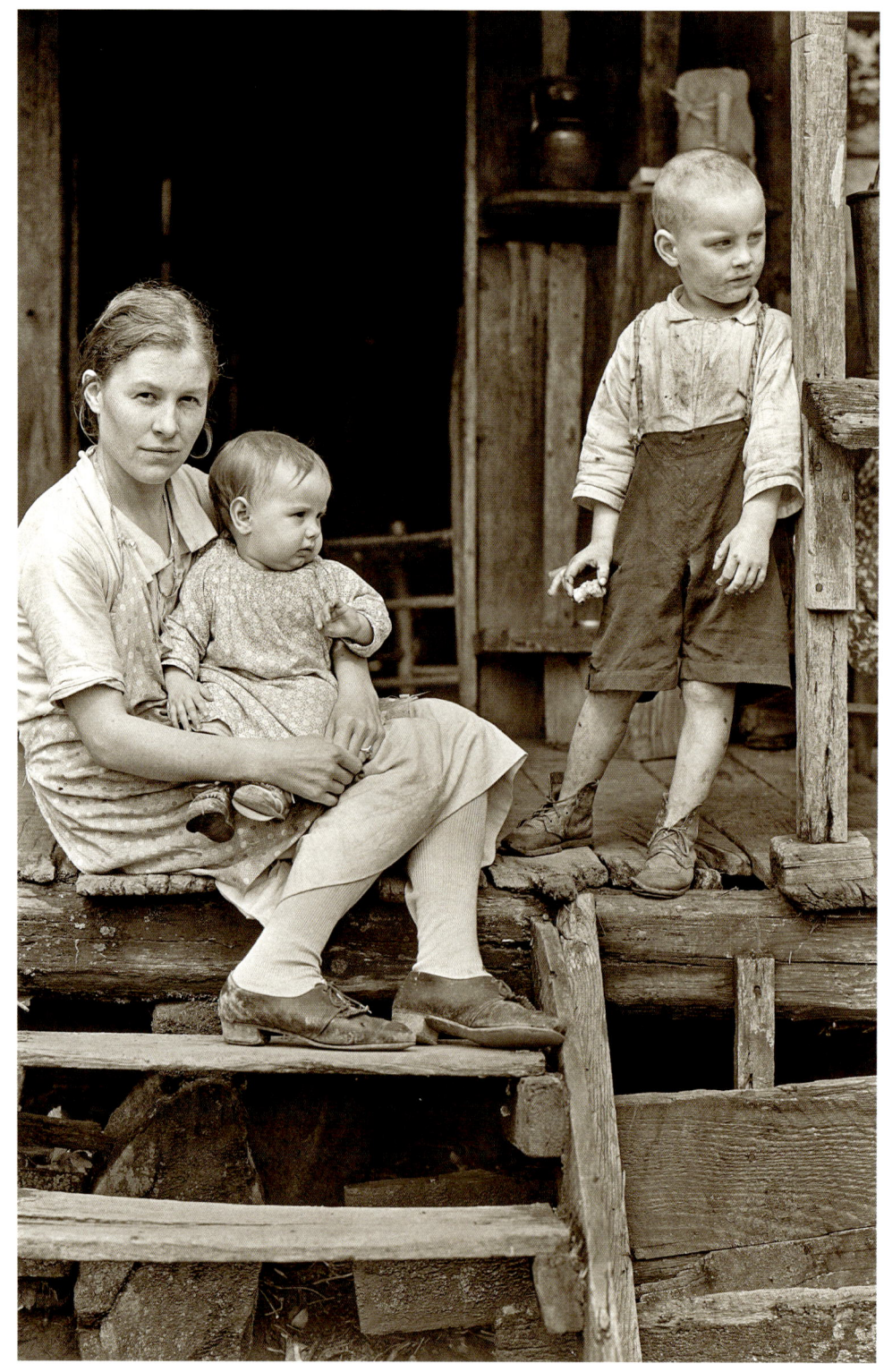

PLATE 29   West Johnson family. Mitchell County, North Carolina, 1930s.

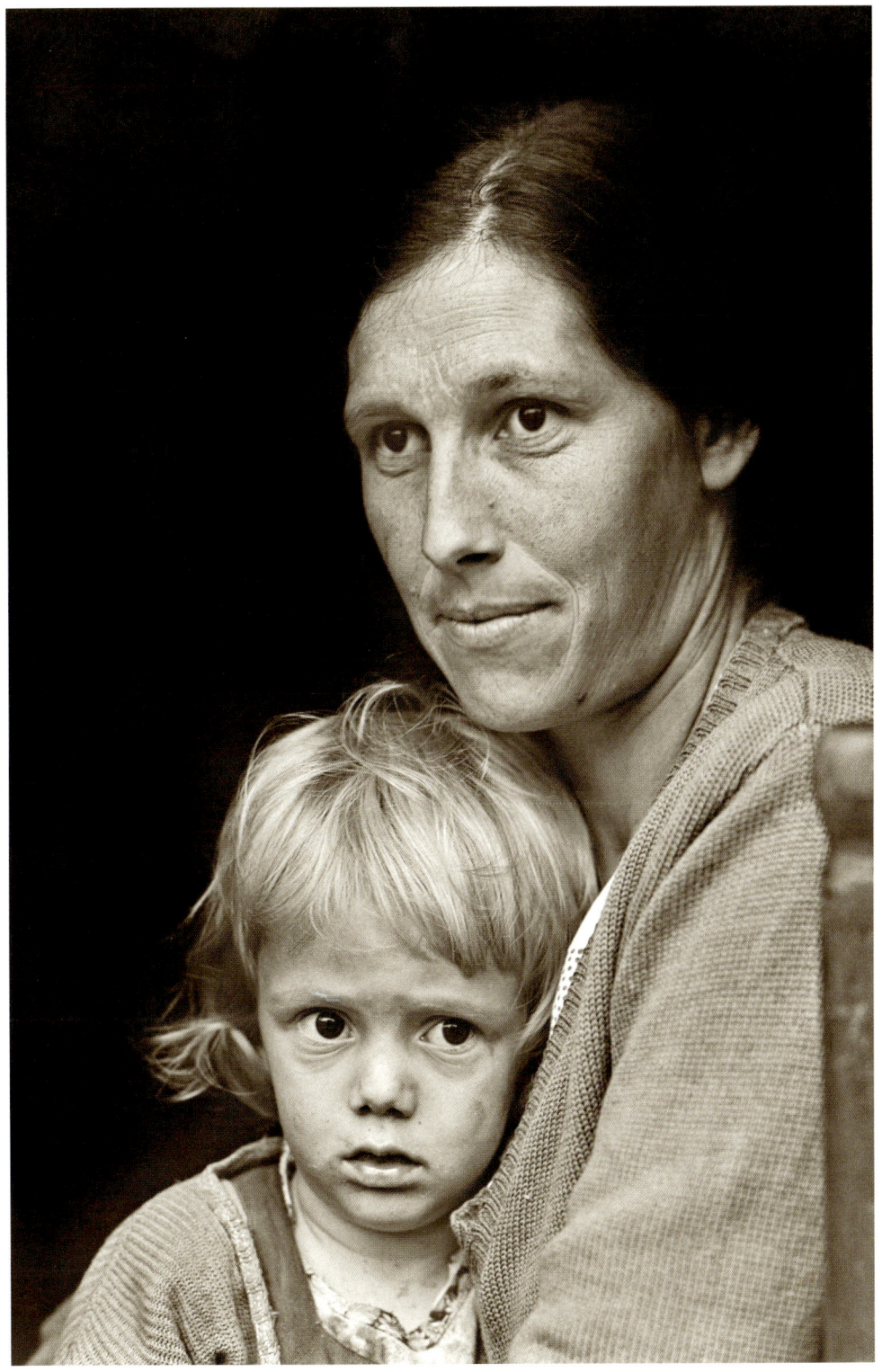

PLATE 30   Mrs. Will Carpenter. Penland, North Carolina, 1930s.

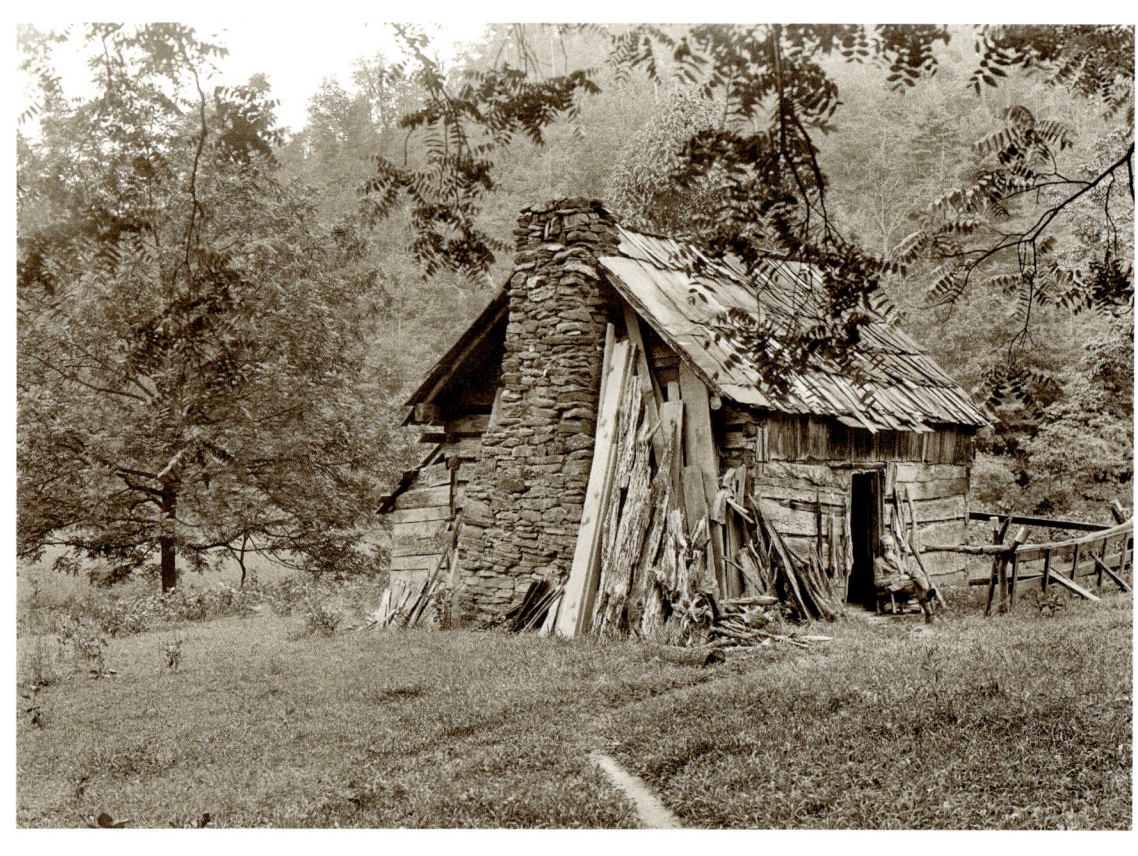

PLATE 31 The cabin of Sam Cresawn, the snake doctor. Little Switzerland, North Carolina, ca. 1934.

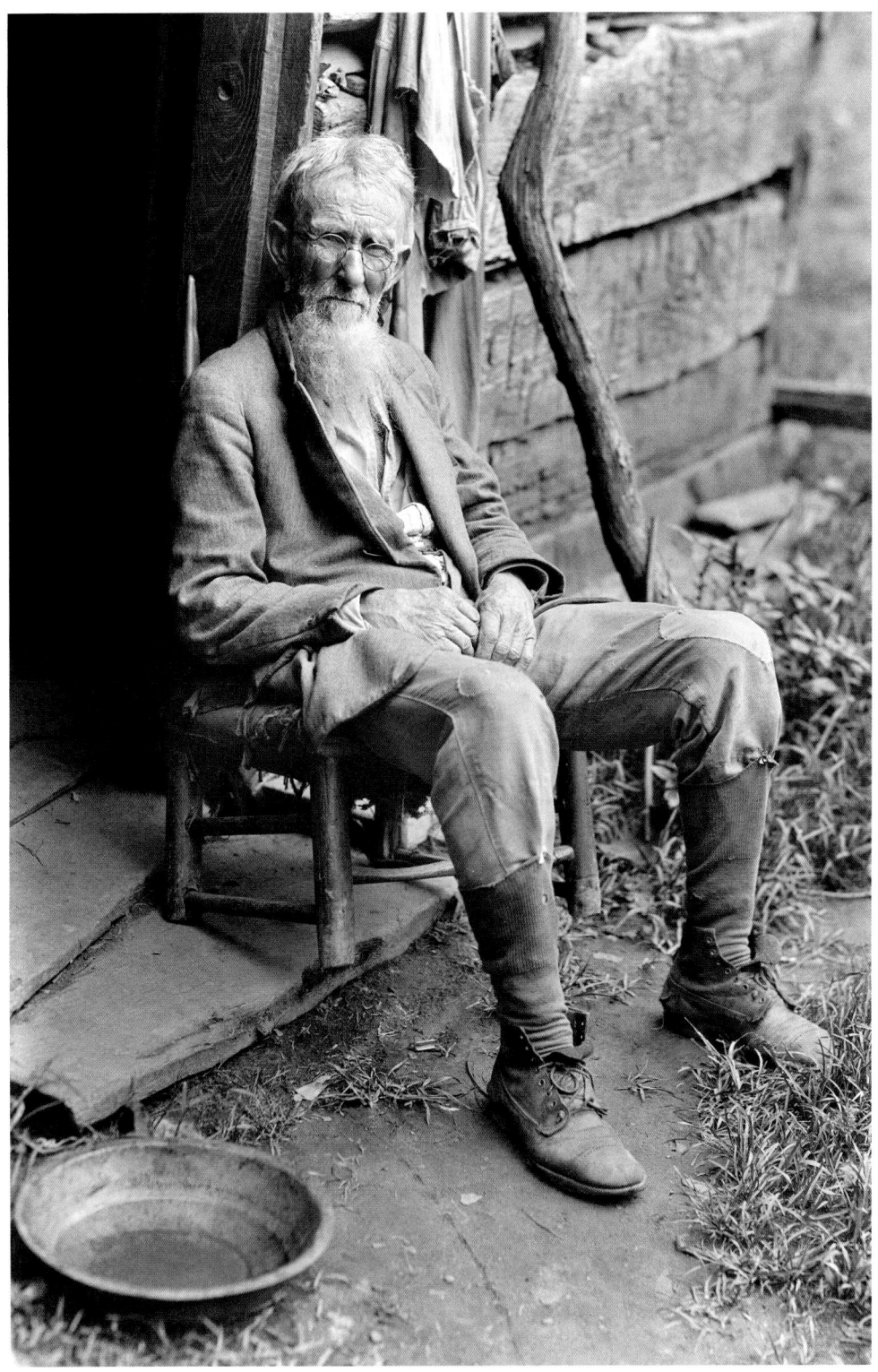

PLATE 32   Sam Cresawn sitting at his cabin door. Little Switzerland,
North Carolina, ca. 1934.

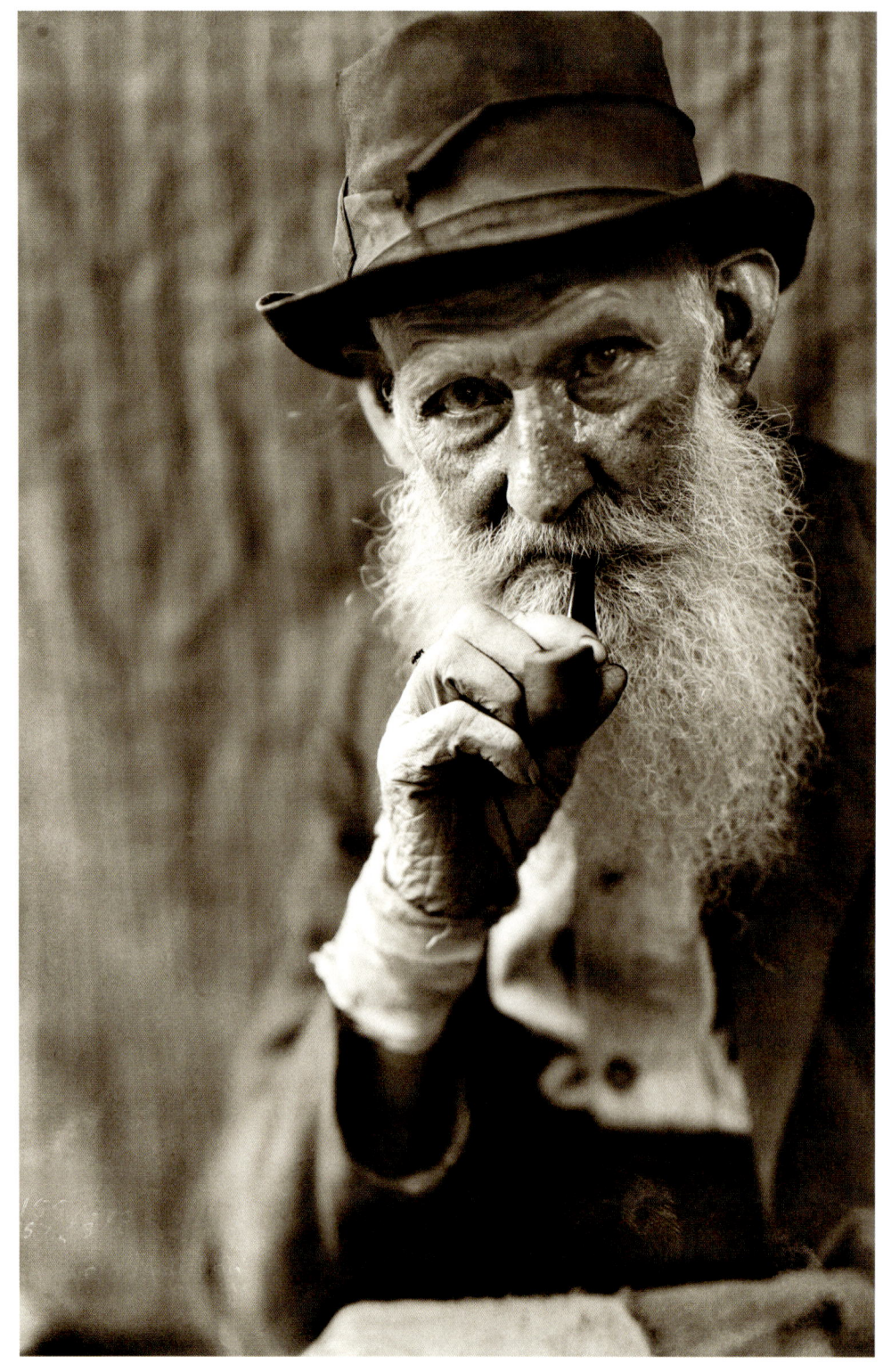

PLATE 33   Tom Sparks. Mitchell County, North Carolina, ca. 1934.

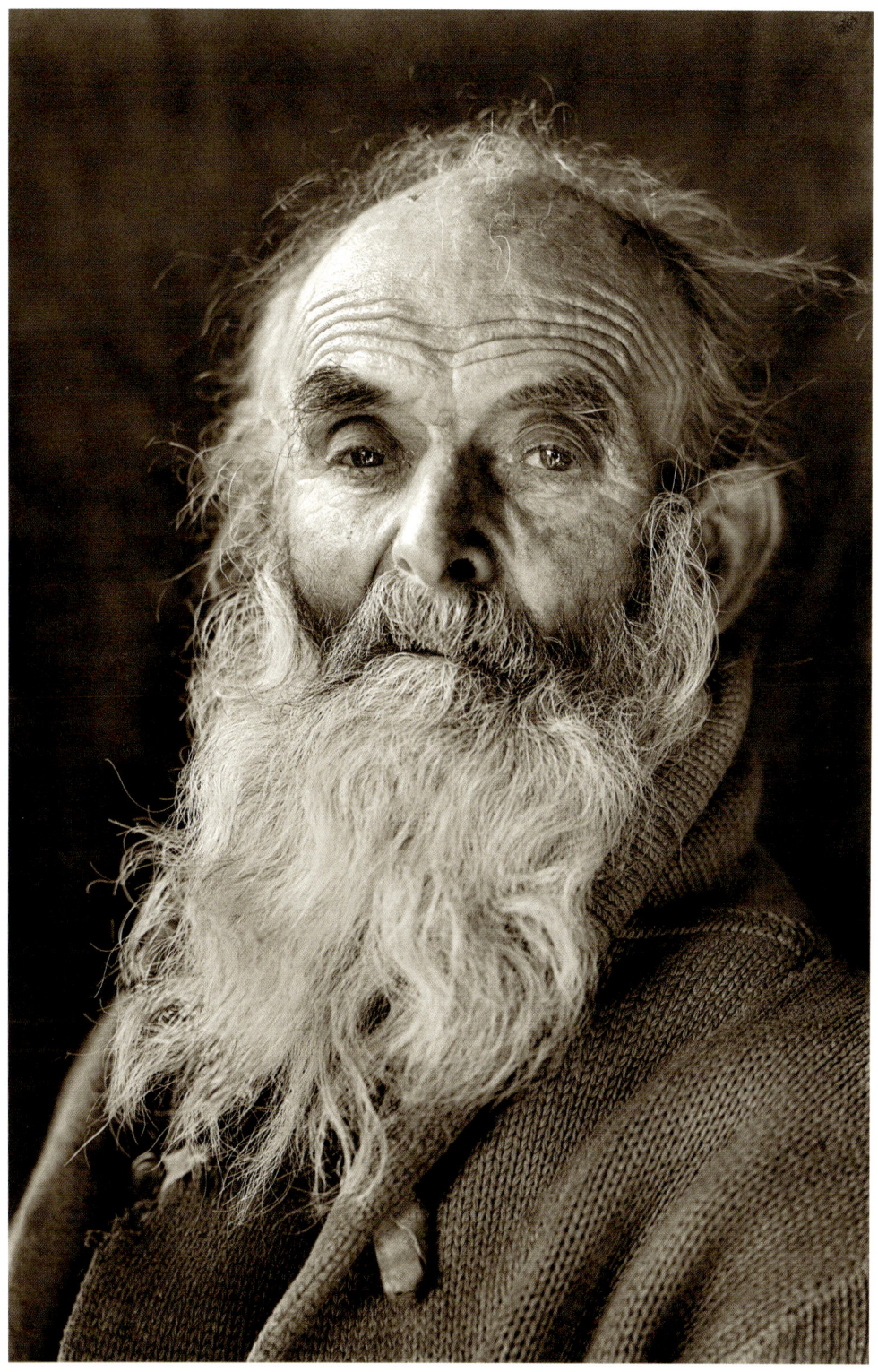

PLATE 34   J. C. Dunsdal. Tryon, North Carolina, 1930s.

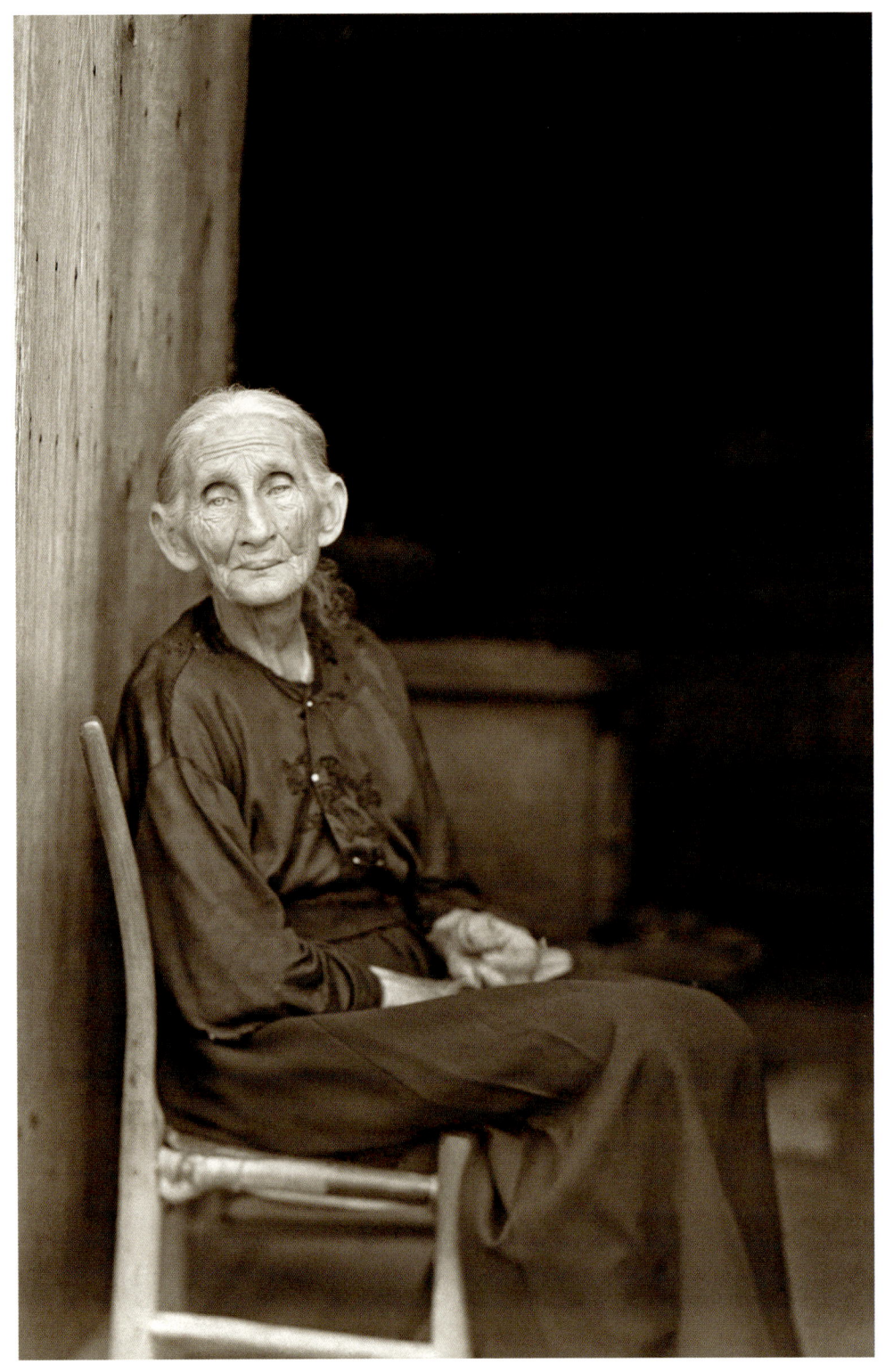

PLATE 35   Clarissa Elizabeth Jane Holyfield. Turkey Cove, McDowell County, North Carolina, ca. 1934.

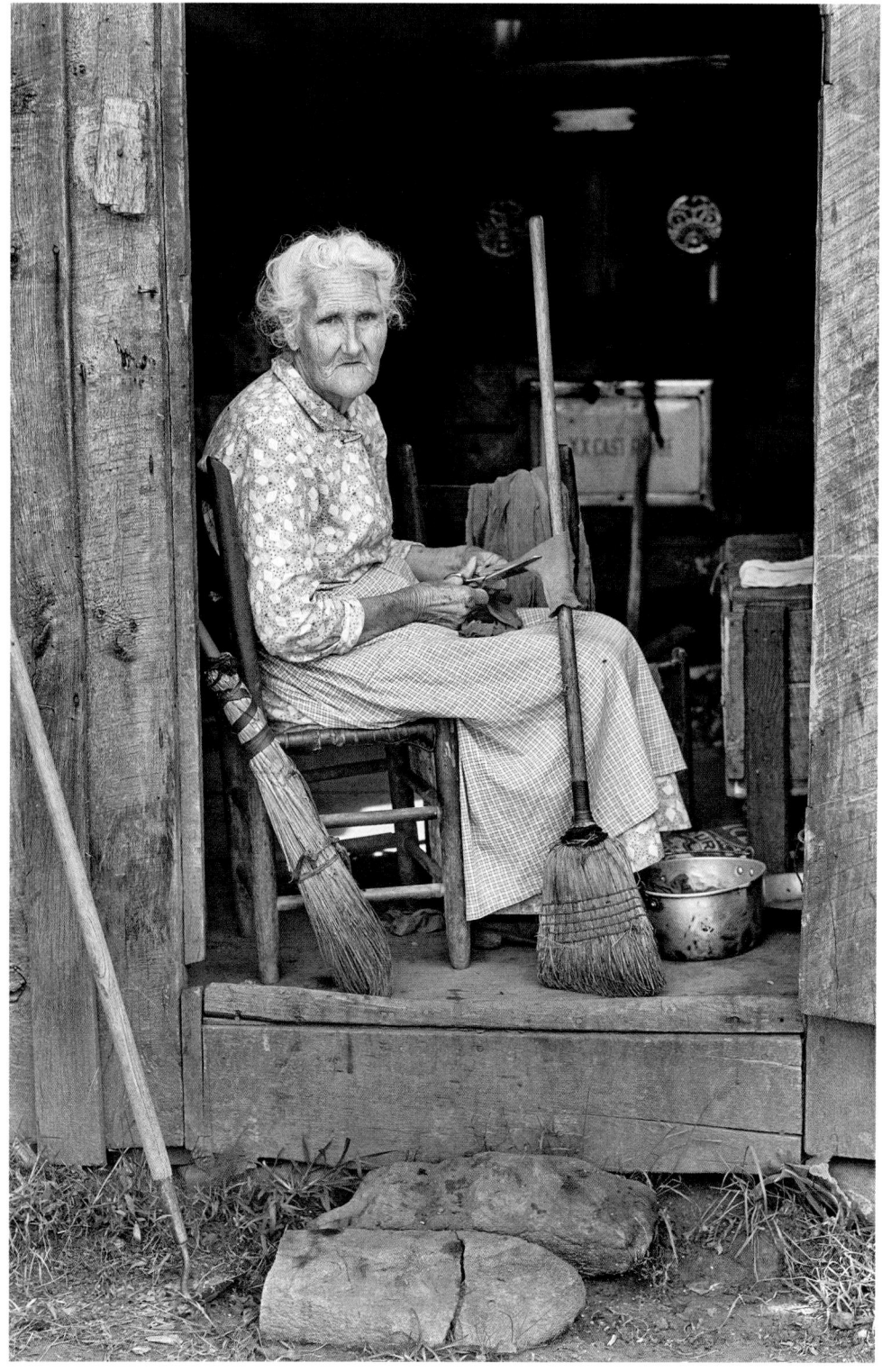

PLATE 36   Polly Jane Wilson. [Mitchell or Yancey County, North Carolina], 1930s.

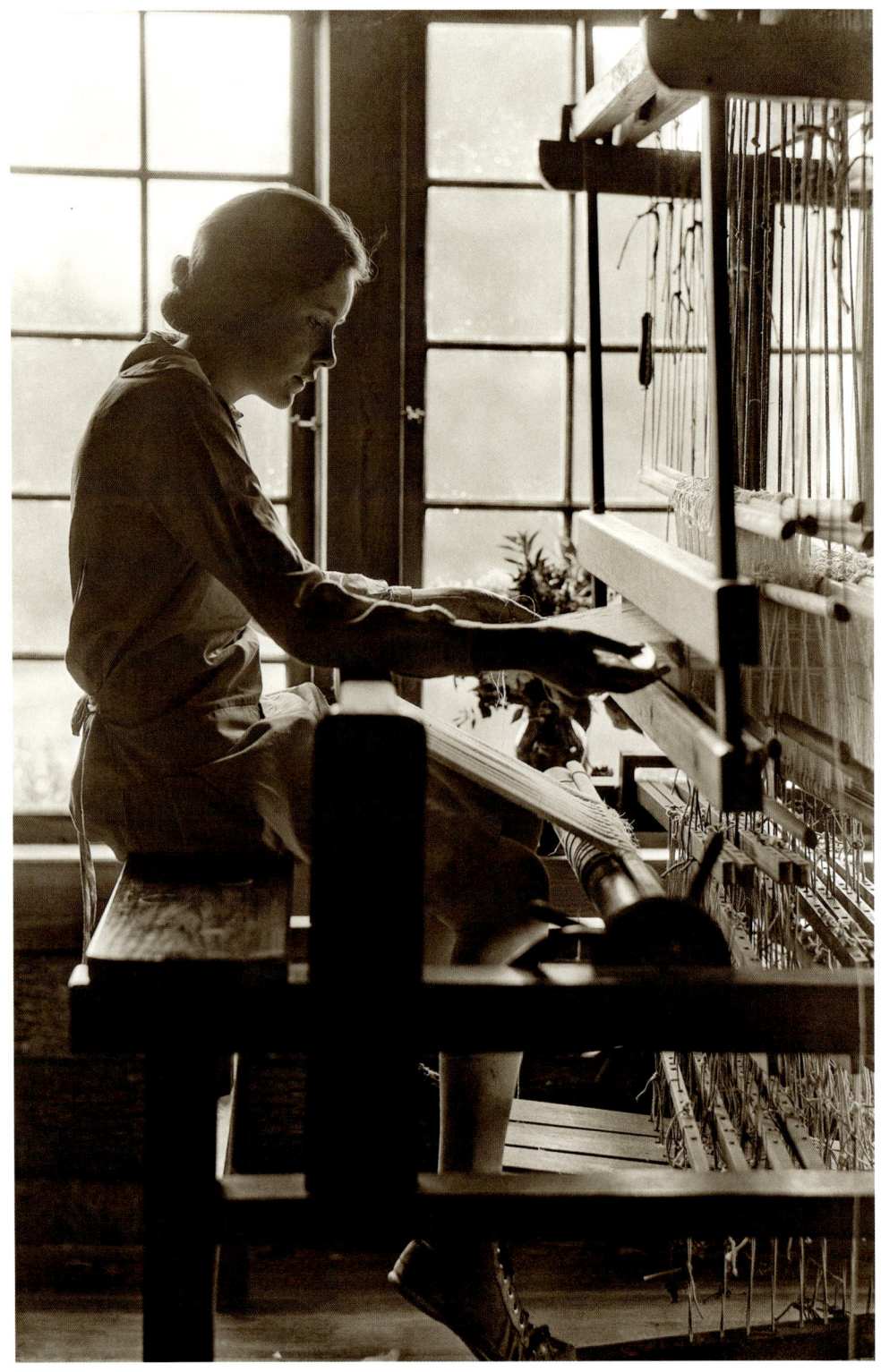

PLATE 37   Mae Gouge weaving. Penland, North Carolina, ca. 1934.

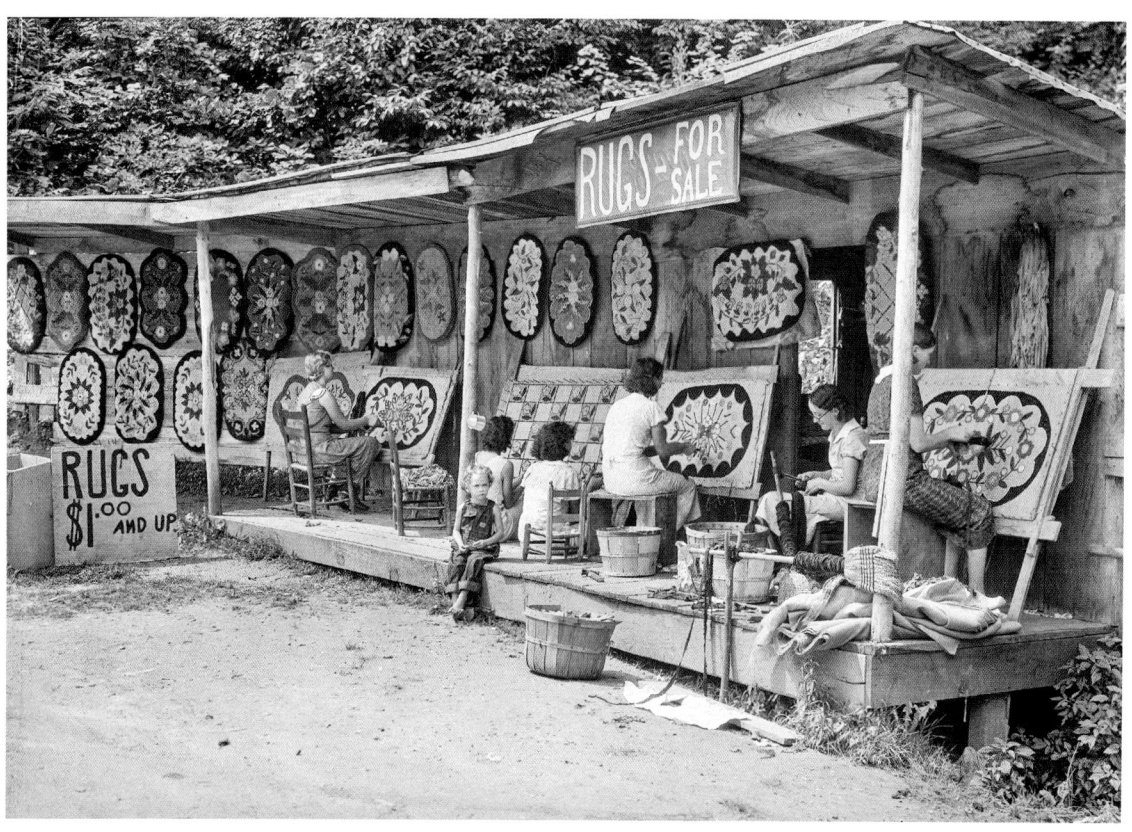

PLATE 38 Rugmakers. [Western North Carolina], 1930s.

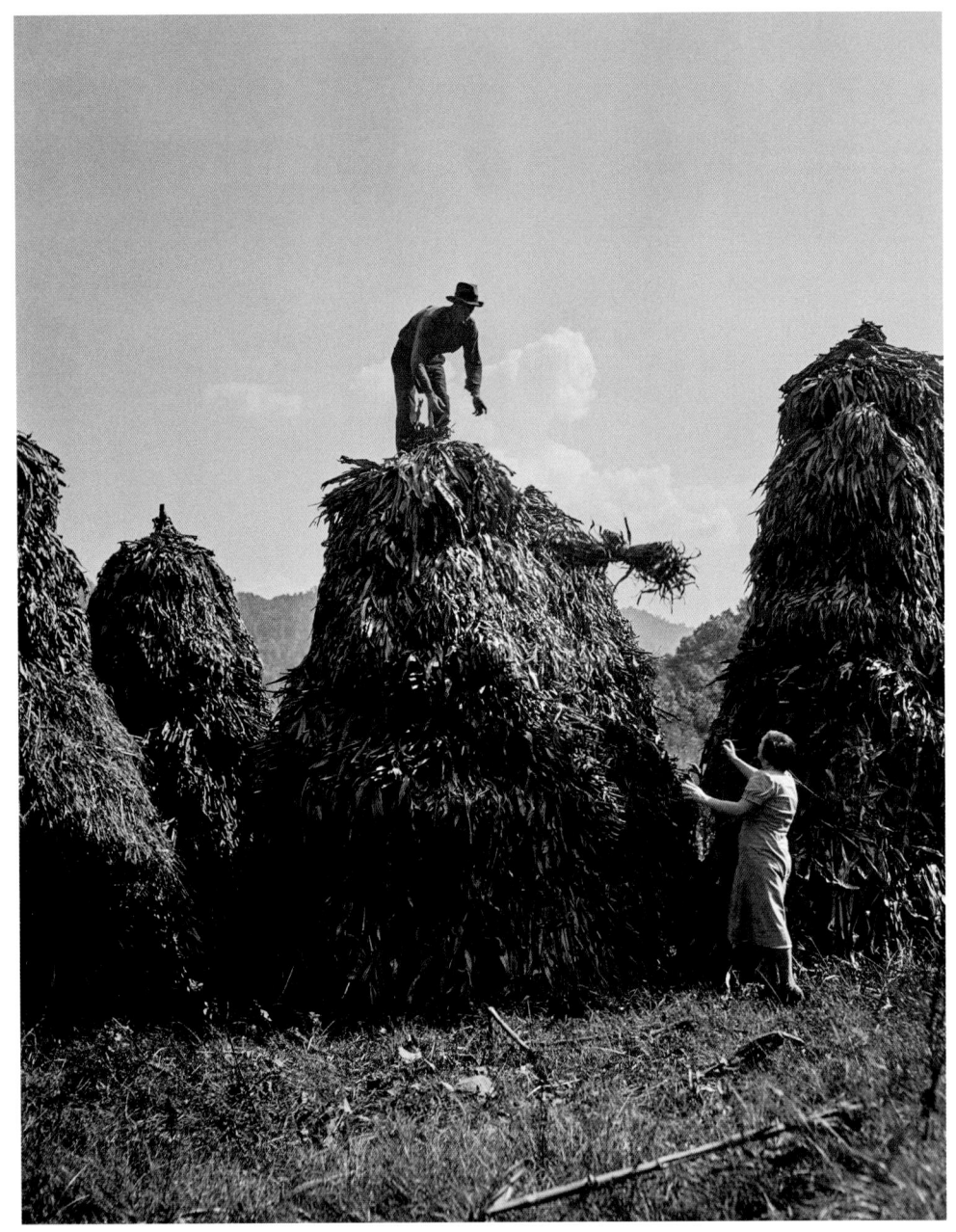

PLATE 39   *Corn Fodder.* [Western North Carolina], ca. 1940.

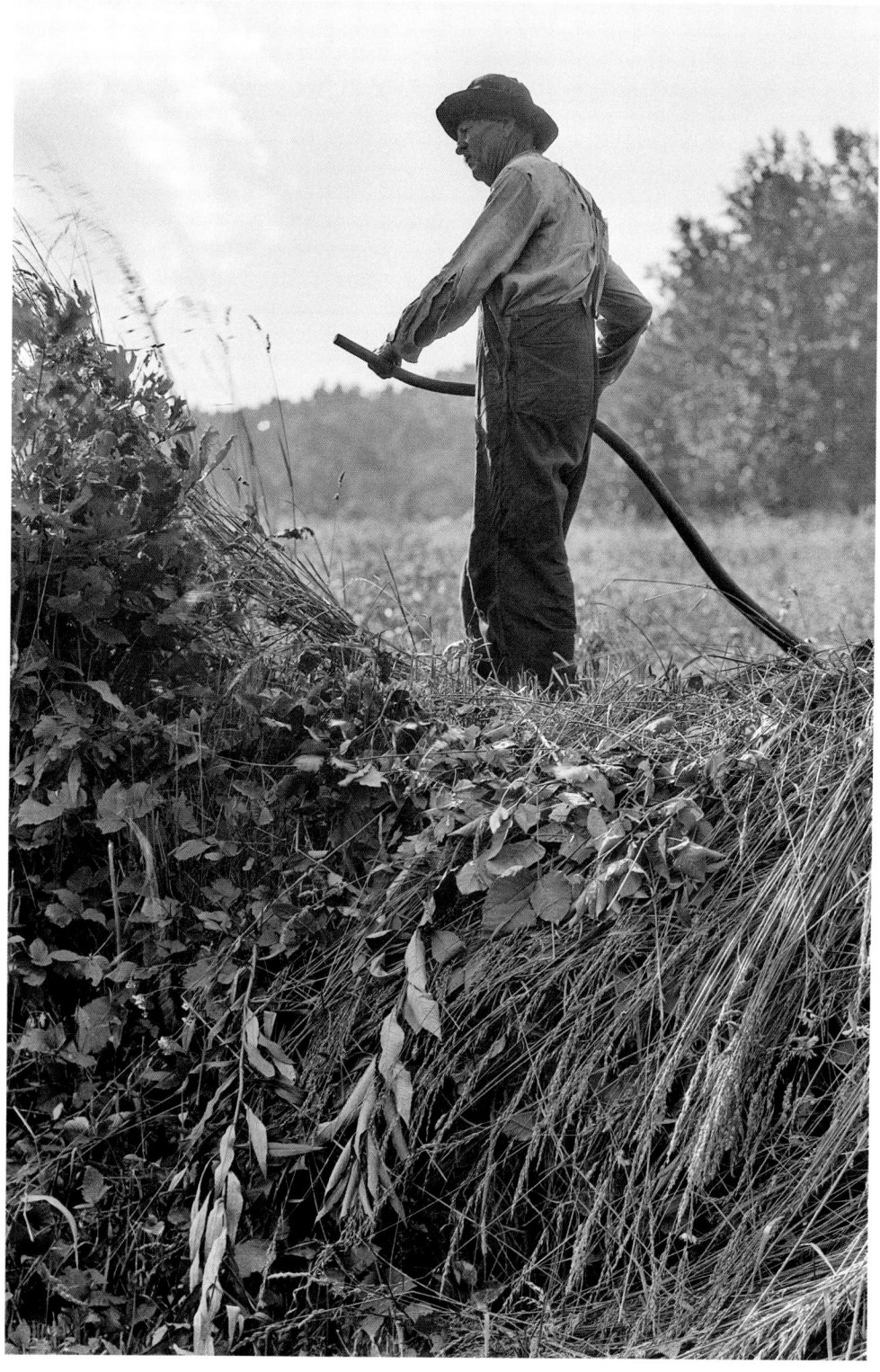

PLATE 40   *Harvesting.* Penland, North Carolina, ca. 1934.

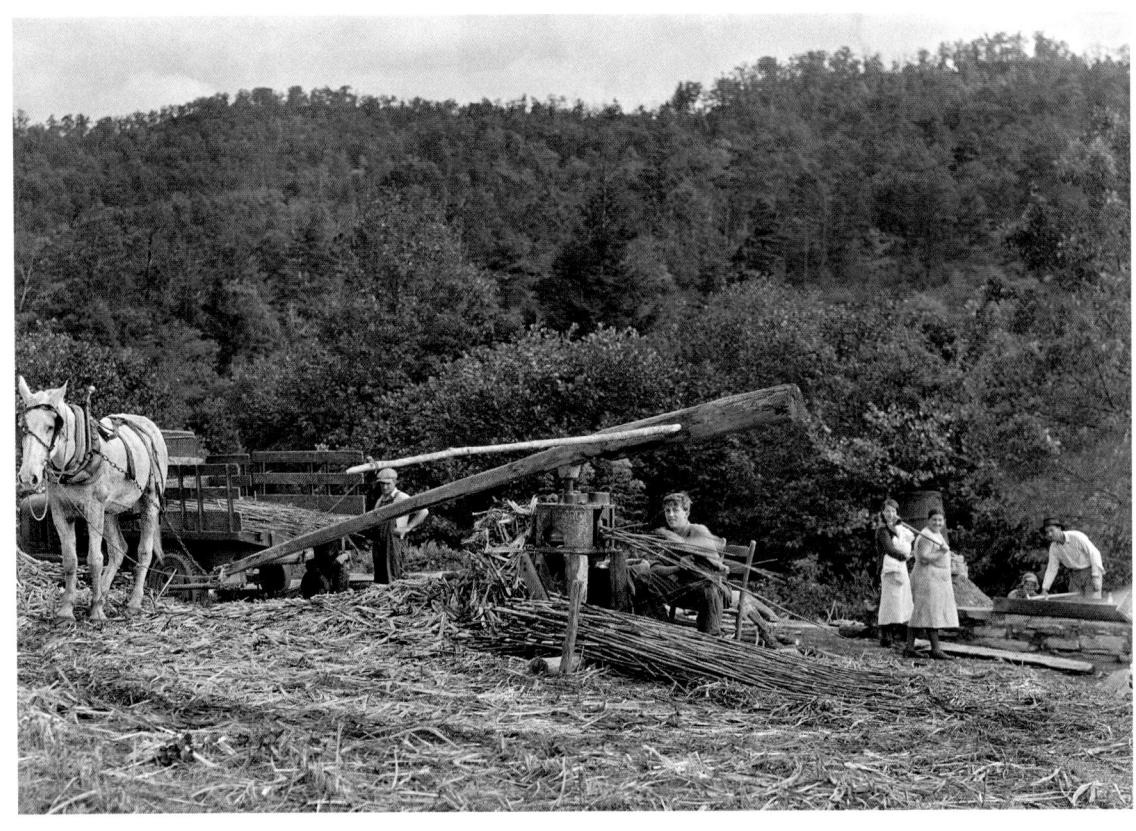

PLATE 41 *Grinding Cane.* [Western North Carolina], 1930s.

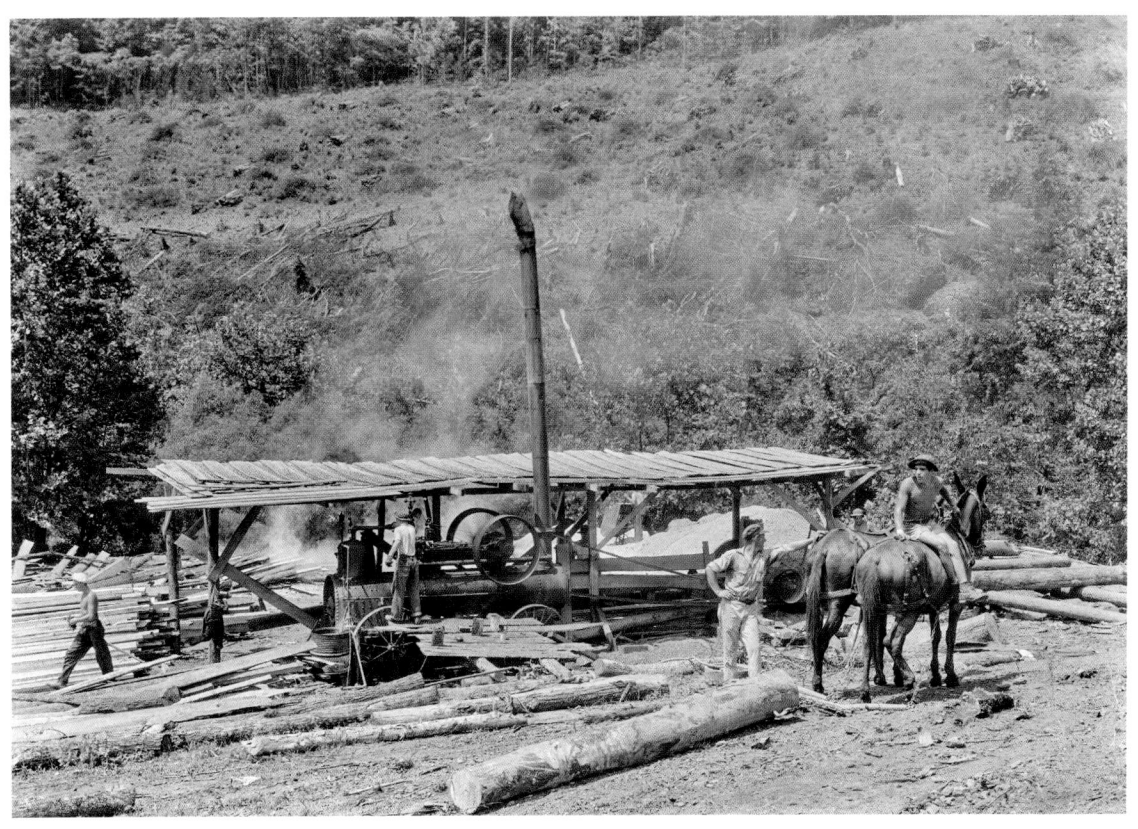

PLATE 42   *Mountain Saw Mill*. [Western North Carolina], 1930s.

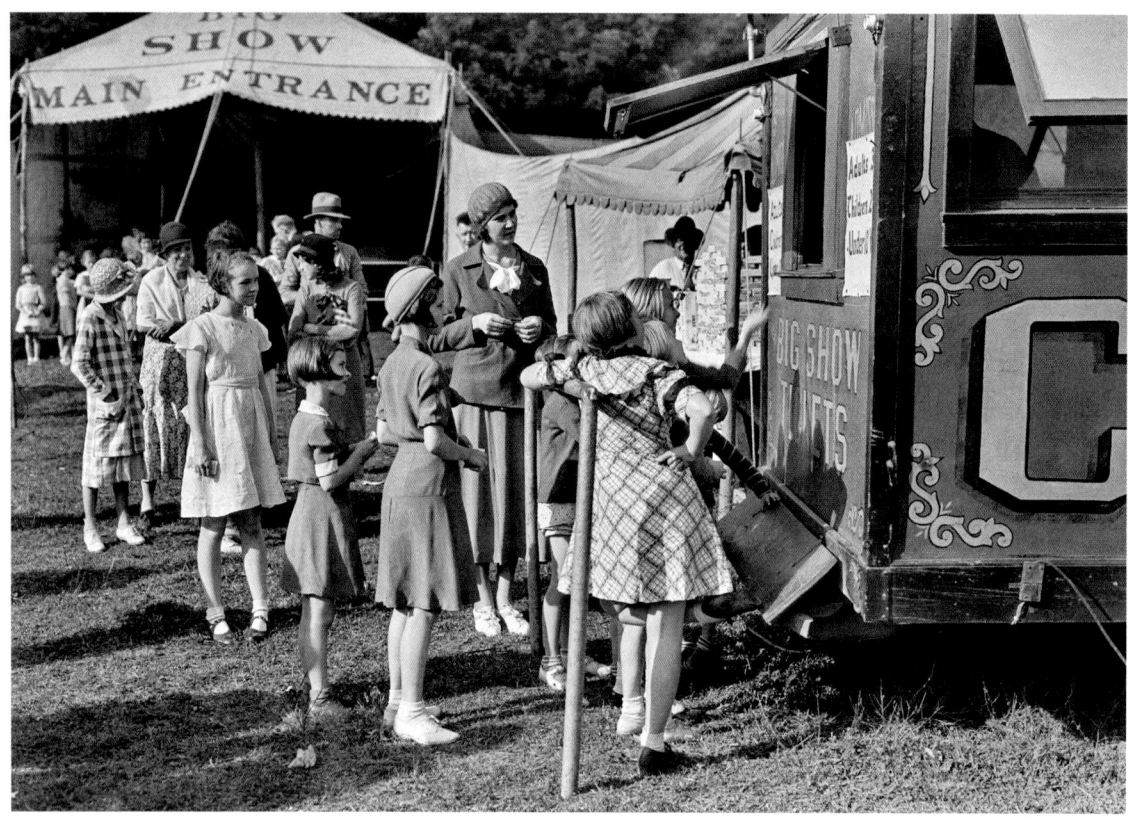

PLATE 43   Ticket buyers at the Mayland Fair. Spruce Pine, North Carolina, ca. 1934.

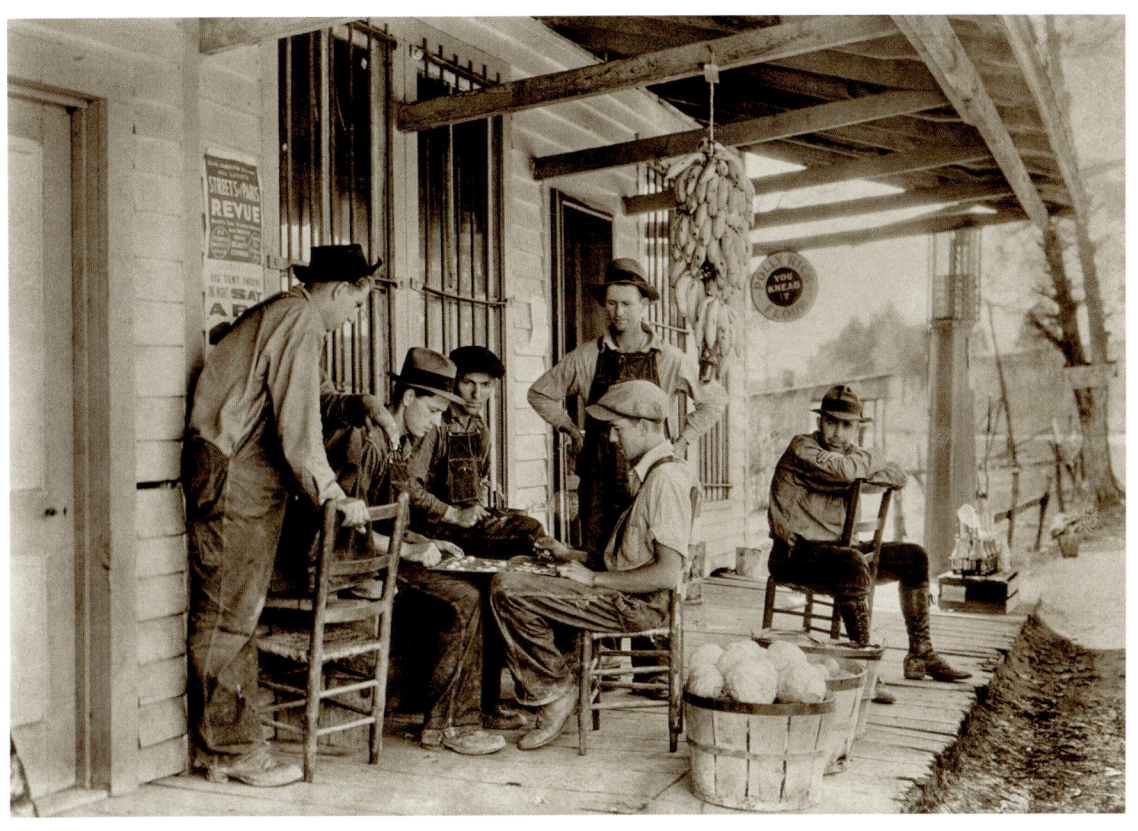

PLATE 44   Checker players at a store. Vicinity of Sevierville, Tennessee, 1930s.

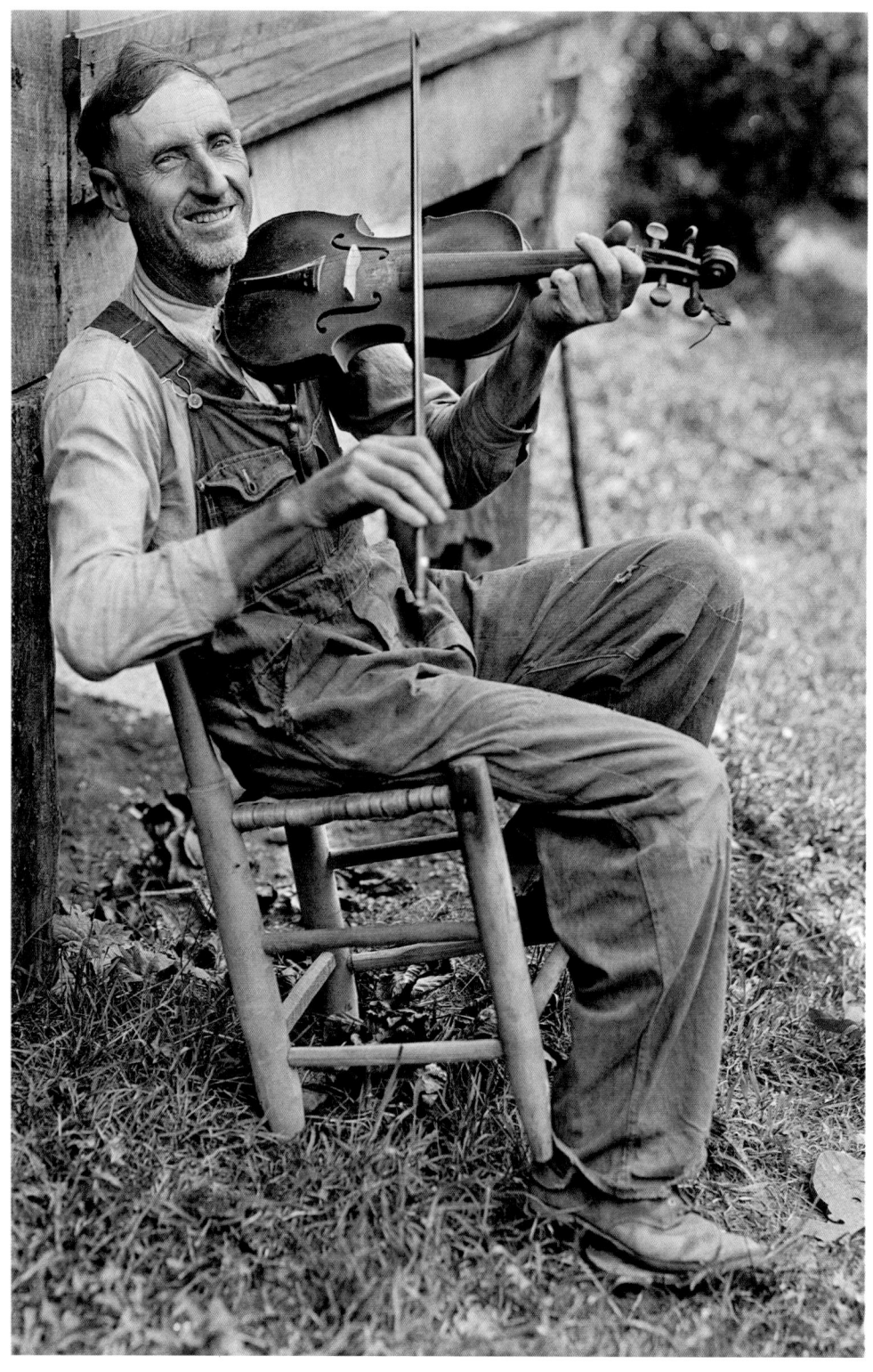

PLATE 45 *Mr. Hoppas Fiddling.* Doc Hoppas. Penland, North Carolina, 1930s.

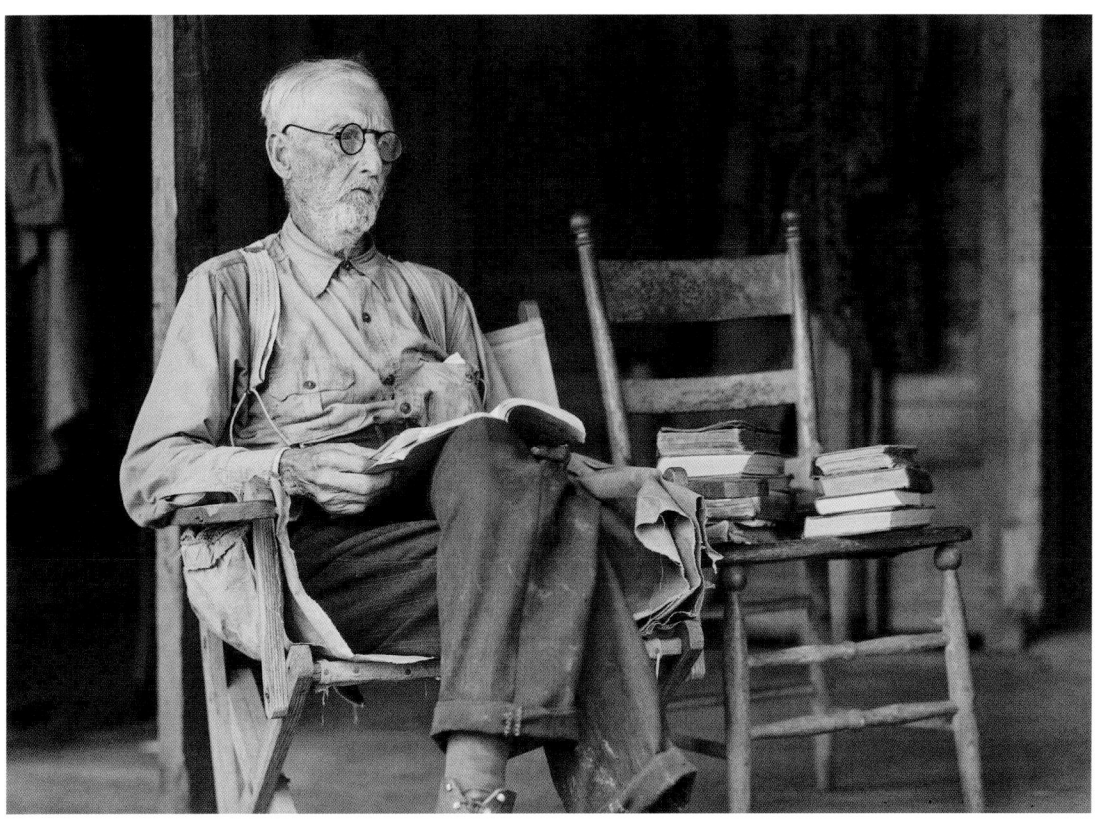

PLATE 46   Zack McHone with his books. Spruce Pine, North Carolina, ca. 1934.

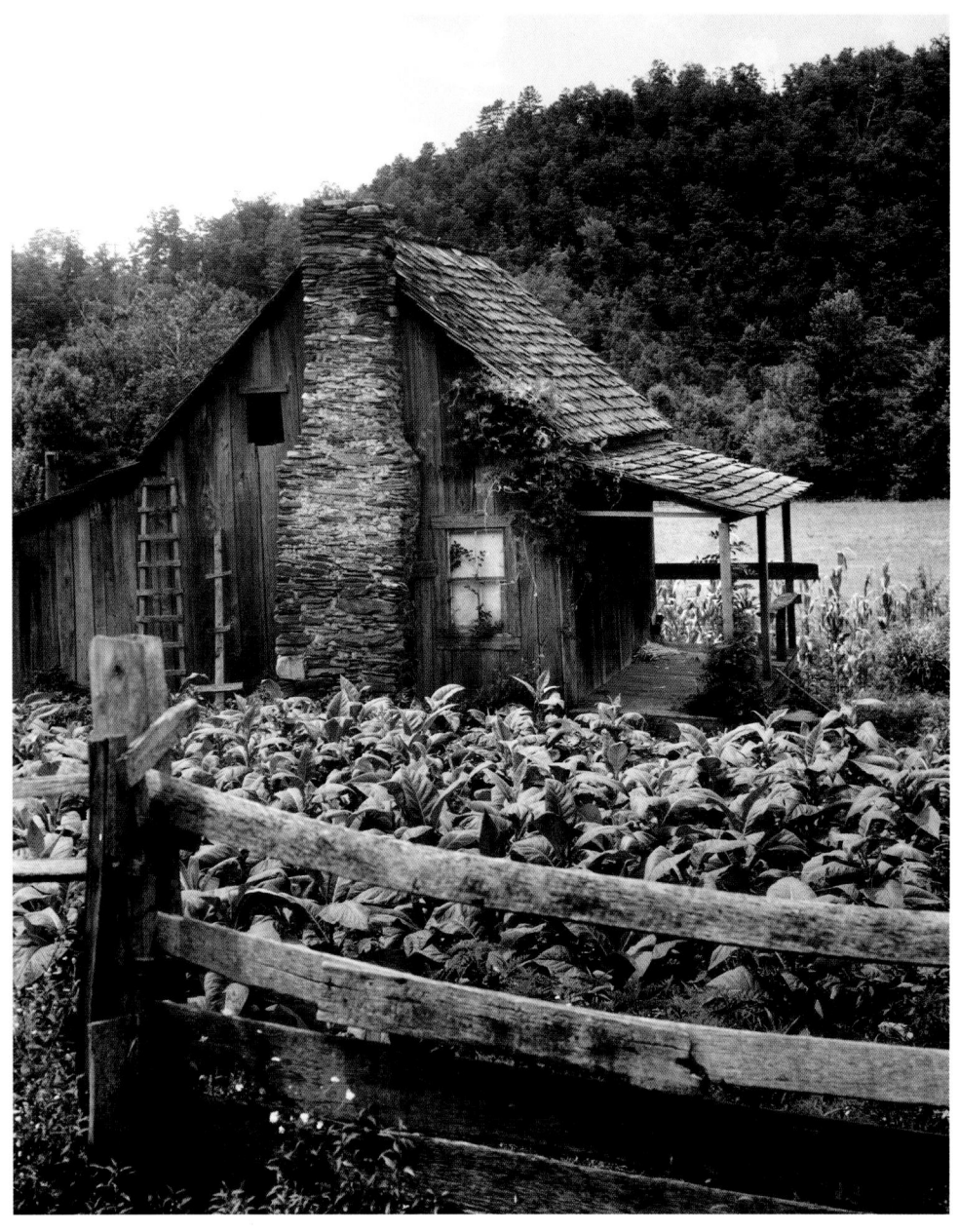

PLATE 47   Abandoned cabin. [Western North Carolina], 1930s.

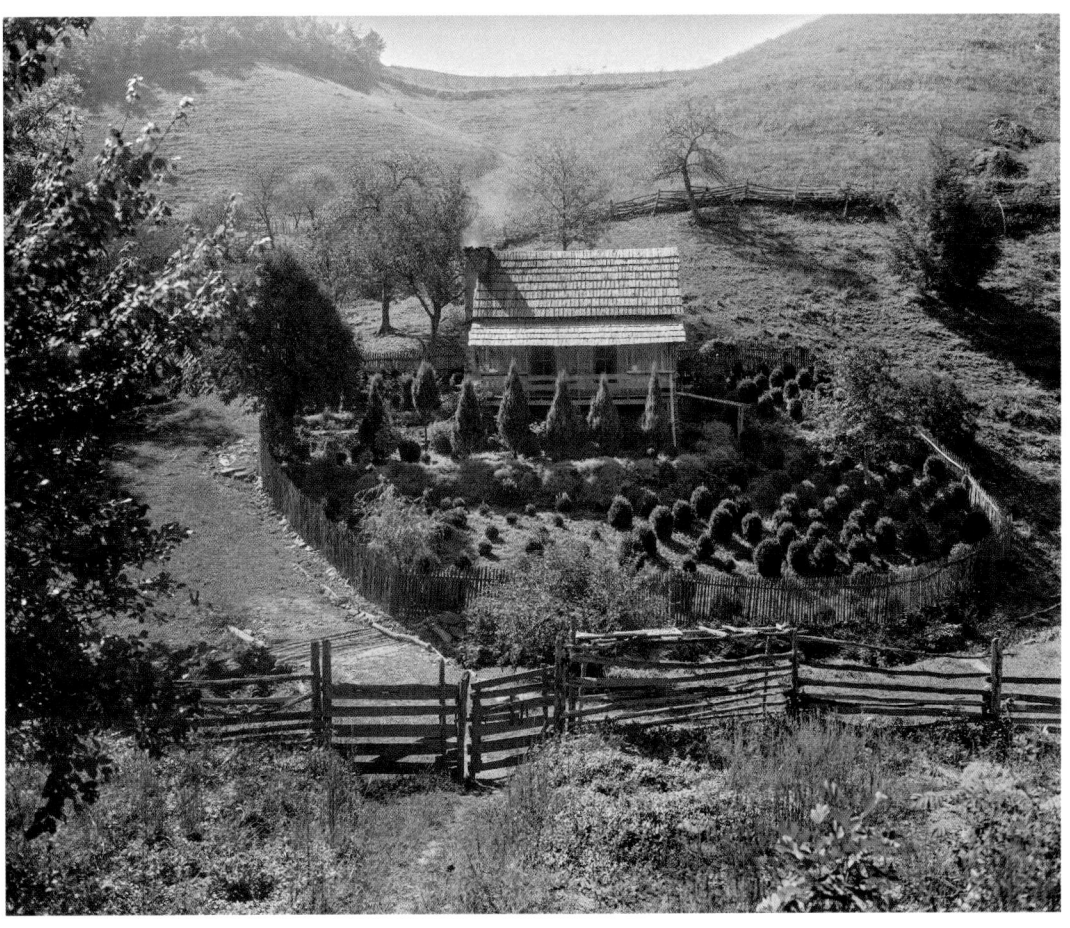

PLATE 48 "Boxwoods and Junipers." Swain County, North Carolina, ca. 1940.

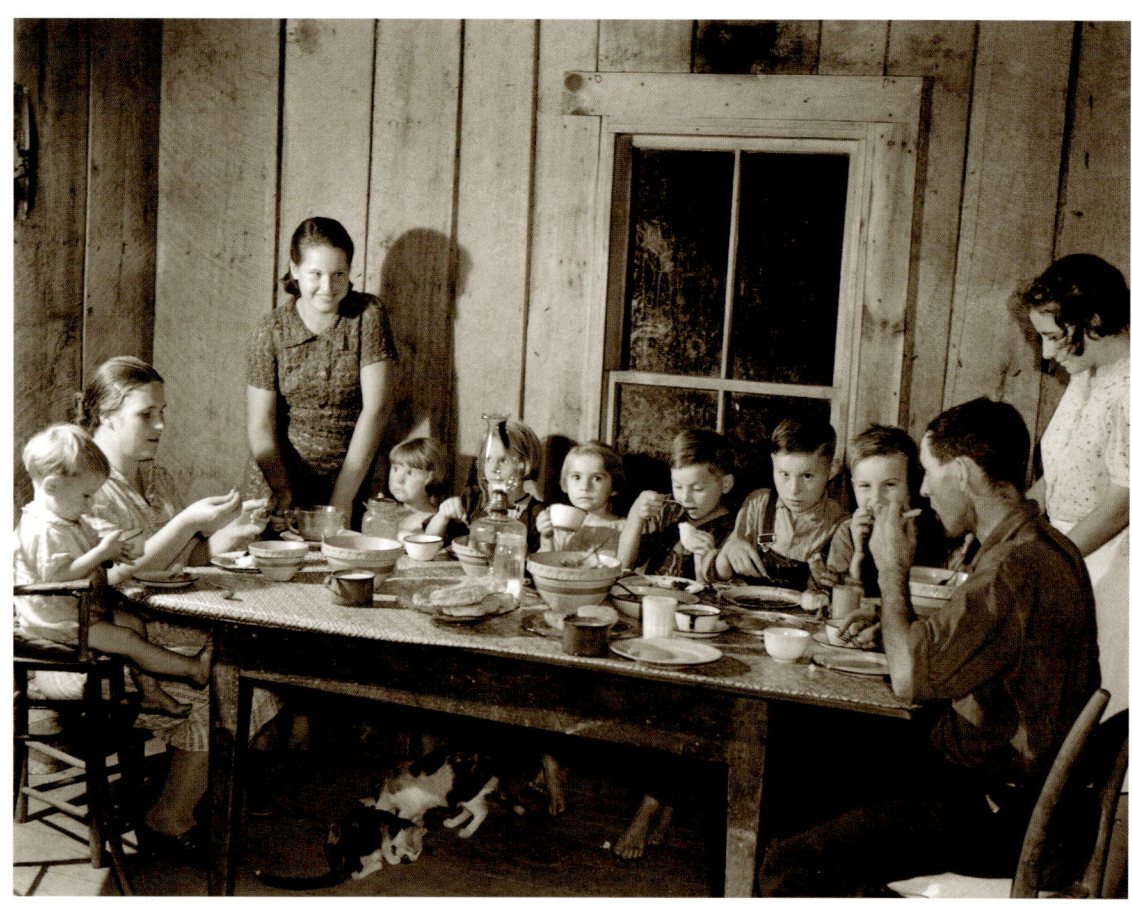

PLATE 49   A family at dinner. Swain County, North Carolina, ca. 1940.

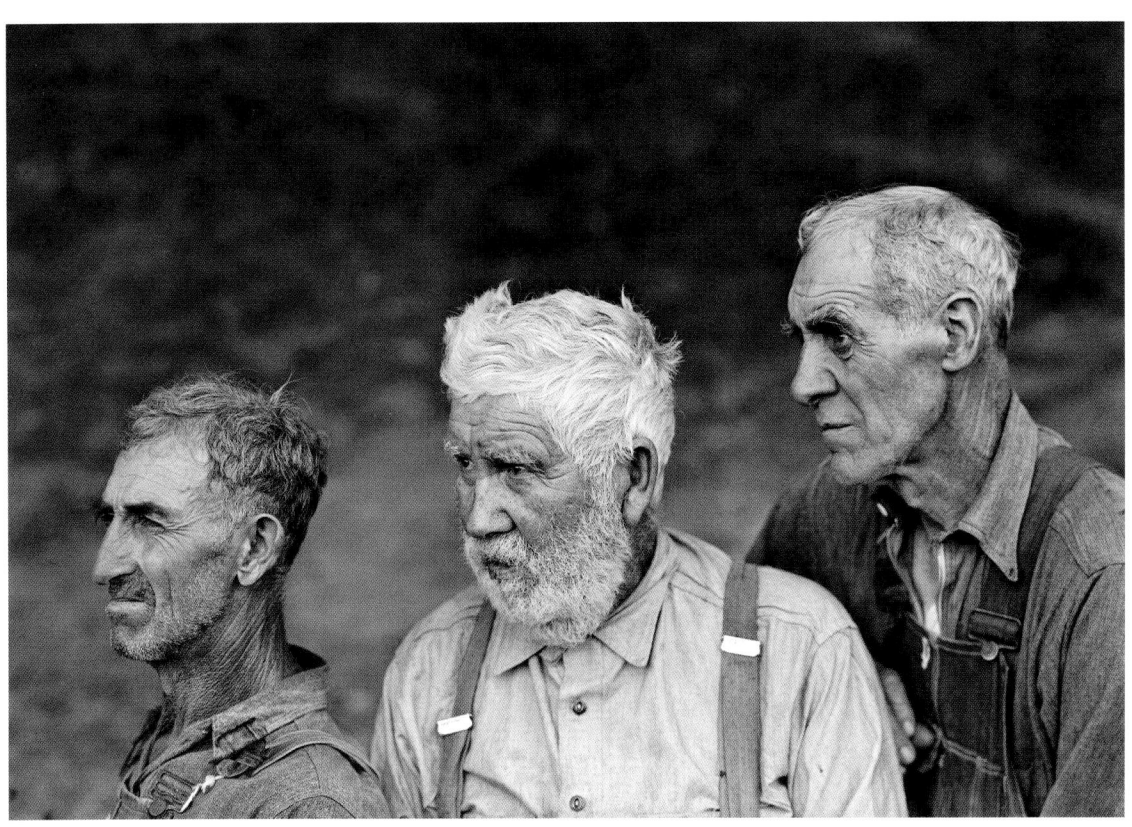

PLATE 50   *Horse Traders.* Bryson City, North Carolina, 1930s.

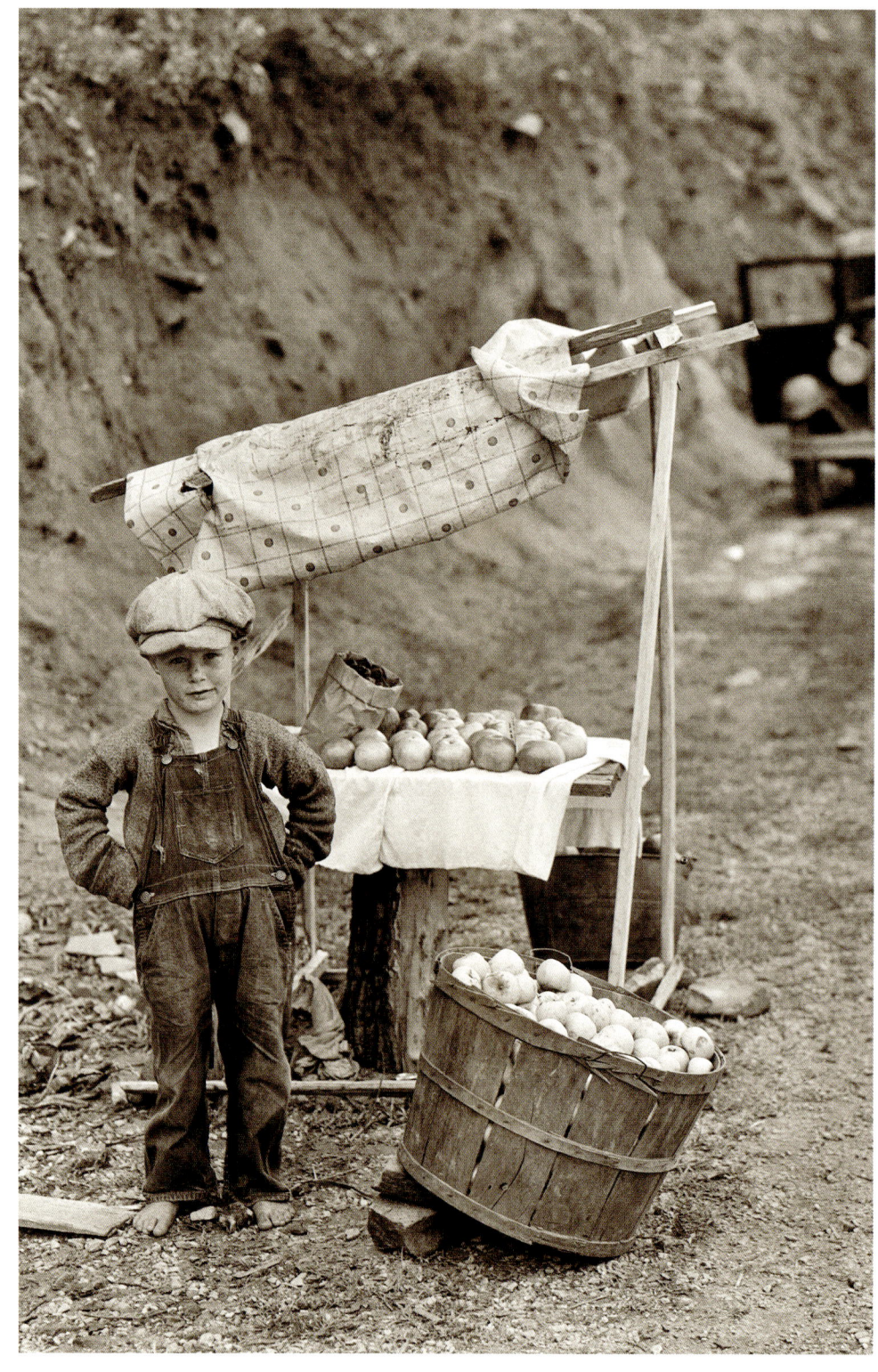

PLATE 51 A boy selling apples beside the road. [Western North Carolina], 1930s.

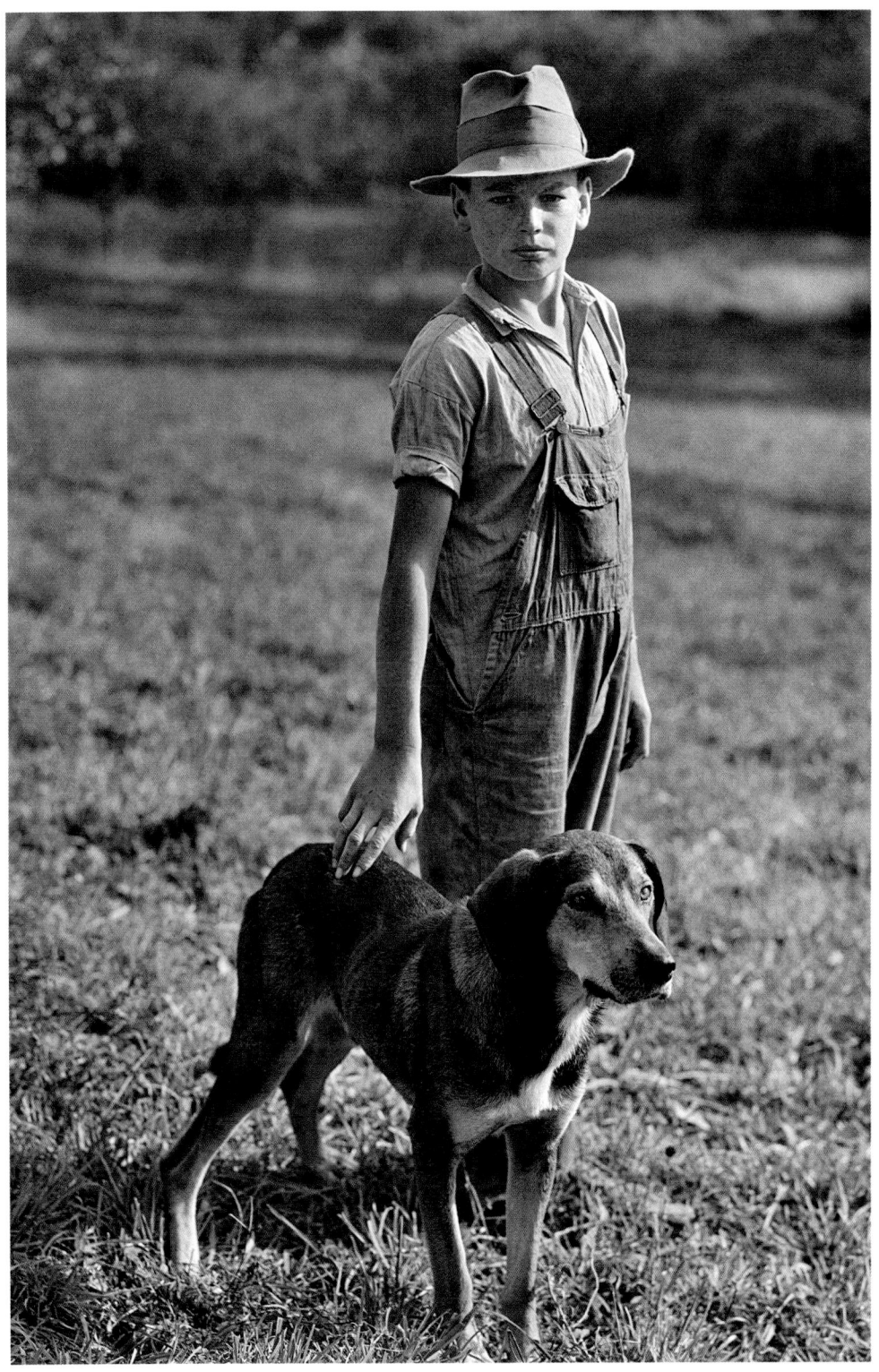

PLATE 52   A boy and his dog. Mitchell or Yancey County, North Carolina, ca. 1934.

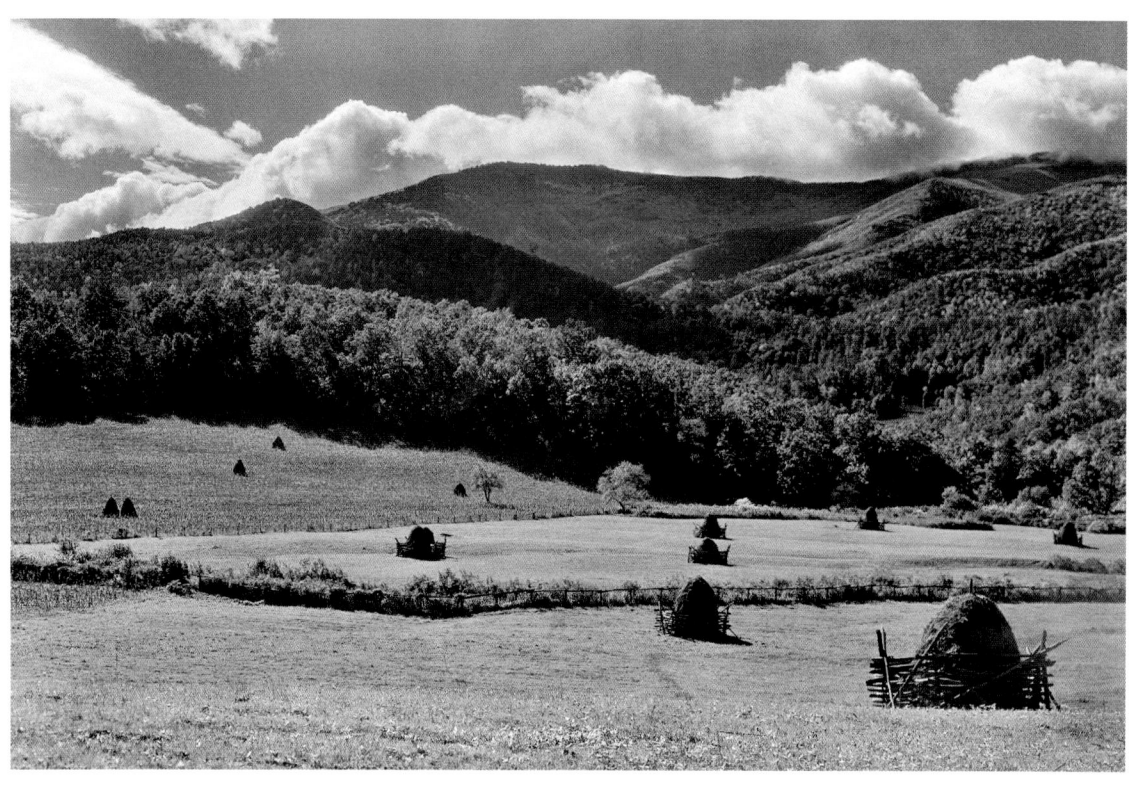

PLATE 53   Haystacks at Celo Mountain. Yancey County, North Carolina, 1930s.

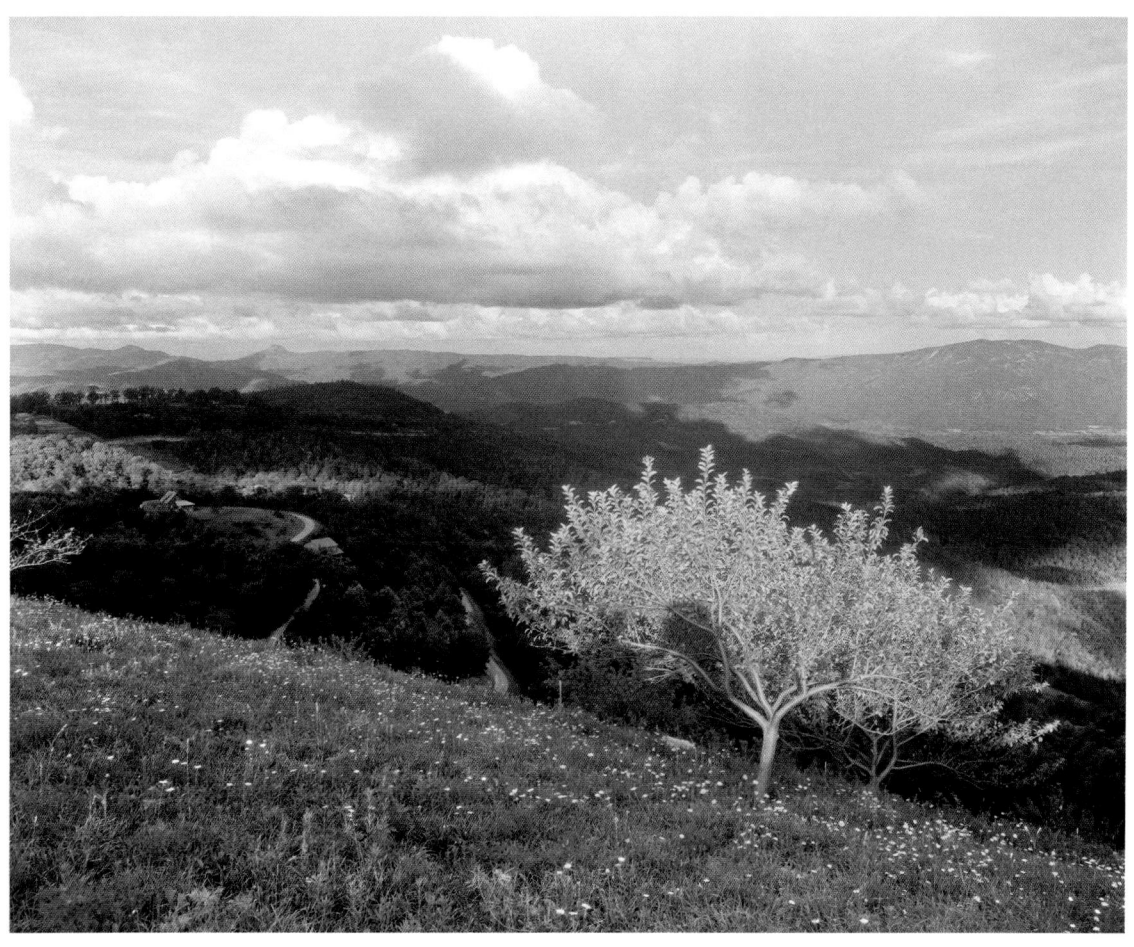

PLATE 54   Apple tree on Clarkson's Knob. Little Switzerland, North Carolina, 1930s.

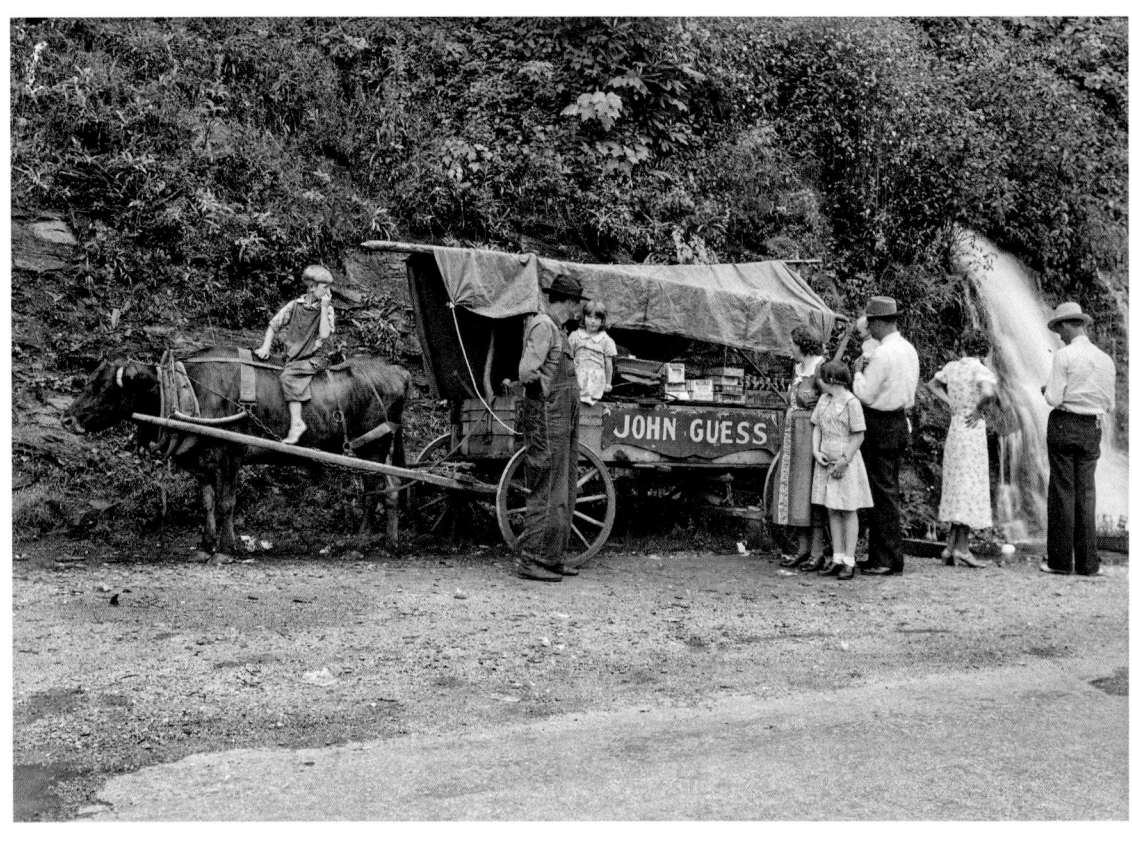

PLATE 55   John Guess, peddler. [Western North Carolina], 1930s.

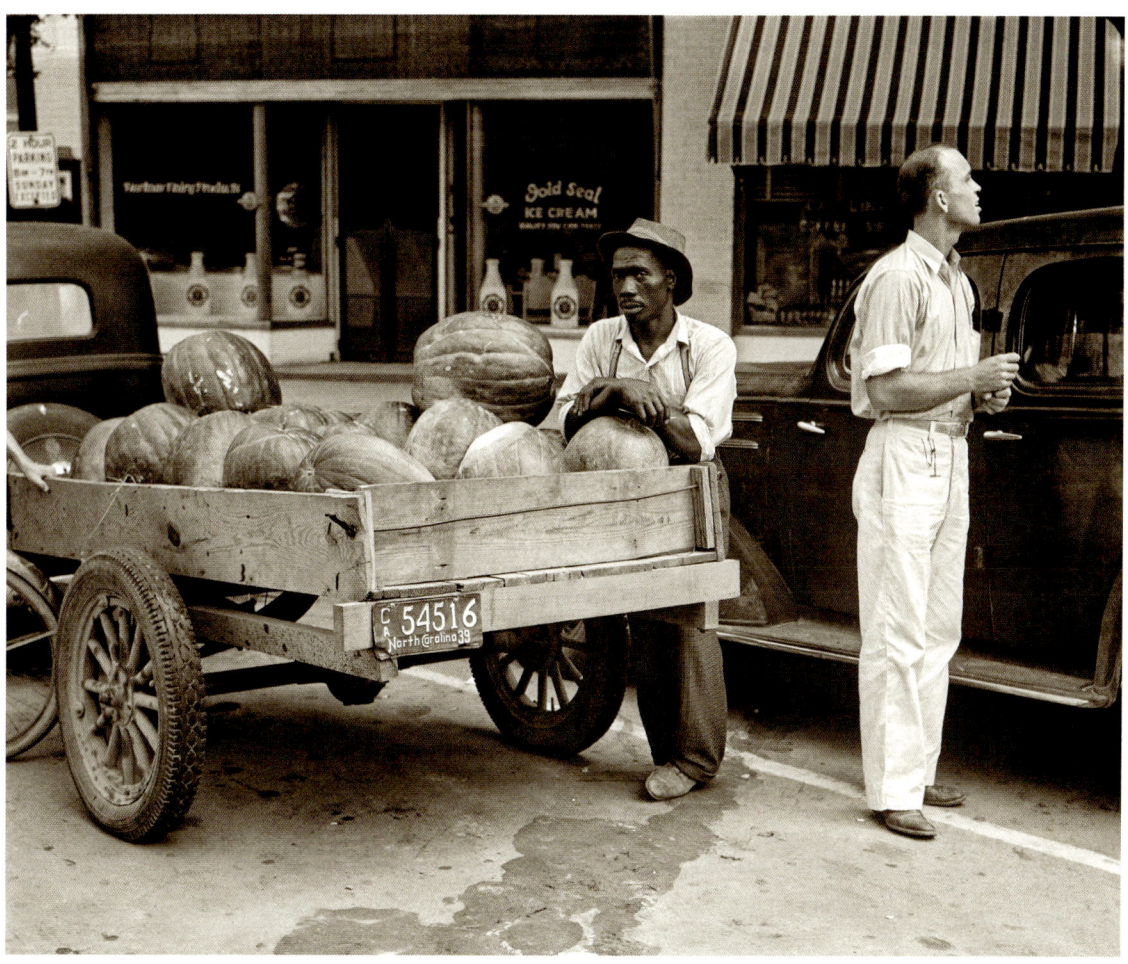

PLATE 56   Franklin Street. Chapel Hill, North Carolina, 1939.

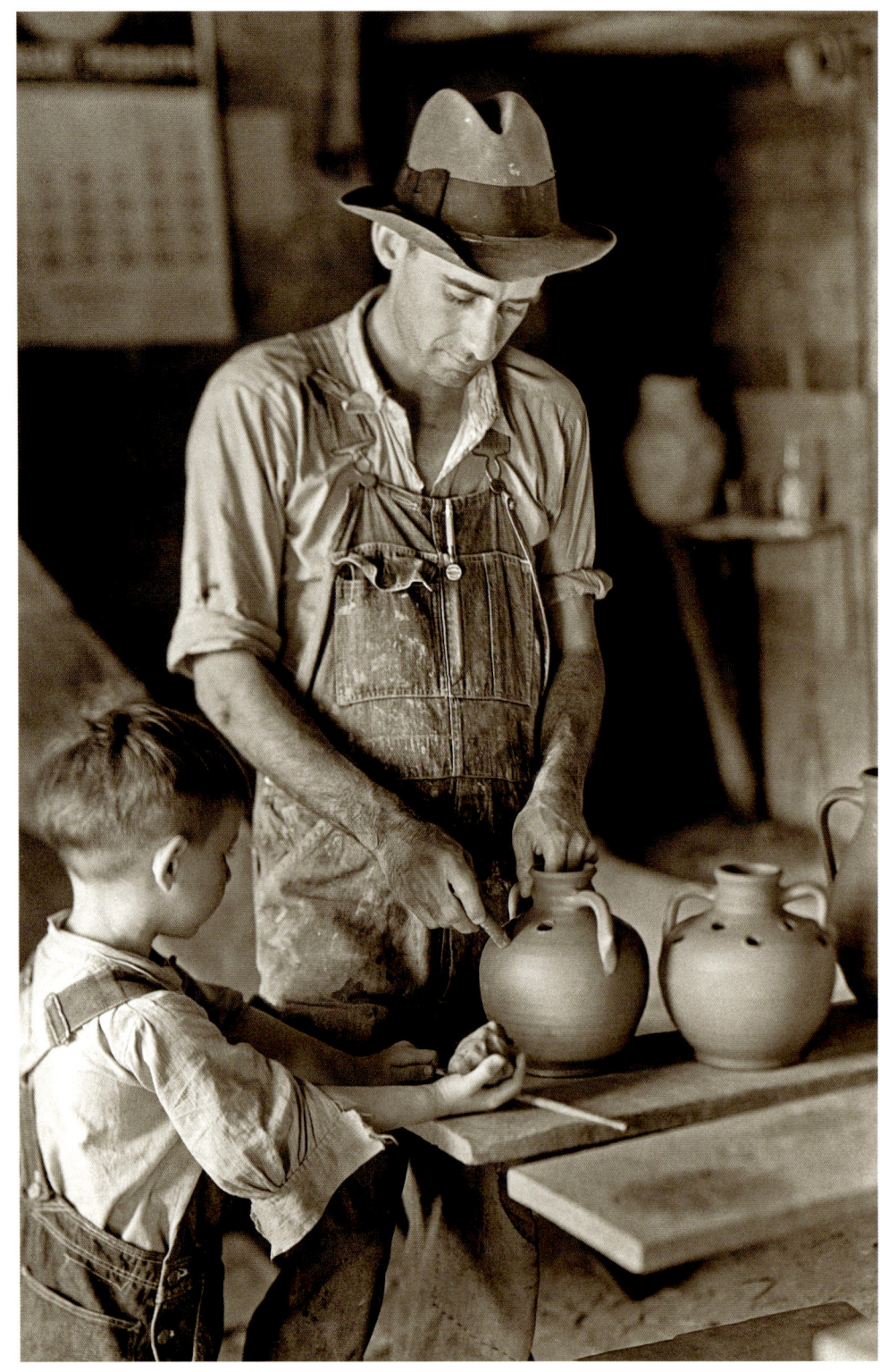

PLATE 57   Waymon Cole making a vase. Steeds, North Carolina, 1930s.

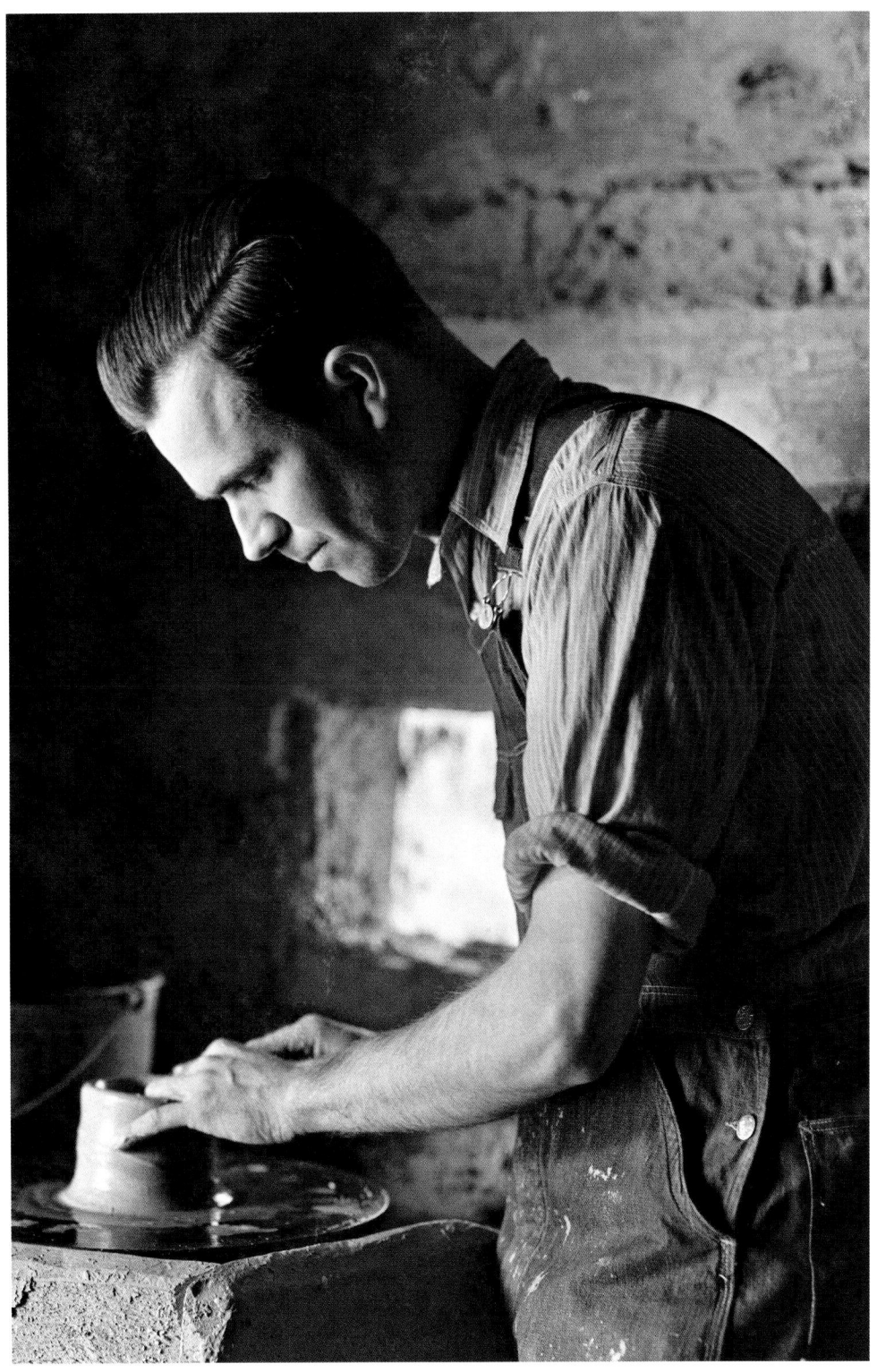

PLATE 58   *Turning Hands.* Ben Owen. Jugtown, North Carolina, 1930s.

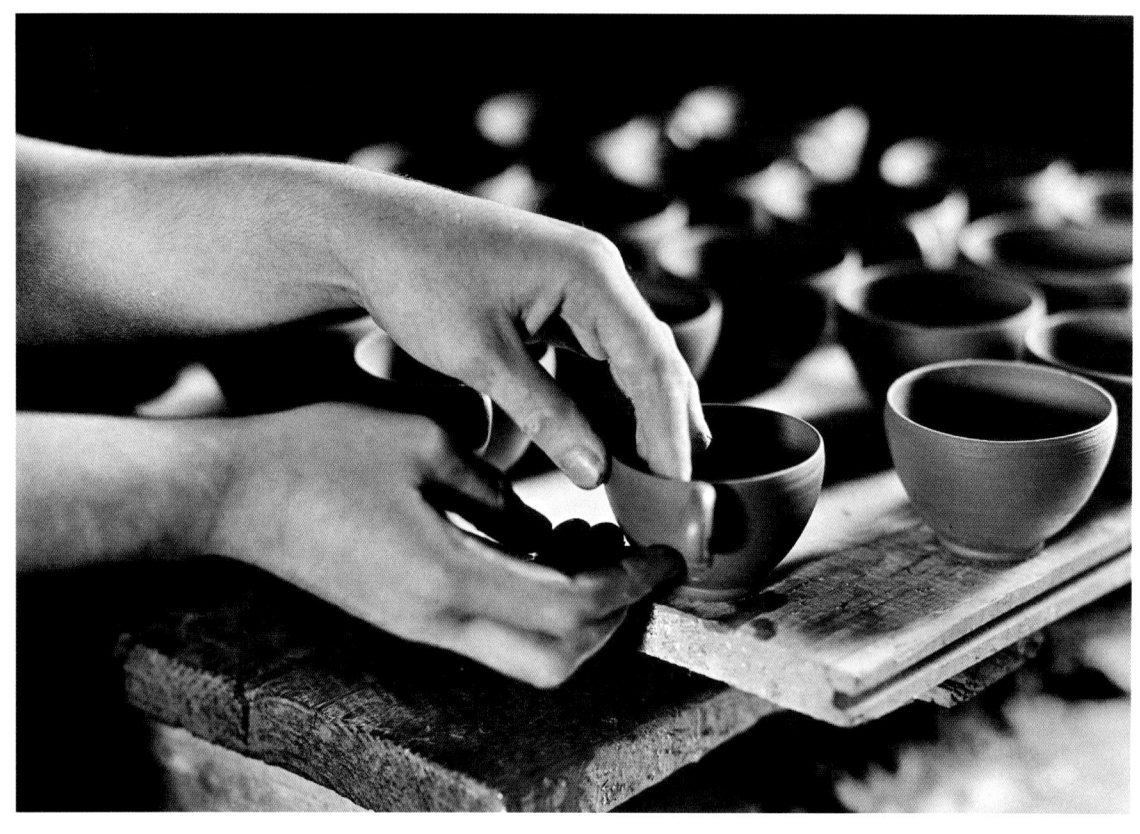

PLATE 59   The hands of Nell Cole Graves. Steeds, North Carolina, 1930s.

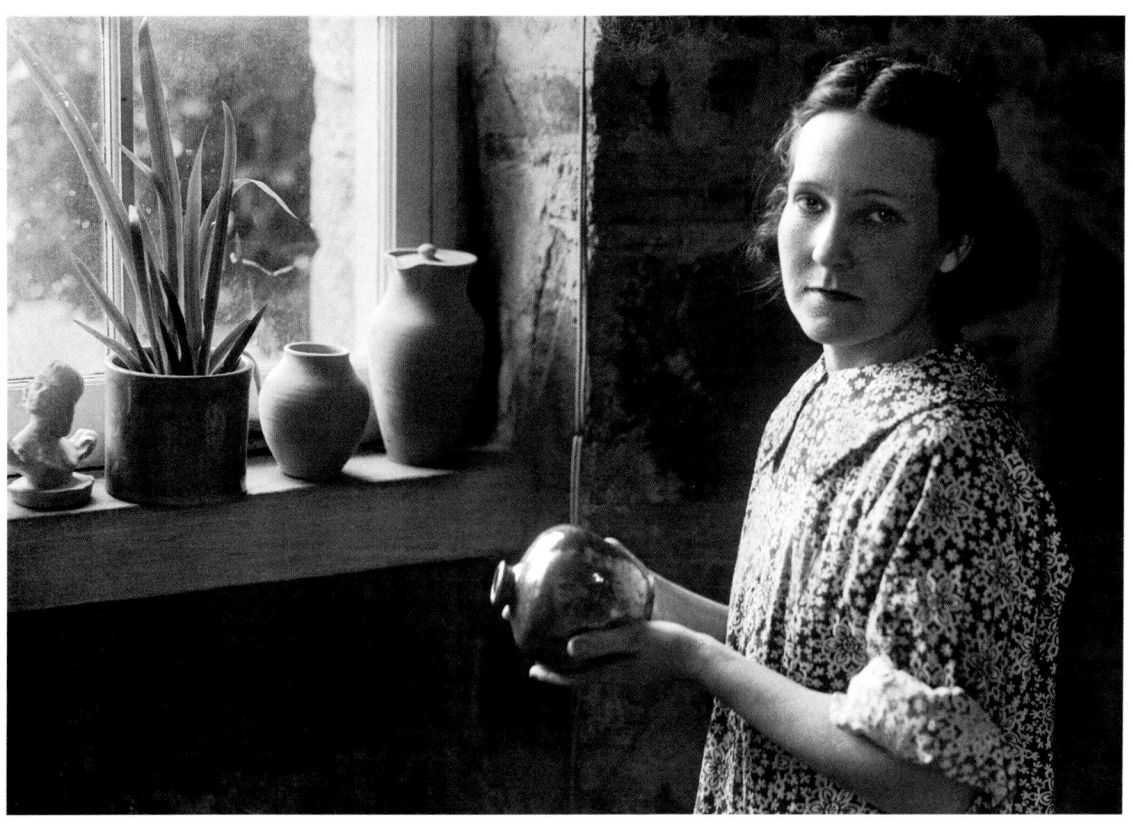

PLATE 60   Edith Harwell. Mecklenburg County, North Carolina, 1930s.

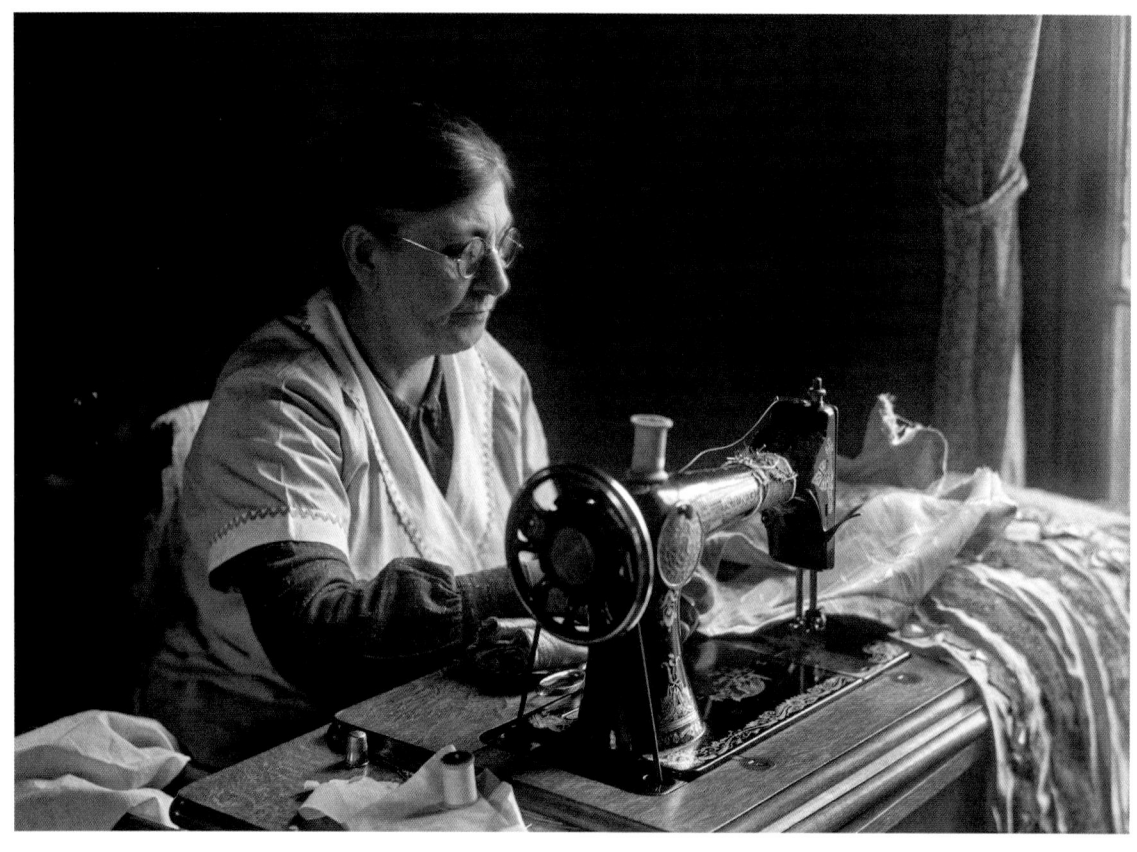

PLATE 61   Costume maker for *The Lost Colony* drama. Manteo, North Carolina, ca. 1937.

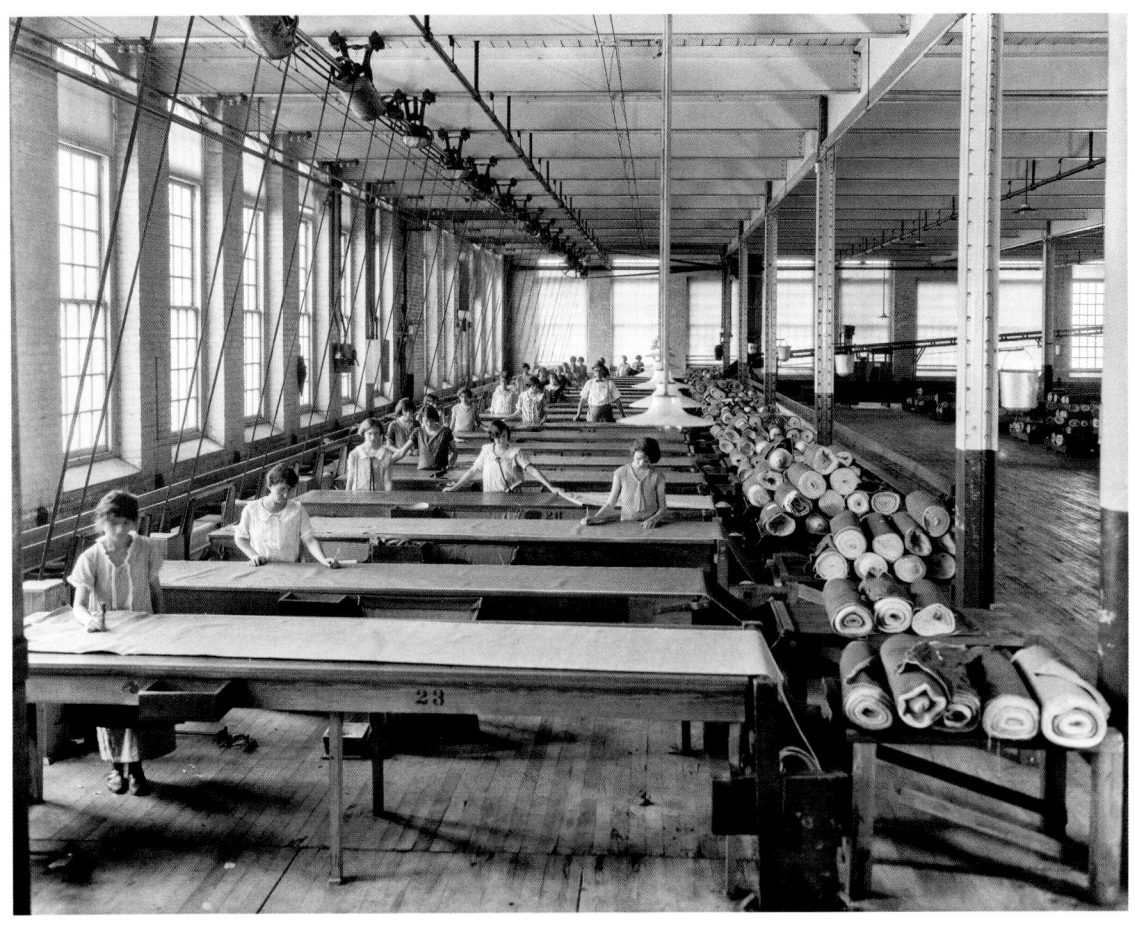

PLATE 62   Cloth inspectors at a textile mill. Greensboro, North Carolina, ca. 1940.

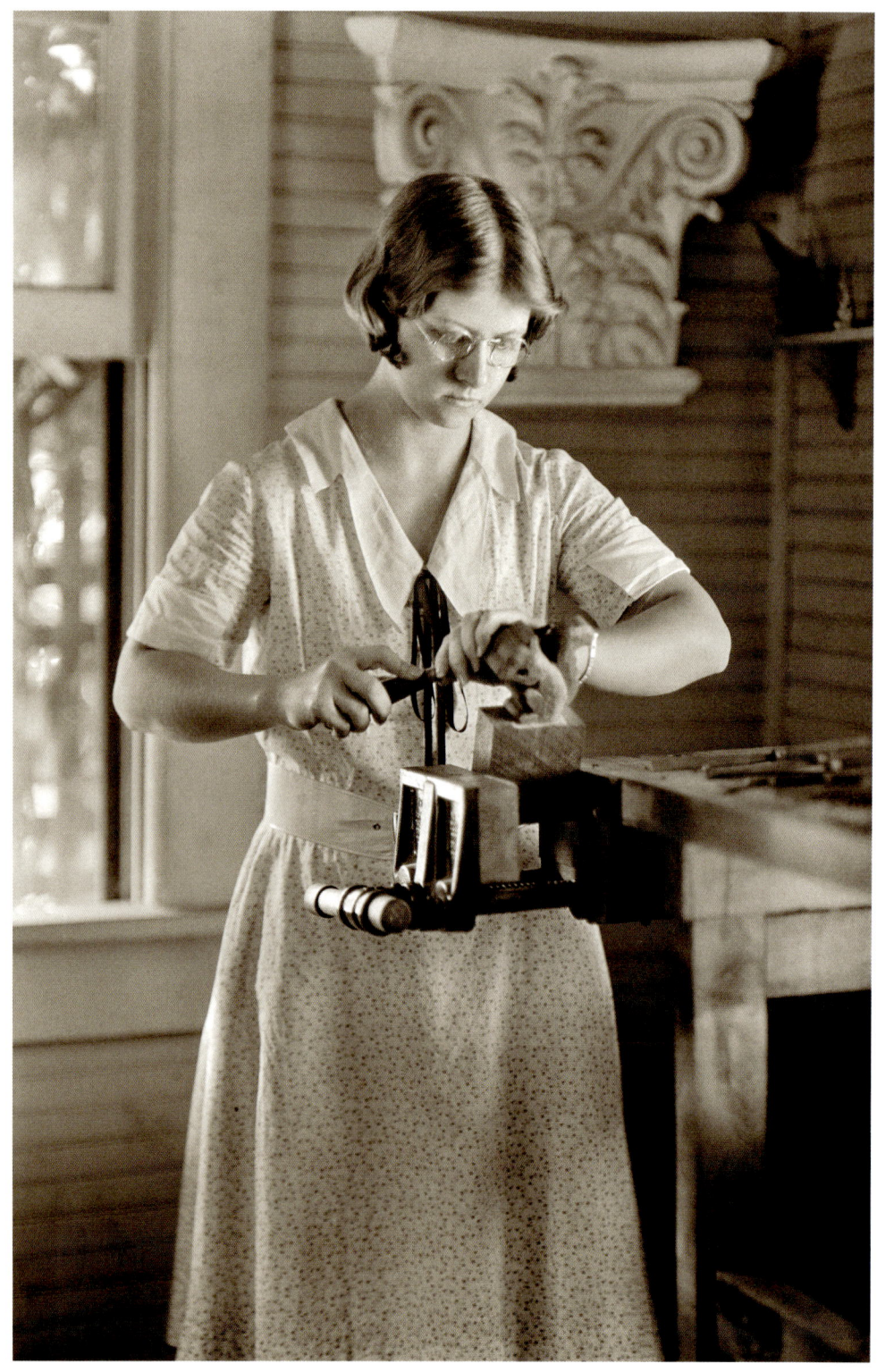

PLATE 63   A toymaker. Tryon, North Carolina, 1930s.

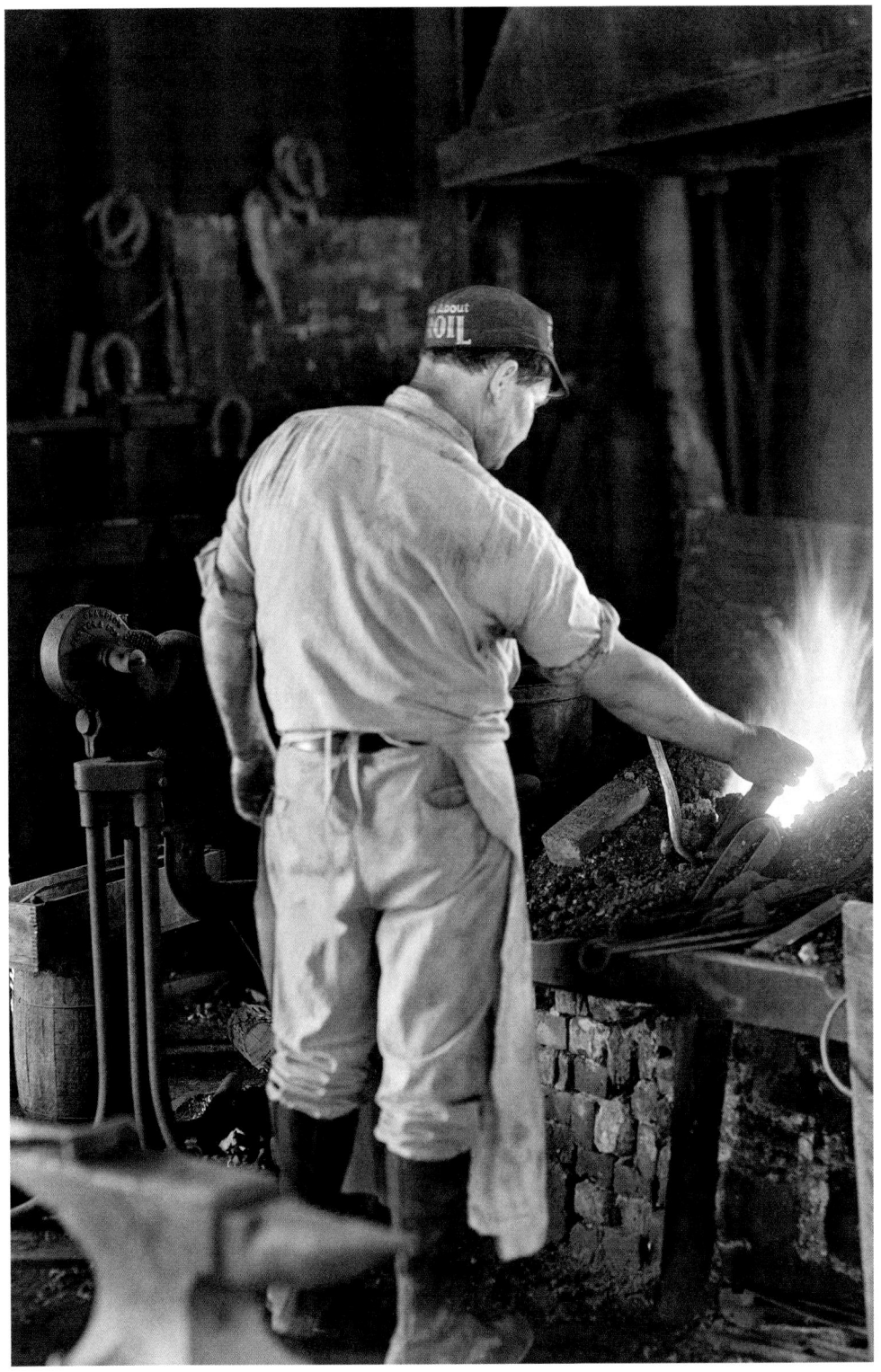

PLATE 64   A blacksmith. Greensboro, North Carolina, 1930s.

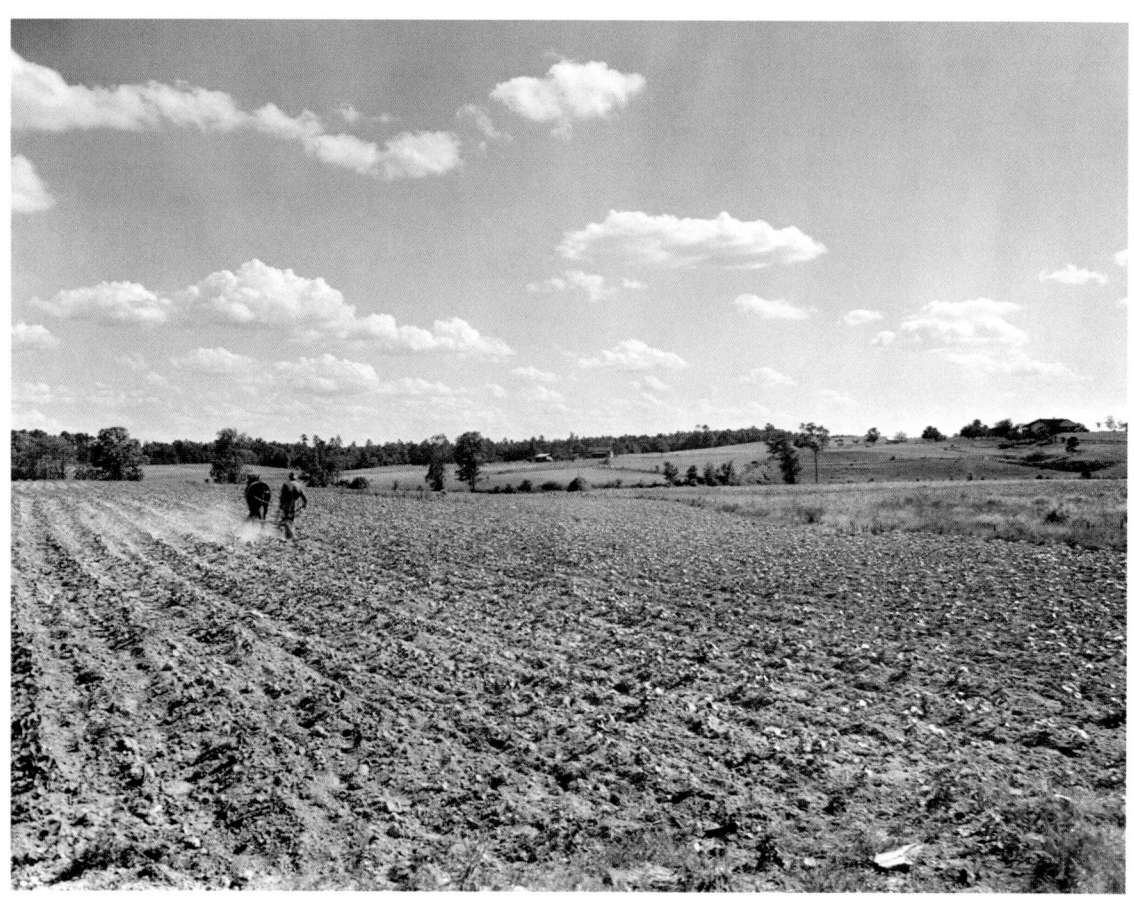

PLATE 65   A farmer plowing. [Eastern North Carolina], 1930s.

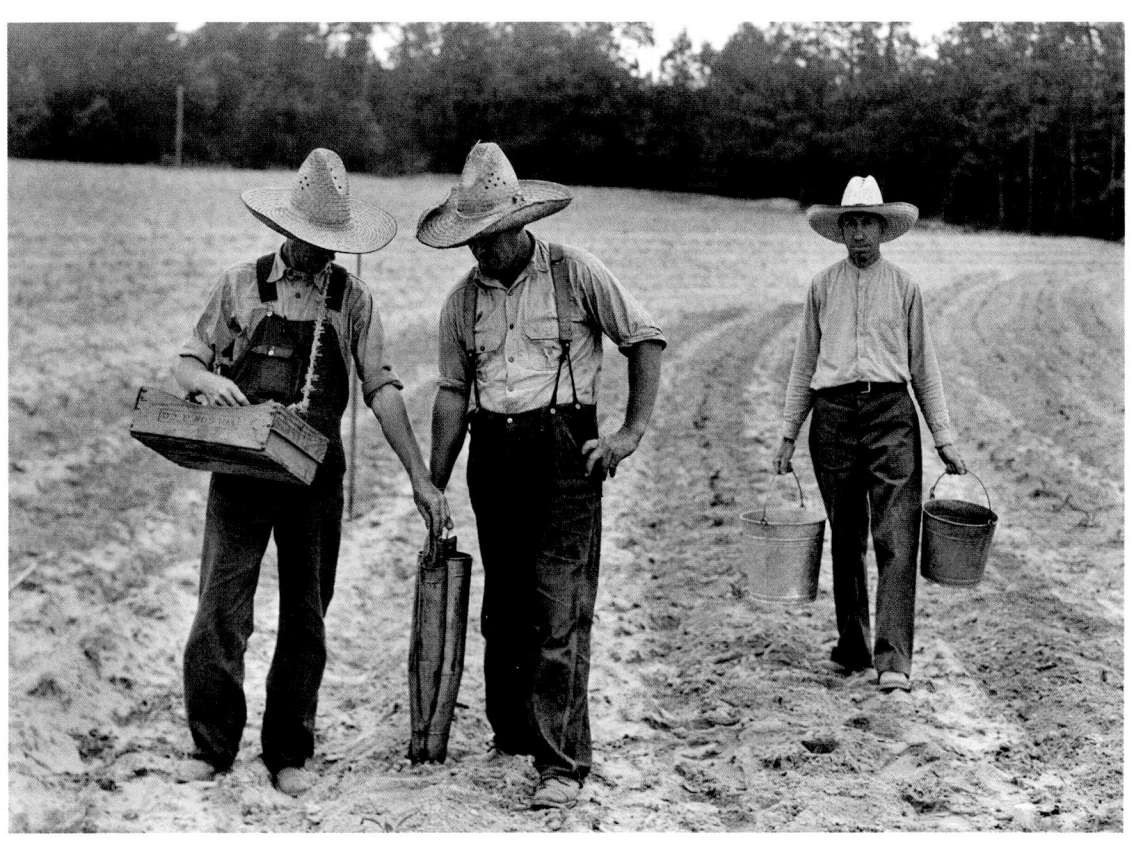

PLATE 66 Tobacco planters. Durham County, North Carolina, 1930s.

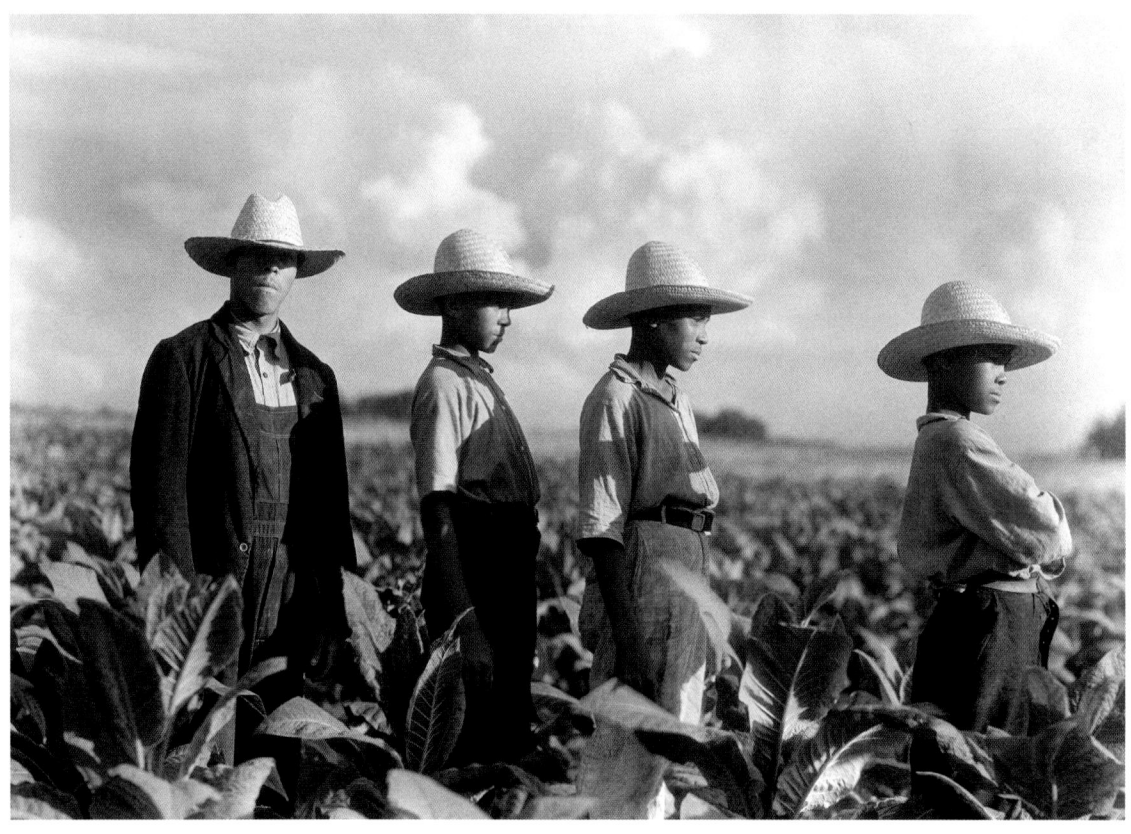

PLATE 67   A tobacco farmer and his three sons. [North Carolina], 1930s.

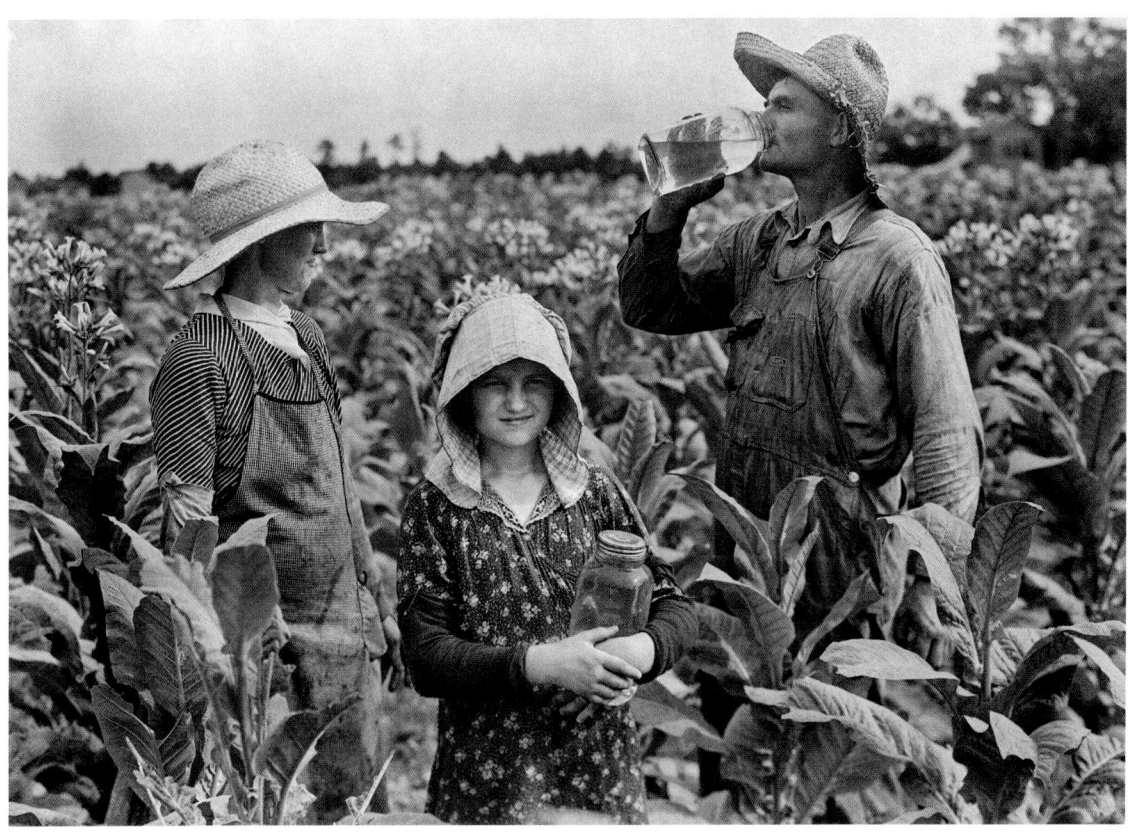

PLATE 68   A tobacco farmer pausing for water. [North Carolina], 1930s.

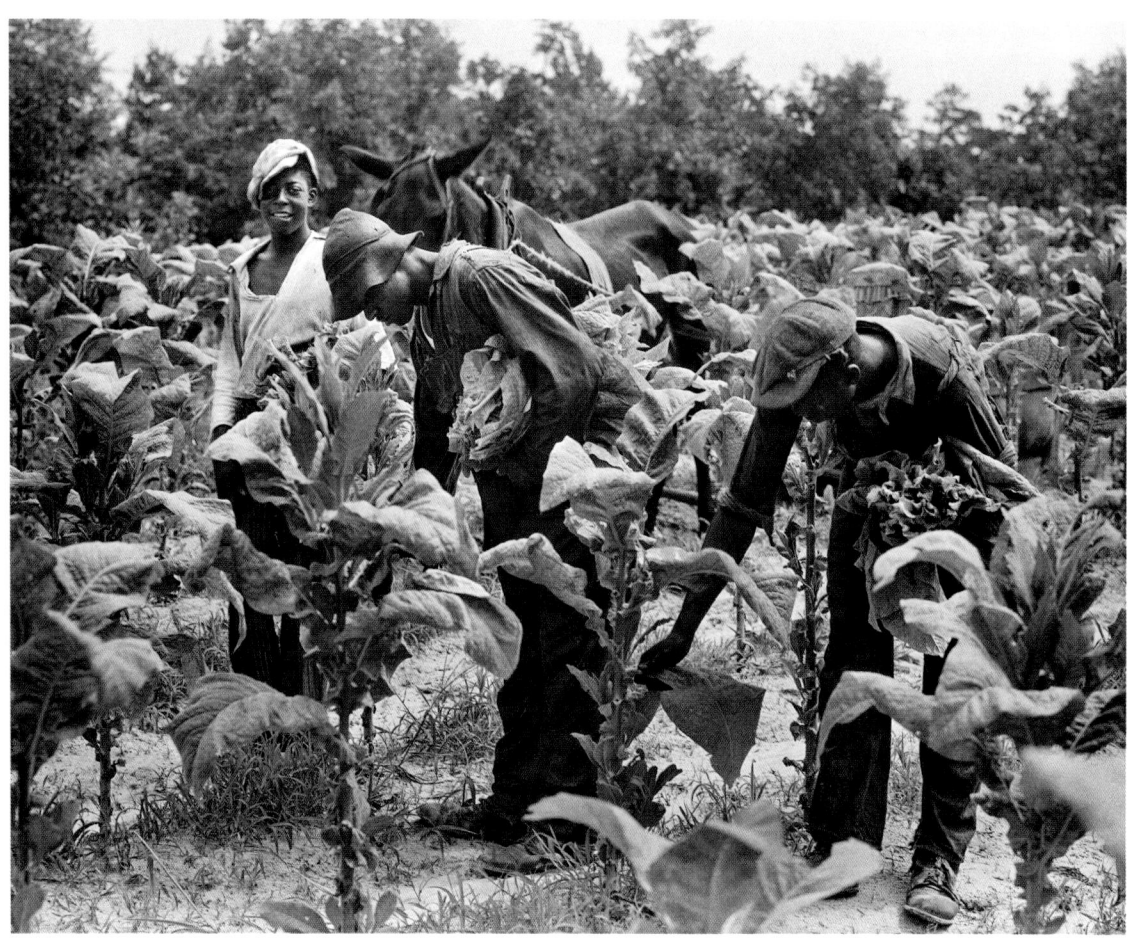

PLATE 69   Harvesting tobacco. [North Carolina], 1930s.

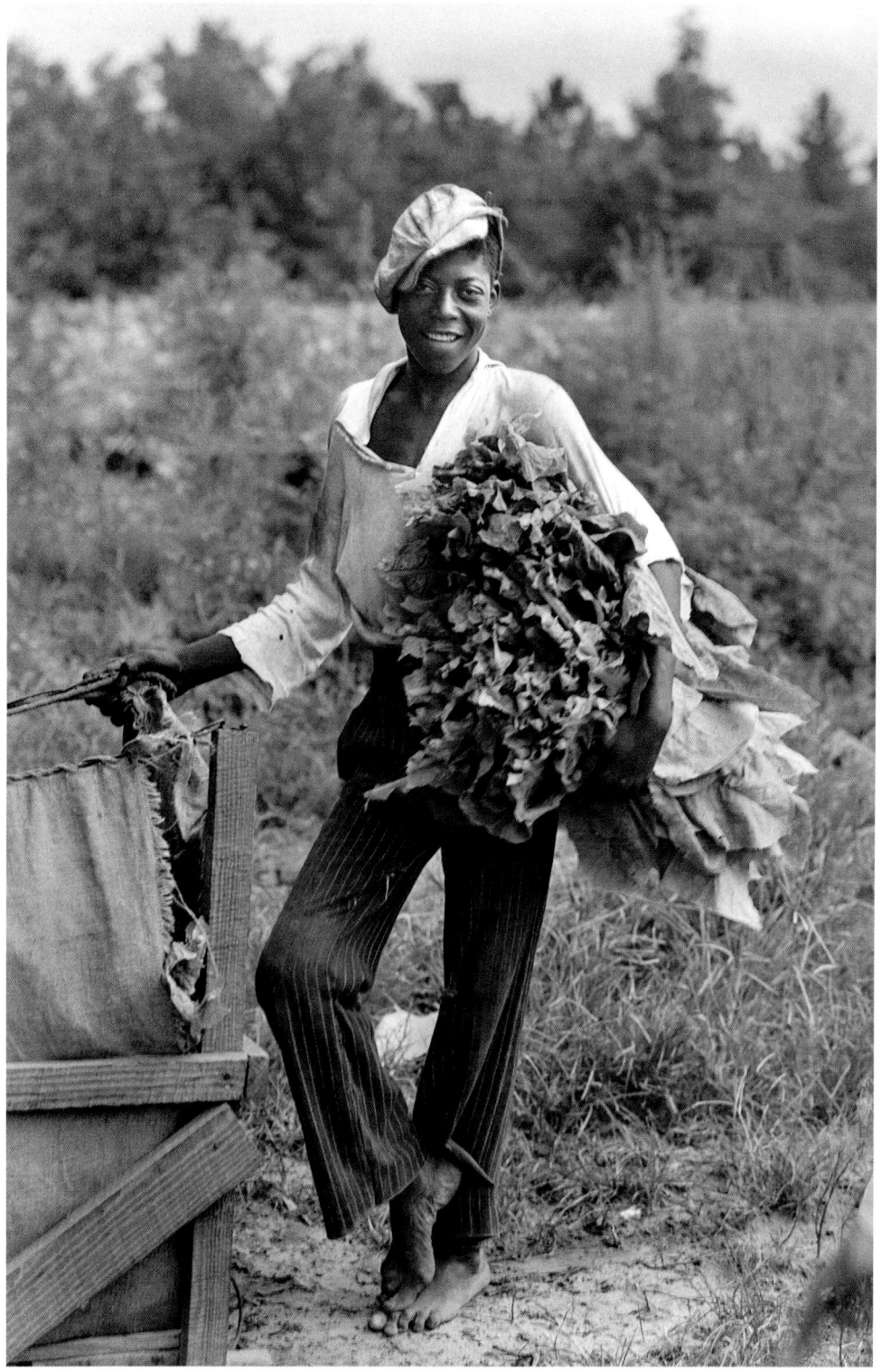

PLATE 70   A tobacco laborer. [North Carolina], 1930s.

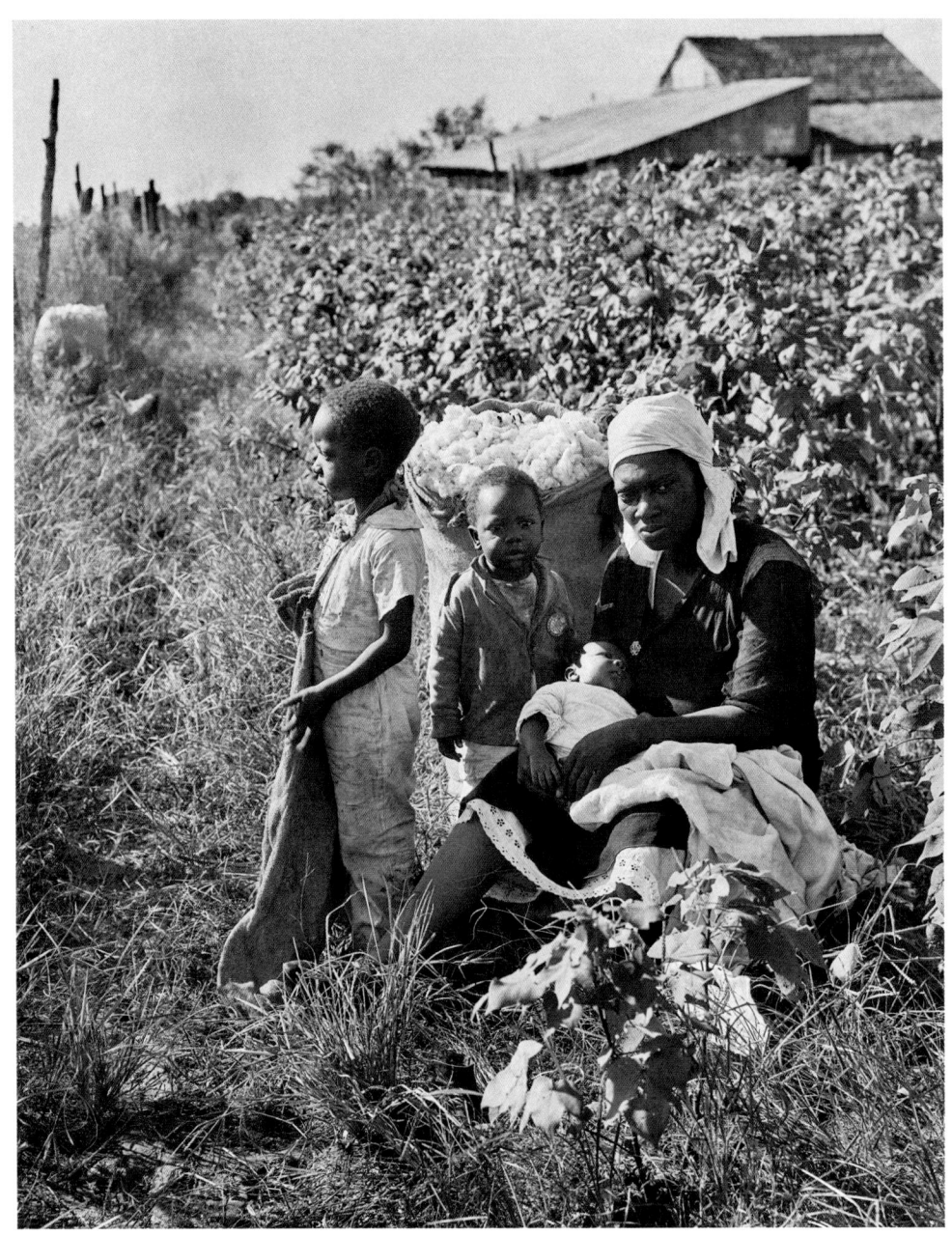

PLATE 71   *A Southern Madonna.* North Carolina, 1930s.

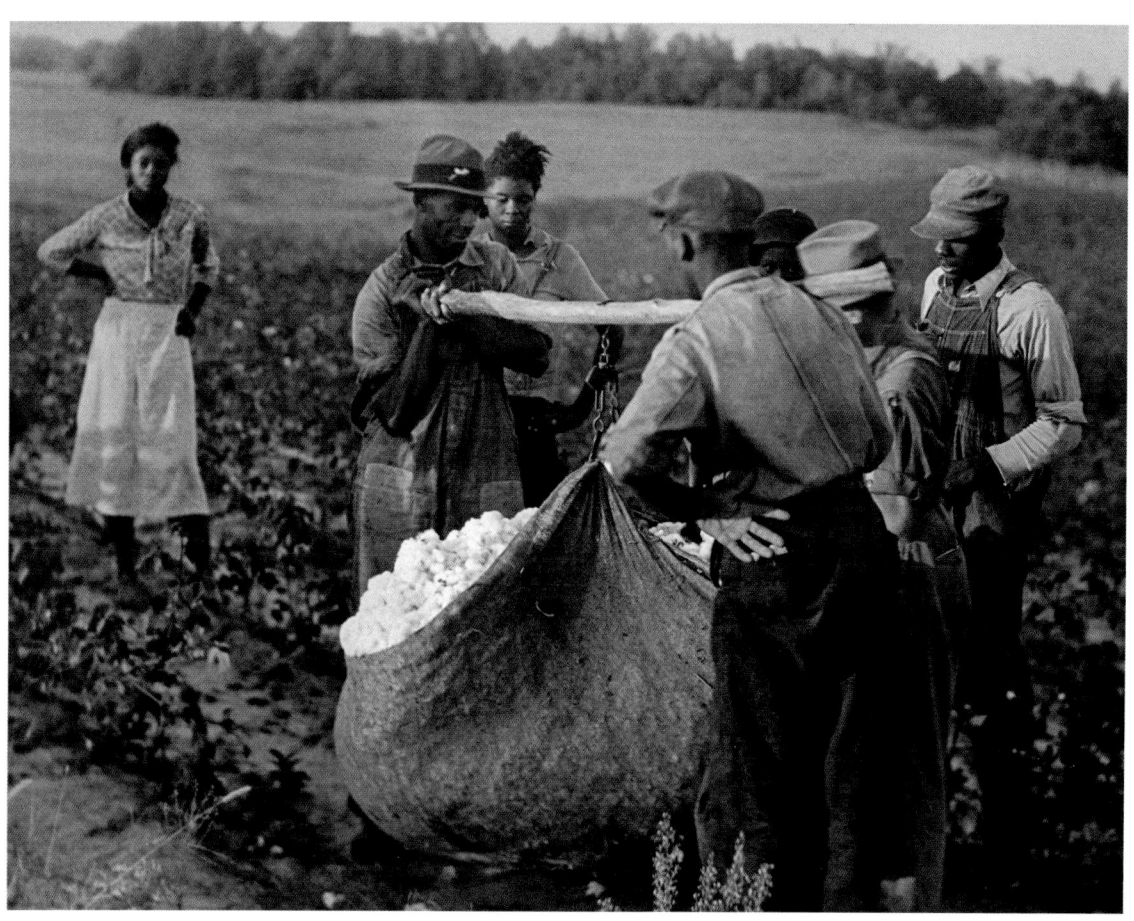

PLATE 72   Weighing cotton. [North Carolina], 1930s.

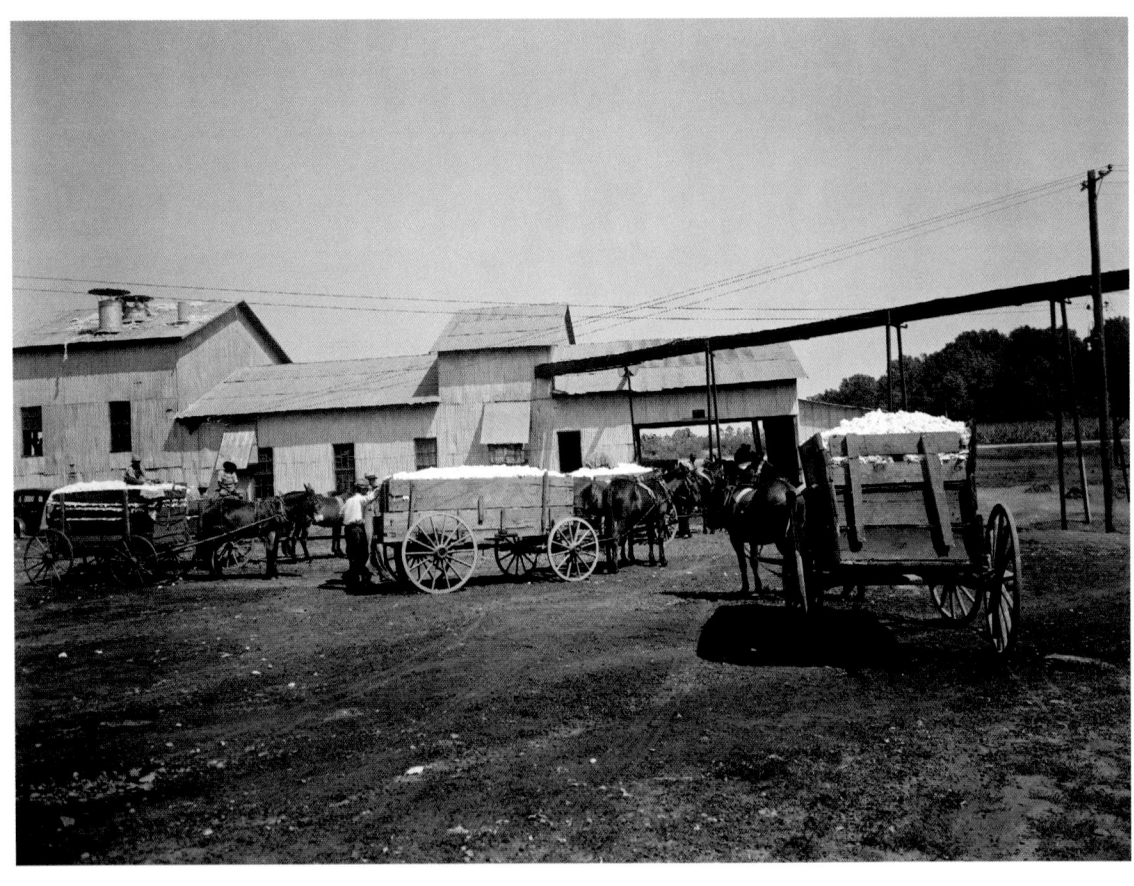

PLATE 73   Farmers waiting in line at a cotton gin. Vicinity of Columbia,
South Carolina, 1930s.

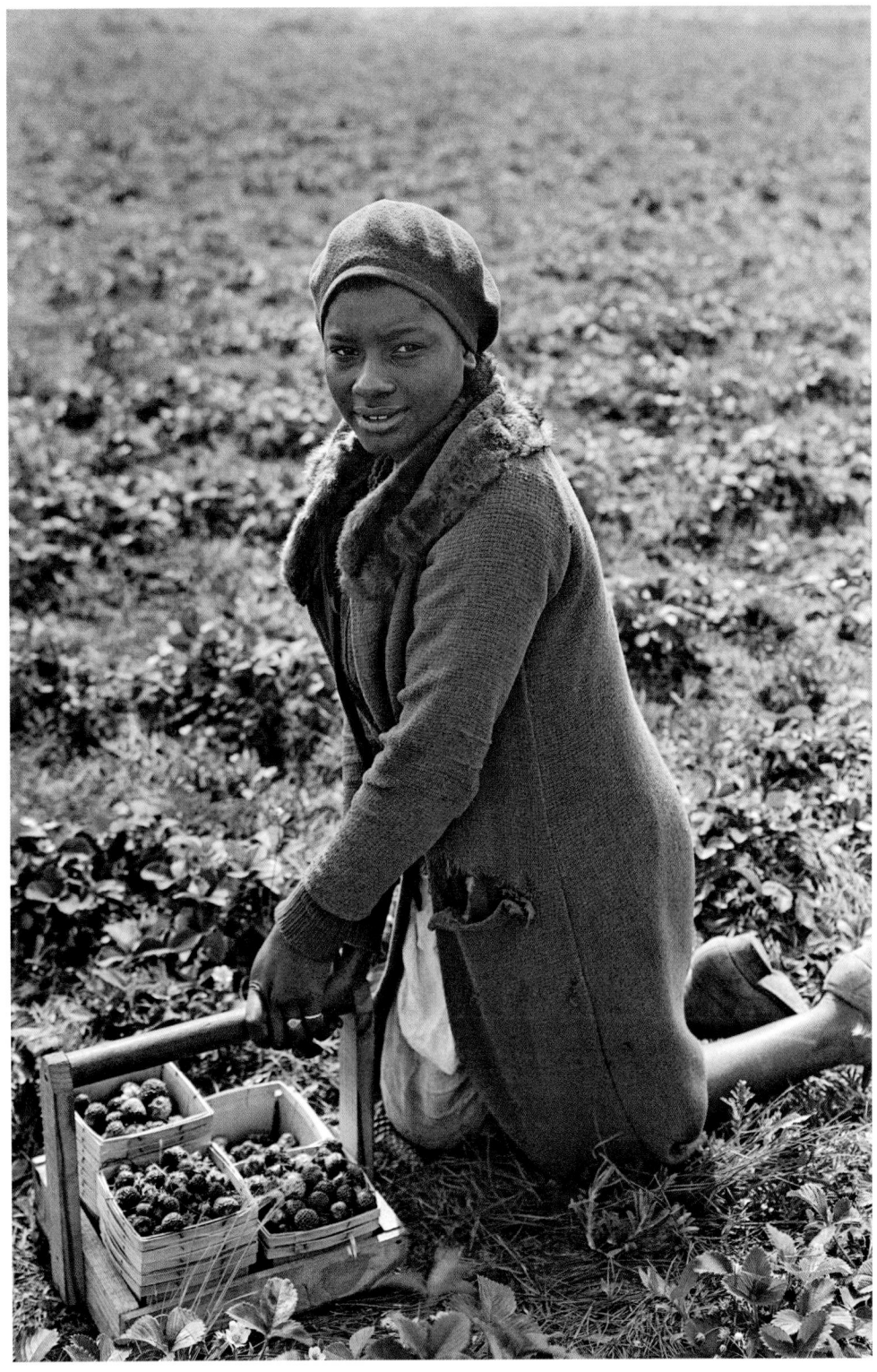

PLATE 74   *A Picker in the Strawberry Fields at Chadbourn.* North Carolina, ca. 1937.

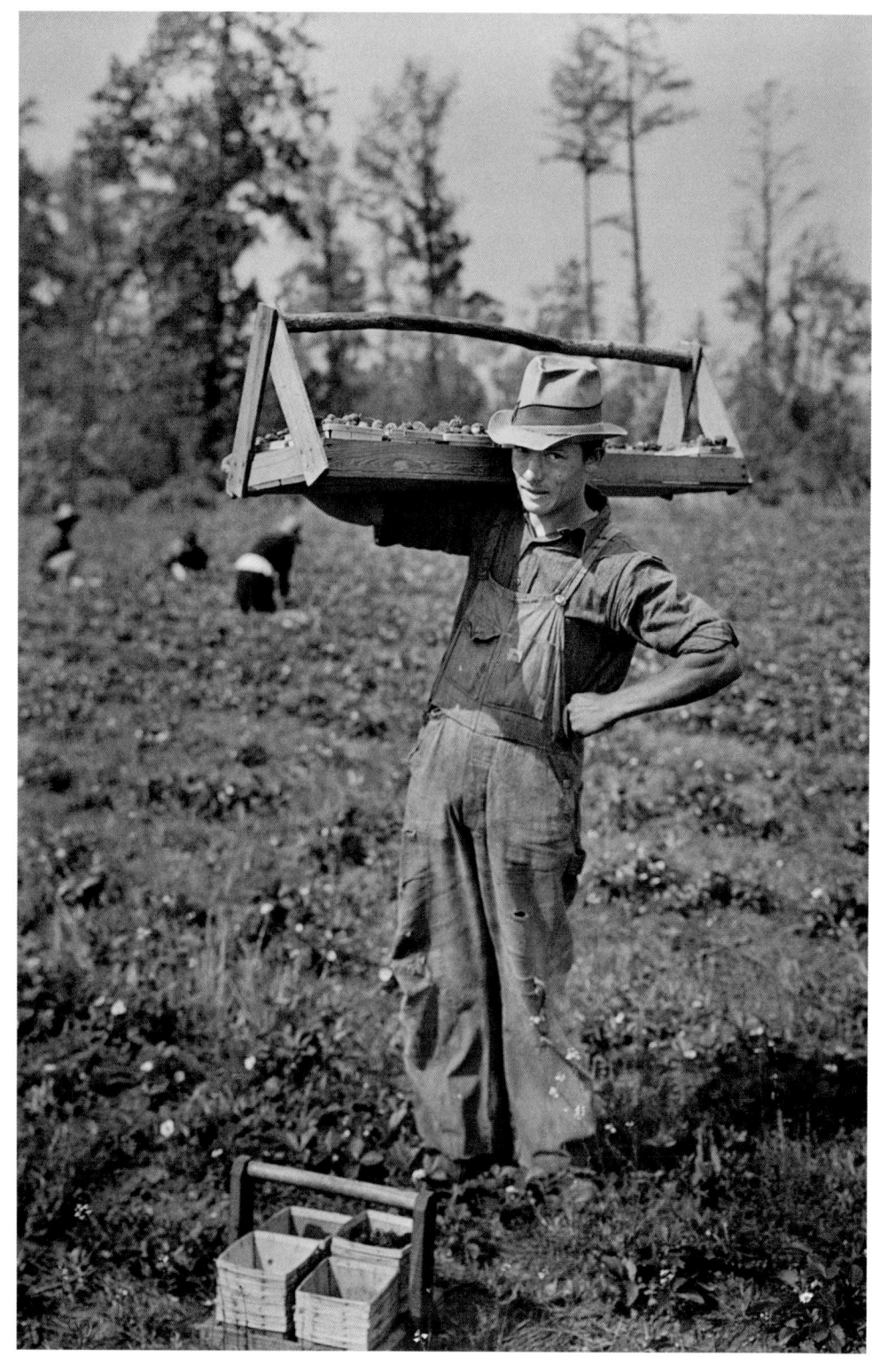

PLATE 75   *Collecting Strawberries for Shipment in Chadbourn.* North Carolina, ca. 1937.

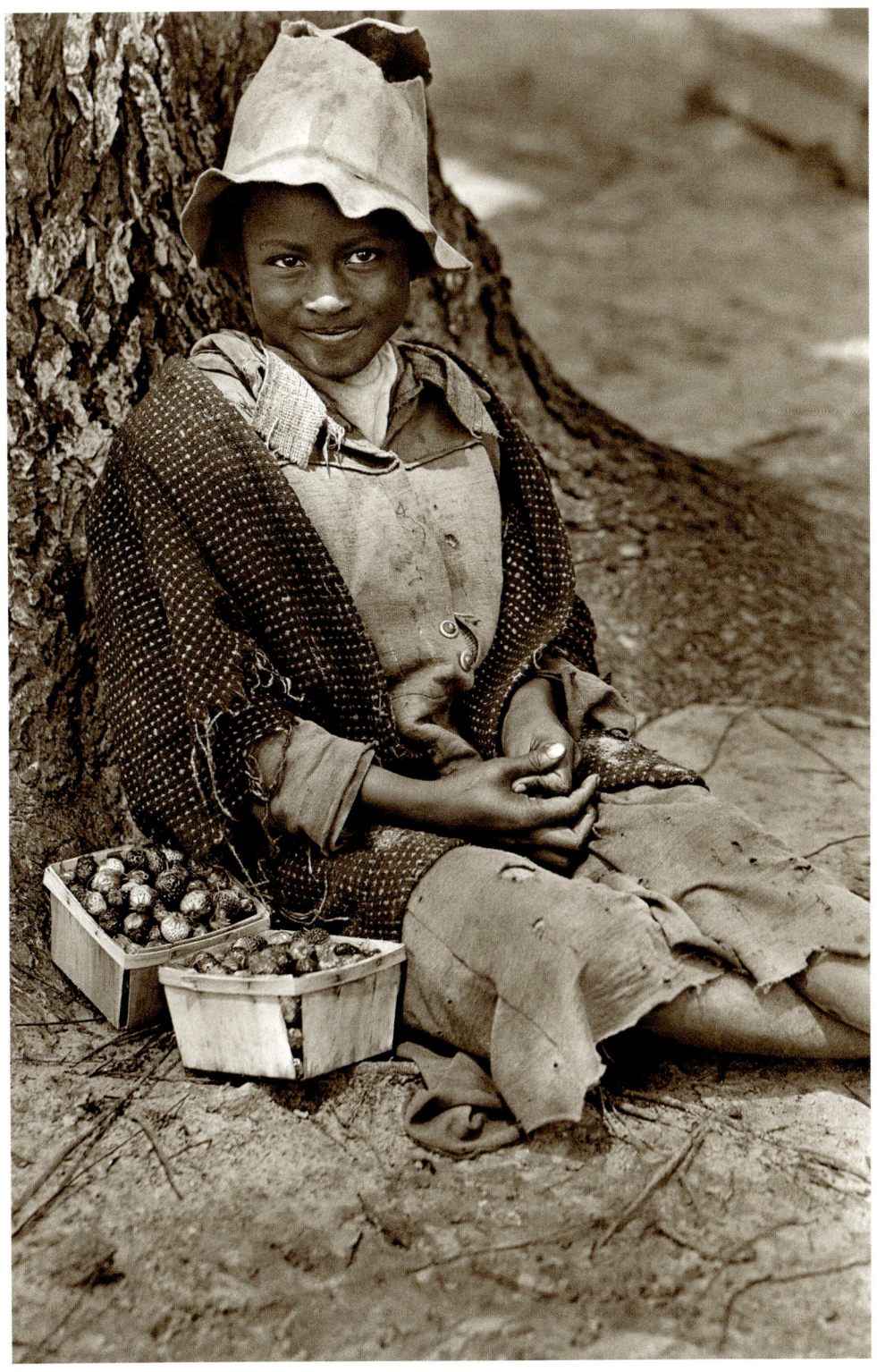

PLATE 76   A girl with strawberries. Chadbourn, North Carolina, ca. 1937.

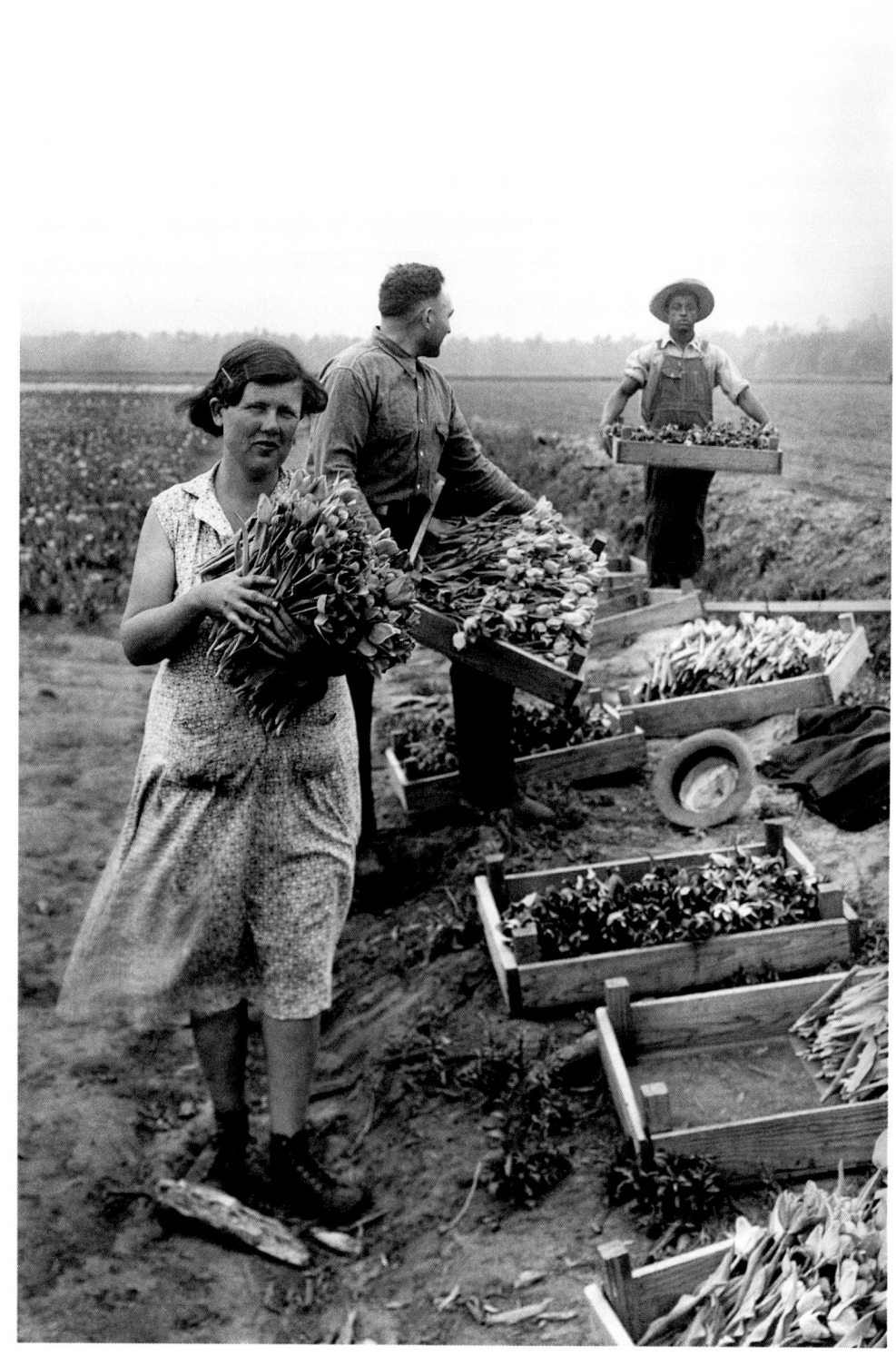

PLATE 77   Gathering tulips. Pinetown, North Carolina, 1930s.

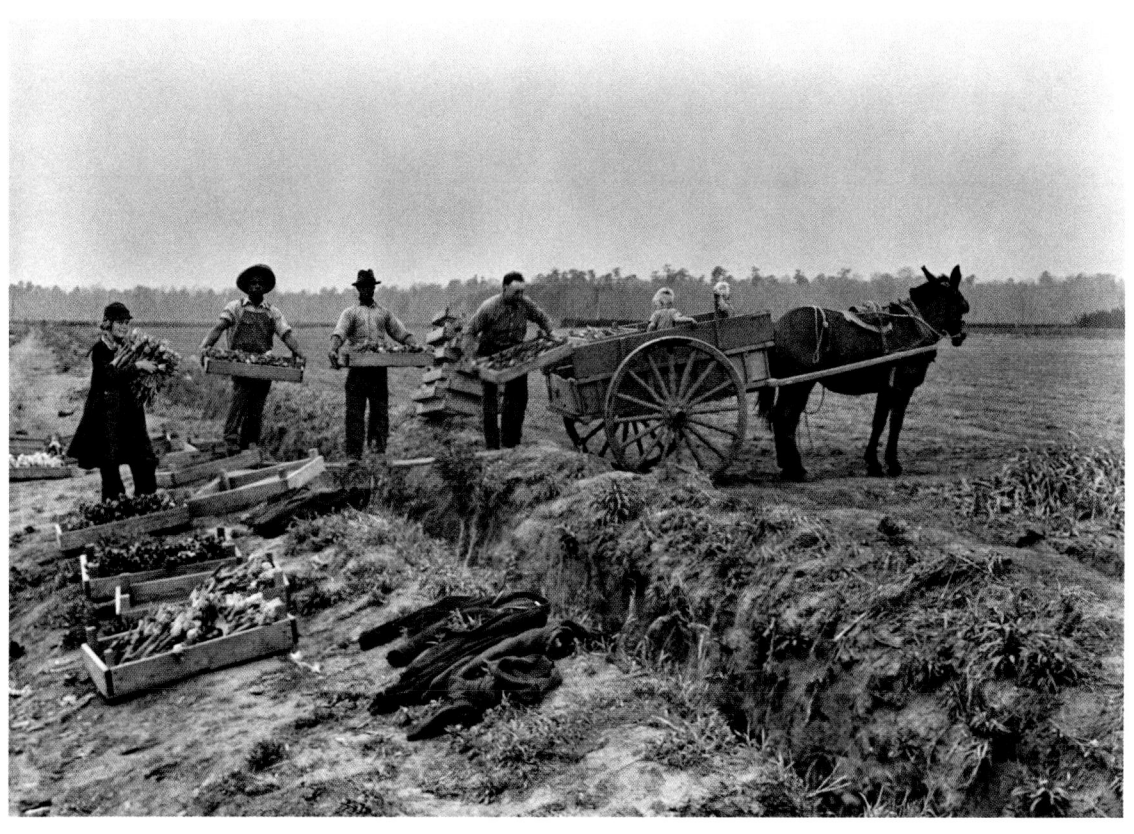

PLATE 78   Loading tulips for market. Pinetown, North Carolina, 1930s.

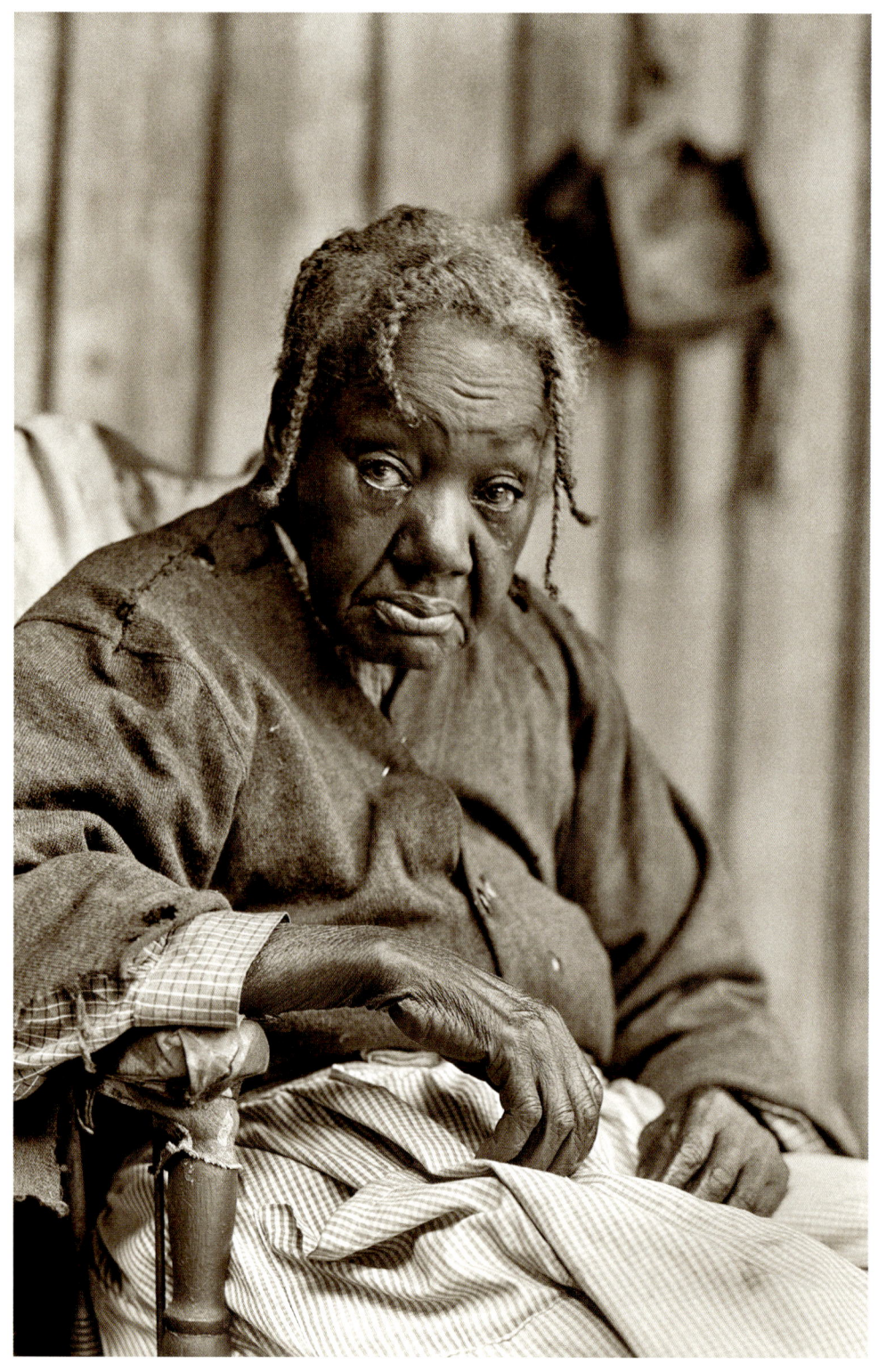

PLATE 79 *Aunt Kate*. Orton Plantation. Brunswick County, North Carolina, 1930s.

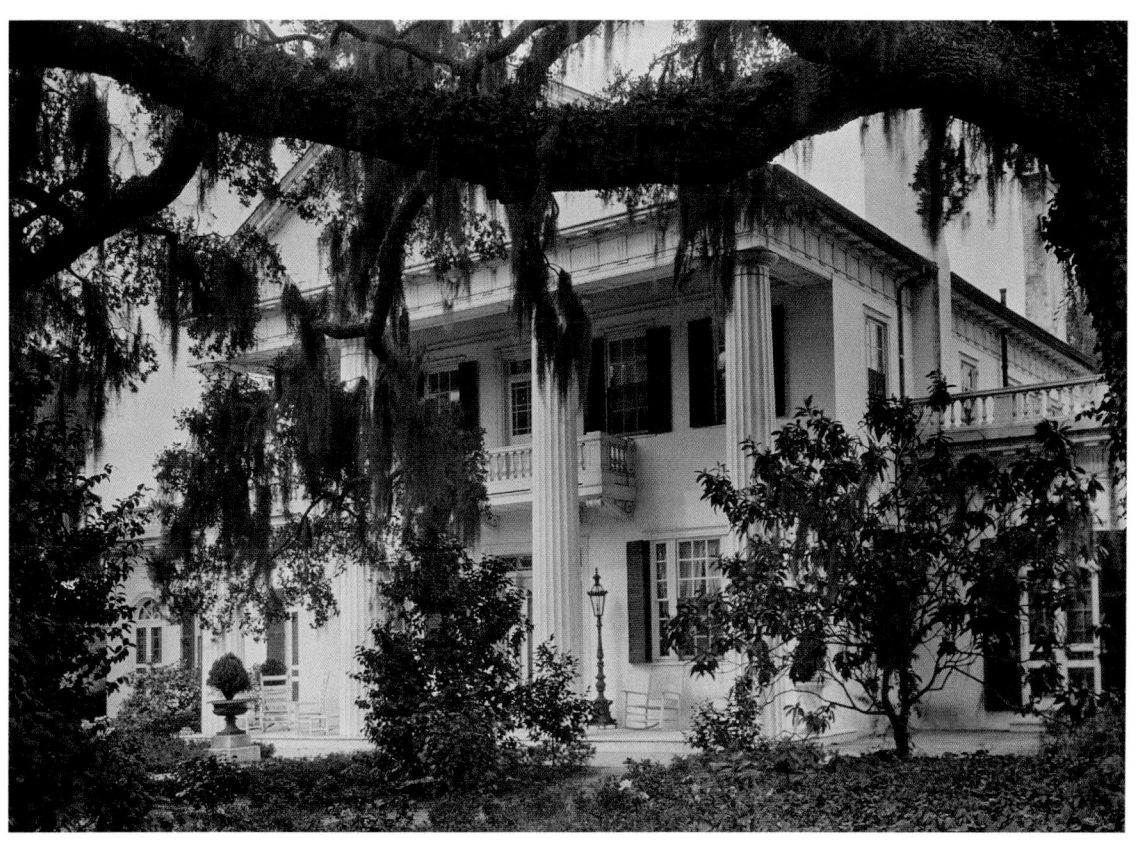

PLATE 80   Orton Plantation. Brunswick County, North Carolina, 1930s.

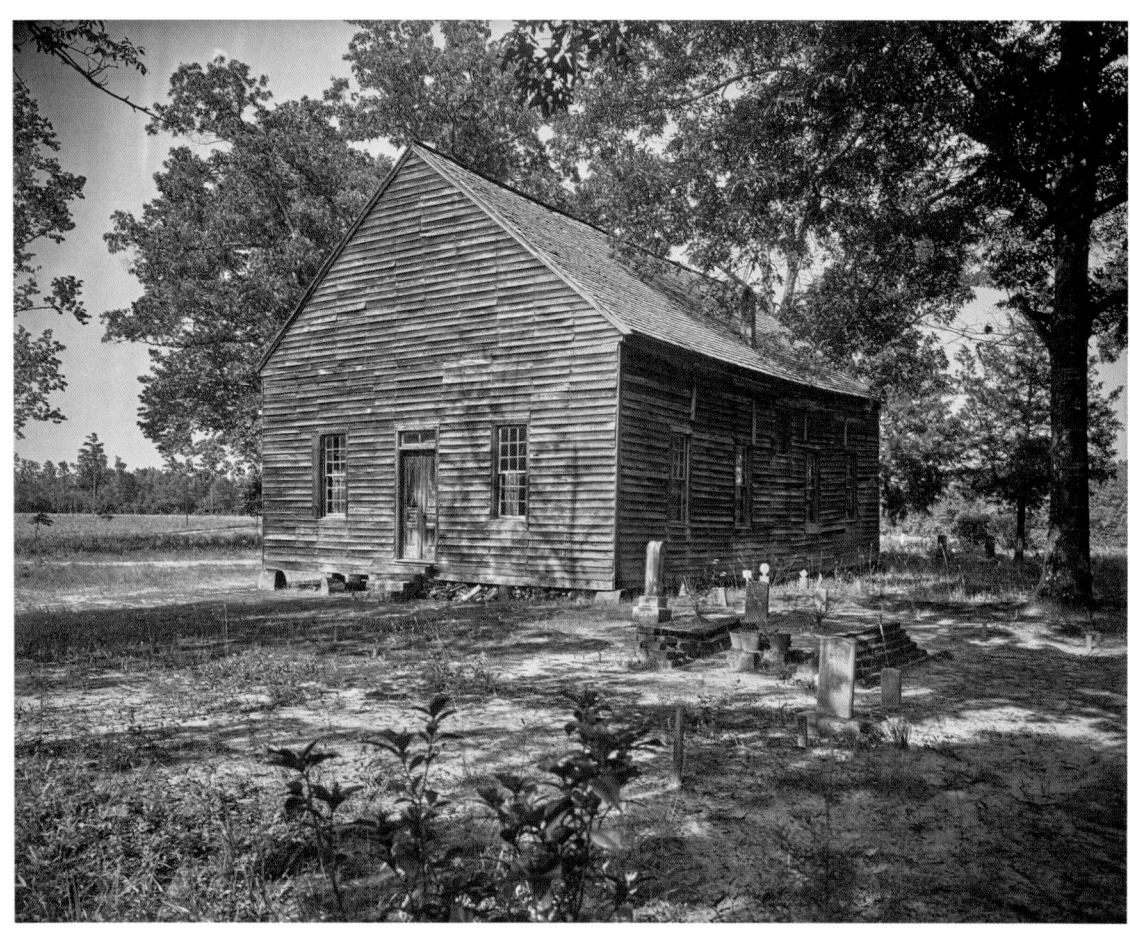

PLATE 81   Brown Marsh Presbyterian Church. Clarkton, North Carolina, 1930s.

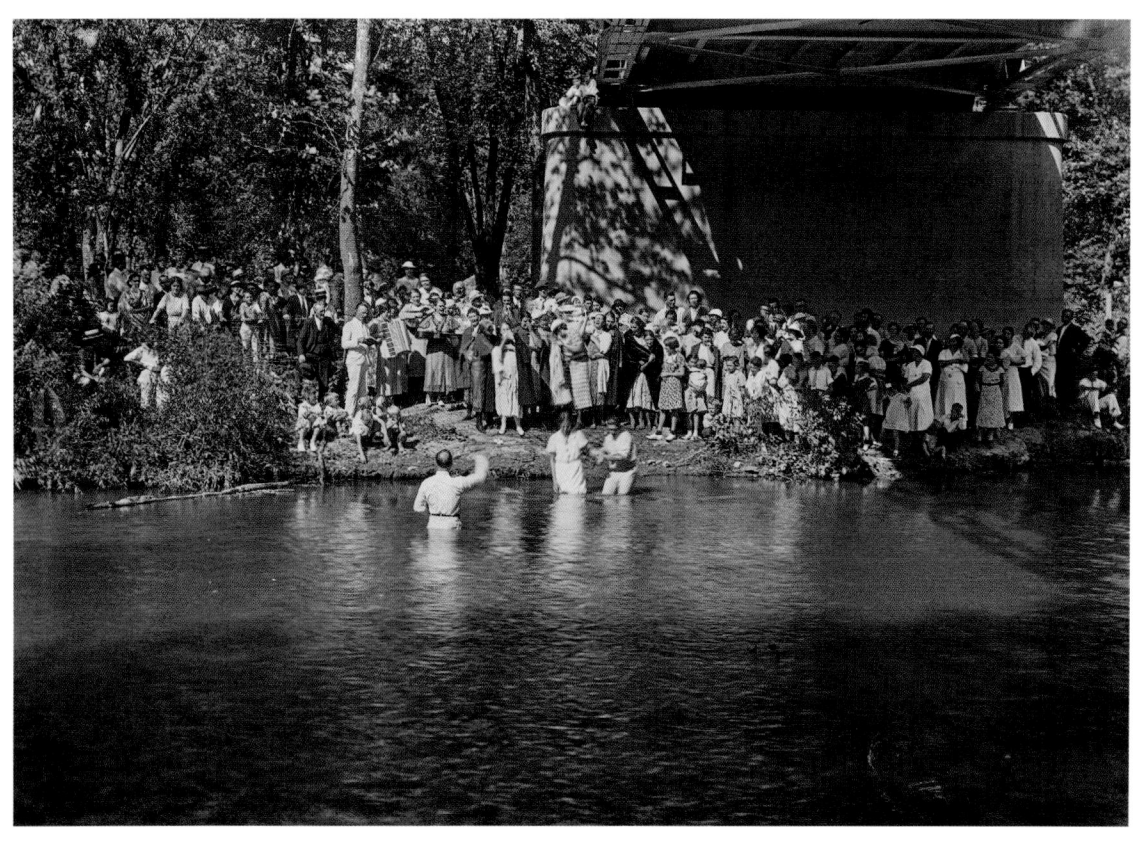

PLATE 82   A baptism. [North Carolina], 1930s.

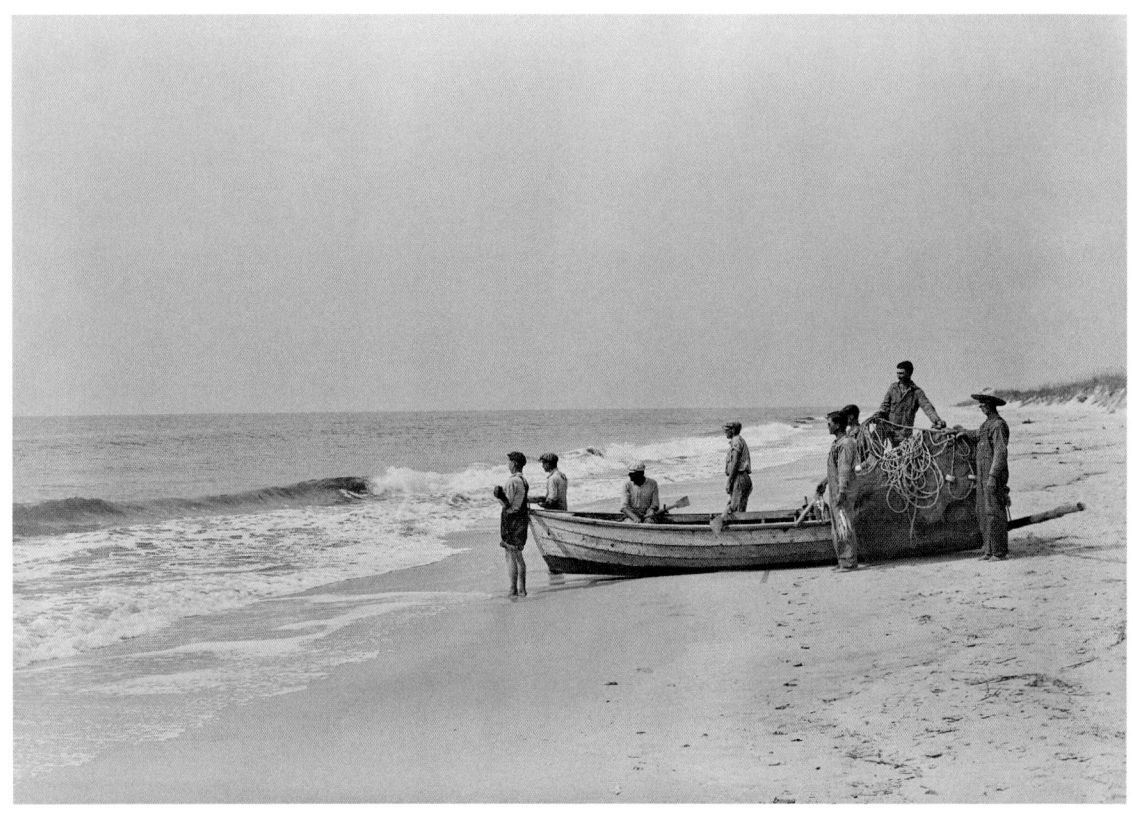

PLATE 83   Fishermen going to sea. Southport, North Carolina, 1930s.

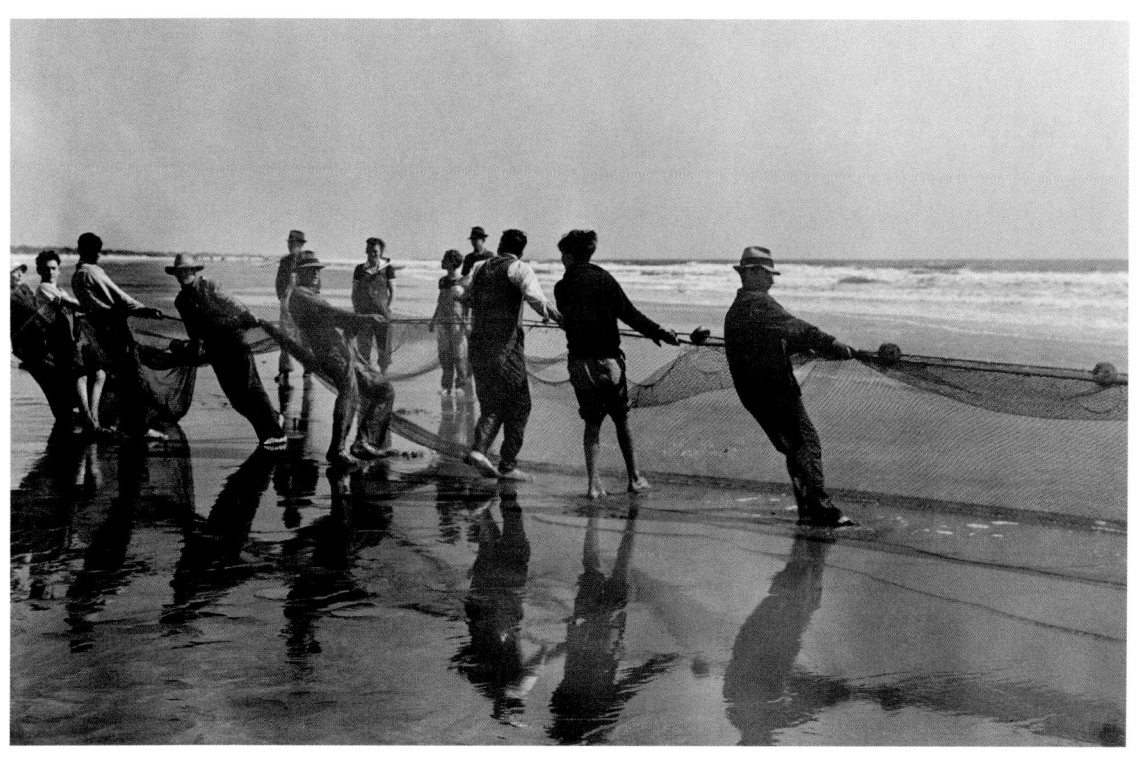

PLATE 84   *Reflections from the East*. Ocean Drive, South Carolina, 1930s.

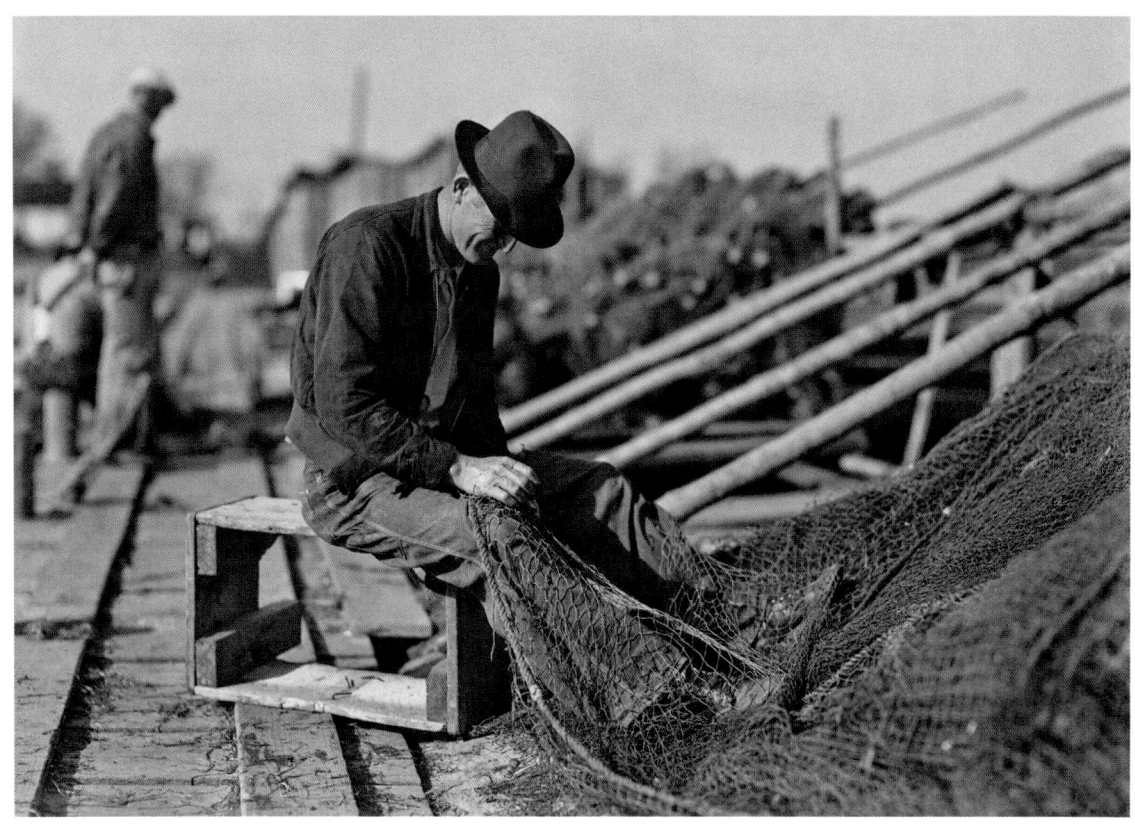

PLATE 85   A fisherman mending nets. [North Carolina], 1930s.

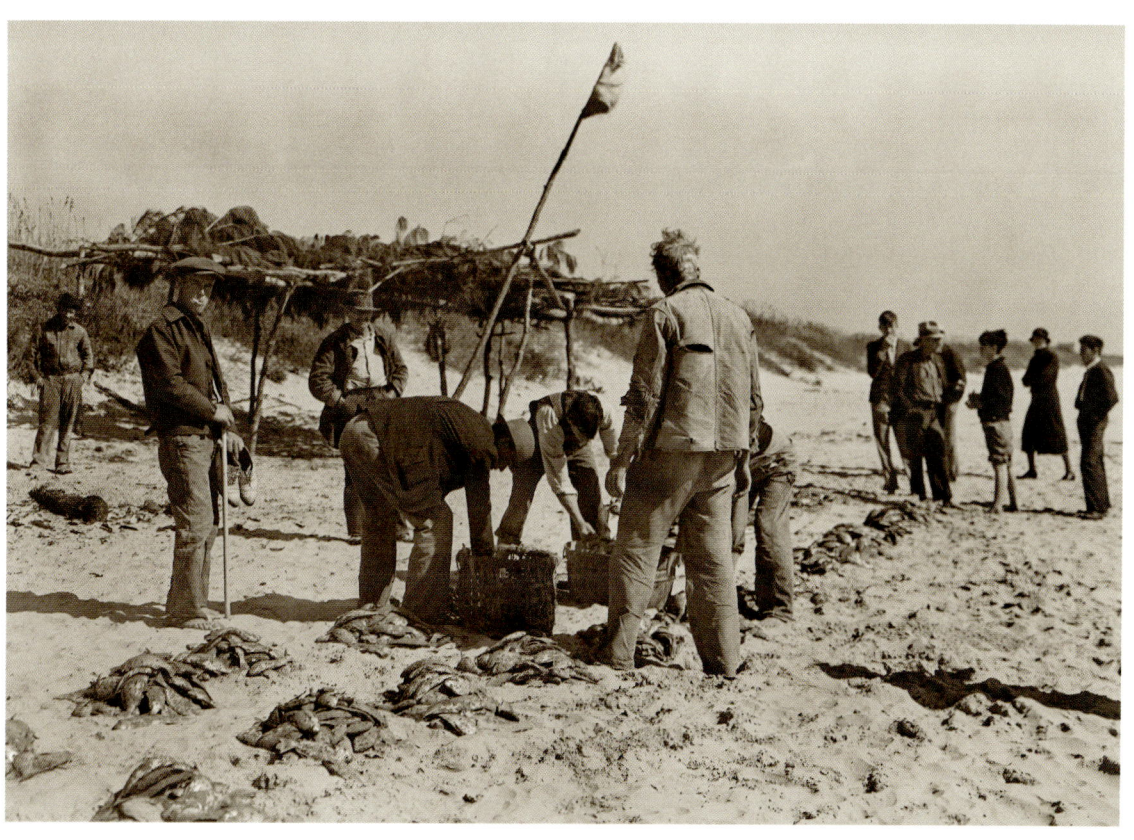

PLATE 86   Fishermen dividing their catch. [North Carolina], ca. 1939.

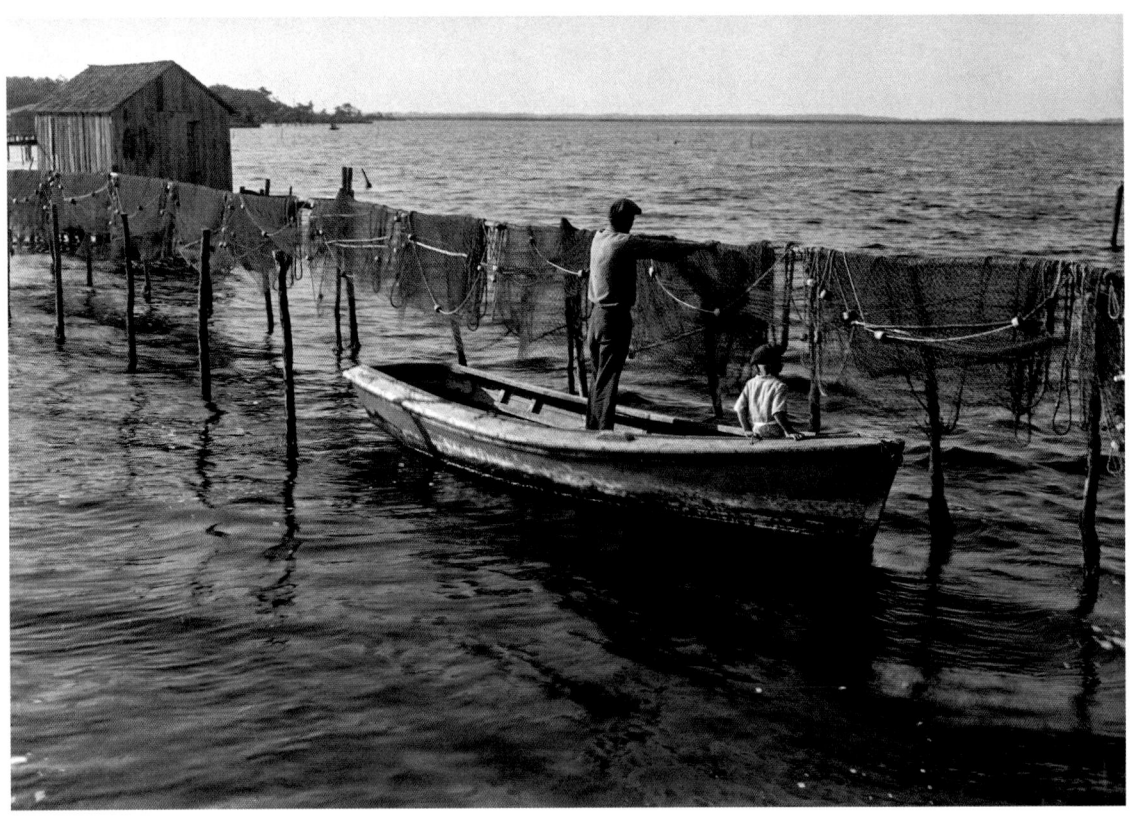

PLATE 87　Spreading nets to dry. [North Carolina], 1930s.

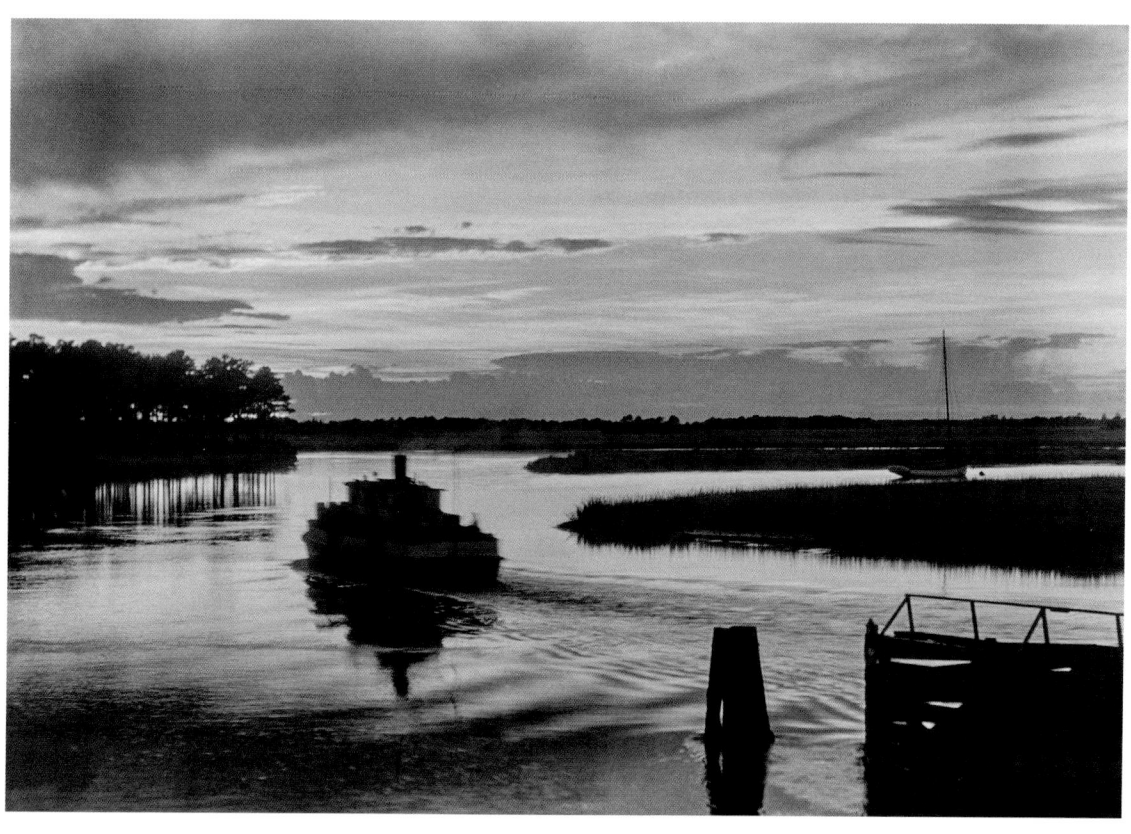

PLATE 88 *Inland Waterway near Wilmington.* North Carolina, 1930s.

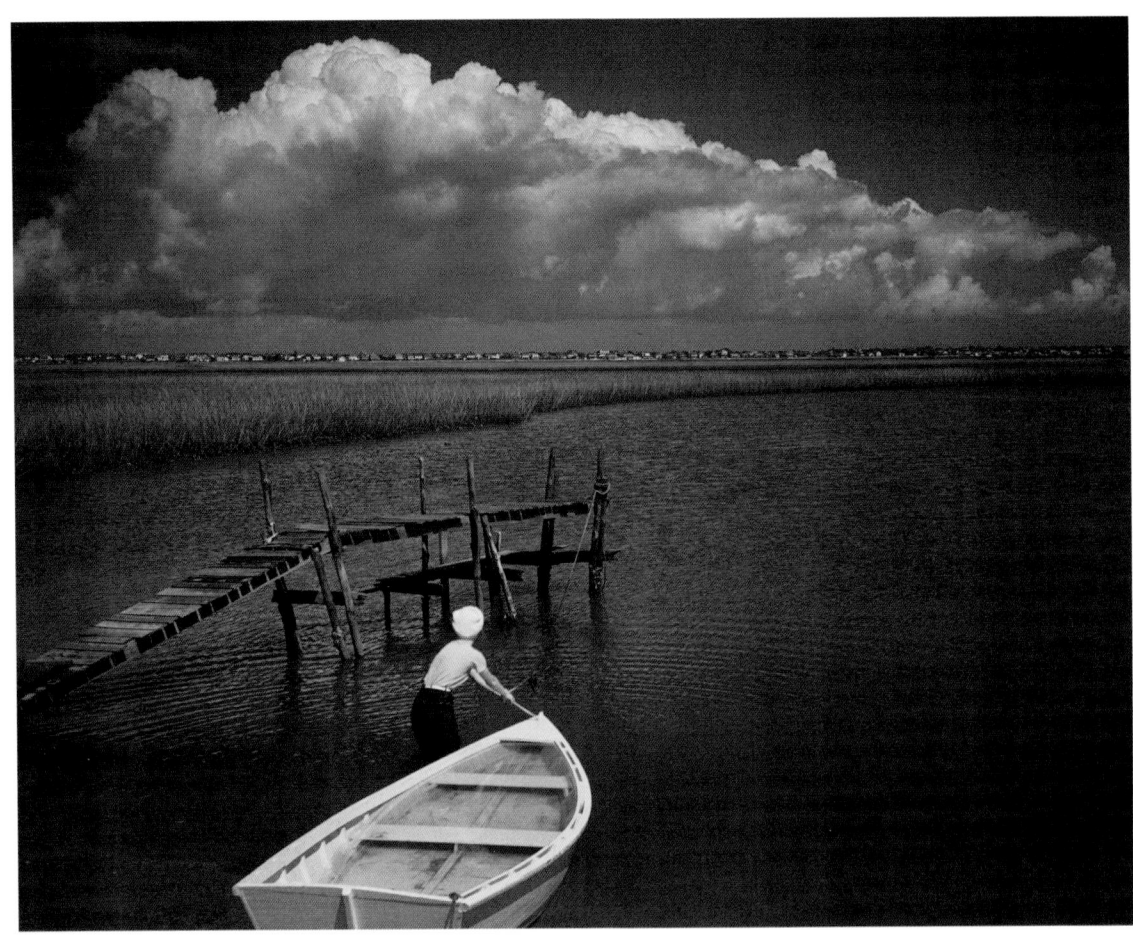

PLATE 89   Woman with a boat. Morehead City, North Carolina, ca. 1939.

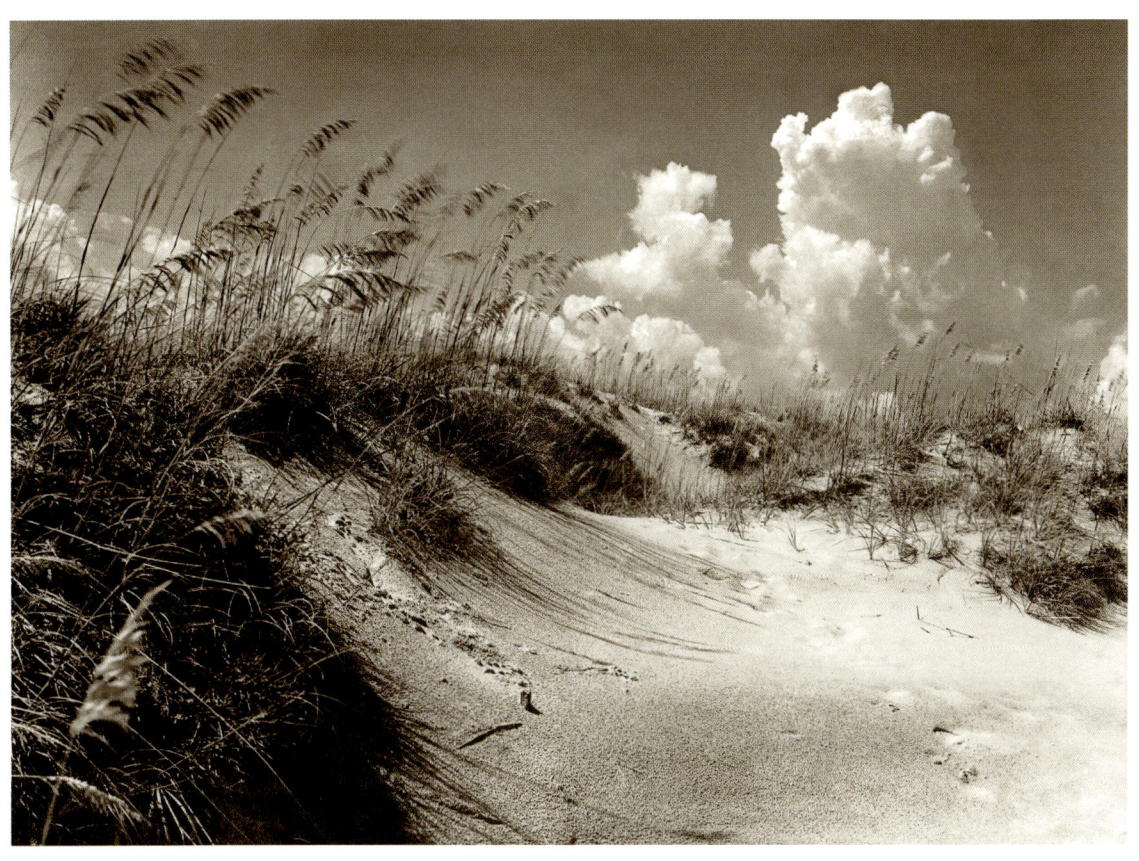

PLATE 90   Sand dunes on the coast. North Carolina, 1930s.

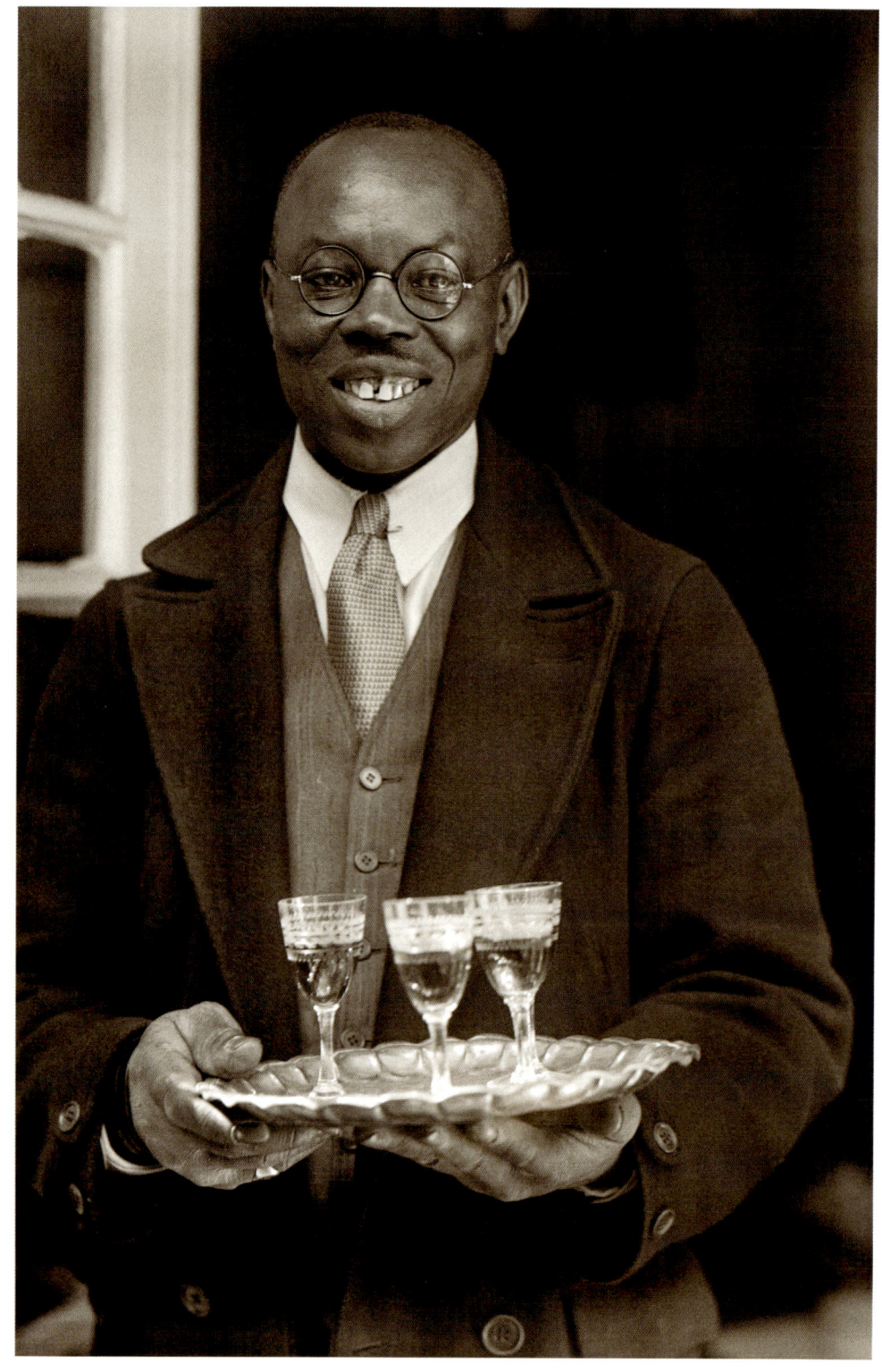

PLATE 91 A waiter serving drinks. [South Carolina], 1930s.

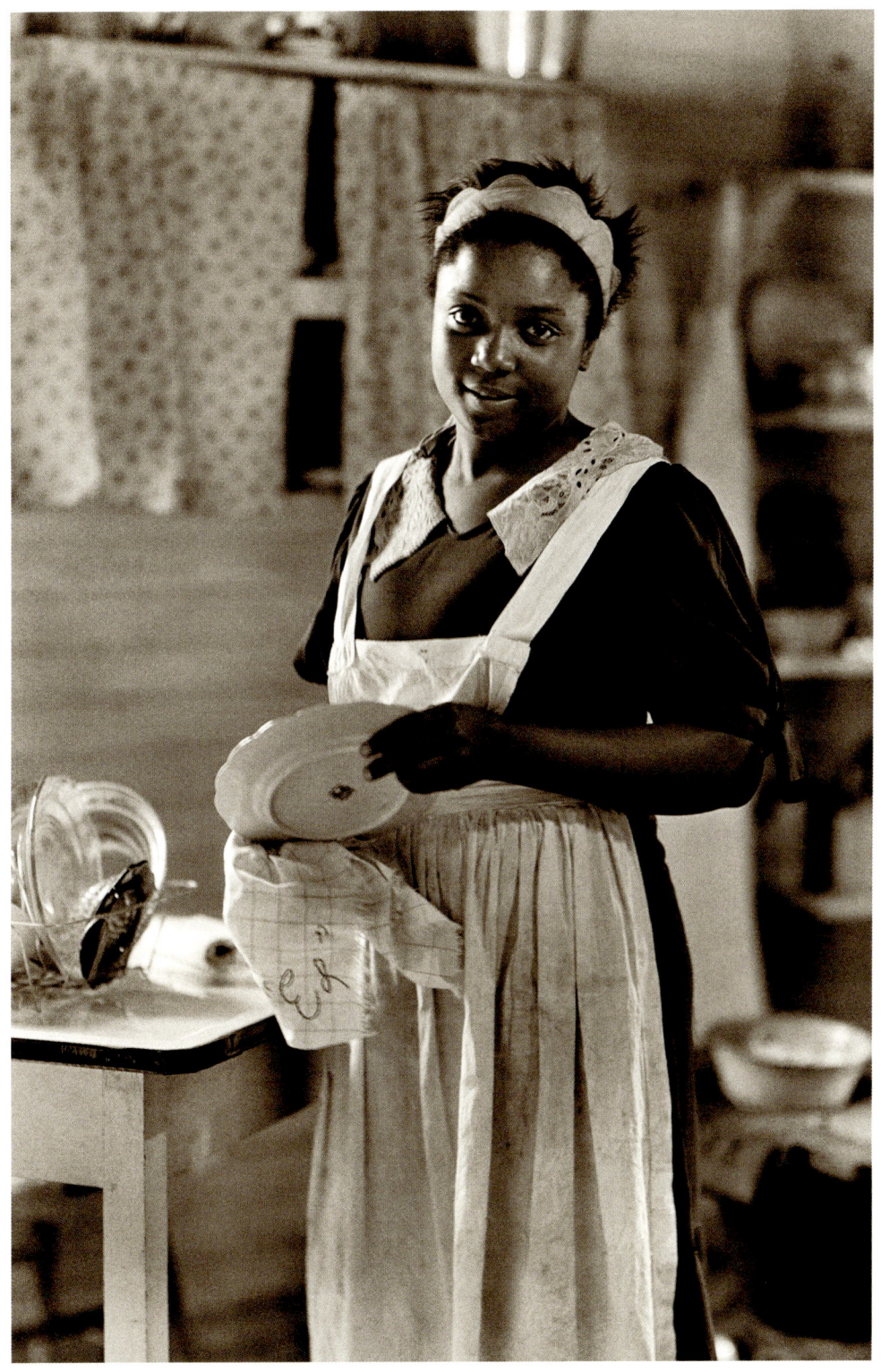

PLATE 92   Woman drying a plate. 1930s.

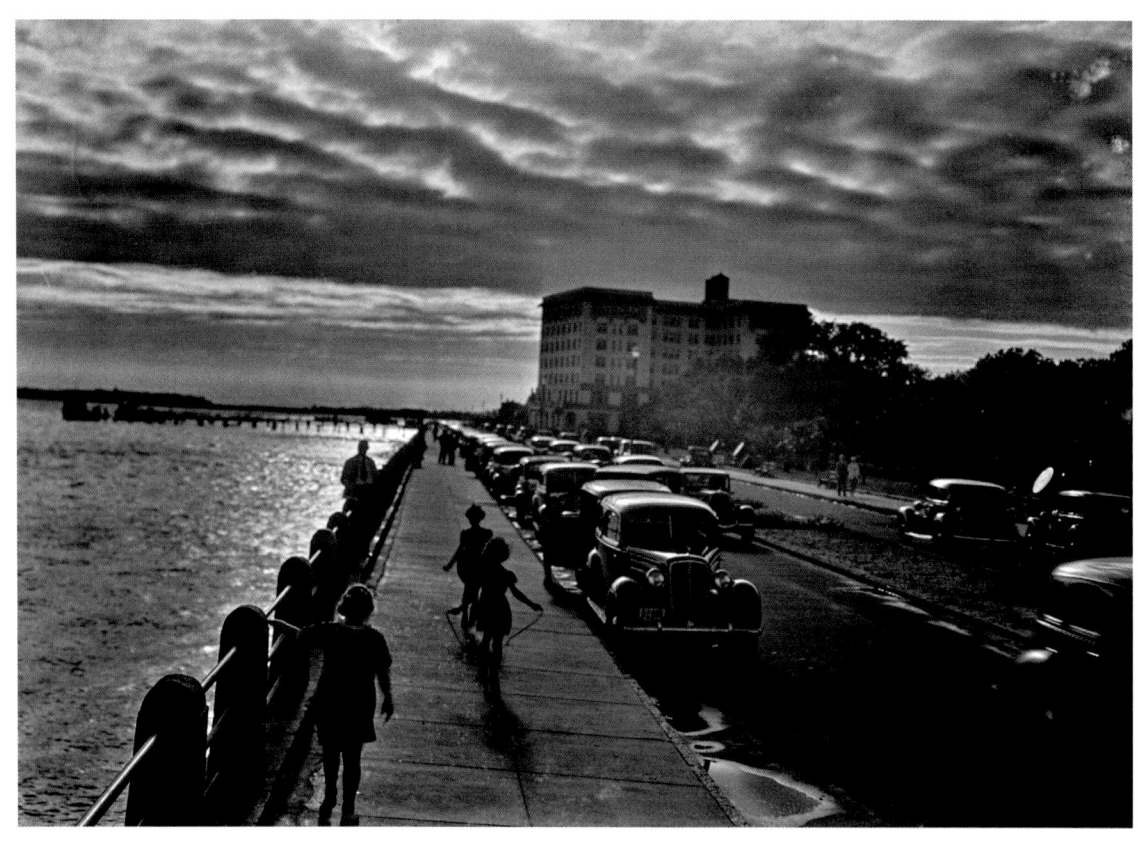

PLATE 93   "Sunset across the Ashley from the Battery." Charleston, South Carolina, 1930s.

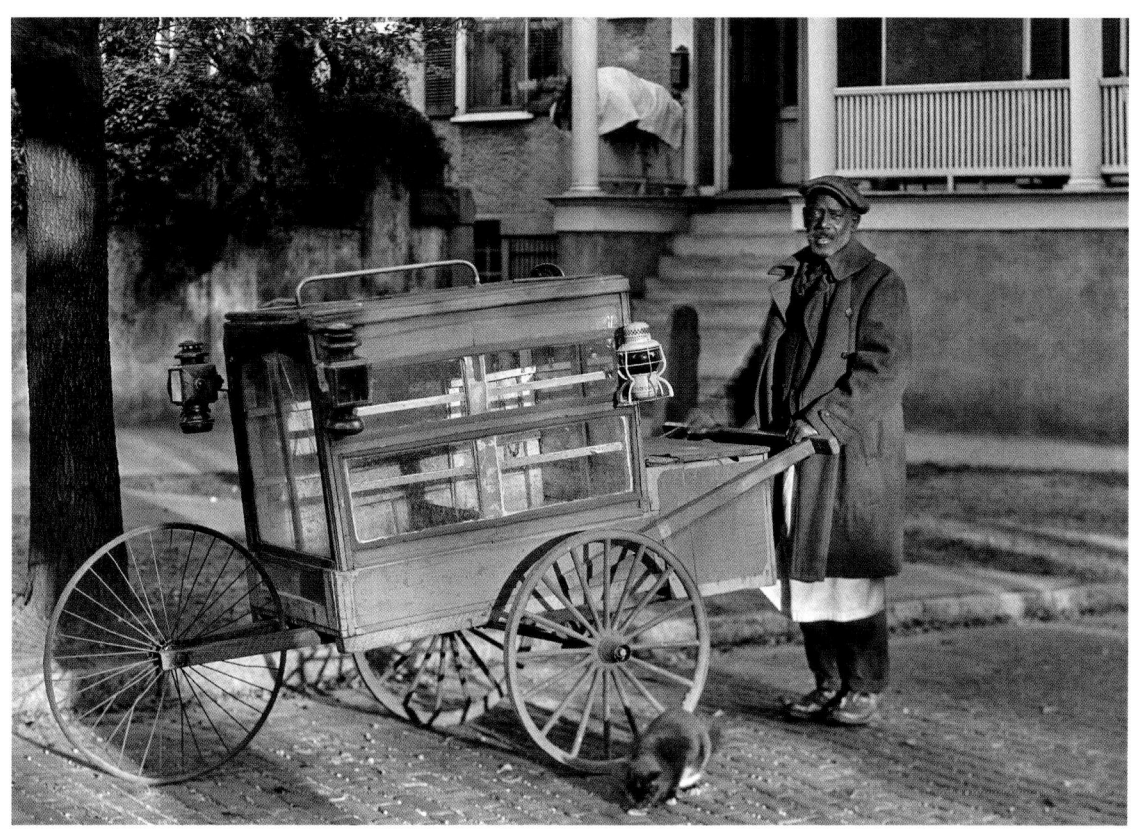

PLATE 94   *A Fishmonger in Old Charleston.* South Carolina, 1930s.

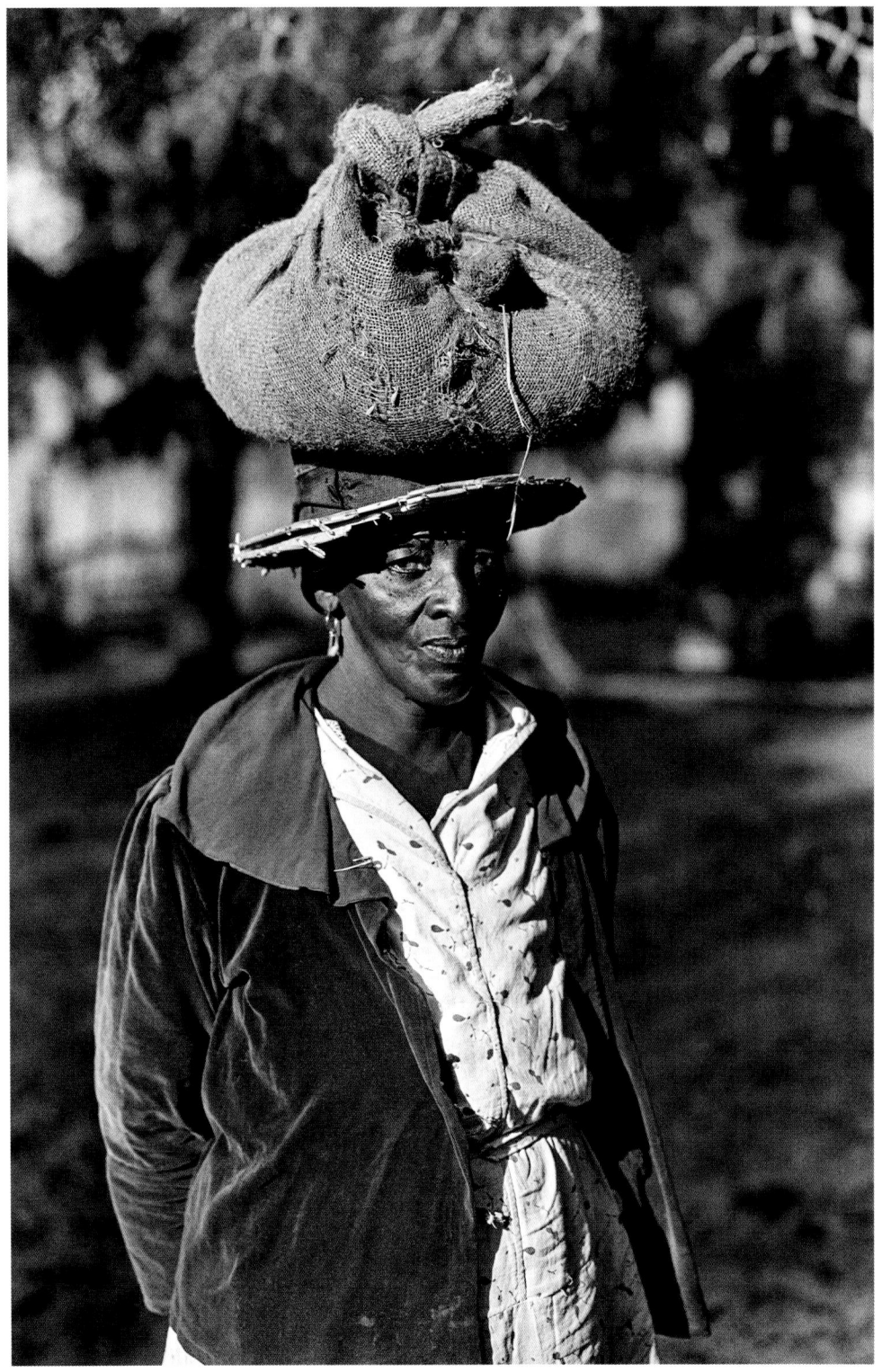

PLATE 95   Woman with a burlap sack. South Carolina, 1930s.

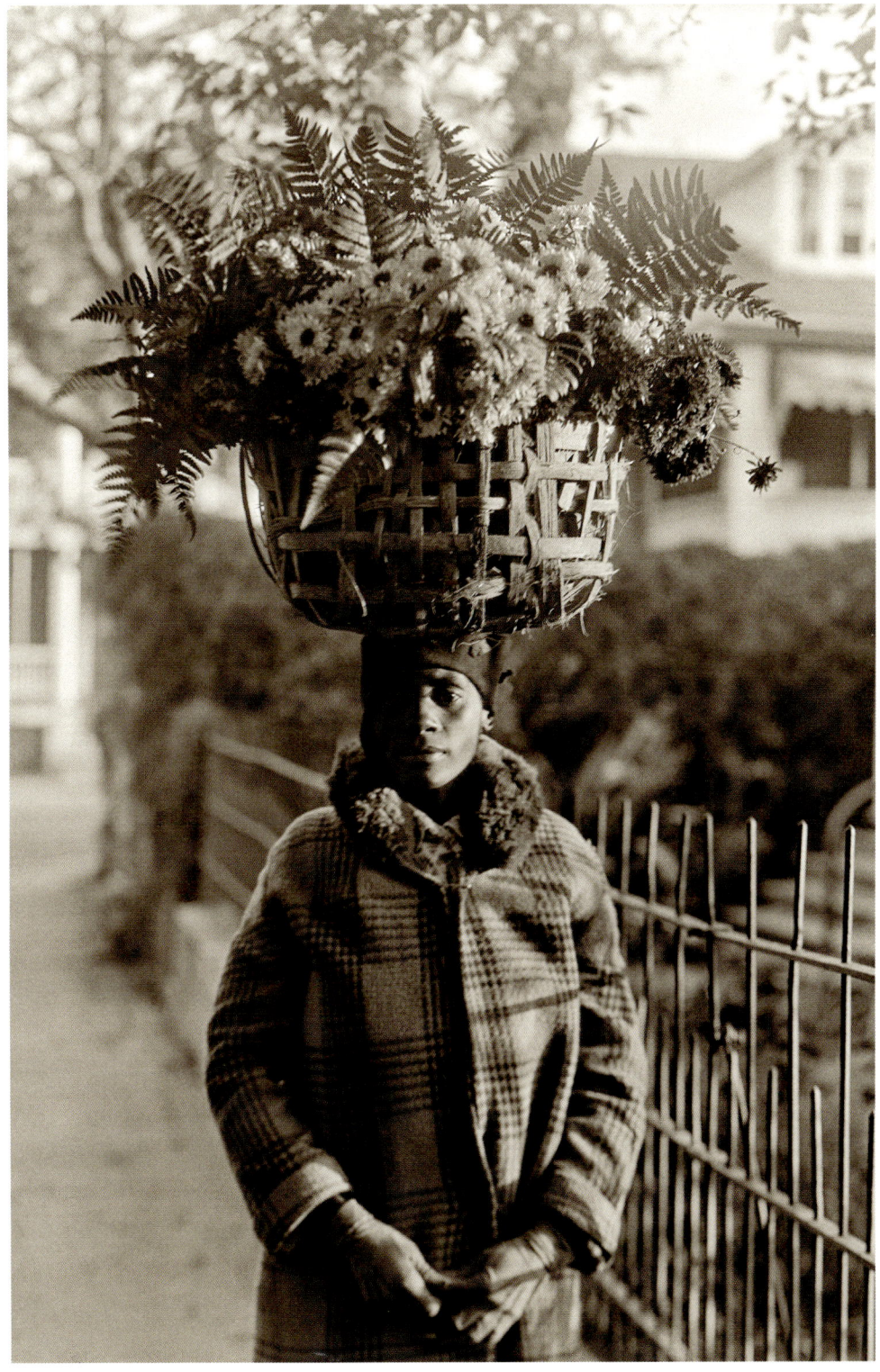

PLATE 96   A seller of ferns and flowers. Charleston, South Carolina, 1930s.

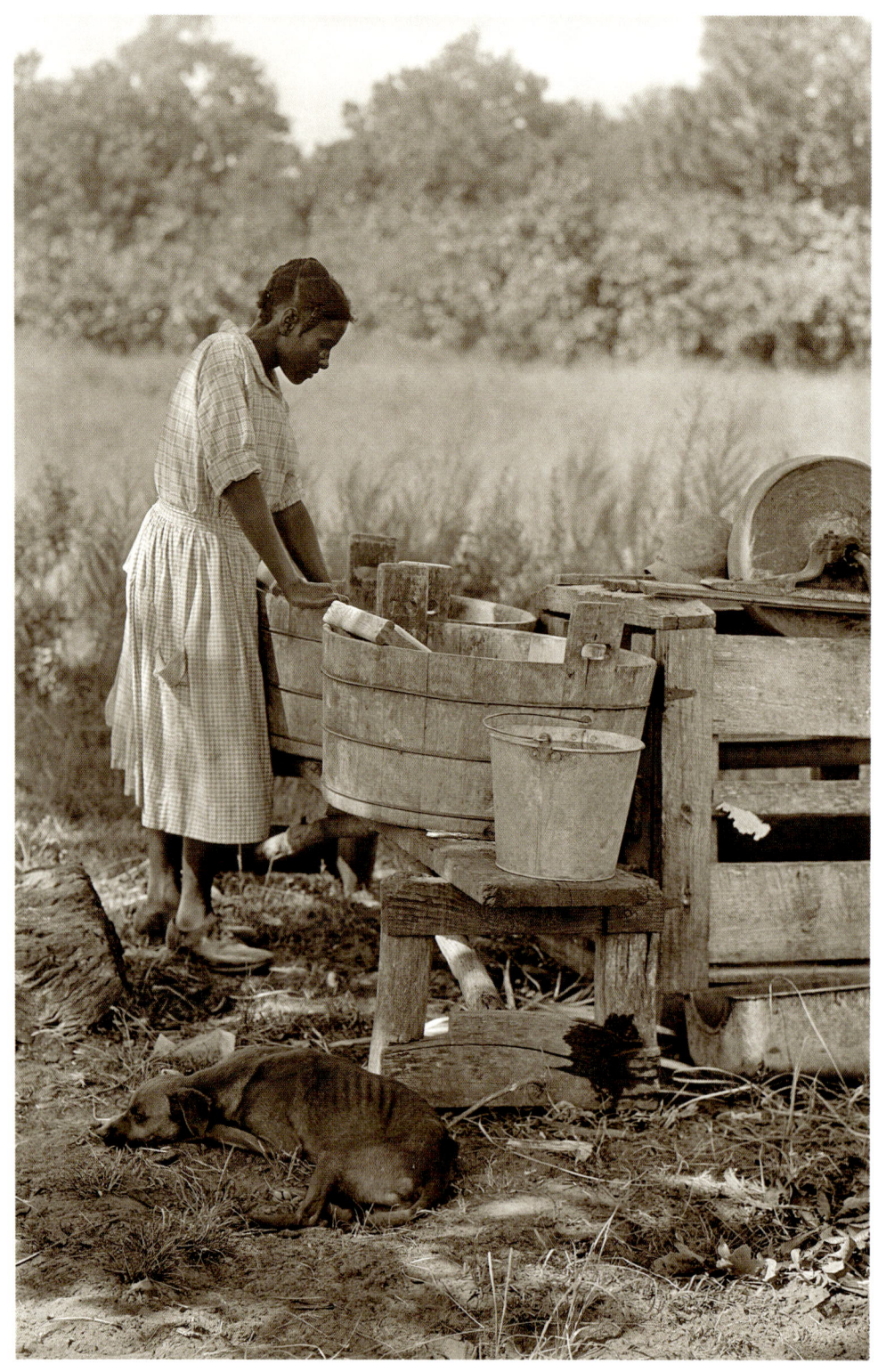

PLATE 97   "Wash Day." Charleston, South Carolina, 1930s.

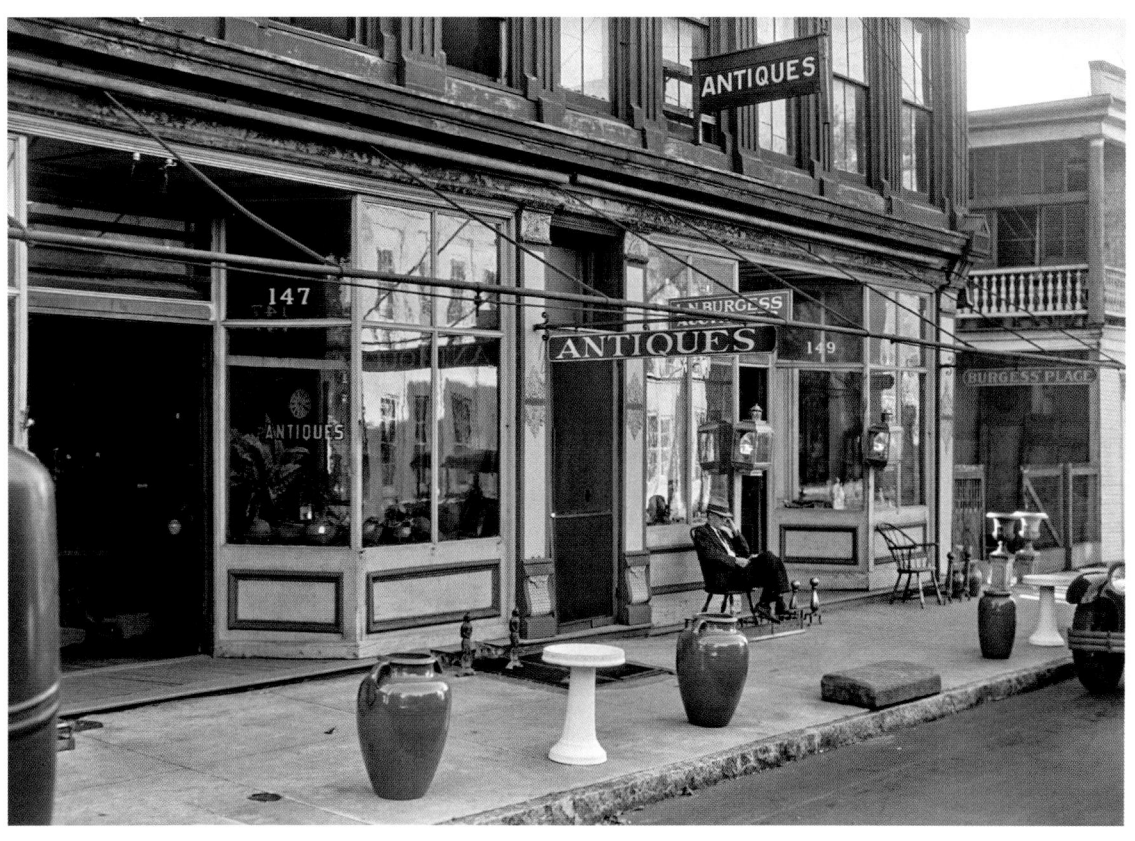

PLATE 98   "Antique Shop." Charleston, South Carolina, 1930s.

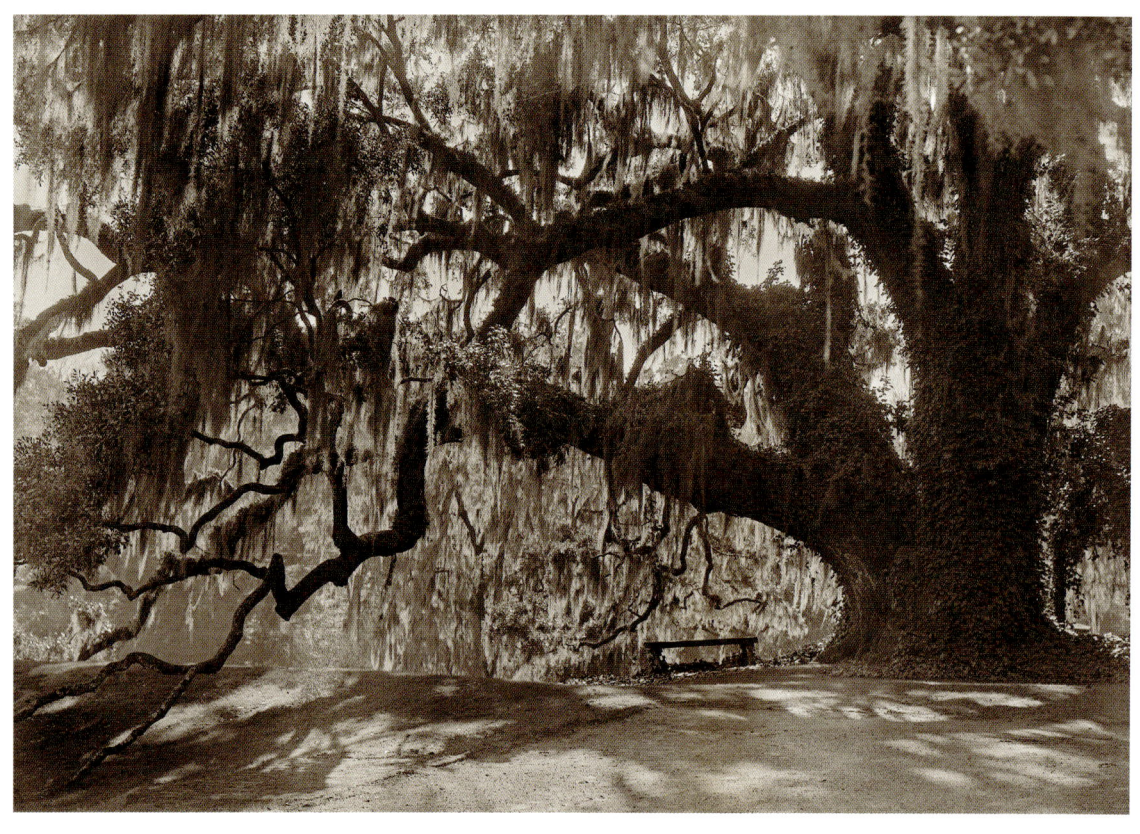

PLATE 99 "Oak at Middleton Place." Charleston, South Carolina, 1930s.

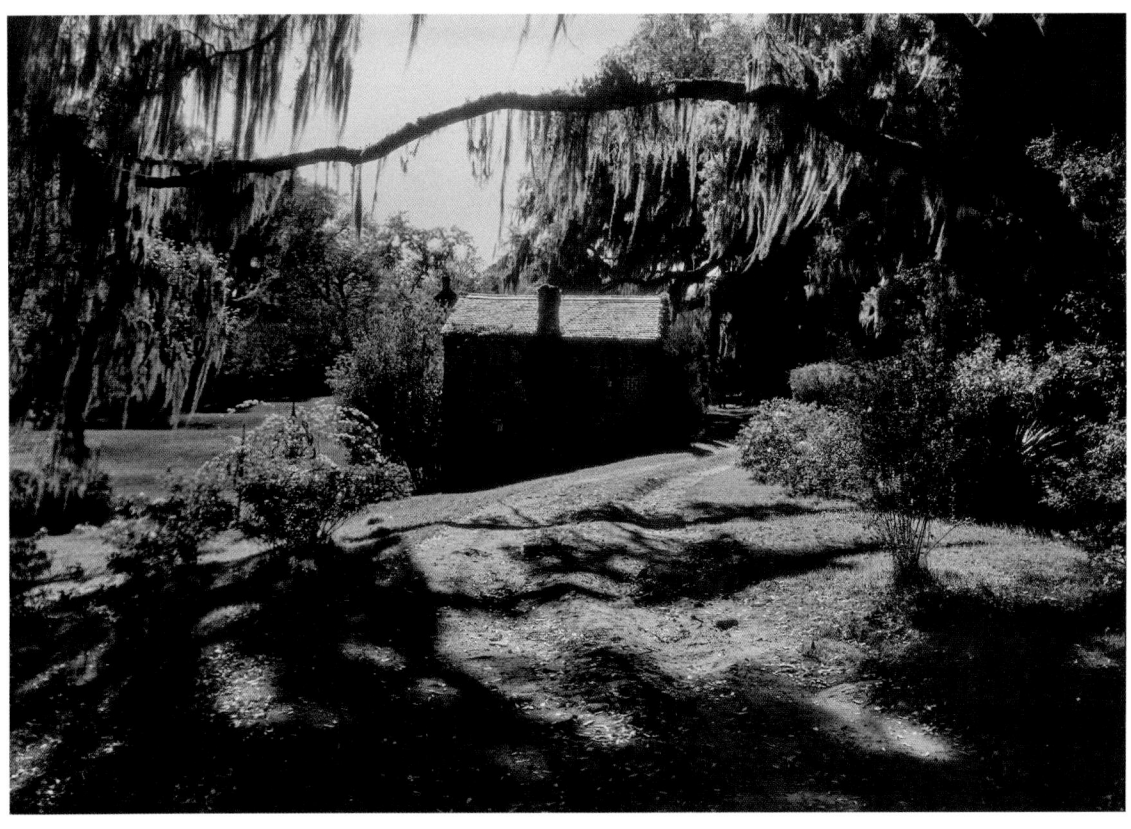

PLATE 100   Low grounds at Middleton Place. Charleston, South Carolina, 1930s.

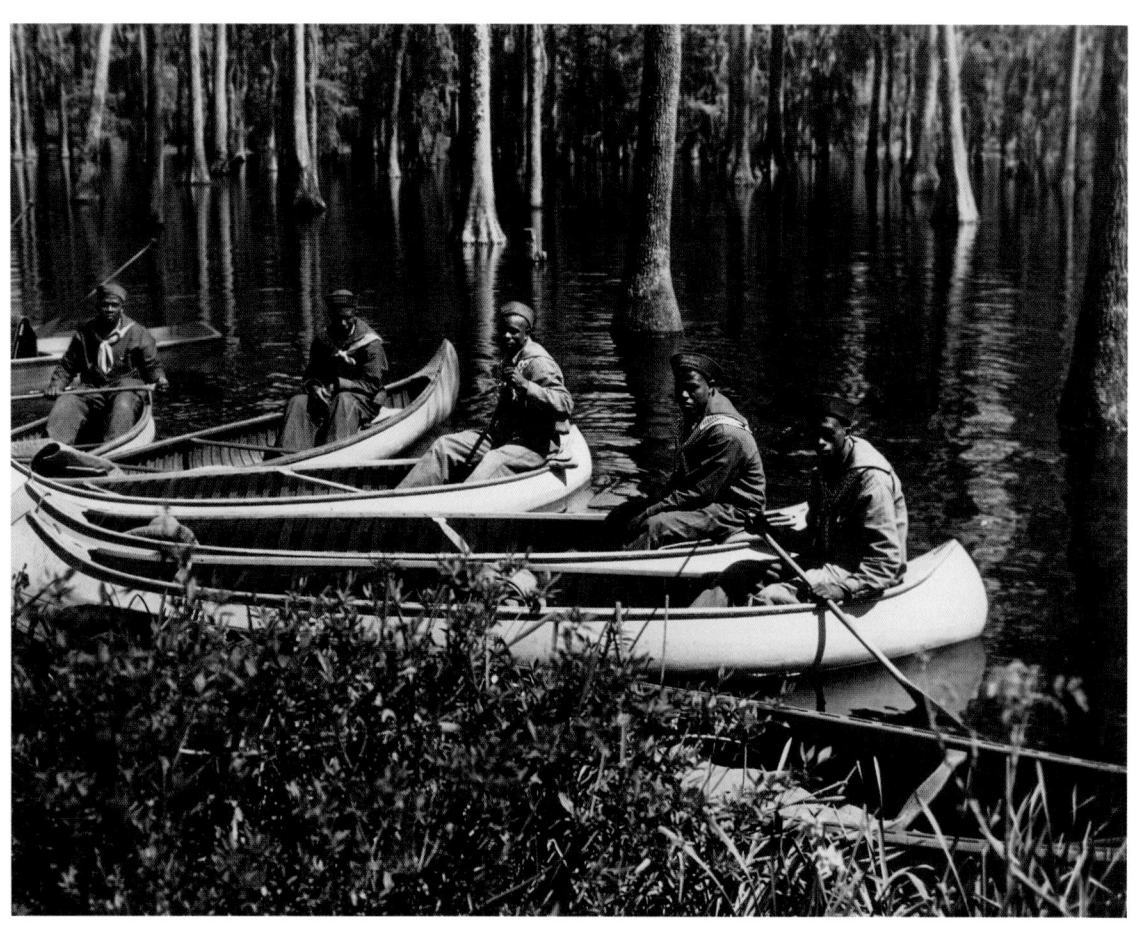

PLATE 101   Oarsmen. Cypress Gardens. South Carolina, 1930s.

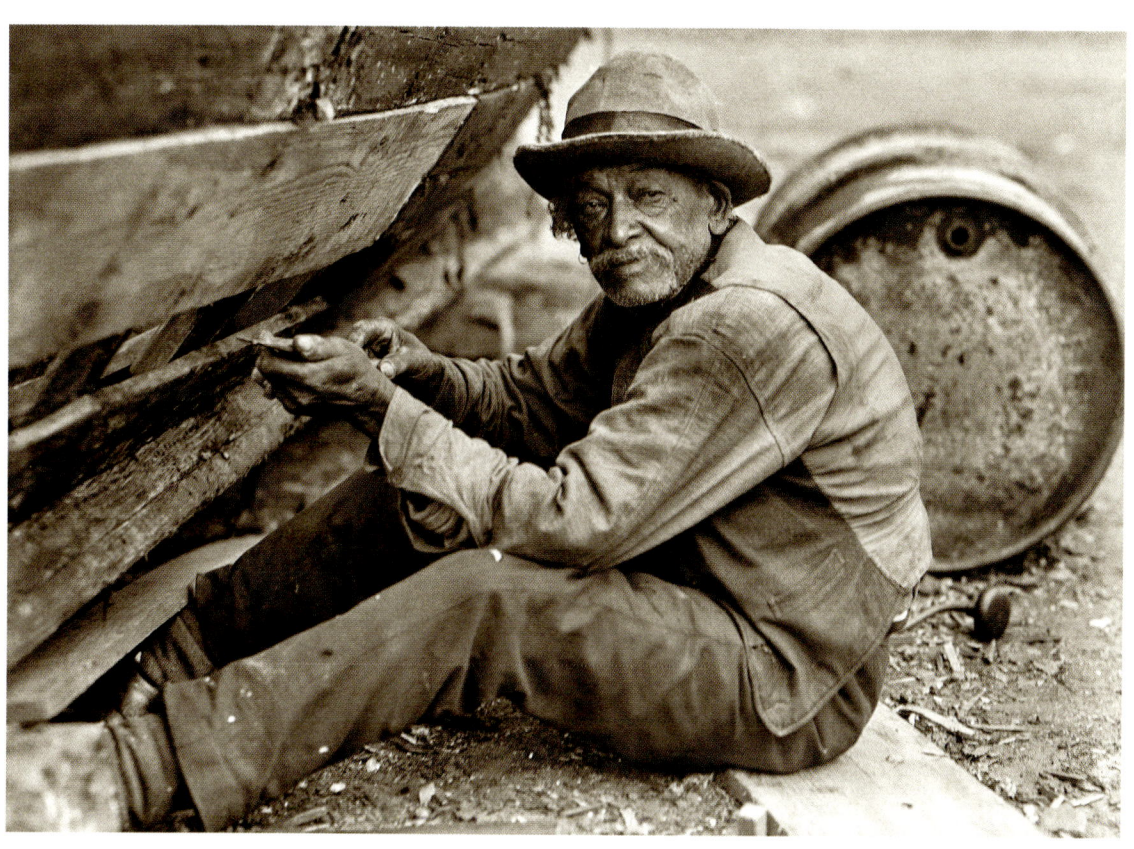

PLATE 102 *Boat Mender.* Charleston, South Carolina, 1930s.

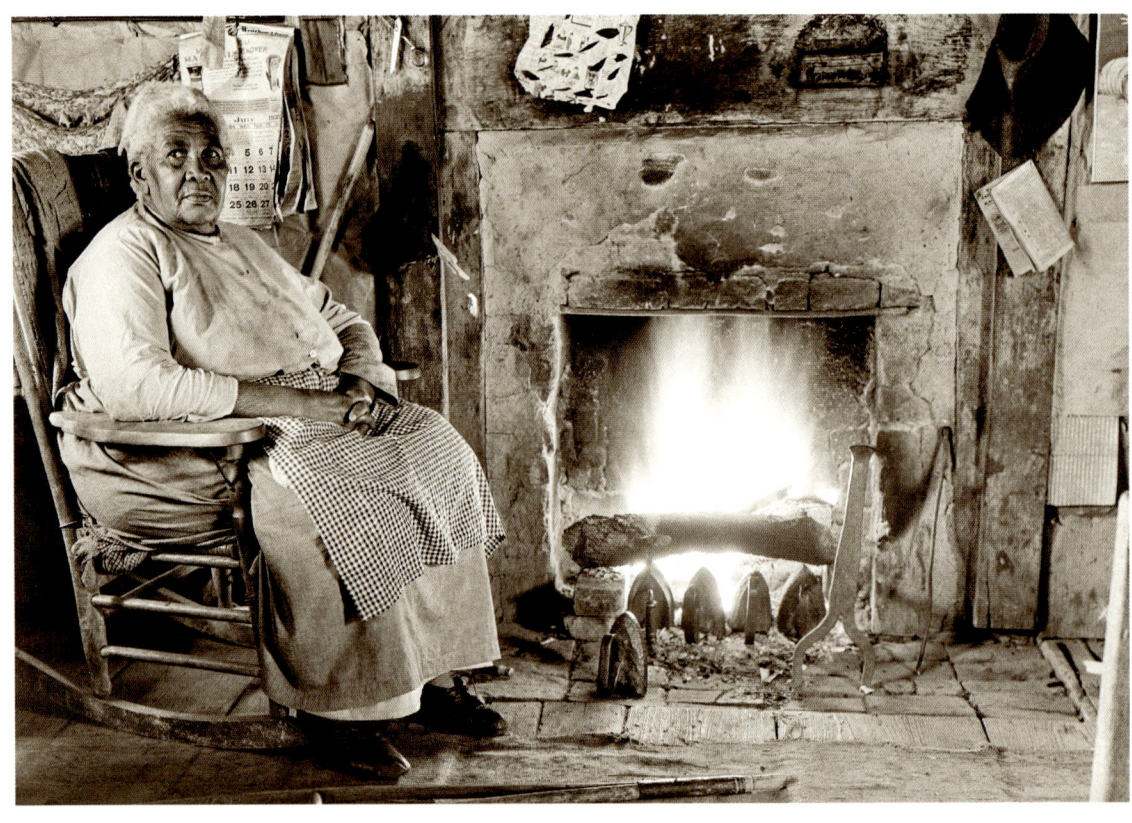

PLATE 103   *Irons in the Fire.* [North Carolina or South Carolina], ca. 1933.

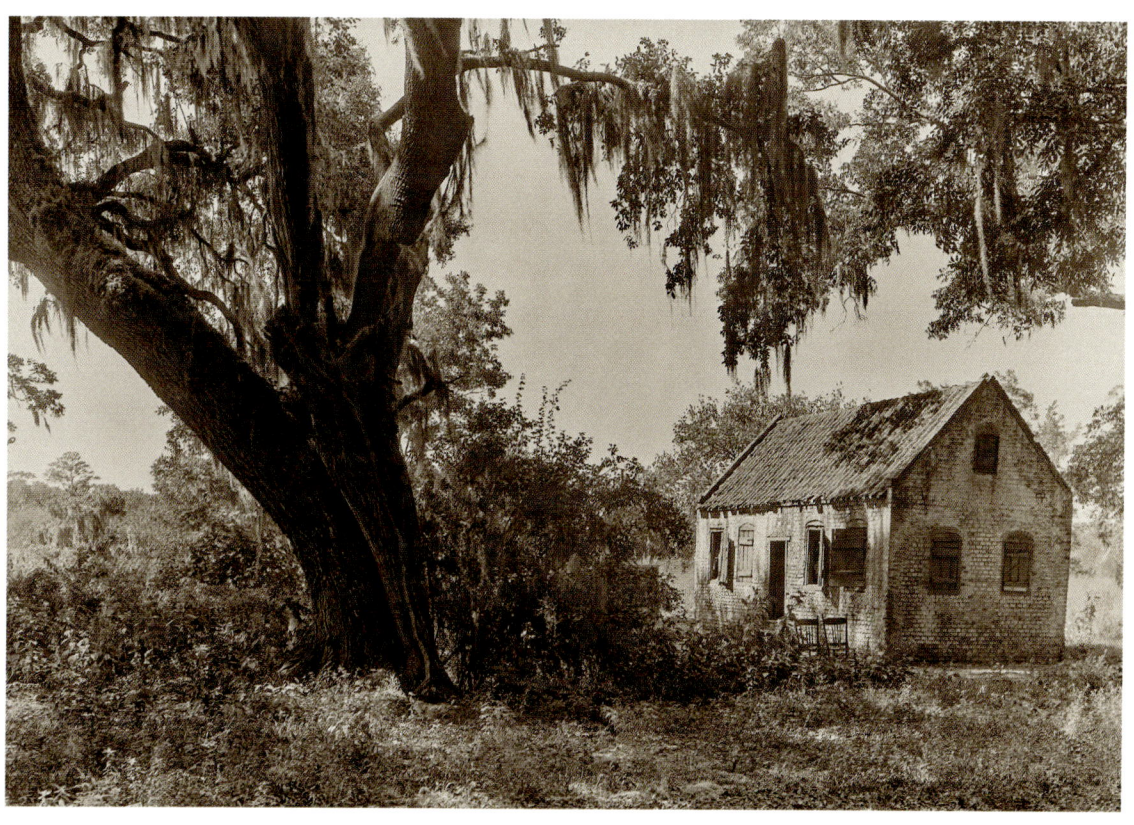

PLATE 104   Slave cabin at Boone Hall Plantation. Charleston, South Carolina, 1930s.

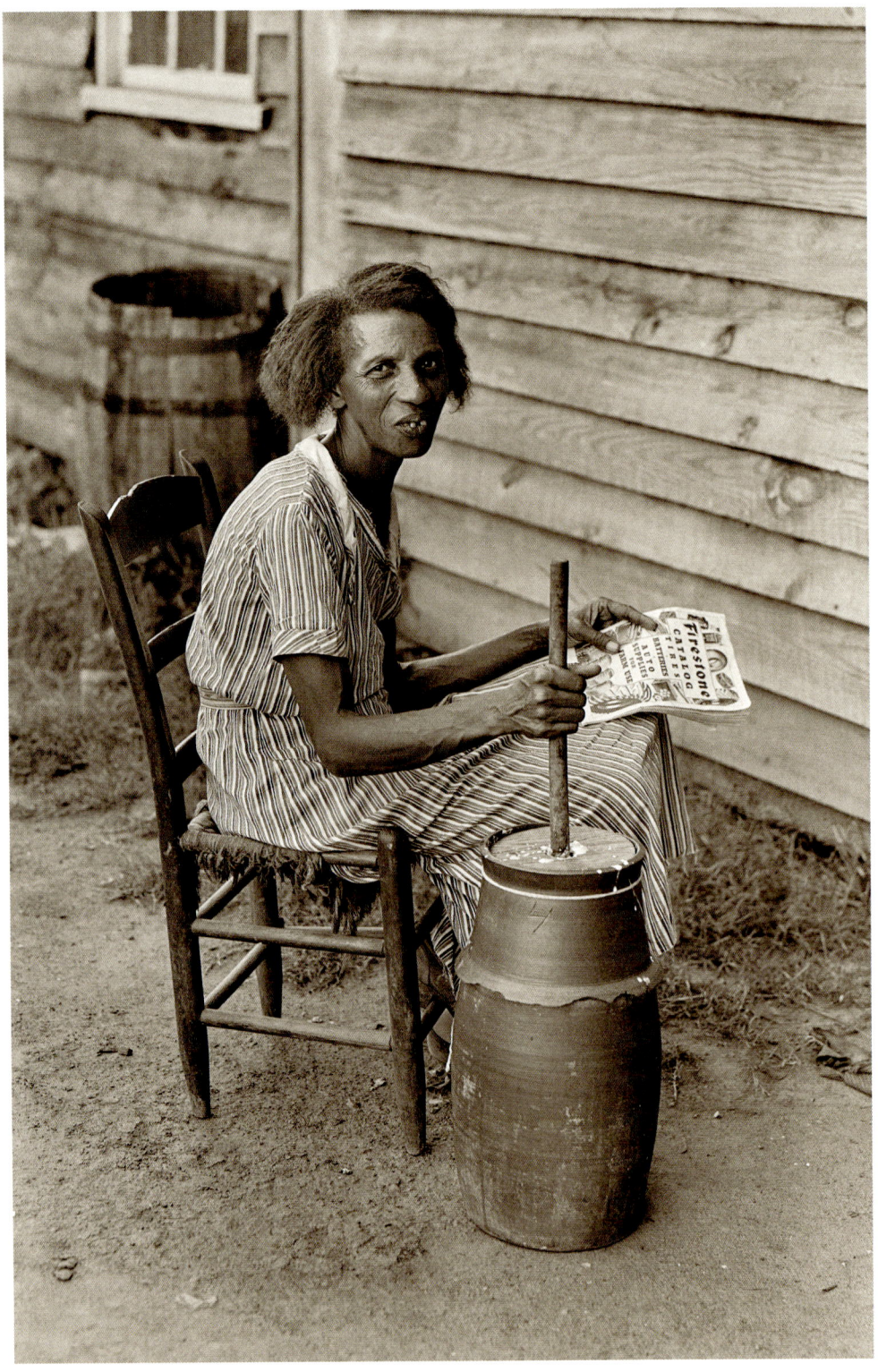

PLATE 105   A woman churning and reading. [South Carolina], ca. 1937.

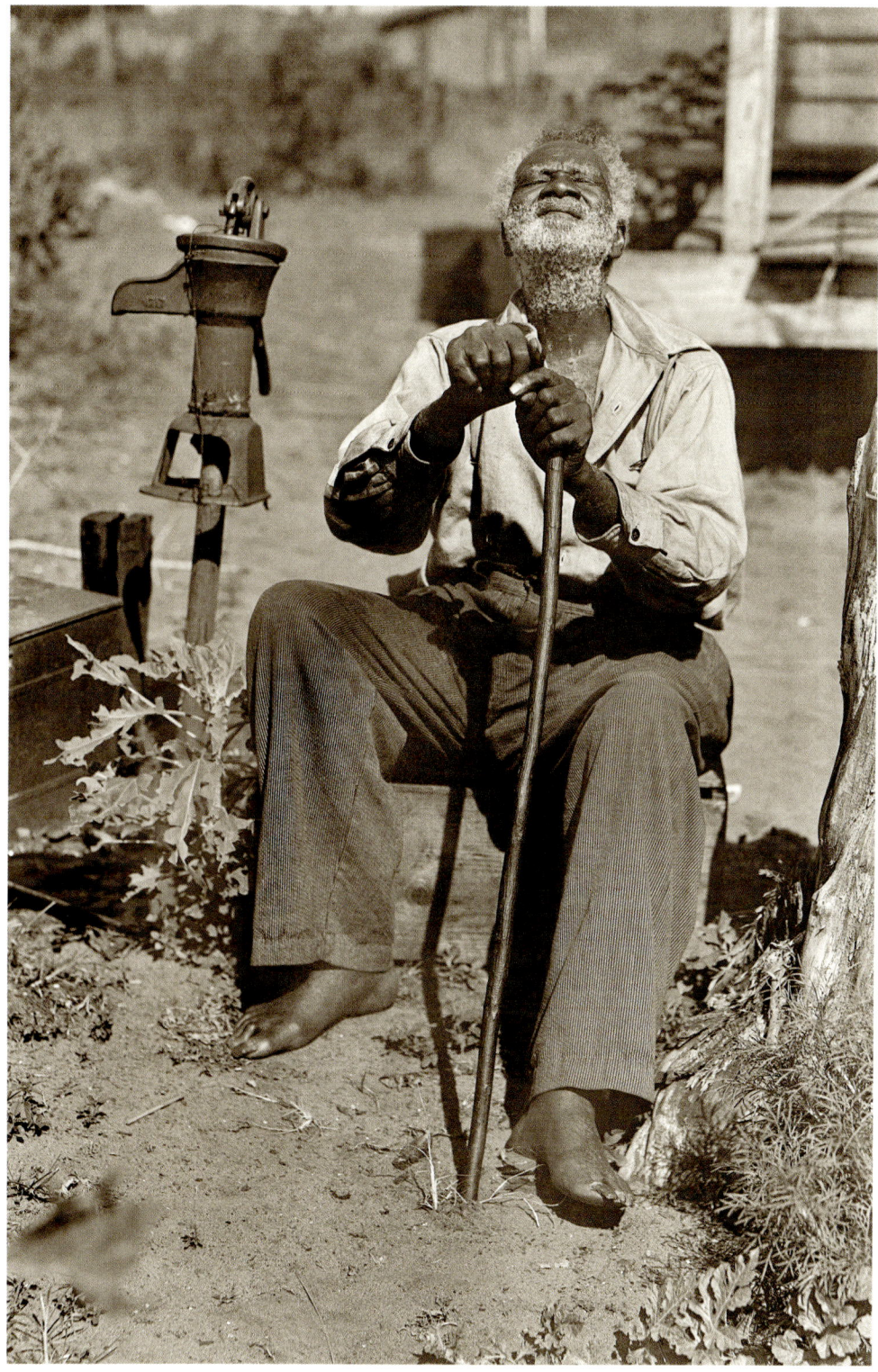

PLATE 106   Welcome Beese. Murrells Inlet, South Carolina, ca. 1937.

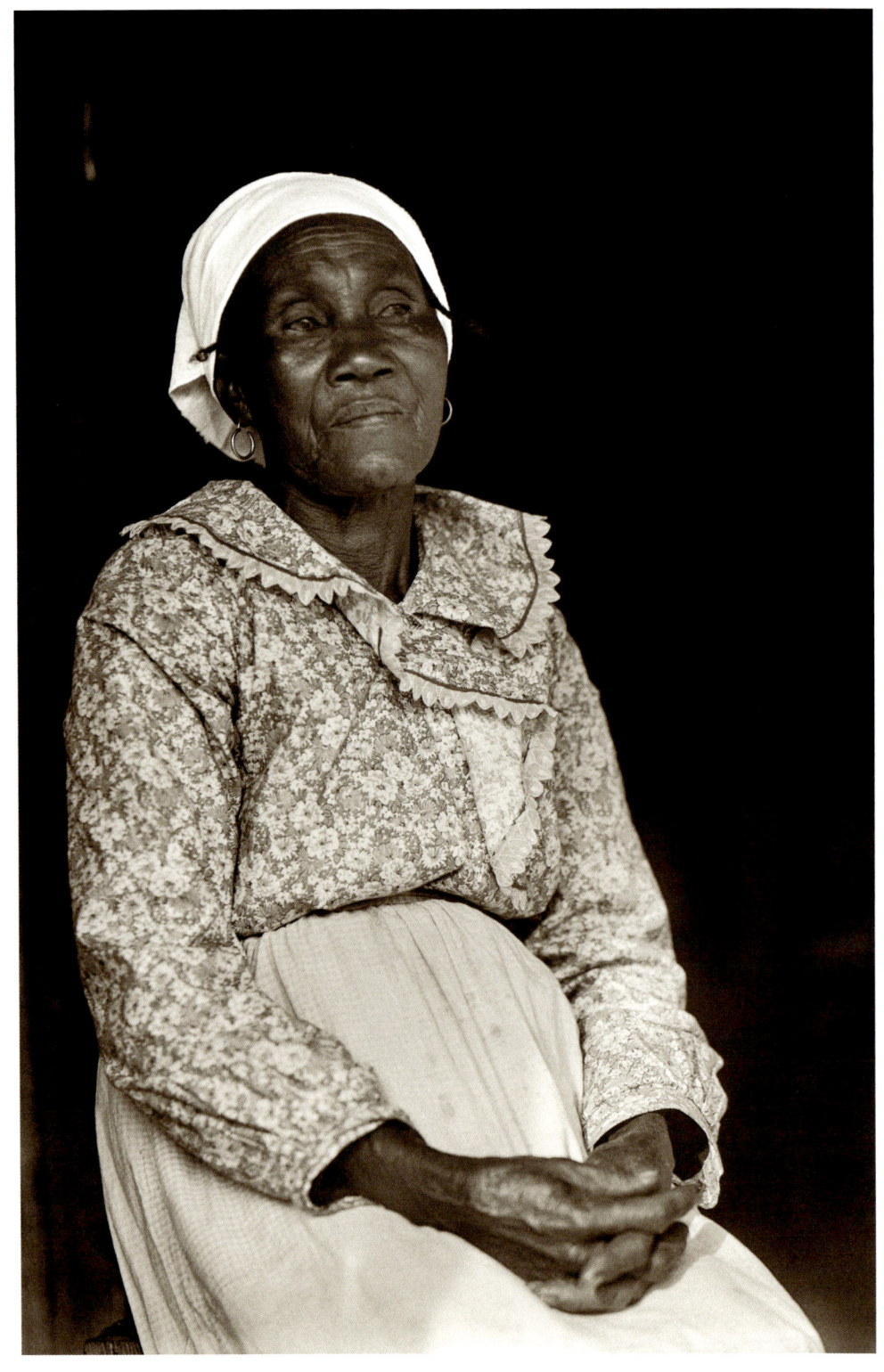

PLATE 107   Hagar Brown. Murrells Inlet, South Carolina, ca. 1937.

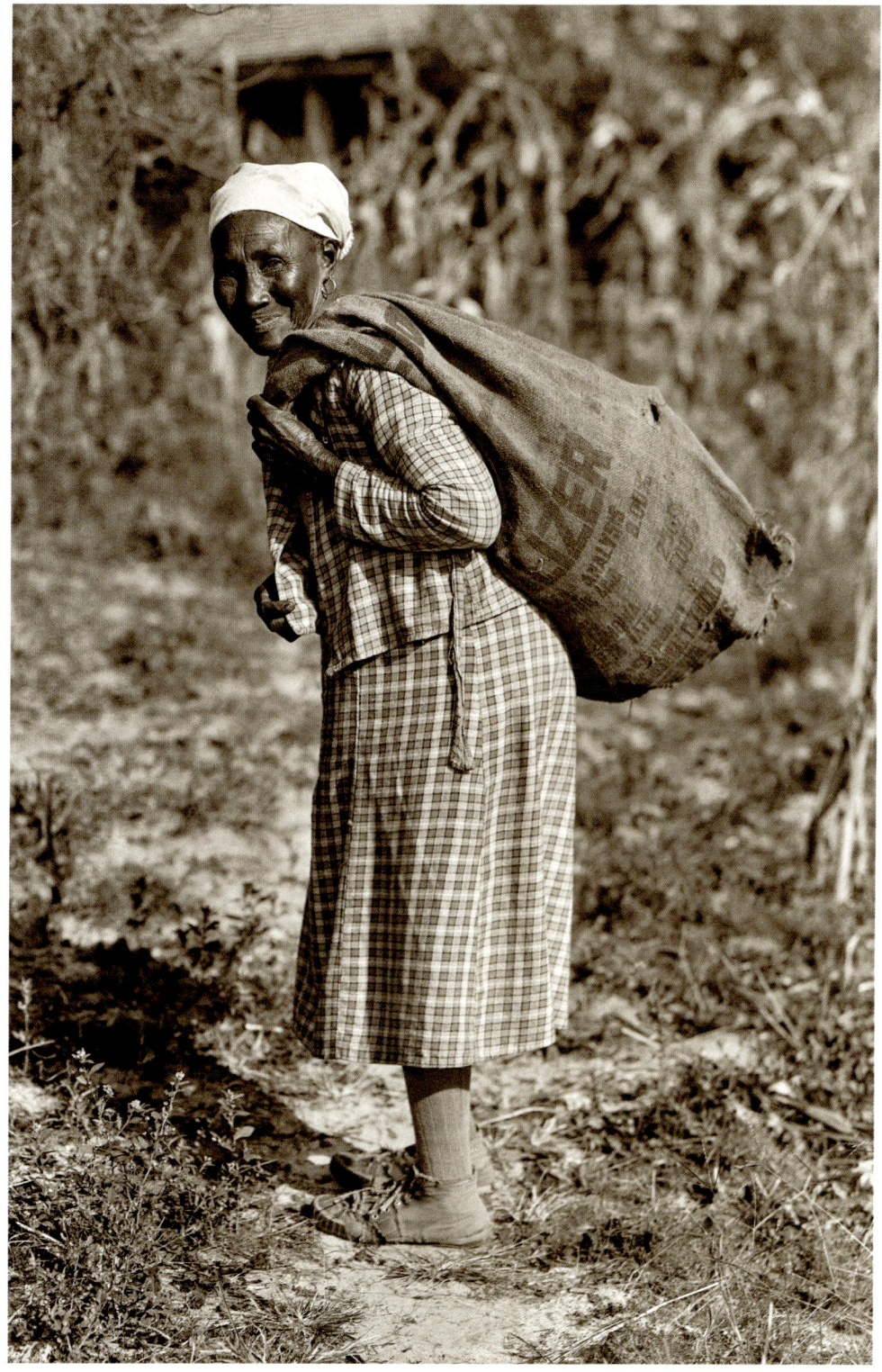

PLATE 108   Hagar Brown going home. Murrells Inlet, South Carolina, ca. 1937.

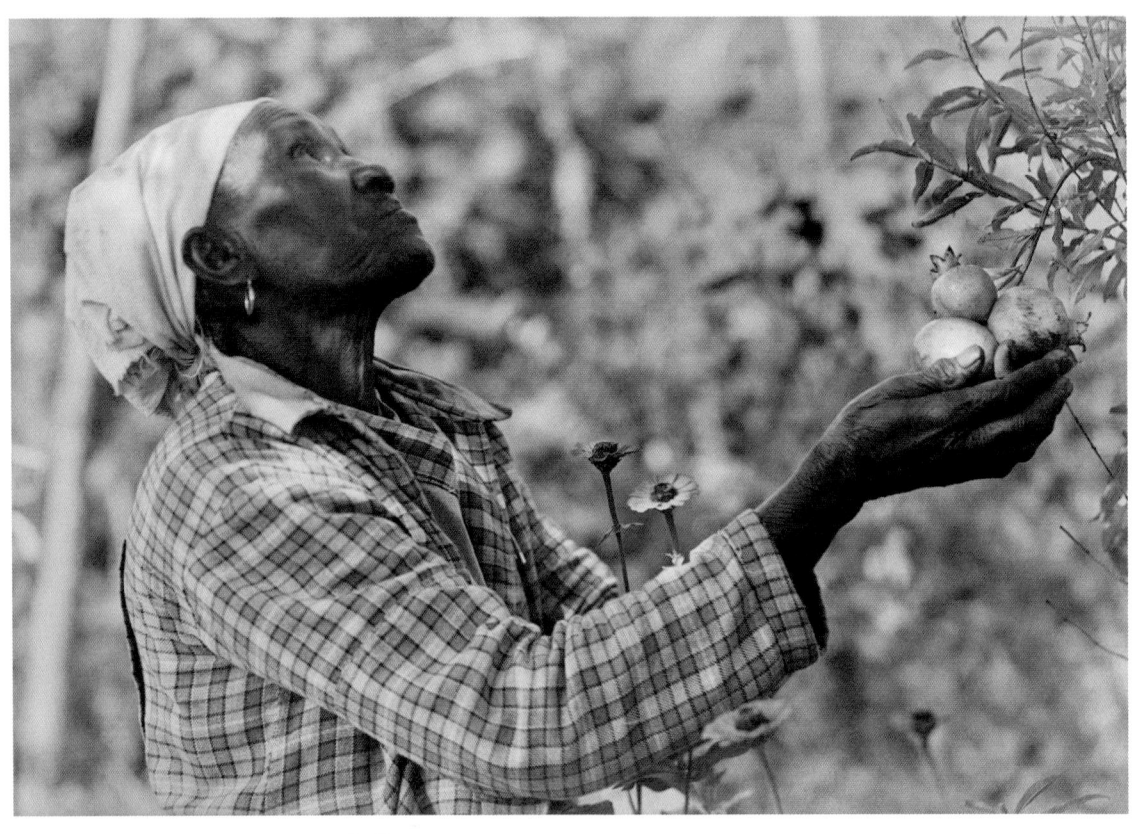

PLATE 109   Hagar Brown holding pomegranates. Murrells Inlet, South Carolina, ca. 1937.

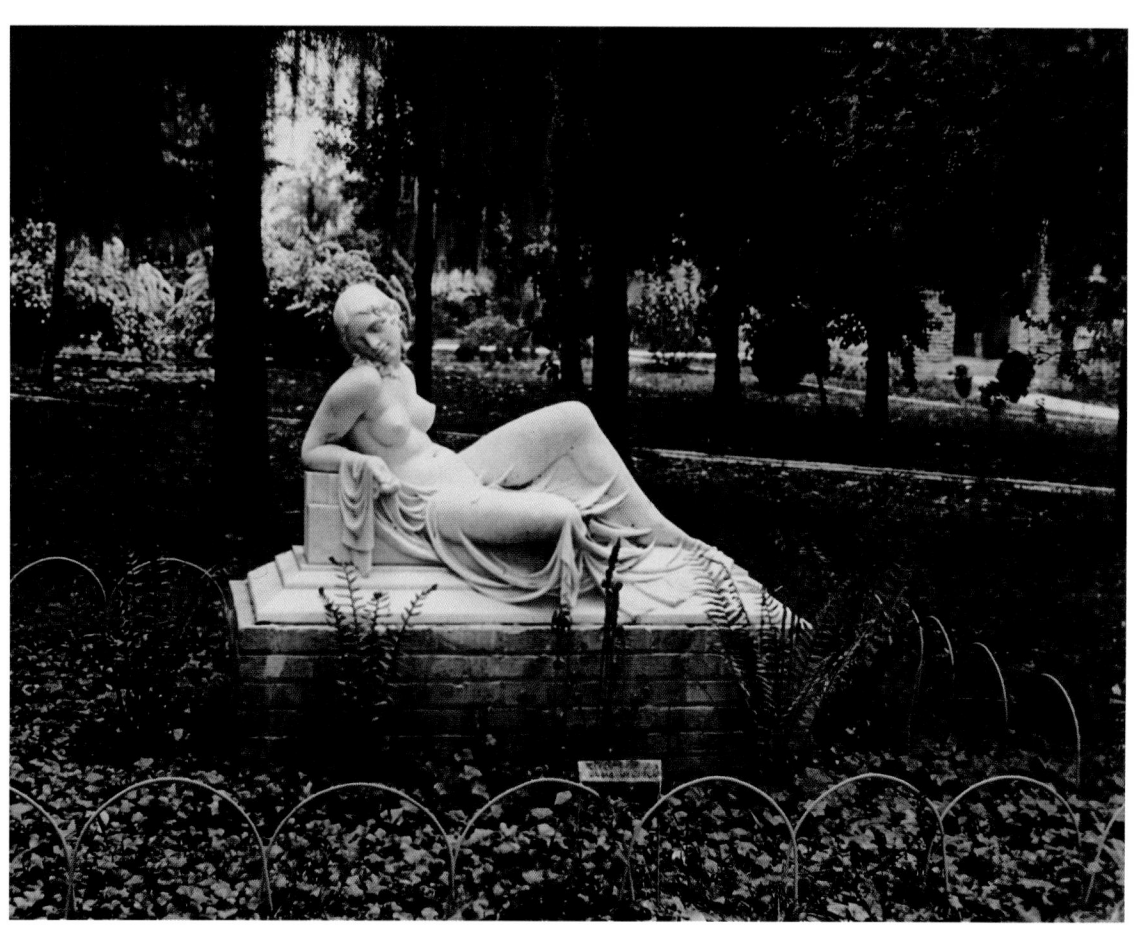

PLATE 110   "Night" by Mario Korbel. Brookgreen Gardens. Murrells Inlet,
South Carolina, ca. 1937.

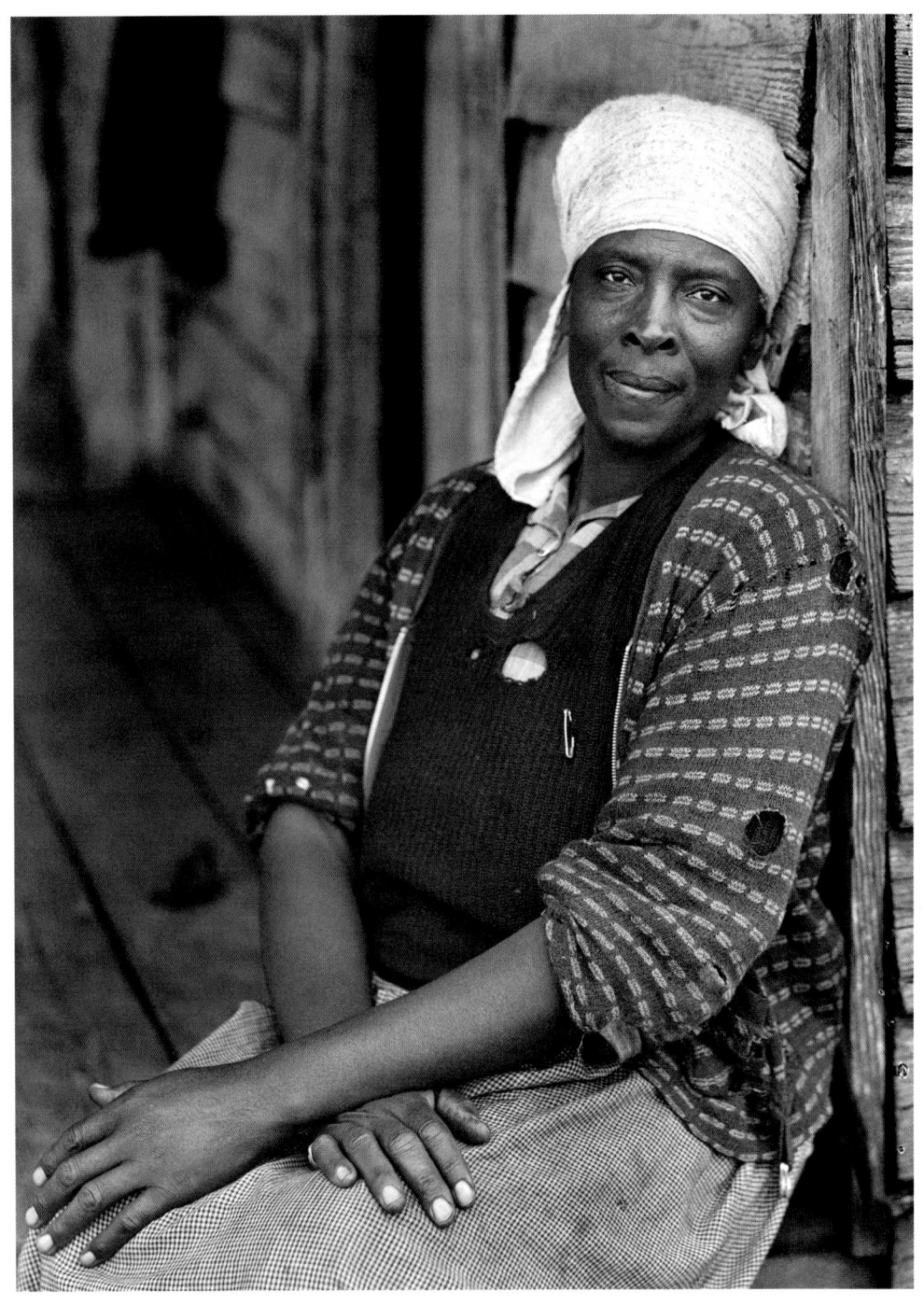

PLATE 111   A woman at rest. [Murrells Inlet, South Carolina], ca. 1937.

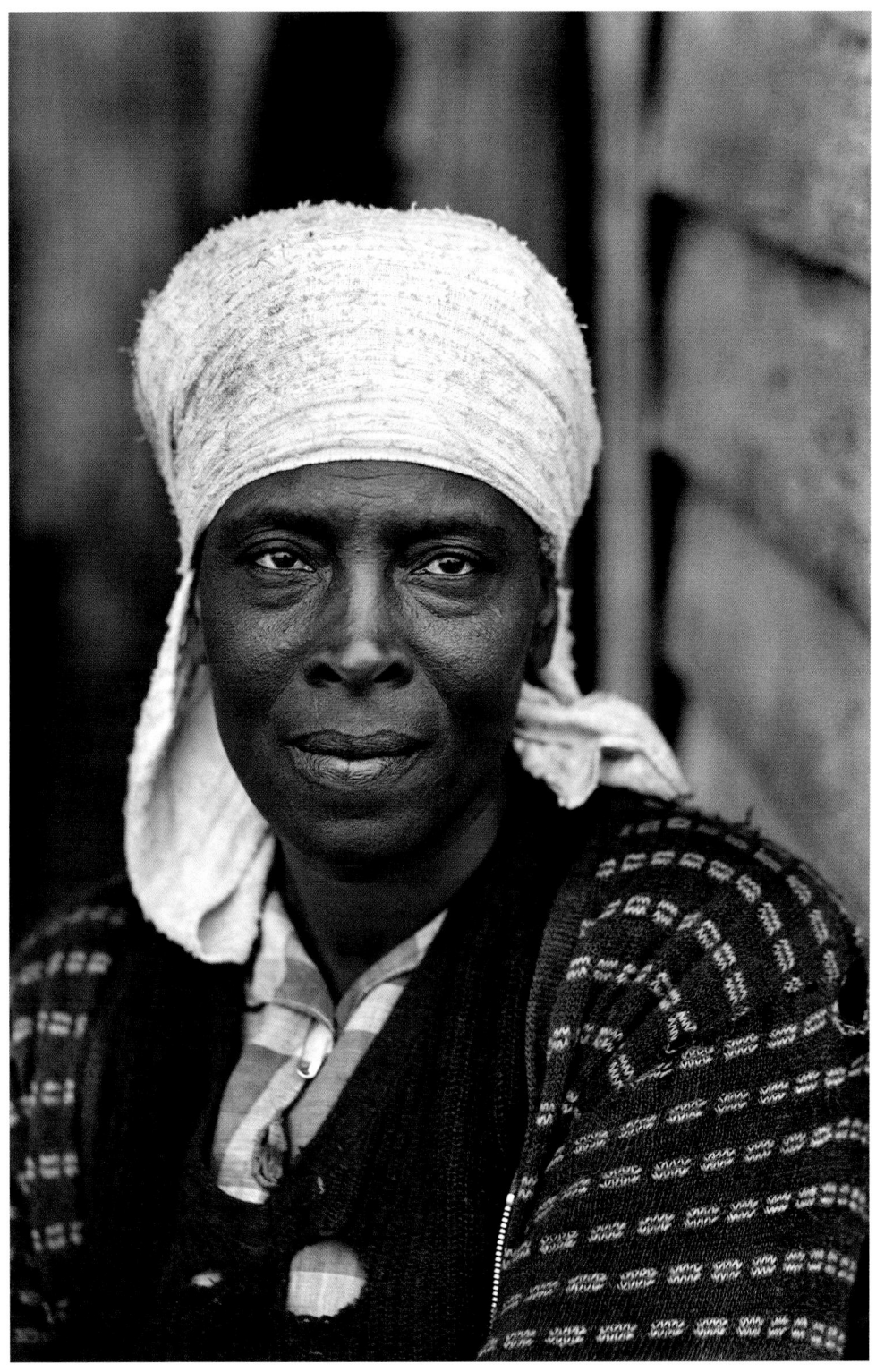

PLATE 112   Portrait of an African American woman.
[Murrells Inlet, South Carolina], ca. 1937.

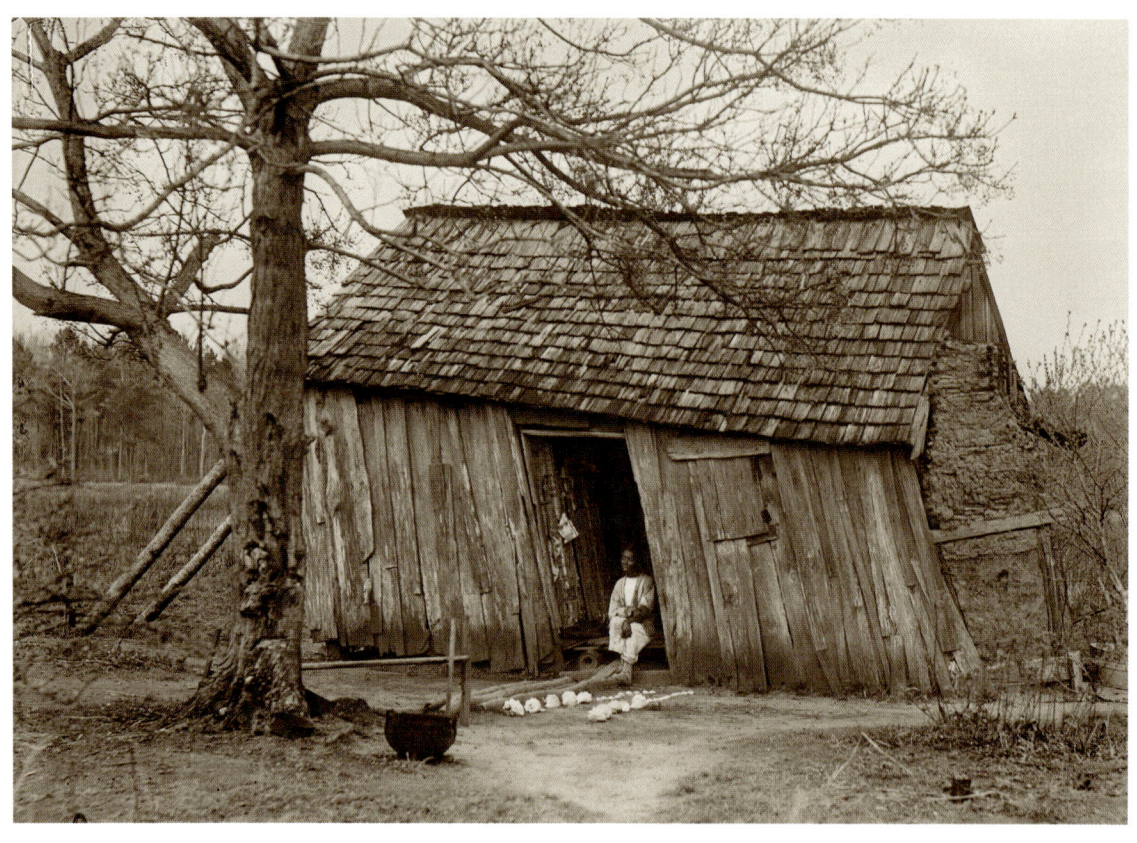

PLATE 113   An old home. [Murrells Inlet, South Carolina], ca. 1937.

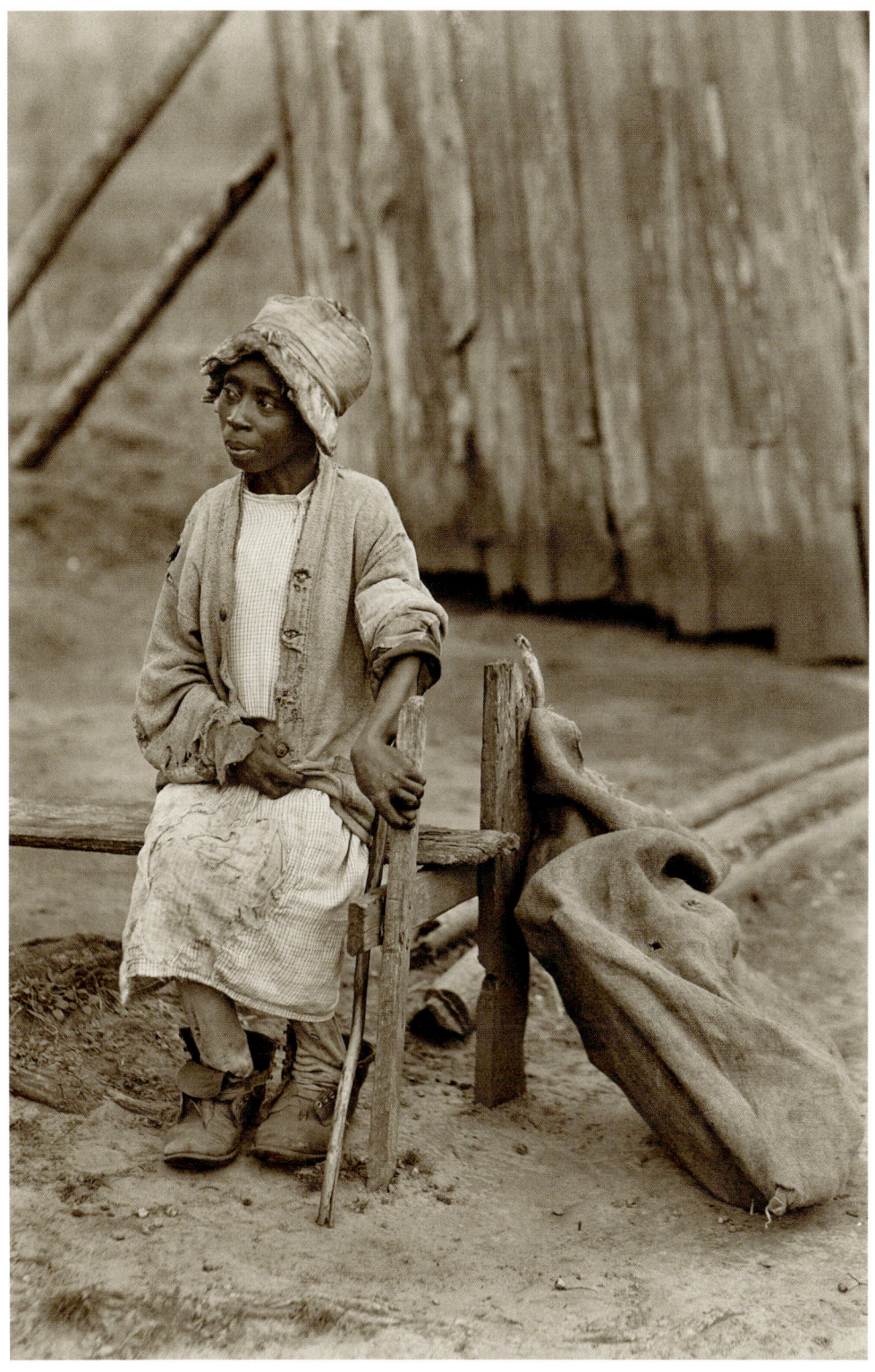

PLATE 114   Woman on a bench. [Murrells Inlet, South Carolina], ca. 1937.

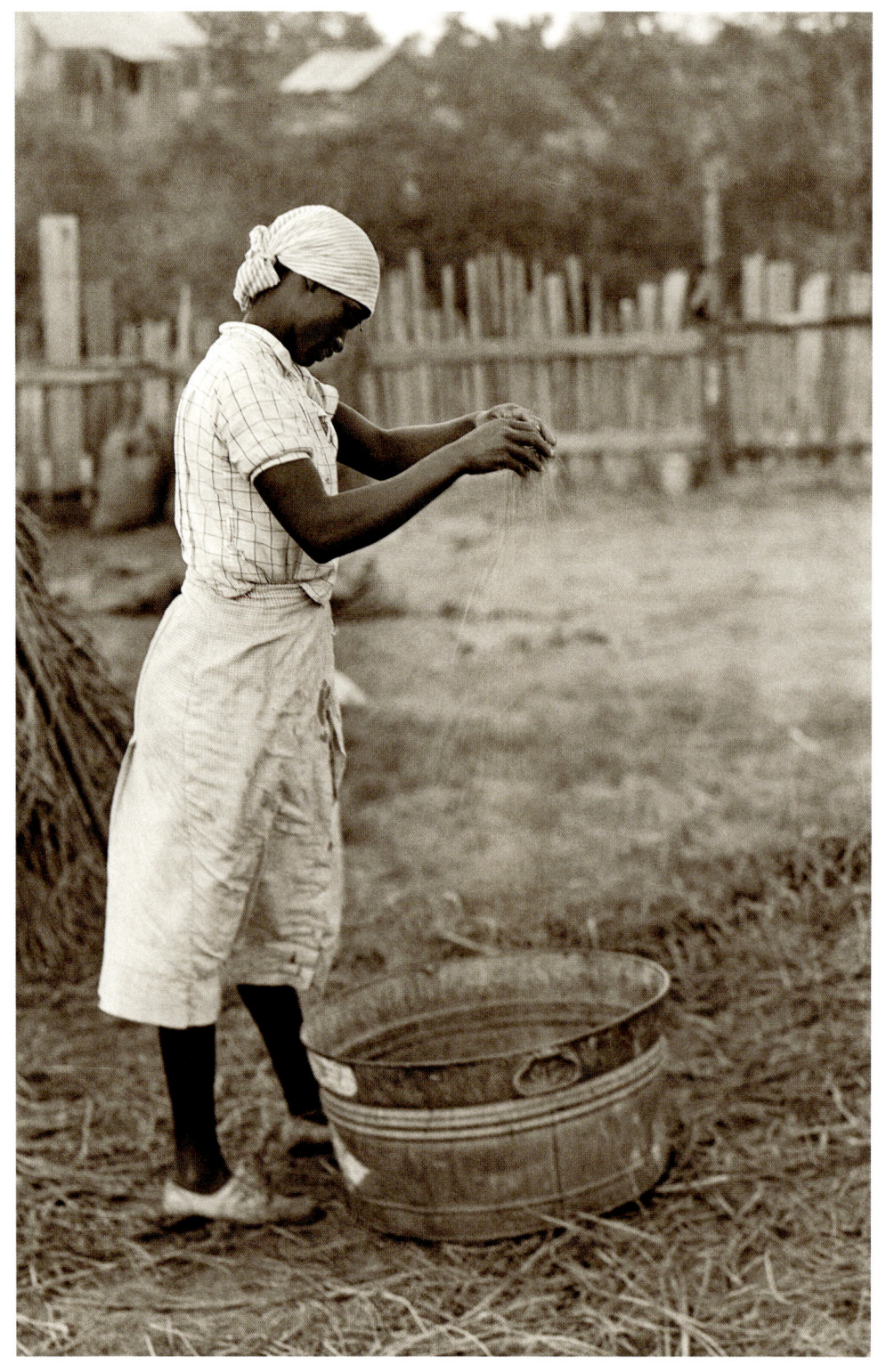

PLATE 115   *Winnowing Rice.* Sandy Island, South Carolina, ca. 1937.

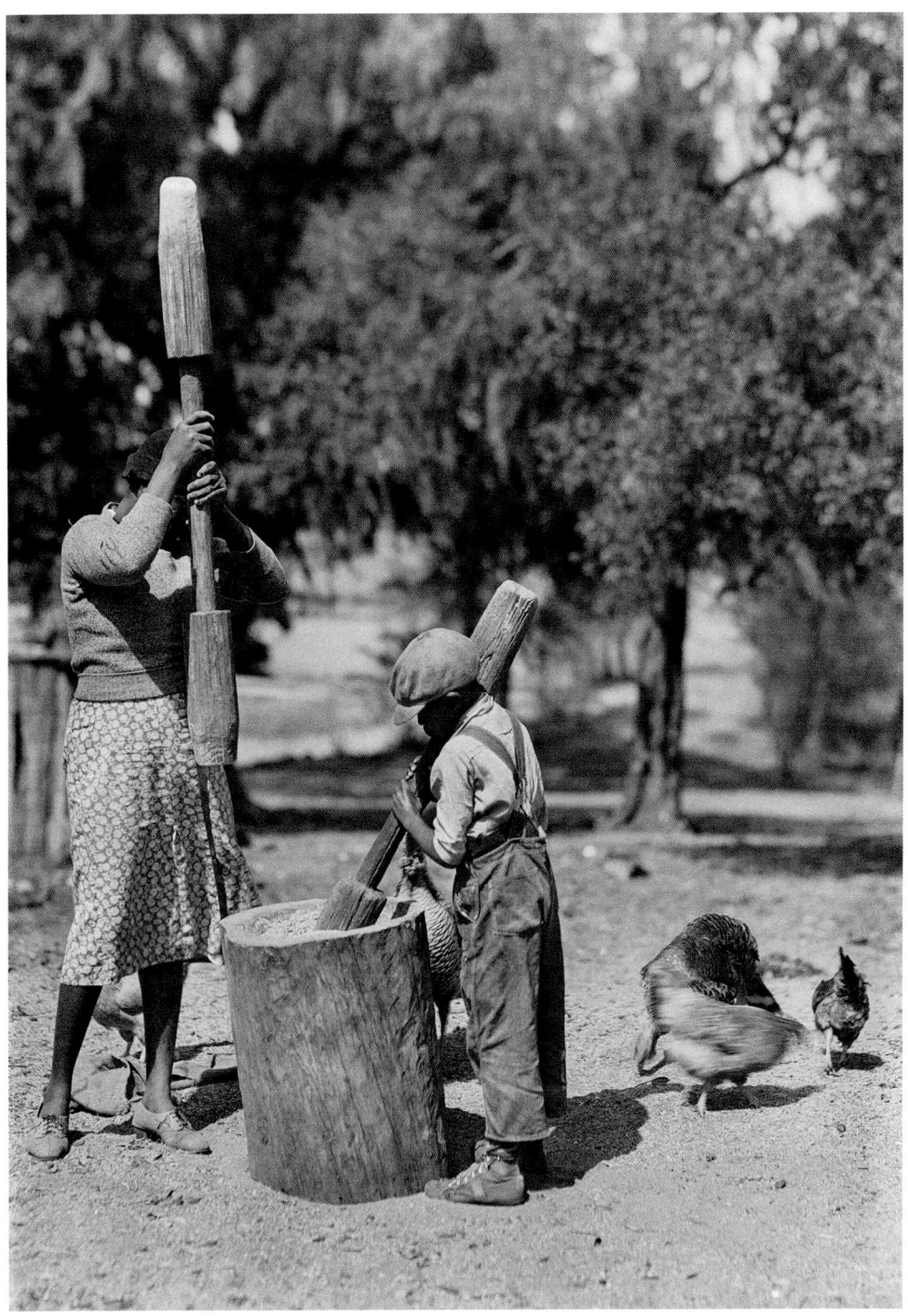

PLATE 116 Grinding rice. Sandy Island, South Carolina, ca. 1937.

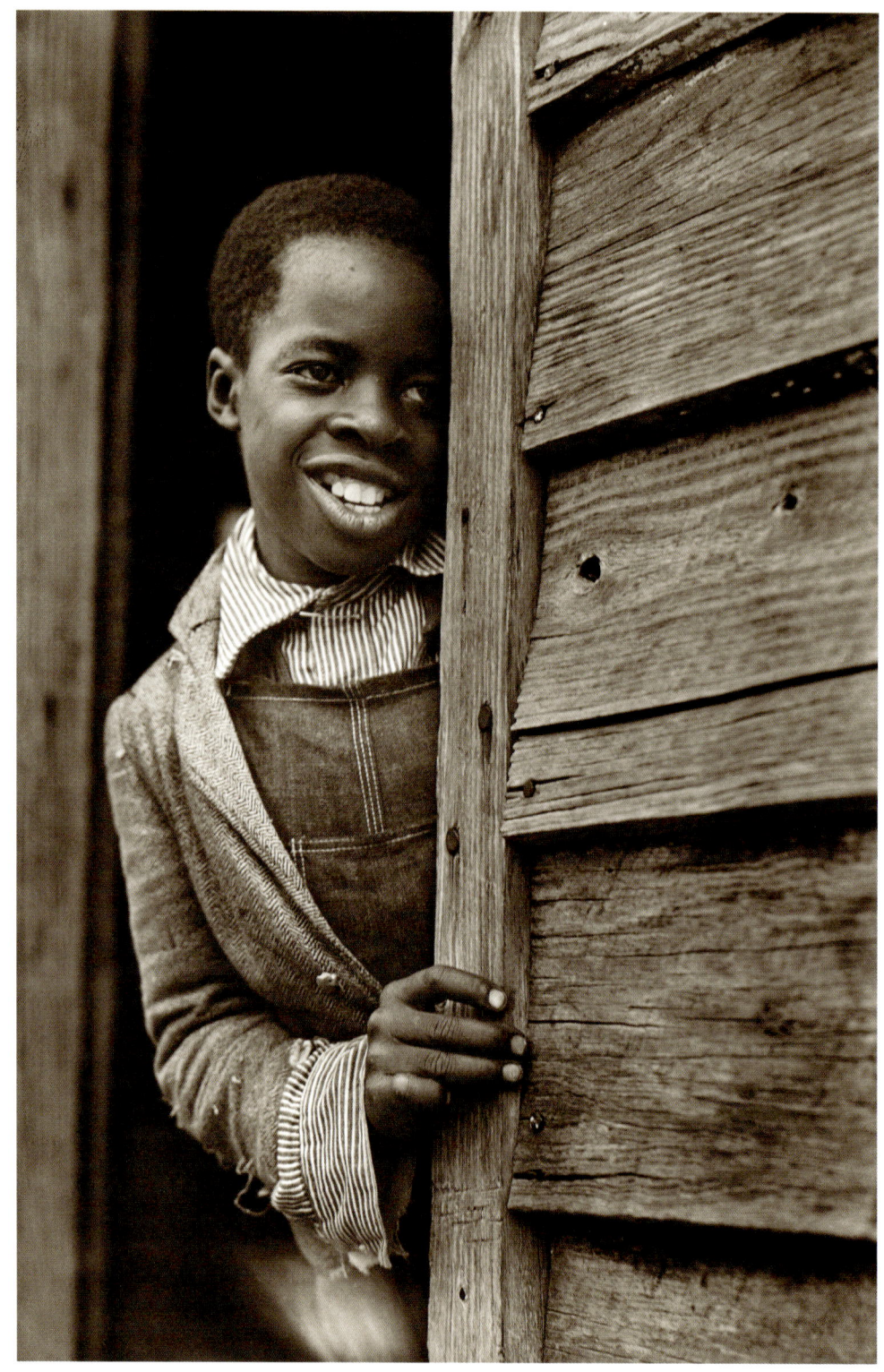

PLATE 117   Boy in a doorway. [Sandy Island, South Carolina], ca. 1937.

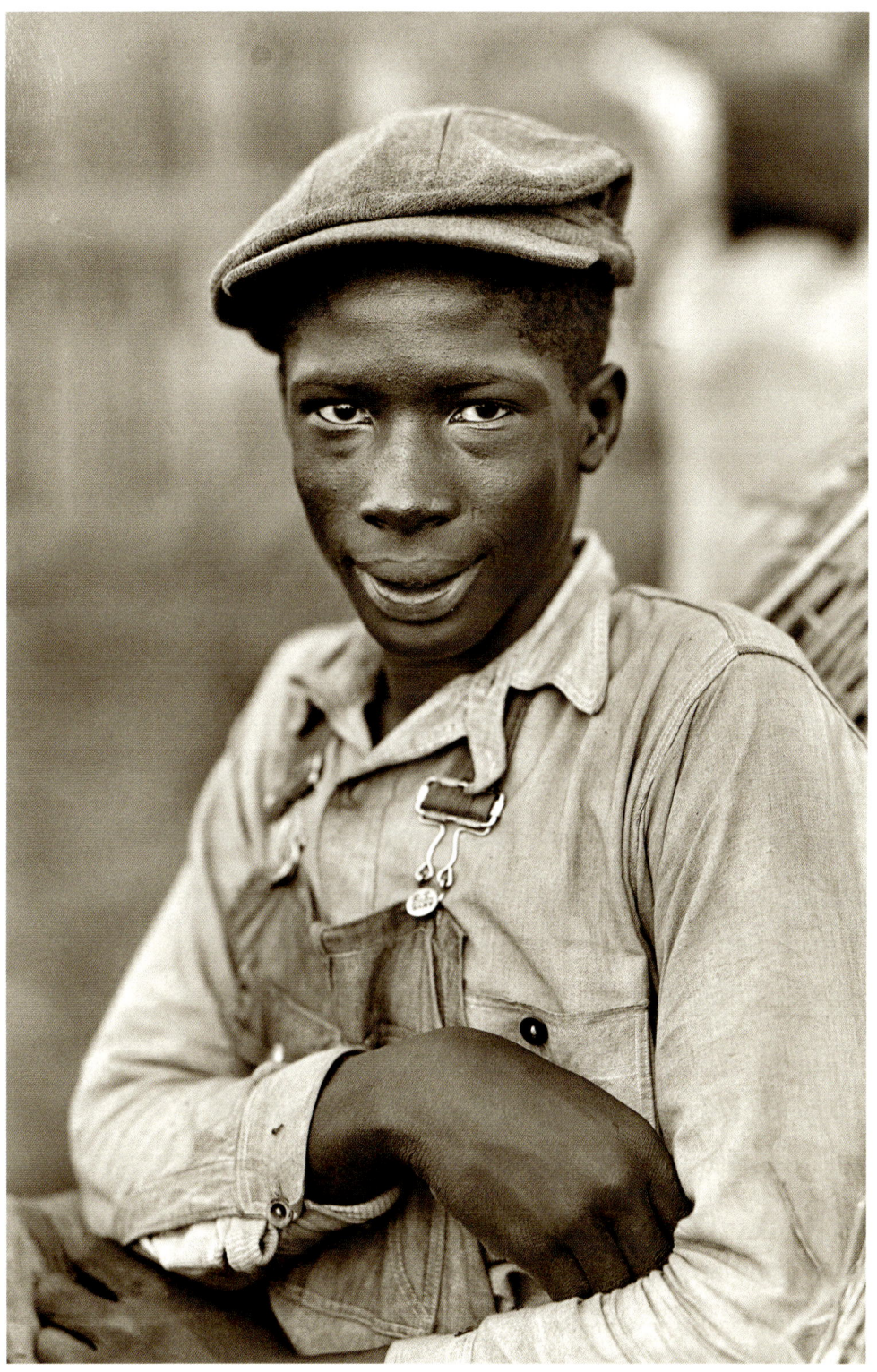

PLATE 118   A youth. Sandy Island, South Carolina, ca. 1937.

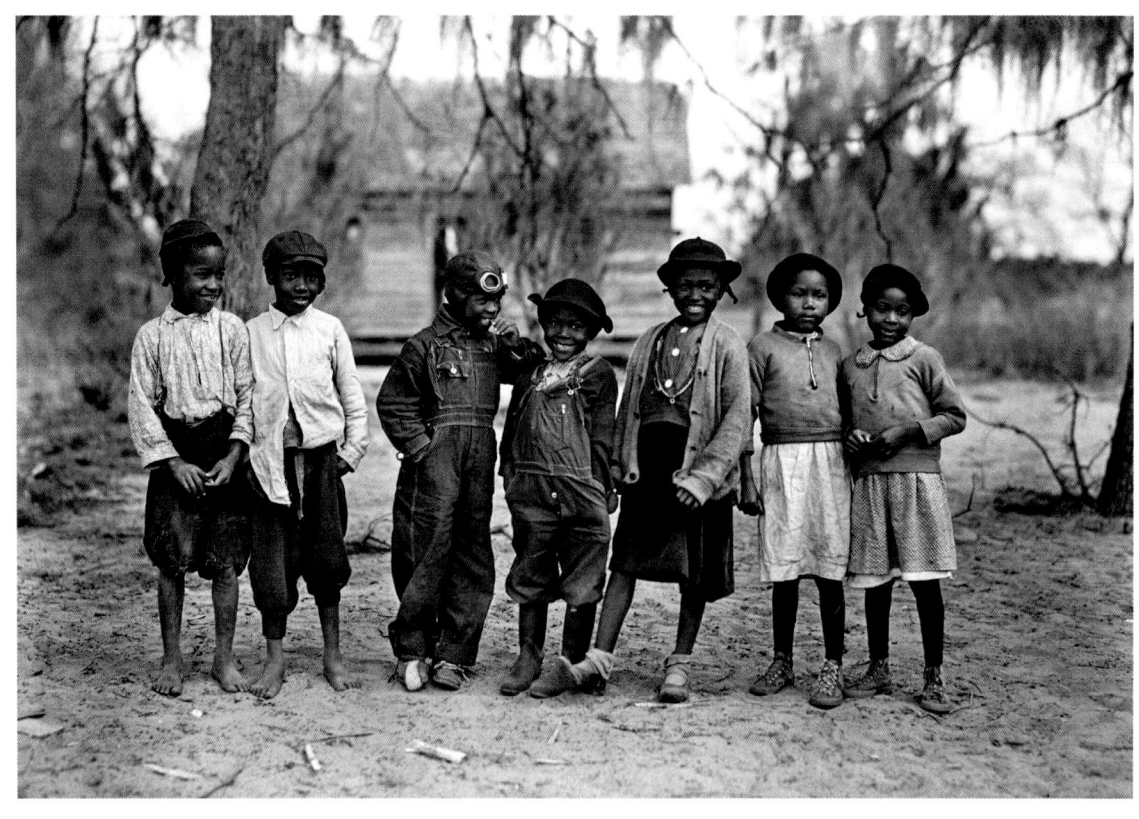

PLATE 119   Children posing. [Murrells Inlet, South Carolina], ca. 1937.

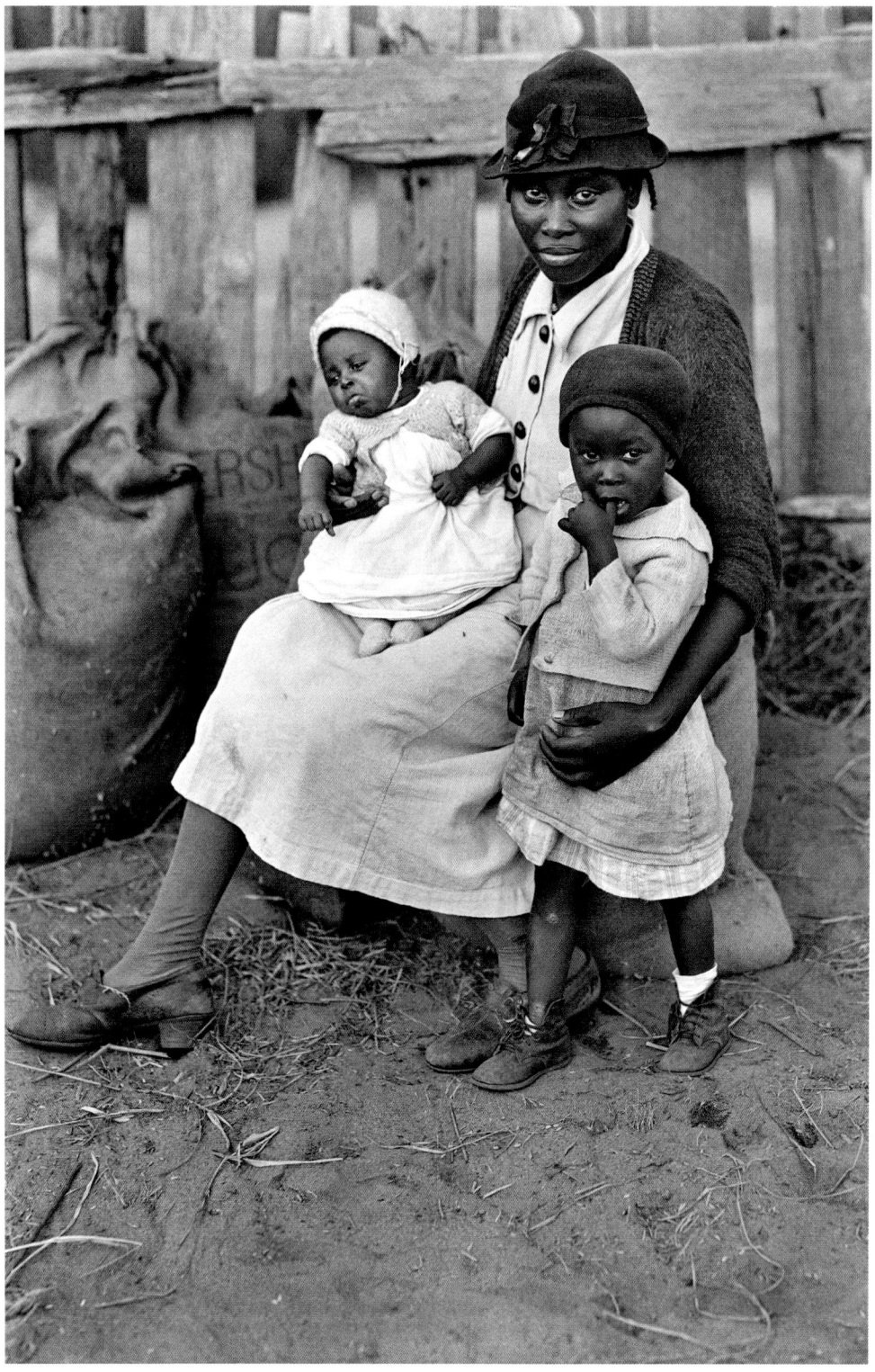

PLATE 120   A mother and children. Sandy Island, South Carolina, ca. 1937.

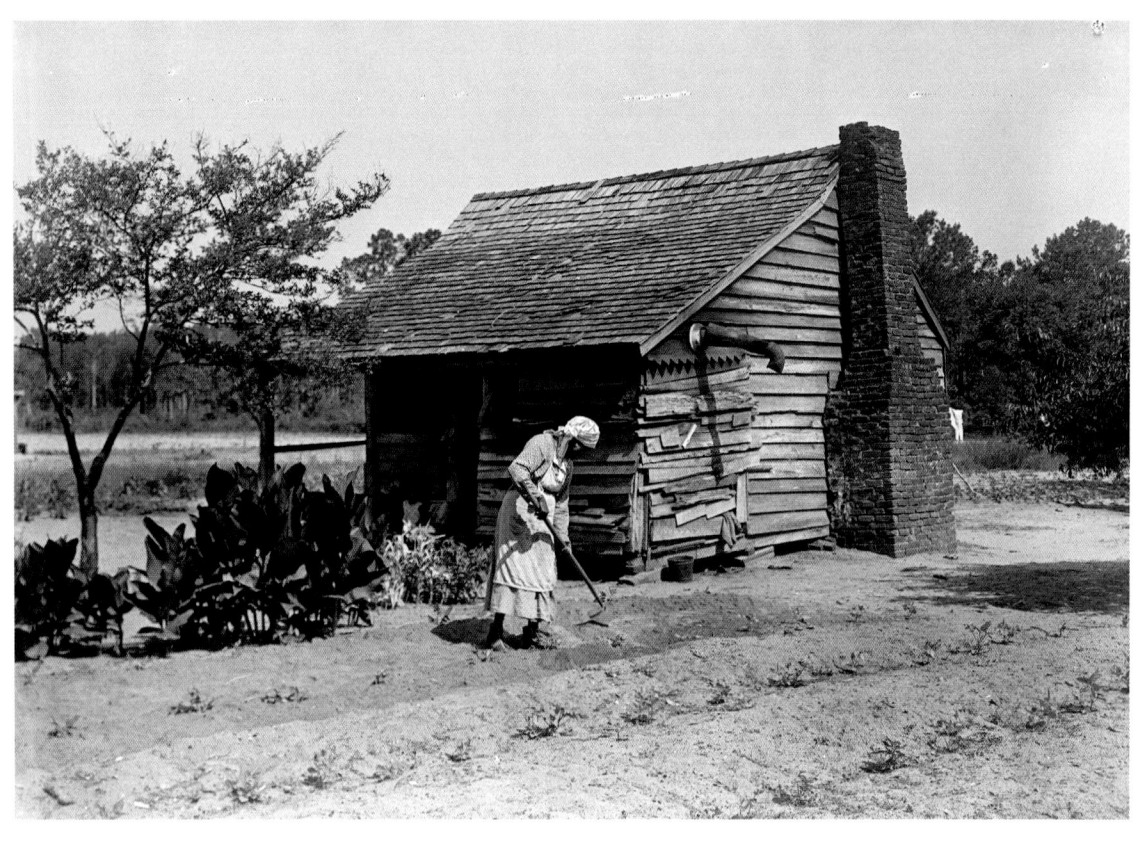

PLATE 121   [Margaret Bryant hoeing her garden. Murrells Inlet, South Carolina], ca. 1937.

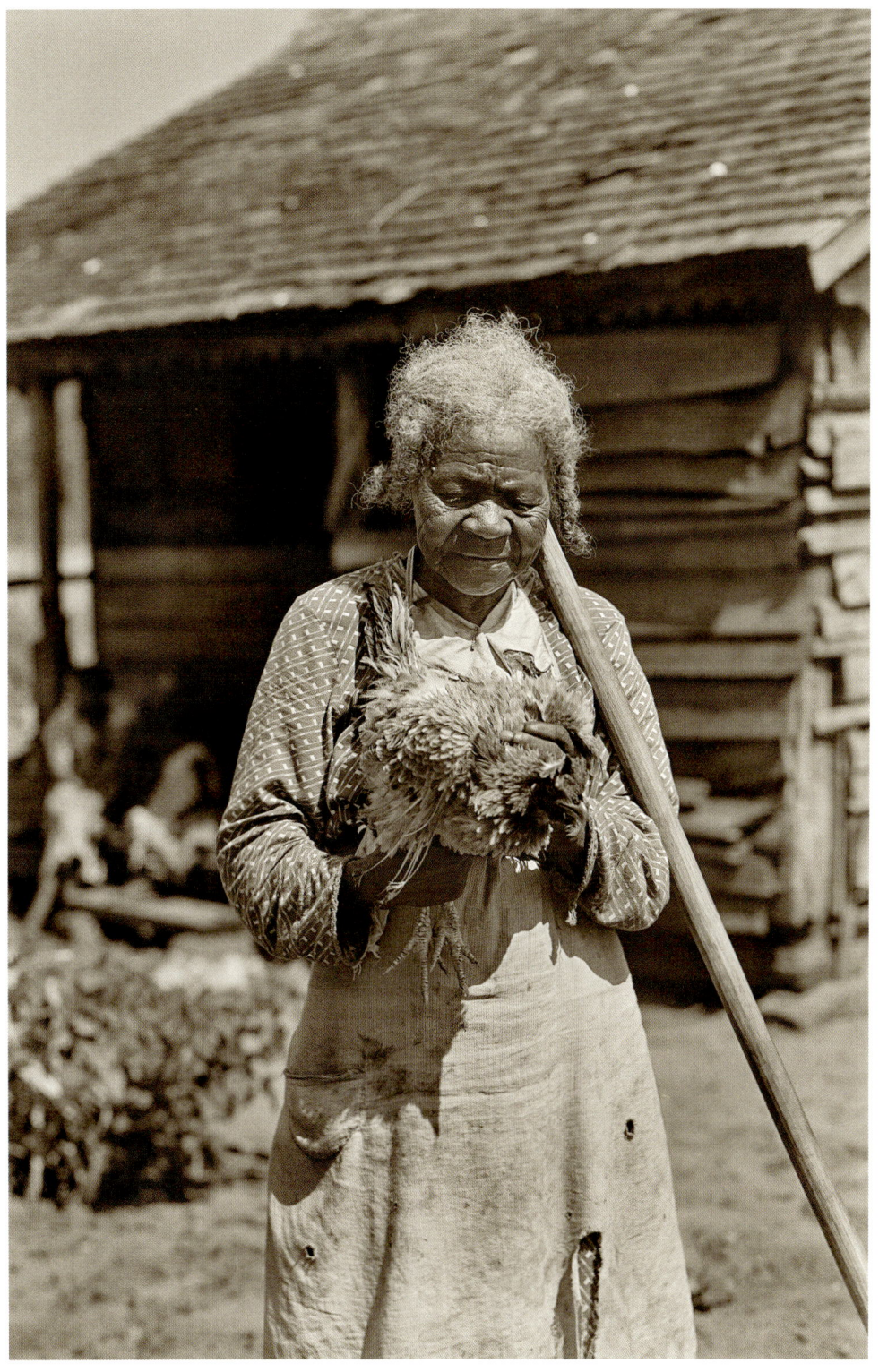

PLATE 122   [Margaret Bryant with a hen. Murrells Inlet, South Carolina], ca. 1937.

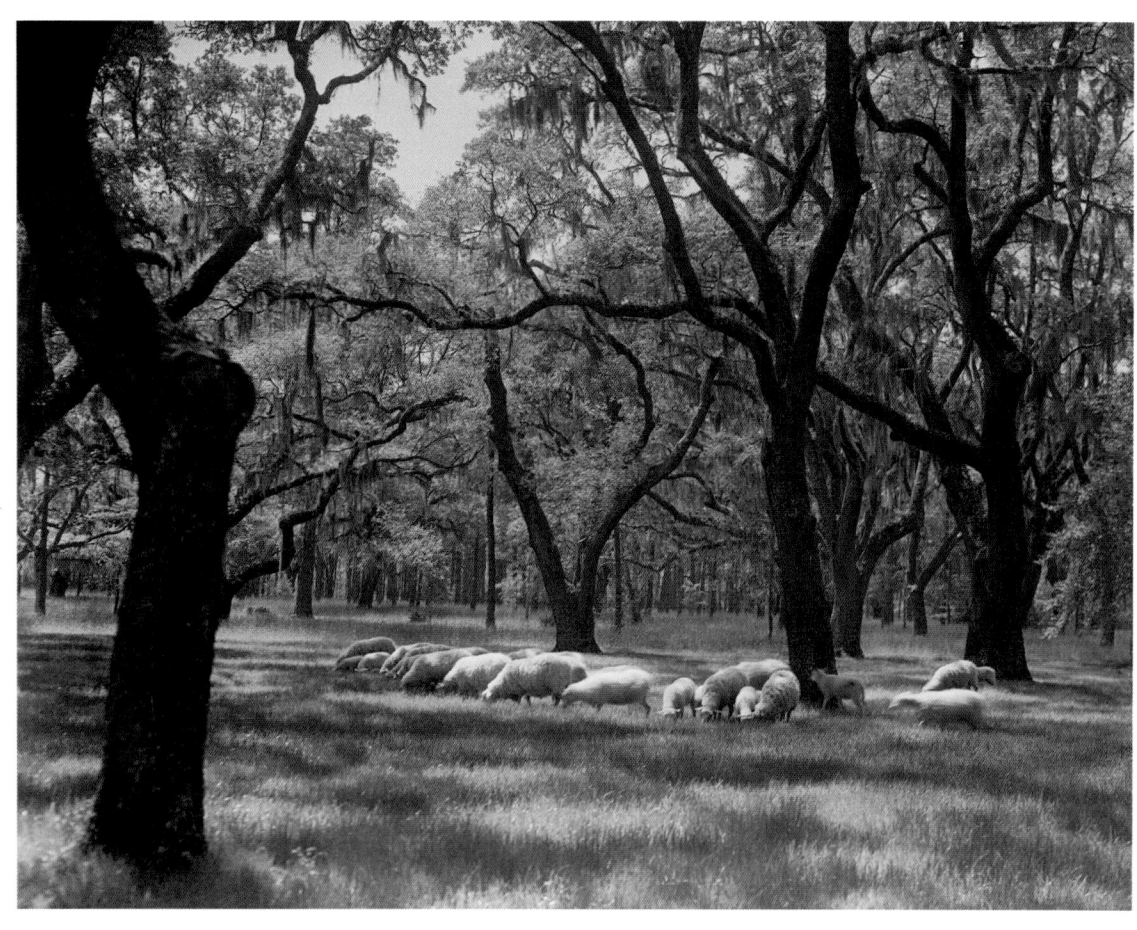

PLATE 123   Grazing sheep. Chicora Woods Plantation. South Carolina, 1930s.

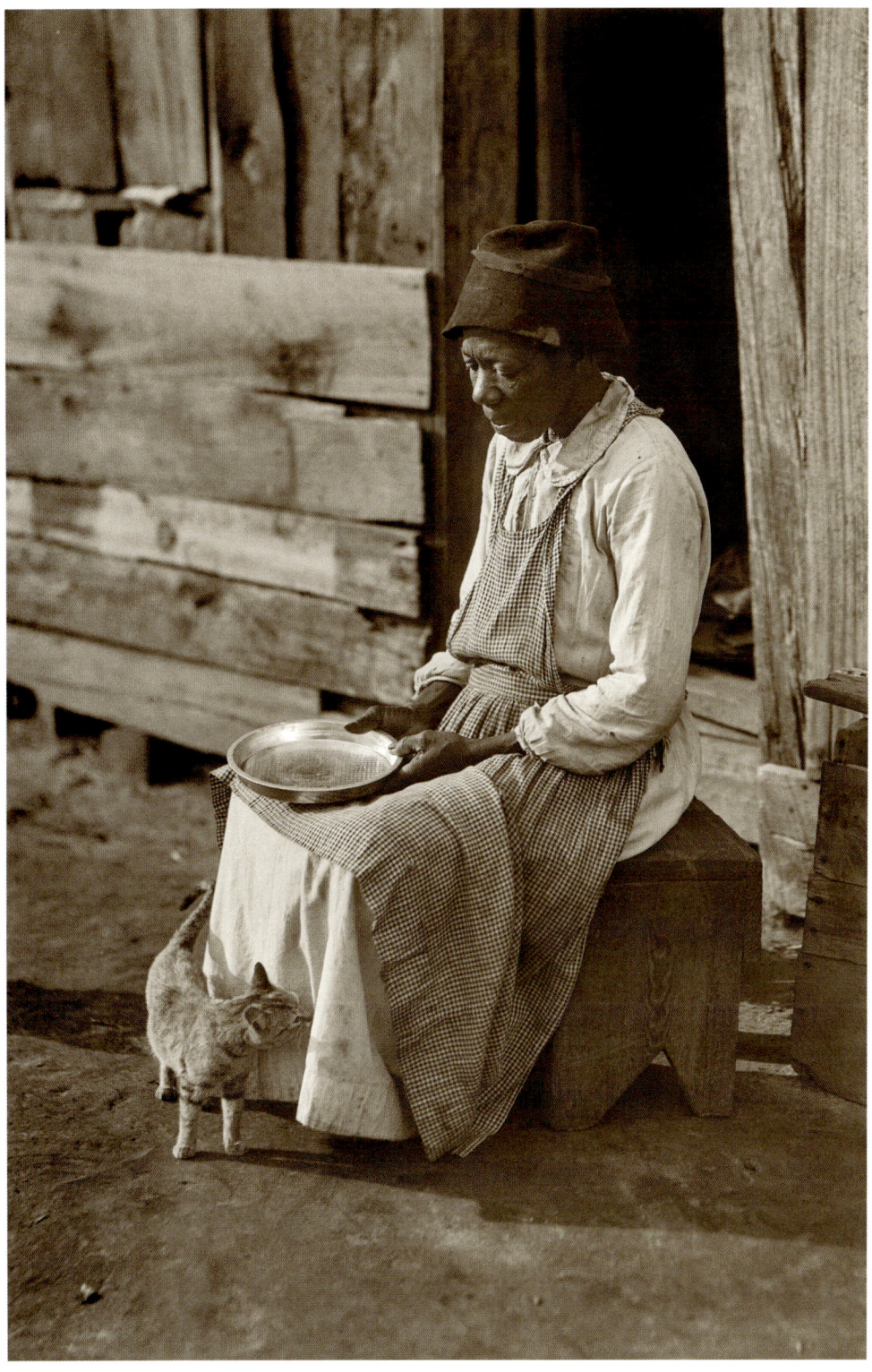

PLATE 124   Woman with an empty plate. [Sandy Island, South Carolina], ca. 1937.

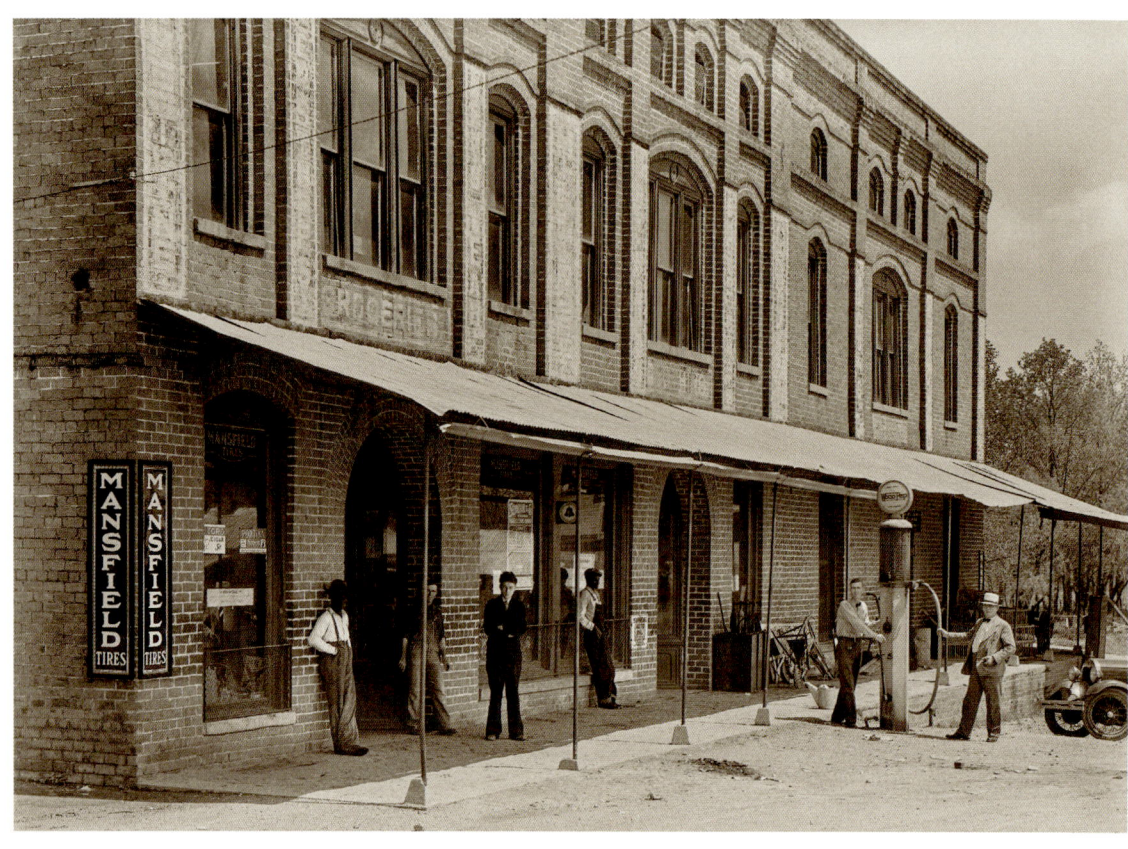

PLATE 125   Storefronts. Wilsonville, Alabama, 1930s.

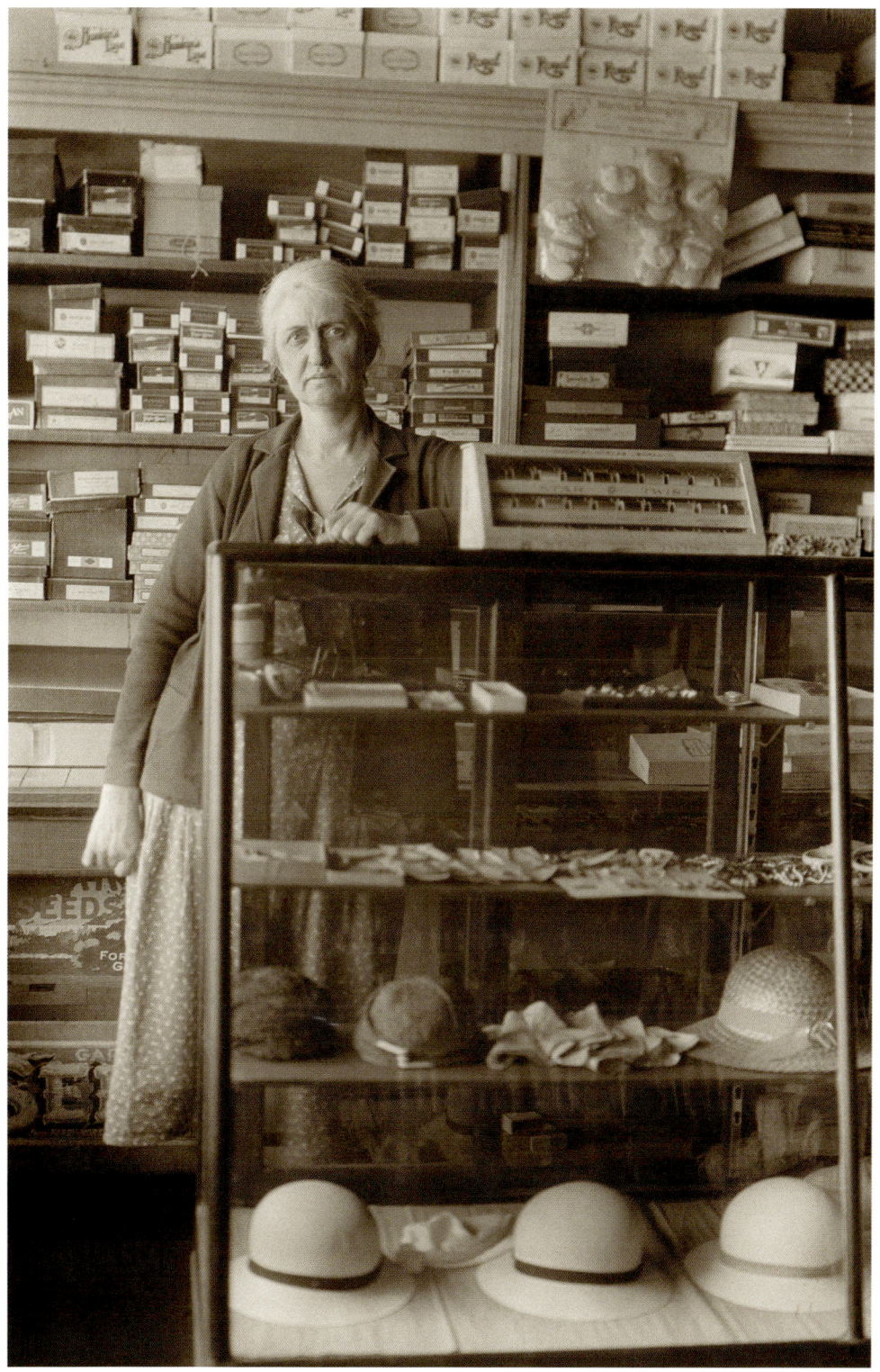

PLATE 126   *Woman Clerk*. Mrs. A. A. Gorman. Vincent, Alabama, 1930s.

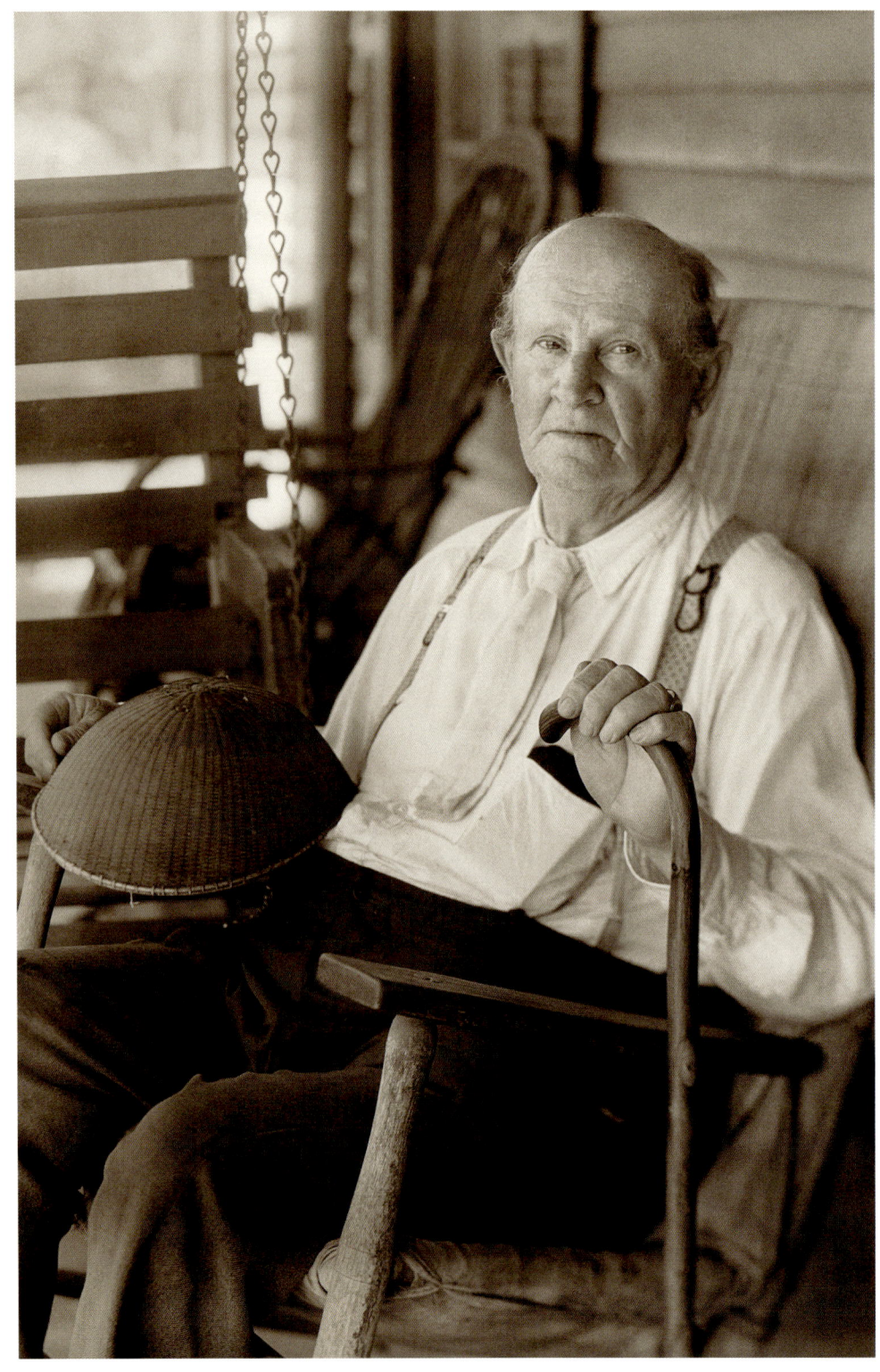

PLATE 127   Dr. J. Buford Boyer. Wilsonville, Alabama, 1930s.

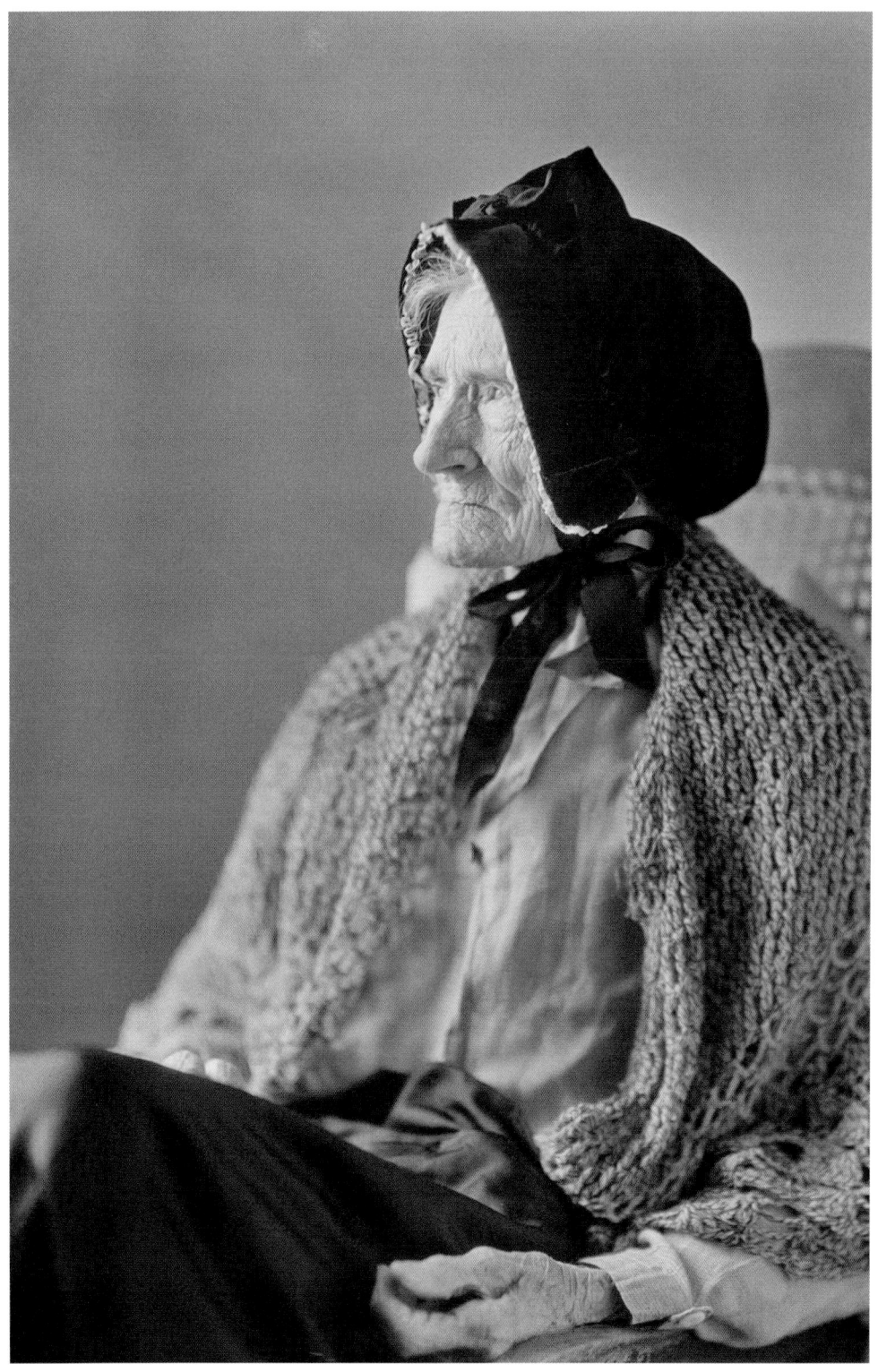

PLATE 128   "Will to Rule." Mrs. S. J. Ackers. Montevallo, Alabama, 1930s.

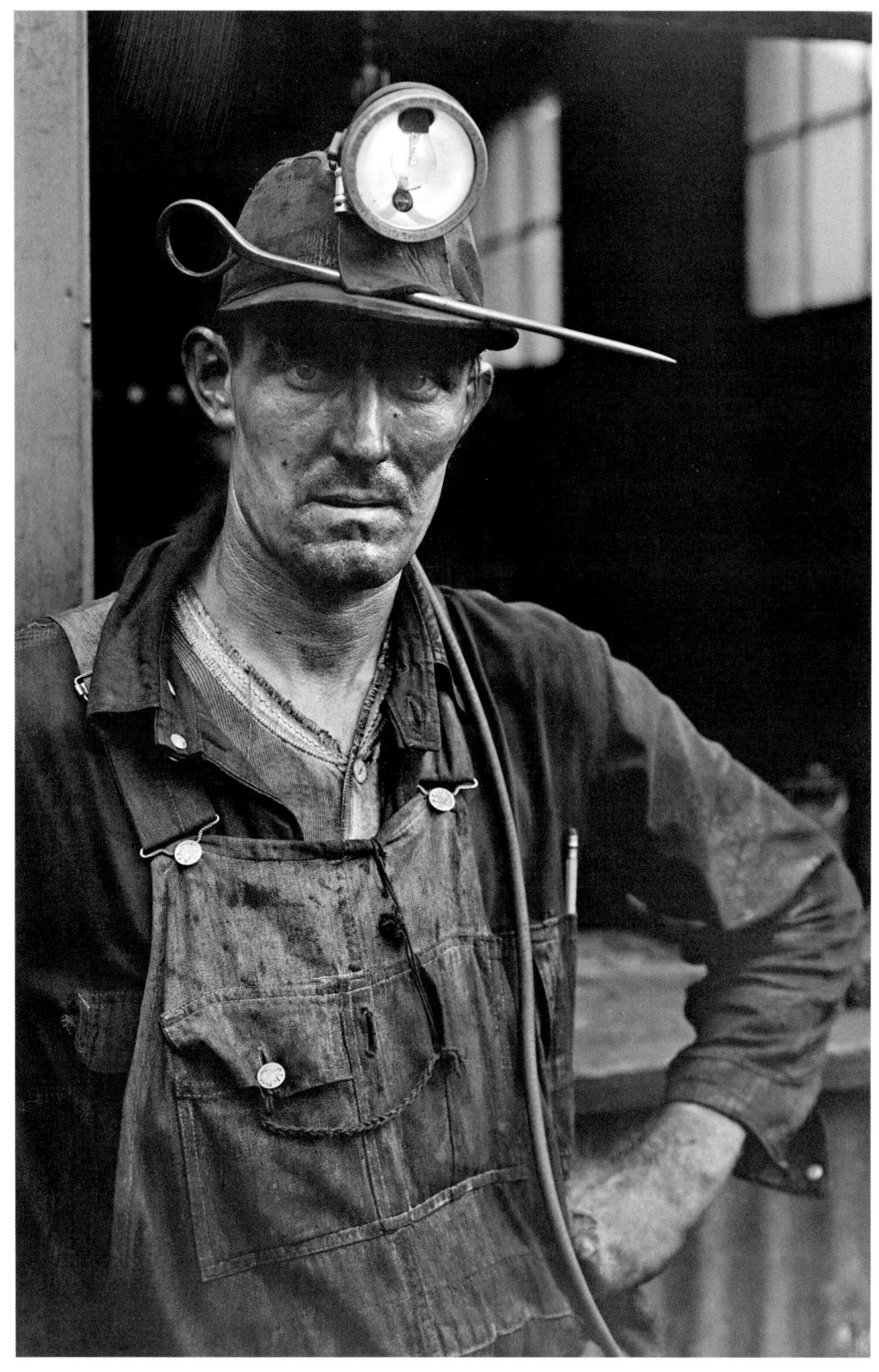

PLATE 129 A miner. Roscoe Dennis. Aldrich, Alabama, 1930s.

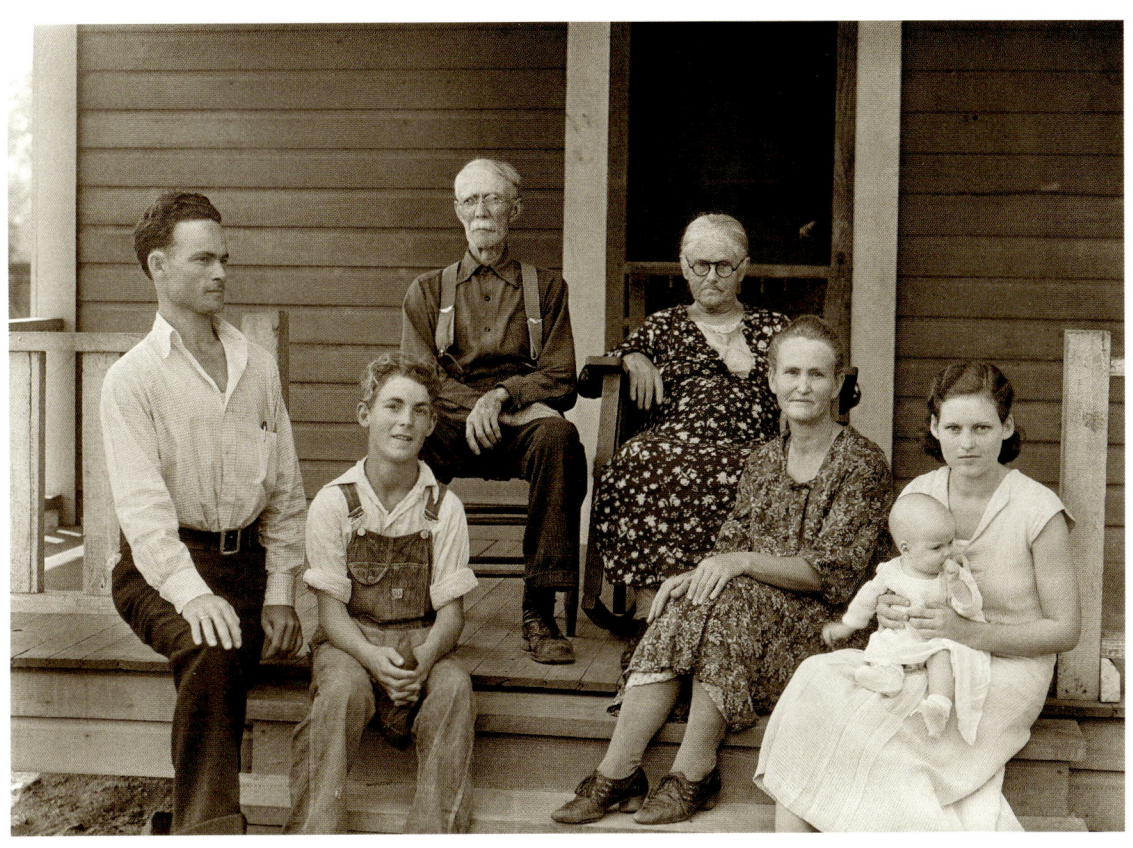

PLATE 130   *Miner's Family*. Shelby County, Alabama, 1930s.

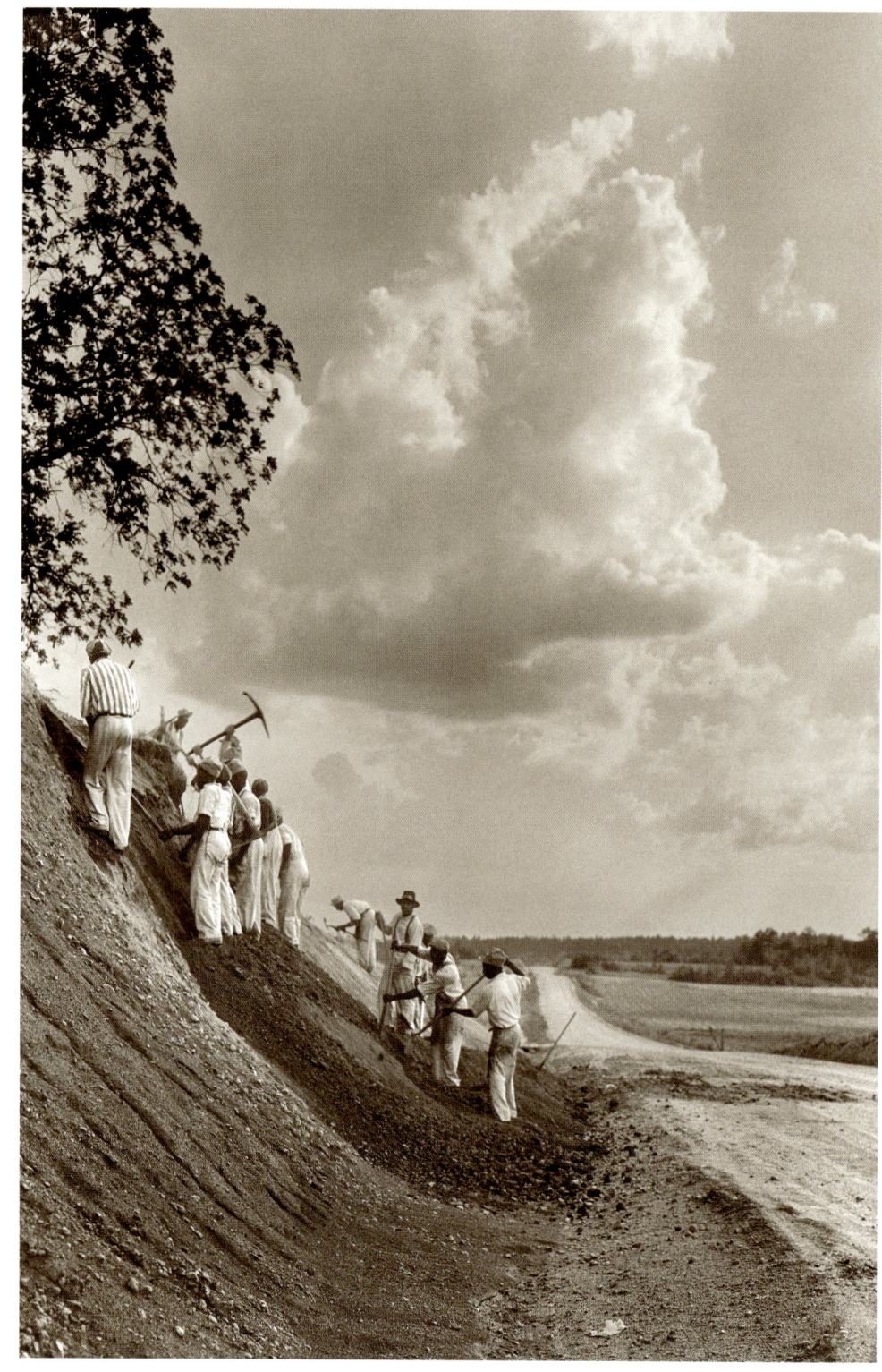

PLATE 131   Convict laborers. Shelby County, Alabama, 1930s.

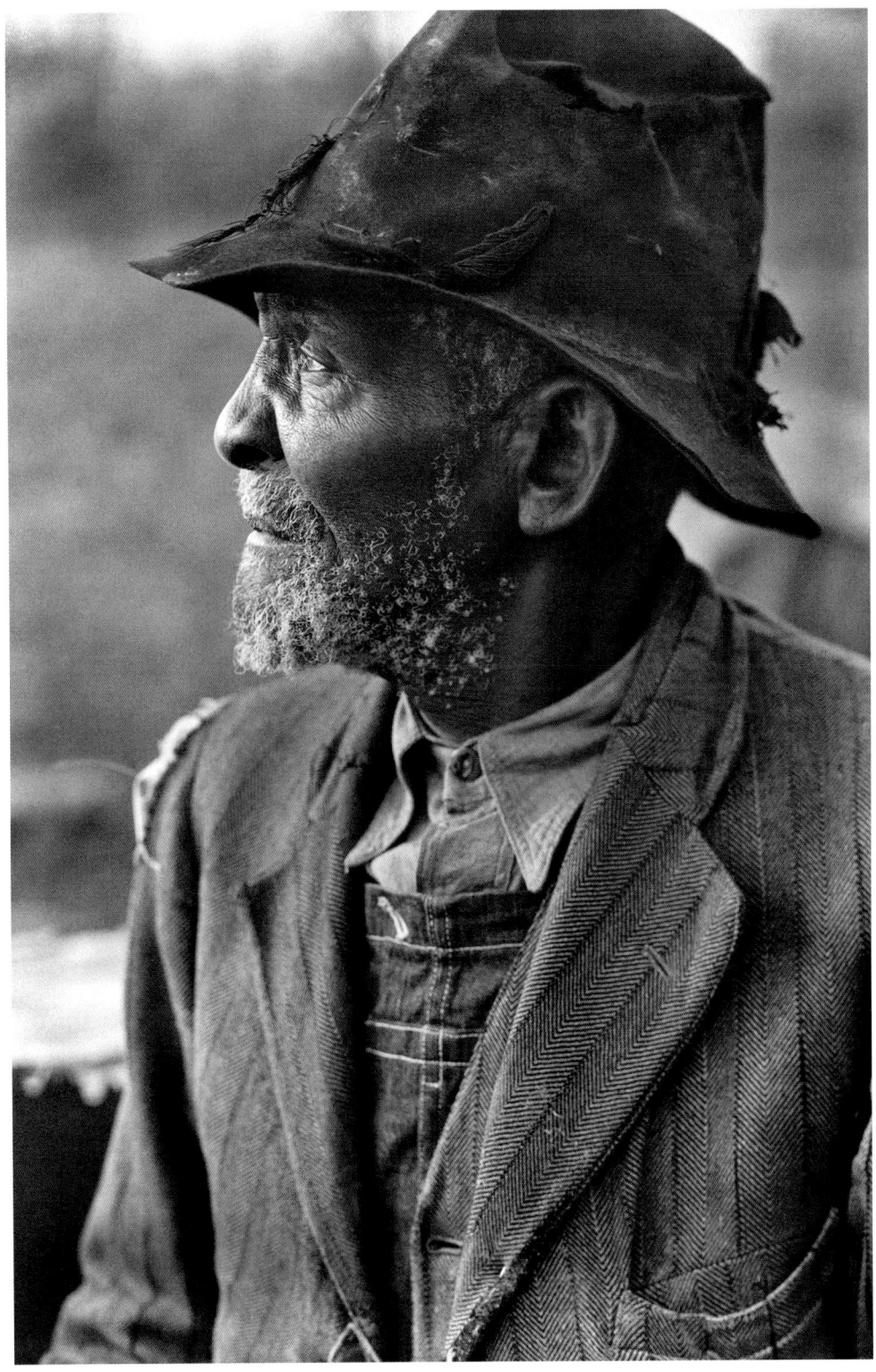

PLATE 132   *Trouble I'se Seen*. Shelby County, Alabama, 1930s.

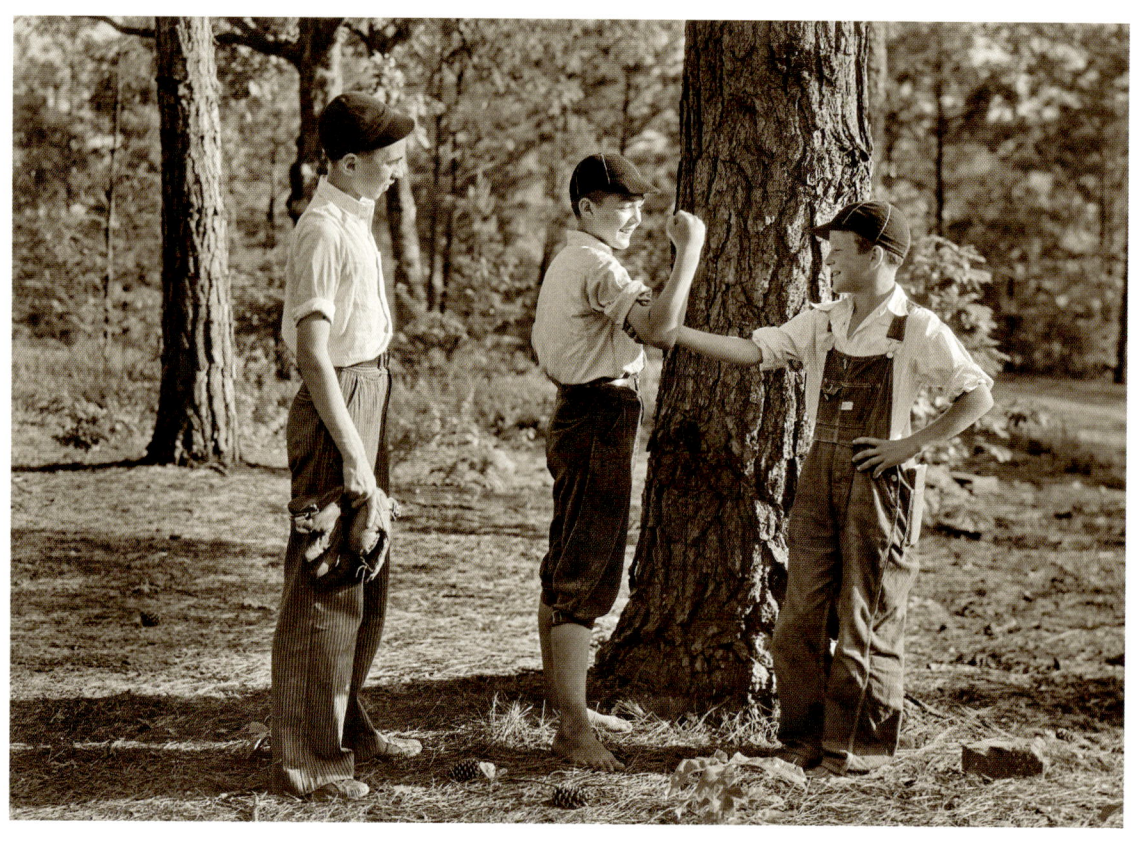

PLATE 133   *Boy Scouts*. Shelby County, Alabama, 1930s.

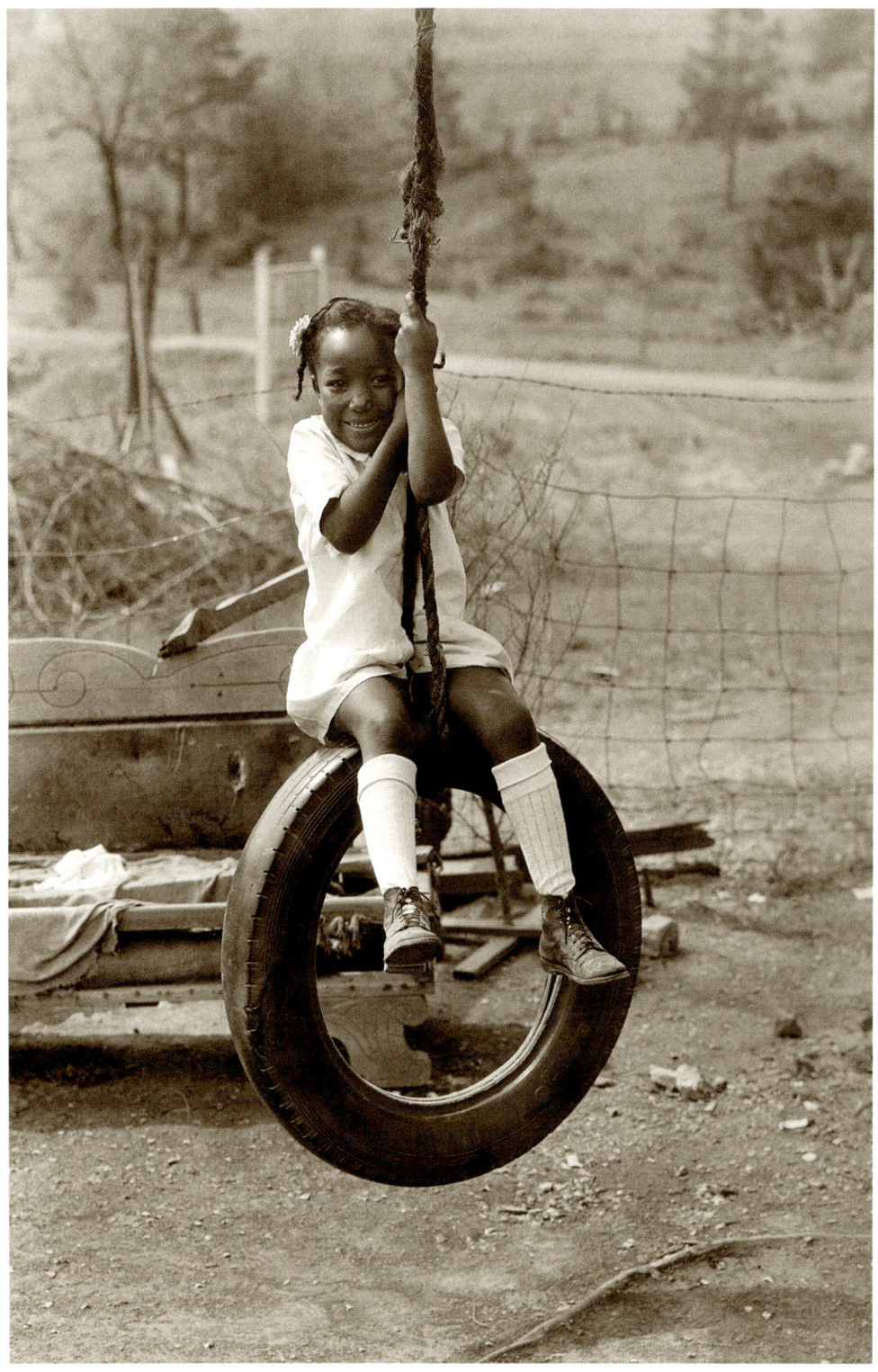

PLATE 134   Girl on a swing. Shelby County, Alabama, 1930s.

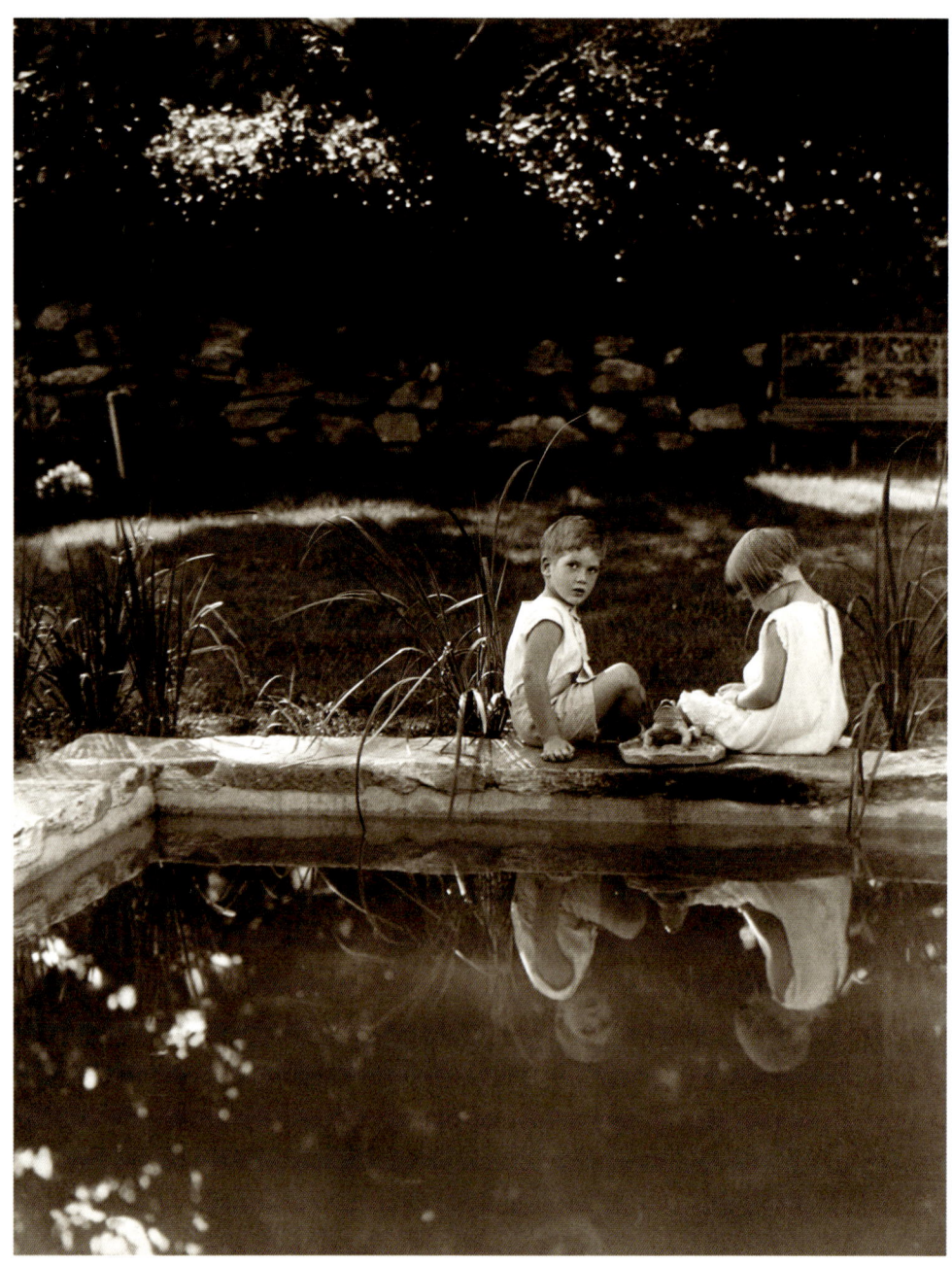

PLATE 135   Moltz children. Lake Toxaway, North Carolina, 1930s.

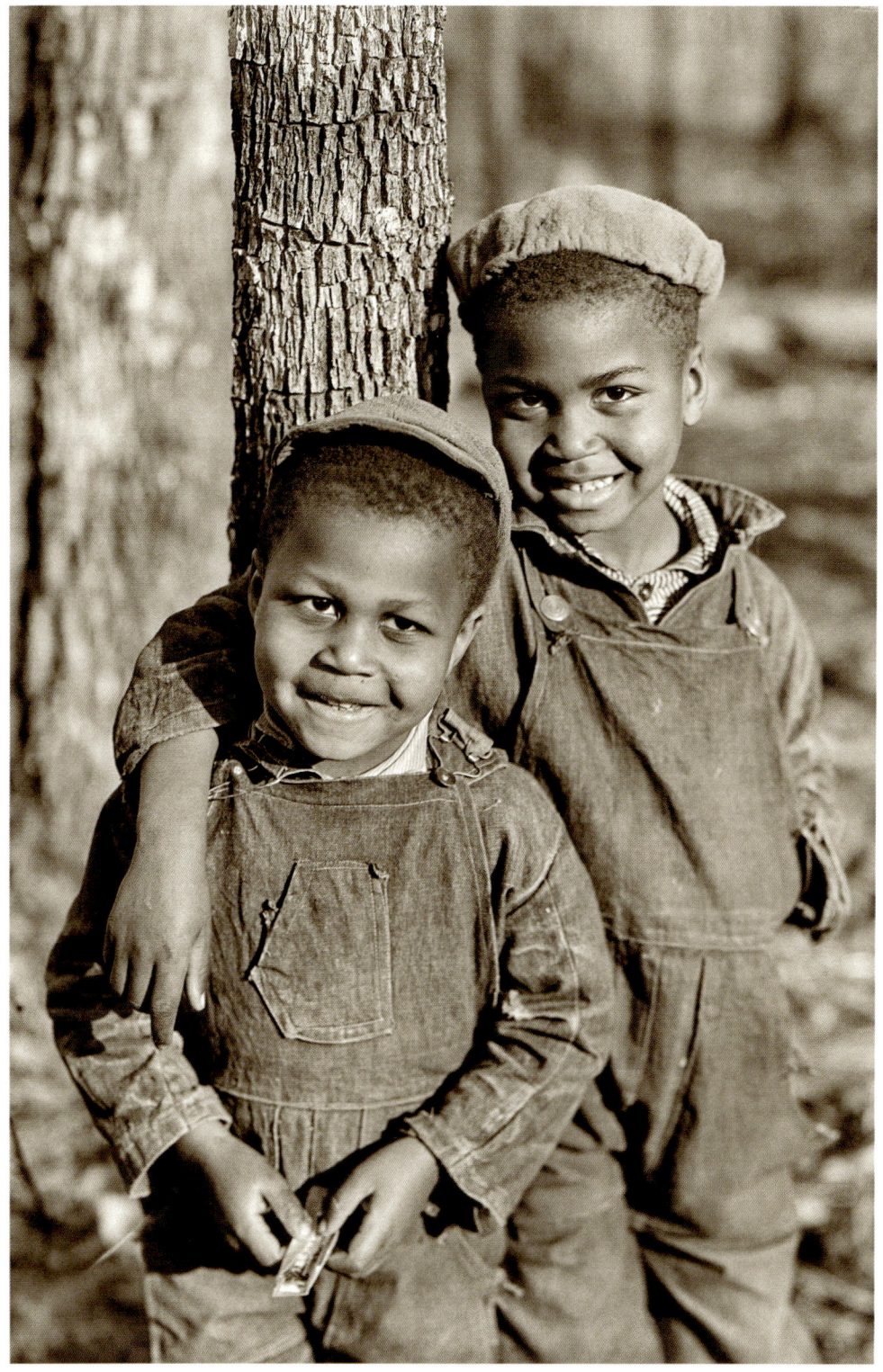

PLATE 136   Two friends. [North Carolina or South Carolina], 1930s.

I have found excitement in the most commonplace

people and localities. True, they have been the same

kinds of people and places you see about you every

day. We all see them, but we do not think about the

beauty of a timeworn face, a workworn hand, or a

God-driven wind. I love people and places and they

have told me a lot about living.

—Bayard Wootten, 1948

Bibliography

Documents

Cambridge, Mass.
  Harvard University, Houghton Library
    Houghton Mifflin Papers, Contracts, MS Storage 228

Chapel Hill, N.C.
  Helen Dugan Allen Collection
  University of North Carolina at Chapel Hill, Wilson Library
    Manuscripts Department
      Bryan Family Papers
      Federal Writers' Project Papers
      Howard Washington Odum Subregional Photographic Study
    North Carolina Collection
      Ignatius Wadsworth Brock Photographic Collection
      Newspaper Clipping File
      Wootten-Moulton Photographic Collection
    University Archives
      University of North Carolina Press Records

Greensboro, N.C.
  University of North Carolina at Greensboro, Walter Clinton Jackson Library
    Charles Duncan McIver Papers

Kinston, N.C.
  Celia Eudy Collection

New Bern, N.C.
  Mary Moulton Barden Collection

Raleigh, N.C.
  North Carolina Division of Archives and History
    Department of Conservation and Development, Travel Information Division Collection

Washington, D.C.
Clare Crawford-Mason and Victor Crawford Collection

Interviews

Allen, Helen Dugan. Interview with author, Chapel Hill, N.C., 1989.
Barden, Mary Moulton. Interview with author, New Bern, N.C., 1989.
Eudy, Celia, and Joseph Eudy. Interview with author, Chapel Hill, N.C., 1990.
Faircloth, Rudolph. Interview with author, Wilmington, N.C., 1990.
Fowler, Margaret Howland. Interview with author, Morehead City, N.C., 1990.

Newspapers

NORTH CAROLINA
Asheville Citizen-Times, 1956
Chapel Hill Weekly, 1923, 1938
Charlotte News, 1935
Charlotte Observer, 1932, 1933, 1935
Durham Morning Herald, 1952
Greensboro Daily News, 1926, 1948
New Bern Daily Journal, 1913, 1914
New Bern New Bernian, 1932
Raleigh News and Observer, 1935, 1937, 1939, 1949
Winston-Salem Twin City Sentinel, 1932

OUT OF STATE
Baltimore Evening Sun, 1935
Detroit News, 1935
Knoxville (Tenn.) News-Sentinel, 1934
New York Herald Tribune, 1935
New York Times Book Review, 1940

Other Sources

Adams, Ansel, and Mary Street Alinder. *Ansel Adams: An Autobiography*. Boston: Little, Brown, 1985.
American Photographers of the Depression: Farm Security Administration Photographs 1935–42. New York: Random House, 1985.
Bartlett, John. "Exhibit of Woman's Federation." *Bulletin of Photography* 11, no. 267 (Sept. 18, 1912): 403–12.
Bonner, Pat, and Charles Nunley. *W. S. Lively and the Southern School of Photography*. McMinnville, Tenn.: Warren County Historical Society, 1984.
Britten, Florence Haxton. "Mountain Folks and Mountain Language." Review of *Cabins in the Laurel*, by Muriel Earley Sheppard and Bayard Wootten. *New York Herald Tribune*, May 5, 1935.

Browne, Turner, and Elaine Partnow. *Macmillan Biographical Encyclopedia of Photographic Artists and Innovators*. New York: Macmillan, 1983.

Buchanan, Paul. *The Picture Man: Photographs by Paul Buchanan*. Edited by Ann Hawthorne. Chapel Hill: University of North Carolina Press, 1993.

Busbee, Mrs. Jacques [Juliana Royster Busbee]. "North Carolina Through the Camera." *North Carolina Teacher* 9, no. 2 (Oct. 1932): 56, 77.

[Catalogue] of Pictures Selected for the Exhibition of the 32d Annual Convention, Photographers' Association of America. Philadelphia: Bulletin of Photograph Press, 1912.

Catalogue of the International Exhibition "Pictorial Photography". Buffalo, N.Y.: Buffalo Fine Arts Academy, 1910.

Chambers, Alice W. "The Woman's Auxiliary at the National." *Bulletin of Photography* 27, no. 684 (Sept. 15, 1920): 252–53.

[Chandler, Genevieve W.] "1930s Federal Writers Project: Collecting Gullah Folklore, Interviews by Genevieve W. Chandler." *Southern Exposure* 5, no. 2–3 (Fall 1977): 119–21, 164.

Crawford, William. *The Keepers of Light: A History and Working Guide to Early Photographic Processes*. Dobbs Ferry, N.Y.: Morgan and Morgan, 1979.

Eaton, Allen. *Handicrafts of the Southern Highlands*. New York: Russell Sage Foundation, 1937.

Featherstone, David. *Doris Ulmann: American Portraits*. Albuquerque: University of New Mexico Press, 1985.

Federal Writers' Project. *North Carolina: A Guide to the Old North State*. Chapel Hill: University of North Carolina Press, 1939.

Garland, Hamlin. "Doris Ulmann's Photographs." *The Mentor* 15, no. 6 (July 1927): 41–48.

Grover, C. Jane. *The Positive Image: Women Photographers in Turn of the Century America*. Albany: State University of New York Press, 1988.

Hickman, Caroline Mesrobian. "Women and the Transformation of Art in Early Twentieth Century North Carolina." In *Nine from North Carolina: An Exhibition of Women Artists*, 13–21. Washington, D.C.: North Carolina State Committee in cooperation with the National Museum of Women in the Arts, [1989].

Hirsch, Jerrold Maury. "Culture on Relief, the Federal Writers' Project in North Carolina, 1935–42." Master's thesis, University of North Carolina at Chapel Hill, 1973.

"How Women Have Won Fame in Photography." *Wilson's Photographic Magazine* 51, no. 5 (May 1914): 199–209.

Hurley, F. Jack. *Portrait of a Decade: Roy Stryker and the Development of Documentary Photography in the Thirties*. Baton Rouge: Louisiana State University Press, 1972.

"Important to Every Member of the P. A. of A.: The Latest and Revised Changes in the Proposed Constitution and By-Laws." Supplement to *Bulletin of Photography* 25, no. 622 (July 9, 1919): a–c.

"Introducing Bayard Wootten." *Coastal Topics* (Charleston, S.C.), Jan. 1937.

Johnston, Frances Benjamin. *The Early Architecture of North Carolina: A Pictorial Survey*. Text by Thomas Tileston Waterman, foreword by Leicester B. Holland, F.A.I.A. Chapel Hill: University of North Carolina Press, 1941.

Joyner, Charles. *Down by the Riverside*. Urbana: University of Illinois Press, 1984.

Linquist, Ruth. "Bayard Wootten—Woman, Photographer, and Artist." *The Tar Heel Woman* 18, no. 3 (Oct. 1945): 5–6.

Loehr, Pearl Grace. "Benefits of the Woman's Federation." *Bulletin of Photography* 11, no. 267 (Sept. 18, 1912): 425–26.

Martin, Milward W. *Twelve Full Ounces*. New York: Holt, Rinehart and Winston, 1962.

Palmquist, Peter E., comp. *A Bibliography of Writings by and about Women in Photography*. Eureka, Calif.: Eureka Printing Co., 1994.

Péladeau, Marius B. *Chansonetta: The Life and Photographs of Chansonetta Stanley Emmons, 1858–1937*. Waldoboro, Maine: Maine Antique Digest, 1977.

Peterson, Christian A. *Index to the Annuals of the Pictorial Photographers of America*. Minneapolis, Minn.: Christian A. Peterson, 1993.

"Photographers' Association of Virginia and the Carolinas, held at Greensboro, N.C., September 1, 2, 3 and 4, 1908." *Bulletin of Photography* 3, no. 58 (Sept. 16, 1908): 190.

[Pictorial Photographers of America]. *Annual Report of the Pictorial Photographers of America*. New York: National Arts Club, 1918.

———. *Pictorial Photography in America, 1926*. New York: Pictorial Photographers of America, 1926.

Rosenblum, Naomi. *Documenting a Myth: The South as Seen by Three Women Photographers— Chansonetta Stanley Emmons, Doris Ulmann, Bayard Wootten, 1910–1940* [exhibition catalogue]. Portland, Oreg.: Douglas F. Cooley Memorial Art Gallery, Reed College, 1998.

———. *A History of Women Photographers*. Paris: Abbeville Press, 1994.

Rothstein, Arthur. *Documentary Photography*. Boston: Butterworth Publishers/Focal Press, 1986.

"Some Old Homes of North Carolina." Review of *Old Homes and Gardens of North Carolina* by Archibald Henderson and Bayard Wootten. *New York Times Book Review*, July 14, 1940.

Spearman, Walter. "Backwoods America Comes to Life in New Books." Review of *Cabins in the Laurel* by Muriel Earley Sheppard and Bayard Wootten. *Charlotte News*, May 5, 1935.

Sutton, Maude Minish. "A Mountain World Sits for Its Picture." Review of *Cabins in the Laurel* by Muriel Earley Sheppard and Bayard Wootten. *Raleigh News and Observer*, Mar. 24, 1935.

Tindall, George Brown. *America: A Narrative History*. Vol. 2. New York: W. W. Norton, 1984.

Ulmann, Doris. *The Appalachian Photographs of Doris Ulmann*. Penland, N.C.: Jargon Society, 1971.

———. *Doris Ulmann: Photographs from the J. Paul Getty Museum*. Malibu, Calif.: J. Paul Getty Museum, 1996.

Van Fleet, Margaret. "Now We Belong—We Are Here." *Bulletin of Photography* 11, no. 267 (Sept. 18, 1912): 428–29.

Wagner, Philip. Review of *Cabins in the Laurel*, by Muriel Earley Sheppard and Bayard Wootten. *Baltimore Evening Sun*, June 1, 1935.

Watkins, Charles Alan. "Merchandising the Mountaineer: Photography, the Great Depression, and *Cabins in the Laurel*." *Appalachian Journal* 12, no. 3 (Spring 1985): 215–38.

Weaver, William Rhodes. "N.C. Guard's Only Woman General Is Official U.N.C. Photographer." *Uplift* 29, no. 44 (Nov. 1, 1941): 14–16.

Who's Who (Sept. 1944), s.v. "Bayard Wootten."

Who's Who in the South and Southwest (1947), s.v. "Bayard Wootten."

Williams, Jonathan. *Blues and Roots, Rue and Bluets: A Garland for the Southern Appalachians*. Durham, N.C.: Duke University Press, 1985.

"Woman's Federation of the P. A. of A., Constitution and By-Laws." *Bulletin of Photography* 11, no. 267 (Sept. 18, 1912): 432.

Wootten, Bayard. "As Seen by One of the Throng." *Bulletin of Photography* 11, no. 267 (Sept. 18, 1912): 429–31.

———. "Modern Portrait Photography." *Bulletin of Photography*, undated extract in the Clare Crawford-Mason and Victor Crawford Collection.

———. "My Experience as a Photographer." *St. Louis and Canadian Photographer* 33, no. 12 (Dec. 1909): 728–30.

———. "The Outlook for Women." *Bulletin of Photography* 6, no. 148 (June 8, 1910): 360–61.

———. "A Three-Minute Survey of Photography." *Alumnae News* (University of North Carolina at Greensboro) 17, no. 1 (July 1927): 33.

———. "Why the Federation Should Have the Earnest Support of All Women Photographers." *Wilson's Photographic Magazine* 51, no. 1 (Jan. 1914): 81–82.

[Wootten, Bayard?]. "A Woman by a Woman." *Bulletin of Photography* 11, no. 267 (Sept. 18, 1912): 416–17.

Wootten, Bayard, and Ida Wilcox. "What Goes On Behind the Camera." *National Altrusan* 12, no. 7 (Mar. 1935): 7–9.

Wootten, Bayard, illus. *The Appalachian School Department of Fireside Industries*. Penland, N.C.: Appalachian School, [1936?].

———. *Backwoods America*. Text by Charles Morrow Wilson. Chapel Hill: University of North Carolina Press, 1934.

———. *Cabins in the Laurel*. Text by Muriel Earley Sheppard. Chapel Hill: University of North Carolina Press, 1935; reprint, 1991.

———. *Carolina Camera Studies*. [Greensboro, N.C.?]: Carolina Motor Club, [1936?].

———. *Charleston: Azaleas and Old Bricks*. Text by Samuel Gaillard Stoney. Boston: Houghton Mifflin, 1937.

———. *From My Highest Hill: Carolina Mountain Folks*. Text by Olive Tilford Dargan. Philadelphia: J. B. Lippincott, 1941.

———. *New Castle, Delaware, 1651–1939*. Text by Anthony Higgins. Boston: Houghton Mifflin, 1939.

———. *Old Homes and Gardens of North Carolina*. Text by Archibald Henderson, compiled by Mrs. Charles A. Cannon, Mrs. Lyman A. Cotten, and Mrs. James E. Latham. Chapel Hill: University of North Carolina Press and the Garden Club of North Carolina, 1939.

———. *The Story of North Carolina*. Text by Alex Mathews Arnett and Walter Clinton Jackson. Chapel Hill: University of North Carolina Press, 1933.

———. *Time Tables of All Passenger Trains: Norfolk & Southern Railway*. Norfolk, [Va.]: Norfolk & Southern Railway, 1909.

———. *Ways and Byways of Chapel Hill*. Text by Ben Bunker. Chapel Hill, N.C.: Wootten-Moulton, 1939.

Wootten, Bayard, and others, illus. *An Exhibition of the Rural Arts, Held in Connection with the 75th Anniversary of the Founding of the Department of Agriculture 1862–1937, November 14–30, 1937*. Washington, D.C.: United States Department of Agriculture, [1937].

Index

Index

Credits

Unless otherwise noted, all photographs are from the North Carolina Collection of the University of North Carolina Library at Chapel Hill.

1. 90-284 (original print in the Clare Crawford-Mason and Victor Crawford Collection)
2. Wootten-Moulton Collection, Eudy Series
3. 90-286 (original print in the Clare Crawford-Mason and Victor Crawford Collection)
4. WMg-189 Eudy Series
5. Wootten-Moulton Collection, Eudy Series
6. Wootten-Moulton Collection, Eudy Series
7. WM-186 z Eudy Series
8. Portrait Collection
9. WMg-A8 Eudy Series
10. Thomas Wolfe Collection
11. 91-128
12. WM-212-47 1226 Eudy Series
13. WM-212-39 2246-1 Eudy Series
14. Wootten-Moulton Collection, Misc. Series
15. WM-212-50 2229 Eudy Series
16. WM-212-50 2229-1 Eudy Series
17. WM-183-1 223 Eudy Series
18. WM-217 1225 Eudy Series
19. WM-215-7 847 Eudy Series
20. WM-212-29 582 Eudy Series
21. WM-C336-98 503 Studio Series
22. WM-224-5 2780 Eudy Series
23. WM-219 1062 SM Eudy Series
24. WM-203 1079-1N Eudy Series
25. WM-212-35 1232-1 Eudy Series
26. WM-212-35 1232 Eudy Series
27. WM-215-2 892 Eudy Series
28. WM-215-2 907 Eudy Series
29. WM-212-28 1312 Eudy Series
30. WM-212-36 1216 Eudy Series
31. WM-215-6 869 Eudy Series
32. WM-216-7 442 Eudy Series
33. WM-212-41 1556-1 Eudy Series
34. WM-217-3 1420 Eudy Series
35. WM-212-7 264 Eudy Series (Some sources list the family name as Hollifield.)
36. WM-212-43 1231 Eudy Series
37. WM-183-30 1560 Eudy Series
38. WM-199 1233 Eudy Series
39. WM-181-2 2749-1 Eudy Series
40. WM-183-19 1501 Eudy Series
41. WM-179-1 1313 Eudy Series
42. WM-175-3 3550 Eudy Series
43. WM-212-19 1321-11 Eudy Series
44. WM-219-6 1071-3 Eudy Series

45. WM-183-16 272-2 Eudy Series
46. WM-212-35 2339-2 Eudy Series
47. Wootten-Moulton Collection,
Misc. Series
48. WM-C336-7 2922 Eudy Series
(caption from *From My Highest Hill*)
49. WM-202-12 2827 Eudy Series
50. WM-202-6 2836 Eudy Series
51. WM-225-2 1236-5 Eudy Series
52. WM-212-3 1270-3 Eudy Series
53. WM-225-11 1318 Eudy Series
54. WM-C336-14 511 Studio Series
55. WM-190-3 2240-1 Eudy Series
56. WM-194 2596-5 Eudy Series
57. WM-201-2 1372-1 Eudy Series
58. WM-201 705-1 Eudy Series
59. WM-201-2 1372-9 Eudy Series
60. WM-201-1 2012-1 Eudy Series
61. WM-178 2215-3 Eudy Series
62. WM-C353-4 4039-19 Studio Series
63. WM-217-10 445-1 Eudy Series
64. WM-30-9 206 Studio Series
65. WM-C353-2 Studio Series
66. WM-166-1 1190-4 Studio Series
67. WM-213-11 1365-9 Eudy Series
68. WM-166-3 1365-7 Eudy Series
69. WM-166-3 1366-6 Eudy Series
70. WM-213-11 1365-19 Eudy Series
71. WM-213-6 1374-1 Eudy Series
72. Wootten-Moulton Collection,
Misc. Series
73. WM-C353 C4016-1 Studio Series
74. WM-177 1648-1 Studio Series
75. WM-177 1843-4 Studio Series
76. WM-177 1648-3 Studio Series
77. WM-176 1947-12 Eudy Series
78. WM-176 1947-9 Eudy Series
79. WM-213-13 3028-2 Eudy Series
80. WM-162-40 1453 Studio Series
81. WM-C340-26 3048 Studio Series
82. WM-200 3539-1 Eudy Series
83. WM-162-51 1527-4 Eudy Series
84. WM-180-3 243 Eudy Series
85. WM-180-1 2640-1 Eudy Series
86. WM-180-4 1989-12 Eudy Series

87. WM-162-11 2218-5 Eudy Series
88. WM-162-26 954 Eudy Series
89. WM-162-33 3526 Eudy Series
90. Wootten-Moulton Collection,
Misc. Series
91. WM-213-10 2108 Eudy Series
92. WM-213-13 3028-1 Eudy Series
93. WM-172-17 [1552] Eudy Series
(caption from *Charleston: Azaleas and
Old Bricks*)
94. WM-172-10 778 Eudy Series
95. WM-213-13 1648-10 Eudy Series
96. WM-172-14 783-1 Eudy Series
97. WM-213-12 988 Eudy Series
(caption from *Charleston: Azaleas and
Old Bricks*)
98. WM-172-5 758 Eudy Series
(caption from *Charleston: Azaleas and
Old Bricks*)
99. WM-168-2 1601-2 Eudy Series
(caption from *Charleston: Azaleas and
Old Bricks*)
100. WM-168 769-8 Eudy Series
101. Wootten-Moulton Collection,
Eudy Series
102. WM-172-21 727-6 Eudy Series
103. WM-213-8 1146 Eudy Series
104. WM-172-3 978-4 Eudy Series
105. WM-213-14 [1913] Eudy Series
106. WM-213-10 1914-1 Eudy Series
107. WM-213-13 1990-6 Eudy Series
108. WM-213-14 1991-20 Eudy Series
109. WM-213-13 1990-4 Eudy Series
110. Wootten-Moulton Collection,
Studio Series
111. WM-213-13 1991-5 Eudy Series
112. WM-213-13 1991-4 Eudy Series
113. WM-213-3 3535-3 Eudy Series
114. WM-213-14 1990-15 Eudy Series
115. WM-196-2 1648-8 Eudy Series
116. WM-196-1 3057-3 Eudy Series
117. WM-213-4 1990 Eudy Series
118. WM-213-4 1648-27 Eudy Series
119. WM-213-4 1991-8 Eudy Series
120. WM-213-9 1648-29 Eudy Series

Credits

121. WM-213-3 1914-12 Eudy Series
122. WM-213-13 1914-8 Eudy Series
123. WM-C117 1410-3 Studio Series
124. WM-213-14 1990-13 Eudy Series
125. WM-182-36 1137 AS Eudy Series
126. WM-182-15 1145-6 SA Eudy Series
127. WM-182-3 1131 AS Eudy Series
128. WM-182 1145-22 SA Eudy Series
    (caption from *Carolina Camera Studies*)

129. WM-182-25 1145-12 SA Eudy Series
130. WM-182-28 1113 AS-1 Eudy Series
131. WM-182-7 1145 SA Eudy Series
132. WM-213-10 1122 AS Eudy Series
133. WM-182-2 1145 SA Eudy Series
134. WM-213-4 1112 AS Eudy Series
135. Wootten-Moulton Collection,
    Studio Series
136. WM-213-4 3028-7 Eudy Series